NARCOTOPIA

NARCOTOPIA

In Search of the
Asian Drug Cartel That
Survived the CIA

Patrick Winn

PUBLICAFFAIRS
New York

PublicAffairs
Hachette Book Group
1290 Avenue of the Americas, New York, NY 10104
www.publicaffairsbooks.com
@Public_Affairs

Printed in the United States of America

First Edition: January 2024

Published by PublicAffairs, an imprint of Hachette Book Group, Inc. The PublicAffairs name and logo is a registered trademark of the Hachette Book Group.

The Hachette Speakers Bureau provides a wide range of authors for speaking events. To find out more, go to hachettespeakersbureau.com or email HachetteSpeakers@hbgusa.com.

PublicAffairs books may be purchased in bulk for business, educational, or promotional use. For more information, please contact your local bookseller or the Hachette Book Group Special Markets Department at special.markets@hbgusa.com.

The publisher is not responsible for websites (or their content) that are not owned by the publisher.

Print book interior design by Bart Dawson

Library of Congress Cataloging-in-Publication Data

Names: Winn, Patrick (Journalist), author.
Title: Narcotopia : in search of the Asian drug cartel that survived the CIA / Patrick Winn.
Description: First edition. | New York : PublicAffairs, 2024. | Includes bibliographical references and index. |
Identifiers: LCCN 2023022650 | ISBN 9781541701953 (hardcover) | ISBN 9781541701977 (ebook)
Subjects: LCSH: United Wa State Army (Burma) | United States. Central Intelligence Agency—Influence. | United States. Drug Enforcement Administration—Influence. | Wa (Asian people)—Politics and government.| Wa (Asian people)—Social conditions. | Drug traffic—Golden Triangle (Southeast Asia)
Classification: LCC DS528.2.W32 W56 2024 | DDC 364.1/33650959—dc23/eng/20230731
LC record available at https://lccn.loc.gov/2023022650

ISBNs: 9781541701953 (hardcover), 9781541701977 (ebook)

LSC-C

Printing 1, 2023

To all the world's highlanders

CONTENTS

Author's Note ix
The Nations and People of Narcotopia xi
Maps xv

Prologue 1

Superstar 5

BOOK ONE

First Encounter 9

Stranger in the Peaks 19

Guns, Drugs, and Espionage 39

The League of Warlords 50

Enslaved No More 64

BOOK TWO

Unspeakable 77

The Prodigy 86

Mr. Success 111

Nativity 124

BOOK THREE

Confidential Informant 149

Kick the Cat 154

The Burn 171

Torpedo 189

The Summit 206

BOOK FOUR

Manifest Destiny 227

The Great Migration 236

Vanilla Speed 248

Whiskey Alpha 258

Mountain Fortress China 278

The Reckoning 292

Epilogue 307

Acknowledgments 315

Appendix: Saw Lu's Manifesto 317

Notes 323

Index 347

AUTHOR'S NOTE

Most accounts of the drug trade are told from the law enforcement perspective. There is a reason for this. Drug Enforcement Administration agents who describe their adventures to journalists are often lionized. They might even score a budget hike for their department.

But drug traffickers have little incentive to tell their stories. In that profession, running your mouth leads to prison or worse. The upshot is that most drug war stories sound the same: valorous detectives battling vile figures—the junkie, the pusher, the kingpin.

It is a genre of half-told tales.

This book does not presume virtue among antinarcotics agents or cruelty among traffickers, or vice versa. I've relied heavily on accounts of lawbreakers in the Golden Triangle, some of whom risked their necks to talk to me. Because few of these sources are scrupulous record keepers, I'm forced to lean on their memories. Every attempt has been made to corroborate their oral histories with other witnesses, but in some cases I can only present recollections as they were told.

Police records and anthropological studies of Wa rituals helped me reconstruct scenes. Central Intelligence Agency and DEA documents proved vital. Some are declassified, others acquired by creative means. For clarity's sake, I've sometimes rendered multiple conversations into one or shifted the order in which certain facts were revealed to me. Most names in this book are genuine, but I've disguised several identities to prevent retribution, from either criminals or government agents.

These are my caveats. They allow for perspectives seldom heard. Few of the stories in this book appear elsewhere. My goal is to present a narrative that is more expansive and truthful, less monochromatic. There is good and evil in this book, but it mostly resides in the heads of its characters, crusading for honor and power and always believing themselves more righteous than their enemies.

Finally, a note about the term *Golden Triangle*, which lacks a formal definition. I use it to describe Southeast Asia's drug-producing heartland: a mountainous area, almost entirely in Burma, that seeps across the borders of China, Laos, and Thailand. It is, to coin a phrase, a *Narcotopia*—a place where narcotics are a defining force shaping commerce, politics, and daily life. This zone powers a regional heroin-and-meth economy that is, according to the United Nations, possibly worth more than the entire GDP of Burma itself.[1]

THE NATIONS AND PEOPLE OF NARCOTOPIA

THE NATIONS

Wa State

Population: 600,000
Size: ~12,000 square miles
Governance: authoritarian
Ruled by the United Wa State Army (UWSA). Split into two
noncontiguous territories, the motherland and Wa South, both
inside Burma's borders but off-limits to Burmese authorities.
Wa State does not seek formal independence status with the
international community; yet it functions, for all intents and
purposes, as a sovereign state.

Burma (officially, Myanmar)

Population: 54 million
Size: 261,000 square miles
Governance: military dictatorship
Former British colony that broke free in 1948. Since 1962,
controlled by an isolationist military regime. This junta fears
both China and the United States—as well as its own citizens,
especially ethnic minorities in the hills. Burmese is the dominant
ethnicity, accounting for two-thirds of the population, living
mostly in the lowlands. Burma's mountainous borderlands are
beyond government control and ruled by indigenous armed
groups, the Wa being the most powerful of them all.

Shanland (defunct)

Peak population: 3–4 million
Peak size: ~5,000 square miles
Governance: authoritarian personality cult
A rogue nation that existed from 1976 to 1996. Controlled
patches of territory along the Thai-Burma border. Led by Khun

Sa, a world-class heroin trafficker. He was also a self-avowed
freedom fighter for the Shan, the largest of Burma's minority
groups and ethnic cousins to Thais. Shanland was targeted
by both the Drug Enforcement Administration and Central
Intelligence Agency.

Thailand
Population: 72 million
Size: 198,000 square miles
Governance: military-dominated quasi-democracy
Major US ally since the Cold War. Then and now, provides a
base of operations for the CIA and DEA. Narcotics produced
in Burma's landlocked mountains flow south through Thailand
to reach global markets, making the Thai-Burma border one of
the world's busiest drug-smuggling zones. Much of that border
is now controlled by the UWSA.

China
Population: 1.4 billion
Size: 3.7 million square miles
Governance: communism (one-party authoritarianism)
US rival. Strives for dominance of Southeast Asia. Ruled since
1949 by the Communist Party of China, which enforces strict
laws against drug use among its own citizens. However, China
is not above colluding with drug traffickers. Beijing supports
the UWSA under an agreement: the Wa can only traffic drugs
to other countries, never China.

Communist Party of Burma (associated group, now defunct)
A disbanded surrogate of China's Communist Party. This
armed group, headed by ethnic Burmese Maoists, hoped
to conquer all of Burma but failed. It only succeeded in
occupying the Wa motherland from the late 1960s to the late
1980s.

United States of America
Population: 332 million
Size: 3.8 million square miles
Governance: democracy, empire

Strives for global supremacy. Competes with China for sway over Southeast Asia. Strongly allied with Thailand. Antagonistic toward Burma's isolationist dictatorship, which resists taking sides. America also seeks the UWSA's downfall. Historically, the United States exerts influence on the Southeast Asian narcotics trade through two agencies: the DEA and the CIA.

US Drug Enforcement Administration

Collaborates with overseas police and troops to seize narcotics and arrest foreign drug traffickers.

US Central Intelligence Agency

Upholds American supremacy by covert means: gathering intel and sabotage. Willing to conspire with criminal organizations, even drug traffickers.

The Exiles (associated group, now defunct)

Once Asia's largest opium-trafficking cartel. Rooted in the Thai-Burma border from the 1960s to the 1980s. Protected from prosecution by the CIA. The Exiles cartel assisted US and Taiwanese spies in espionage operations along the Burma-China border, sometimes using Wa warlords as assets.

The League of Warlords (associated group, now defunct)

A short-lived coalition of Wa warlords in the late 1960s to early 1970s. Sold opium to the Exiles. Some members aided CIA operations against China. Led by four warlords: Saw Lu, Shah, Mahasang, and Master of Creation.

THE PEOPLE

Saw Lu (Wa): Born in 1944 on the China-Burma border. Raised in an American Baptist missionary sect. An anticommunist warlord in his youth. Later a top UWSA leader—and DEA asset.

Jacob (Wa): Saw Lu's pious son-in-law, married to his daughter, Grace. Born in the late 1970s.

Lai (Wa): Born circa 1940 in the Wa highlands. Full name: Zhao Nyi Lai. A Maoist guerrilla in his youth but later rejected the ideology in favor of Wa nationalism. Founding father of Wa State.

Bao (Wa): Wa State's current leader. Born in 1949 in Wa highlands. Full name: Bao Youxiang. Former communist guerrilla commander turned Wa ethnonationalist.

Wei Xuegang (Wa-Chinese): The most successful drug lord of the twenty-first century so far. Born mid-1940s in the Wa peaks. Former Khun Sa protégé. Finance czar of the UWSA since 1989.

Khun Sa (Shan-Chinese): The most powerful Asian drug lord of the latter twentieth century. Born in 1934 in Burma's Shan foothills. Original name: Zhang Qifu. Founder of Shanland and a former mentor to Wei Xuegang.

Gen. Lee Wen-huan (Chinese): Born in 1917 in China's Yunnan province near the Burma border. Scion of an opium-merchant clan. A die-hard anticommunist, he fled to Burma after China's Maoist takeover in 1949. A founder of the Exiles. Protected by the CIA and the Thai military.

Angelo Saladino (American): Lead DEA agent in Burma from 1989 to 1992. Formerly posted in Chiang Mai, Thailand.

Rick Horn (American): Lead DEA agent in Burma in 1992 and 1993.

John Whalen (American): Longest-running DEA agent in Burma. Arrived in 1997 and retired in 2014.

Franklin "Pancho" Huddle (American): Top US State Department official (chargé d'affaires) in Burma from 1990 to 1994. Oversaw feuding DEA and CIA bureaus inside the US embassy.

Bill Young (American): DEA operative based in Chiang Mai. Former CIA officer who became disgruntled with the spy agency. Grandson of legendary Baptist missionary William Marcus Young, known as the "Man-God."

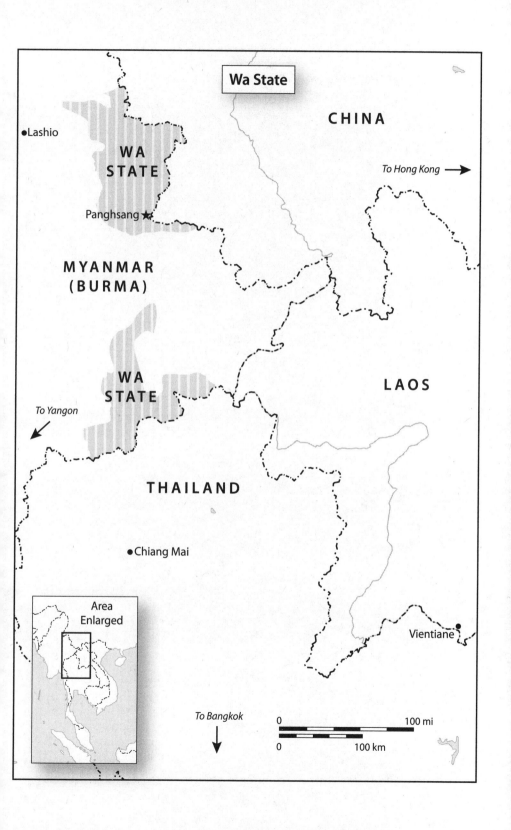

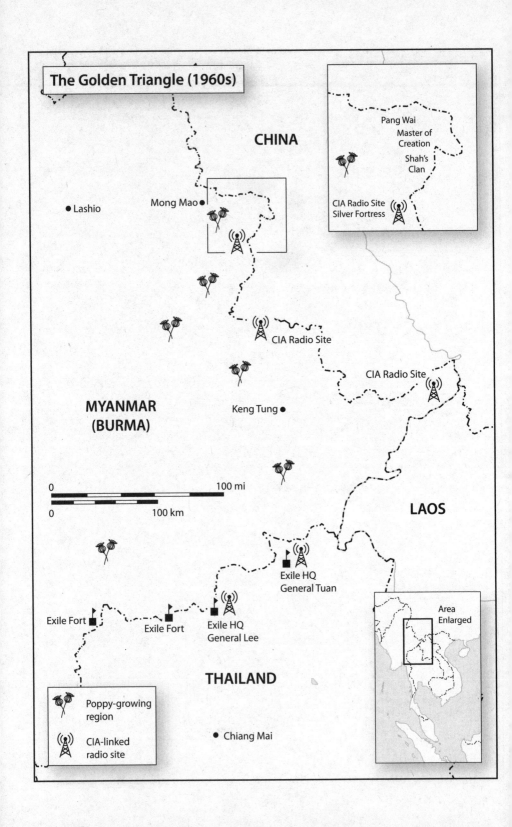

The Golden Triangle (1960s)

CHINA

Lashio

Mong Mao

CIA Radio Site

MYANMAR
(BURMA)

CIA Radio Site

Keng Tung

LAOS

0   100 mi
0   100 km

Pang Wai
Master of
Creation
Shah's
Clan

CIA Radio Site
Silver Fortress

Exile HQ
General Tuan

Exile Fort

Exile Fort

Exile HQ
General Lee

THAILAND

Area
Enlarged

Poppy-growing
region

CIA-linked
radio site

Chiang Mai

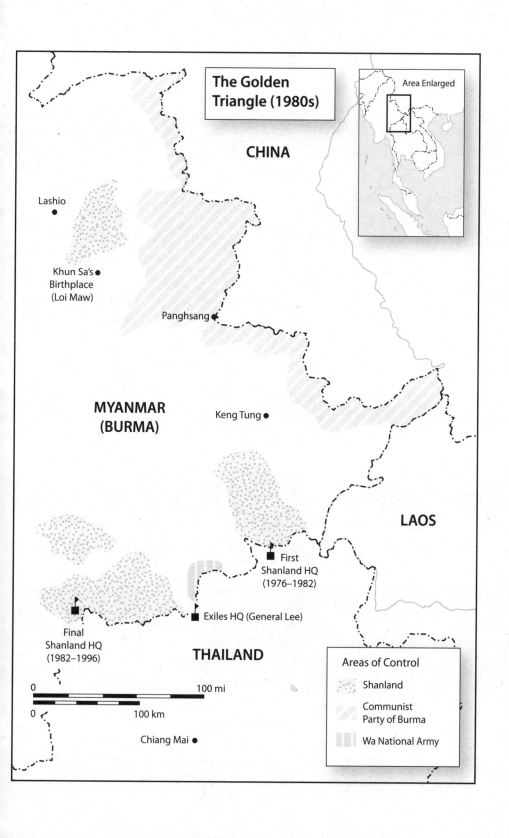

The Golden Triangle (1980s)

Area Enlarged

CHINA

Lashio ●

Khun Sa's ●
Birthplace
(Loi Maw)

Panghsang ●

MYANMAR
(BURMA)

Keng Tung ●

LAOS

■ First
Shanland HQ
(1976–1982)

■ Exiles HQ (General Lee)

Final
Shanland HQ
(1982–1996)

THAILAND

0   100 mi

0   100 km

Chiang Mai ●

Areas of Control

Shanland

Communist
Party of Burma

Wa National Army

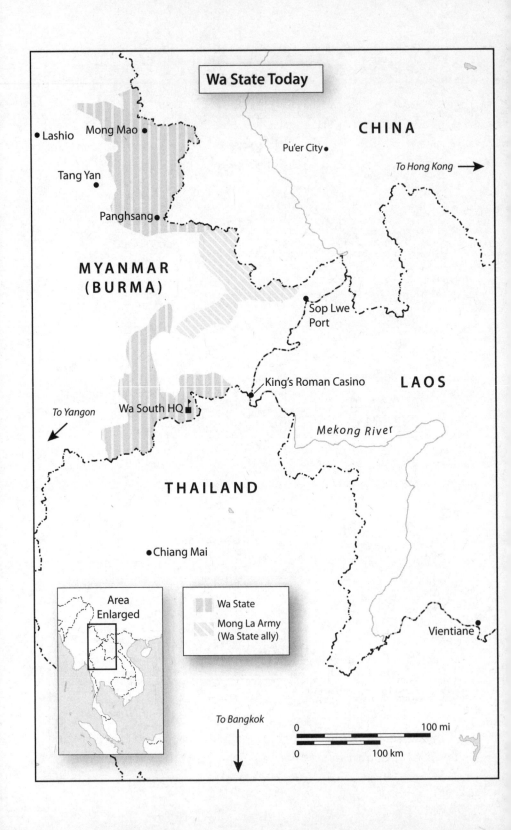

Wa State Today

CHINA

Lashio

Mong Mao

Pu'er City

To Hong Kong →

Tang Yan

Panghsang

MYANMAR
(BURMA)

Sop Lwe
Port

LAOS

King's Roman Casino

To Yangon

Wa South HQ

Mekong River

THAILAND

Chiang Mai

Area
Enlarged

Wa State

Mong La Army
(Wa State ally)

Vientiane

To Bangkok

| 0 | | | 100 mi |
| 0 | | | 100 km |

PROLOGUE

The Wa are among the most vilified people in Asia, if not the world. This has been true for ages. To the Imperial British, they were "filthy" and "undoubtedly savage." Before that, China's Qing dynasty deemed them the "most obstinate among the barbarians."[1]

Even Vasco da Gama slandered the Wa, though the sixteenth-century explorer never reached their homeland: a jagged stretch of mountains dividing Burma and China. He'd only heard rumors about the tribe, which he immortalized in a poem:[2]

> *On human flesh, with brutal hunger they feed*
> *And with hot irons stamp their own—rude deed!*

He was wrong. The Wa weren't cannibals. They were headhunters, ritually planting enemies' heads on spikes. Like Scottish clans and French revolutionaries, they had their reasons.

From the Middle Ages to the twenty-first century, the Wa have been steadily denigrated. They quit head-hunting a few generations ago—the last skulls were lopped off sometime between Beatlemania and disco—but the stigma endures. They're now branded as a narco-tribe. Practically everything written about the Wa portrays them as vicious hill people who churn out illegal drugs.

Few cultures are so strongly linked to a commodity. The Amish build furniture. The Swiss make watches. The Wa cook meth—and before meth was in vogue, the Wa churned out heroin. Their soil is cold and bitter, terrible for vegetables but ideal for heroin's raw ingredient: *Papaver somniferum*, the opium poppy.

Like mountain peoples from Chechnya to the Ozarks, the Wa like to do things their own way. A tribal authority called the United Wa State

1

Army (UWSA) controls their native terrain, even though every inch technically sits inside Myanmar, also known as Burma. The UWSA makes laws, defends its motherland, builds roads, and collects taxes. It even issues driver's licenses. In every sense, it is a government. Yet to the United States of America, the latest empire to target the Wa, the UWSA is just a cabal of "kingpins" and "drug lords" presiding over a "dangerous criminal syndicate." Dangerous to whom? Americans, we are told. That may surprise the Americans who've never heard of the Wa people, which is practically all of them. Still the Drug Enforcement Administration insists that the Wa foster "crime, violence and terrible social damage here in the US."

Illegal drugs are indeed one of the UWSA's top revenue sources. Over the years, tons of narcotics produced on Wa soil have hit the black market, and traffickers have smuggled them onto American shores. The DEA therefore sees the UWSA as a Mastodon-sized trophy kill. America's stated goal is to "disrupt and dismantle" the entire system of Wa governance.

Herein lies the problem. The UWSA isn't some jungle-dwelling mafia. It's running an honest-to-God nation called Wa State, home to more than half a million people. It has its own schools, electricity grid, anthems, and flags. Because it is not sanctified by the United Nations, its territory isn't marked on official maps, but it comprises more than twelve thousand square miles. Wa State controls nearly as much soil as the Netherlands.

Wa State's army commands thirty thousand troops and twenty thousand reservists, more than the militaries of Sweden or Kenya. The Wa possess high-tech weaponry: artillery, drones, and missiles that can knock jets out of the sky. When it comes to firepower, the UWSA makes Mexican cartels look like street gangs. The Wa stockpile guns for a reason. America isn't the only country they've had to worry about. Wa people are indigenous to China's frontier, just like Tibetans and Uyghurs, minorities who've suffered deeply under a Chinese government that micromanages their every move. The Wa have faced the same threat.

So why is there a "Free Tibet" movement but none to free the Wa? Because they freed themselves. Yet, through Western eyes, they did it the wrong way: by producing illegal drugs, spending the profits on weapons, and daring outsiders to come take their land.

There's no getting around it. Just as Haiti was built on sugar and Saudi Arabia on oil, Wa State was built on heroin and methamphetamine. The UWSA sits at the core of a Southeast Asian drug trade generating $60 billion each year in meth alone.[3] The national economies of most "real" countries are smaller than that.

Wa leaders are indeed sovereigns of a narco-state. But to capture them and toss them into American prisons would wipe out the executive branch of a foreign government. In other words, it would constitute regime change. This book is based on a modest conviction: when a superpower tries to undermine an entire civilization and doom its people as untouchables on the world stage, it is essential to seek out the underdog's side of the story. That is what I've spent years trying to do.

I'm an American journalist who has lived and worked in Bangkok for more than fifteen years. In my day job with *The World*, a foreign affairs show airing on National Public Radio stations, I might cover anything from pop groups to riots. But I'm also a part-time *narcoperiodista*: a reporter specializing in drugs and organized crime. The premise of my first book (*Hello, Shadowlands*) is that lawbreakers tend to be rational actors, not just black-hearted ghouls. It's a collection of real-life stories about smugglers and rebels in Southeast Asia. You might suppose it would offer the UWSA more than a cameo, but that was all I could muster. Like Vasco da Gama, I'd only encountered the Wa through secondhand tales.

I've been fascinated with Wa State—a forbidden republic hiding in plain sight—since the moment I learned of its existence. Growing up in a factory town in the Appalachian foothills, I have a soft spot for mountain peoples and always assumed the Wa couldn't be as sinister as their reputation. But it is hard—no, really damn hard—to get to Wa State, vastly more difficult than traveling to North Korea or Antarctica. Americans face the highest bar to entry because the UWSA regards all US citizens as potential spies. Harder still is sitting down with UWSA leaders, many of whom are wanted by the DEA. Still I set out to meet the supposed super-villains of Asia's drug trade and understand their worldview.

This book is the result. It is the saga of an indigenous people who've tapped the power of narcotics to create a nation where there was none before. But much more is at stake here than the struggle of a little-known tribal group. Hollywood and cable news would have us think the War on Drugs is a conflict solely waged in the Americas. They've wrung dry every last detail about Latin kingpins. Meanwhile, Asia's underworld goes ignored. It is treated as a fringe curiosity that has little to do with the United States.

That is a dangerous lie.

When I began peering into the UWSA's inner workings, I didn't expect to find puppies and marshmallows, but what I uncovered was far stranger than I ever imagined. As it turns out, the origin story of this narco-army is smudged with American fingerprints. Not only did the Central Intelligence Agency create the conditions for its inception, but one of its foremost leaders was also a DEA asset.

The American government tells us the UWSA is a monster "poisoning our society for profit." But this is a beast that US agents, through malice and incompetence, have secretly nurtured.

Every empire needs its barbarians.

SUPERSTAR

They called him Superstar.

His former Drug Enforcement Administration handlers still speak of him with reverence, which is unusual, because confidential informants are seldom praised by anyone. CIs rat out fellow criminals to spare themselves from prison. Some CIs snitch for envelopes of cash, others to help police arrest their underworld rivals. As DEA agents see it, most are liars and squirmers who believe in nothing bigger than themselves.

But Superstar was different. Unlike other CIs, he brought a grad student's intensity to the informant role. His DEA handlers would go to a rendezvous in some Burmese safe house and find him already waiting inside, a sheaf of papers on his lap. His handwritten reports contained coordinates of heroin refineries and upcountry poppy farms, even rosters of corrupt police. They read like almanacs of crime.

"My God," said one DEA analyst, "the intel he gave us and the things he did to get it." Said a DEA agent, "I don't want to give away any sensitive secrets. But he certainly earned it—the name Superstar." And yet another agent said, "I'd never met a CI who was also an idealist."

As DEA agents extracted information from Superstar, he sought to extract something in return: a promise that America would honor its Christian soul and uplift the world's downtrodden, including his own people: the Wa. Superstar had a dream that, one day, Wa children would tote schoolbooks instead of Kalashnikovs. That Wa elders, once prone to decapitating outsiders on sight, would welcome foreigners into their homes. He imagined a doctor on every mountain to spare the sick from pointless death. A Wa nation of which he could feel proud.

Superstar told the DEA that the Wa wanted to go clean. They would torch their poppy fields, demolish their heroin labs, and stop making the white poison that so entranced addicts in New York and Los Angeles, a people clueless about the Wa yet spellbound by the silky powder they produced. In exchange, Superstar wanted American aid: schools, hospitals, expertise in building a modern nation, and the glory that comes from friendship with the United States.

Superstar believed divine forces sought to bind together the world's most powerful country and its most despised tribe—and that he was God's intermediary. He was a CI who talked like a messiah. "Like the heroin addicts that result from opium we grow, we too are in bondage," he wrote in one of his classified reports. "We are searching for help to break that bondage."

He dreamed of an alliance between the DEA and the United Wa State Army—known to the United States as a drug cartel. The agents had every reason to laugh. Yet, one by one, Superstar seduced them with this radical idea: that the DEA might bring about the largest narcotics eradication in history without firing a single bullet. For a brief time, there emerged on the horizon the glimmers of a bloodless alternative to the War on Drugs.

The DEA called him Superstar. But by the time I met him, no one had used his code name in a very long time. He was an old man with scars and a conviction somehow undiminished by a tragic life.

He made me call him by his Wa name: Saw Lu.

BOOK ONE

FIRST ENCOUNTER

I t's been said there are two ways to enter Wa lands: fight your way in or get invited.[1] Since my last fight was in middle school (I lost), I'd have to invite myself. If only I knew how to start the conversation.

The United Wa State Army (UWSA) has many trappings of government: a central committee and departments of finance, health, and education, but it does not have a press bureau that actively courts international media. The UWSA would rather starve journalists of contact, particularly Westerners, assuming anything we write will further the same old "narco-tribe" narrative. Google UWSA and you'll see why. The acronym conjures thirdhand stories about meth labs and child soldiers inside what the BBC calls "one of the most secretive places on earth."

Over the years, I'd requested permission to visit Wa State through various interlocutors. Sometimes I'd get a curt no. Usually I was ignored. But in 2019 my stubbornness generated a twinkle of hope. My emails to a senior UWSA officer—an envoy of sorts—received a reply written by the envoy's assistant in Google Translate–assisted English. First he asked for scans of my passport, which I sent reluctantly. Then he told me to come to their office later in the week—a de facto UWSA embassy, located in a Burmese city called Lashio, roughly fifty miles west of Wa territory.

The assistant did not provide a street address or a date or time. I tried to nail down the particulars, but his follow-ups made little sense.

> *Good morning, Patrick, thanks to received your*
> *concerning.*
> *Yours, Wa State*
> *Sent from Mail for Windows 10*

Screw it, I thought. An invite's an invite. I bought a ticket from Bangkok to Lashio and started packing. In my luggage: envelopes full of pristine $100 bills (always good to have in Burma) and a box of chocolates for the envoy. My wife was skeptical—"Is this a date?"—but the chocolates, I explained, were treats for his children, a gesture that might skirt the Kingpin Act, a piece of US legislation that can put anyone conducting "dealings" with the UWSA in prison for ten years.

Then I scrambled to line up a translator, ideally a Wa person in Lashio who could articulate my long-shot request: to enter the UWSA's territory and interview its leaders. I contacted a local travel agency, usually a good source of people who are bilingual and outgoing. Over email, they put me in touch with a "high-character Wa guy around 40 years old with a history of working for the Wa government." Perfect.

The interpreter introduced himself in an email—I'll call him Jacob—and wrote that he looked forward to meeting me at Lashio's airport. I told him not to bother. I could make my way to the hotel just fine on my own. But he wouldn't have it. Jacob was waiting outside the arrival hall, among the taxi touts and ladies with *thanaka*, tree-bark paste, painted on their cheeks. He was scanning for a pale face coming out of baggage claim. When I emerged, he jostled forth, flip-flops squeaking on the tile floor—a stranger coming straight at me with a handshake. His free hand relieved me of my luggage.

"Oh, Jacob? I can carry that."

"No, Mr. Patrick. Let me do it. It is a pleasure to make fellowship with you."

Bespectacled, his onyx hair gelled into a schoolboy part, Jacob wore a clean sweater and gray jogging pants in lieu of the usual sarong, worn by men and women alike in Burma. We walked toward his car, parked beyond a security booth manned by officers with shotguns. My wheeled suitcase rattled behind him.

"Your first time in Lashio," Jacob said. I took it as a question.

"Yes, though I can't count how many times I've been to—"

I stopped myself from saying either Burma or Myanmar. A person's preference between these names indicates their politics, and I did not want to reveal much about myself, not just yet.

"—this country."

I detected a stagger in Jacob's walk, more pronounced as he wheeled my luggage. Most Wa males have served in the UWSA—each household must hand over at least one son for a few years, sometimes at the tender age of twelve—and I wondered if he'd been injured while soldiering.

"Did police bother you inside the airport?" he said.

"Not really." When I came off the plane, two vacant-eyed Burmese cops waved me aside and took camera-phone snaps of my face. Nothing atypical. I was relieved they didn't ask the purpose of my visit.

"I don't think police will be a problem on your visit," said Jacob, sliding my suitcase into the trunk of his old Japanese hatchback. "Don't worry. We will take care of you here."

JACOB TOLD ME my hotel was close to the airport distance-wise, "but we'll have to take the long way around." There was something in the way: Northeast Command Headquarters, a giant Burmese military base.

Lashio is an army town and has been since the British colonial days. It sits on a plateau with mountains hunkering on the horizon. As far back as Queen Victoria's time, British troops used it as a staging ground for raids into the peaks. They were hellbent on conquering native tribes.

This subjugation drive remains unfinished. When the Brits pulled out after World War II, ending more than a century of occupation, Burma became an independent country. Its military picked up where their colonizers left off, deploying brute force into the borderlands. The old colonial machinery creaks on—only now the generals are Buddhist and ethnically Burmese, the country's majority race, native to the balmy lowlands. Their mission is to dominate everyone inside the former colony's borders, especially the unruly mountain folk. They're not very good at it though.

Beyond Lashio, eastward in the direction of China, military rule weakens and the country shatters into pieces. It is an archipelago of rebellions—the scattered domains of hill-dwelling minorities: the Shan, Kachin, Kokang, and Lahu, to name a few of Burma's minorities, which number in the dozens. They intend to rule themselves, and most have their own mini-governments, complete with armed wings defending patches of homeland with rifles and rockets. Among these groups, the UWSA is the mightiest. Just as the Wa terrified the British in the 1800s, they terrify the Burmese military now.

Cruising past Northeast Command HQ, I took in a sprawling fortress secured behind spiky iron gates. Seeing Burmese platoons running drills on a dusty field, I wondered which indigenous group they'd attack next. "It's good you didn't need to fly here last month," Jacob told me. Apparently some guerrillas crept down from the hills, lobbed mortars at the army base, missed, and blew up the airport runway. "There were no flights for a while."

Jacob was full of questions. Was I married? Yes. Is your wife American? Thai-American and we live in Bangkok. In which American state did I grow up? Carolina. I omitted the "North" so he wouldn't mistake me for a northerner, but Jacob knew his US states, asking if I was from the Carolina that touches Tennessee. Impressive.

My turn. You work for that travel agency? No, I am well known in town, and they just connected us as a courtesy. Where do you work? I have various jobs, he said, failing to elaborate. Family? Yes, wife and kids. Languages? Wa, Burmese, English, some Chinese.

Are you friendly with the UWSA envoy? Yes, he said, the Wa community here is small. Jacob said he was finalizing a meeting for me inside the UWSA "embassy," a compound where the Wa conduct diplomacy with lowlanders.

"That's great. So wait. Are you in the UWSA too?" Jacob hesitated. After a long pause, he said no.

It was late afternoon. Lashio appeared typical of any second-tier Burmese city. Leafy creepers running up concrete walls. Metal rooftops splotched coffee-orange with rust. Sun-bleached billboards for instant coffee powder or jade necklaces. A patina of dust cast a sepia tint over the streetscape.

Jacob braked in front of my hotel. A sign out front depicted a handgun x-ed out: a "no weapons" pictogram. "Patrick, I have prepared a schedule," Jacob said as he retrieved my luggage from the car. "Tomorrow, I will greet you here at 8:15 a.m. We will eat breakfast from 8:20 to 8:45. Then we will arrive at the UWSA office at 9 a.m. for your meeting."

I'd only seen that degree of punctuality in Germans and military officers. Jacob was not German.

"That's very specific," I said teasingly. He did not smile.

"I like to be on time. Enjoy your rest and God bless."

THE NEXT MORNING, I took the stairs down to the lobby, declining the elevator over fears that a citywide power outage could trap me in that metal box and sabotage my precious appointment. I descended to find Jacob sitting on a sofa, his forehead crumpled in a pained expression.

"Oh, Patrick. I am very sorry. I just found out. Our meeting is canceled. The envoy was called urgently to Panghsang."

Wa State's capital, UWSA headquarters. Located on the China-Burma border, roughly one hundred miles and a zillion checkpoints away. Jacob stared down at his phone, holding it like a kid presenting a bad report card.

"When will he return?"

"In a few days maybe. It is not certain."

"What if I just hang out in Lashio until he comes back?"

That was fine; Jacob's week was open. But even as I voiced the suggestion, I thought it sounded risky. There was no way to know if there had been a genuine scheduling mishap or the envoy had zero intention of ever seeing me. The envoy's main role was smoothing relations with Burma, the country that Wa State awkwardly nests inside. That made him a bureaucrat, and in my experience, bureaucrats in Southeast Asia never tell you to get lost. They'd rather ghost you or rain-check the meeting eternally.

Jacob took me to a tea shop for breakfast. Then we cruised around town, two strangers with an ocean of time ahead of us. I assumed he was driving aimlessly until his car strained up a hill and he announced, "Here it is. Our Wa village."

In a typical village in Burma, you see bamboo shelters bent by gravity and mothers squatting over charcoal fires. Here the streets were arranged in blocks lined with two-story homes. There were middle-class signifiers: satellite dishes, trucks in driveways, balconies with wrought-iron banisters. Painted on the sides of a few homes were buffalo skulls, a Wa symbol of vitality.

"A village? This looks more like a neighborhood."

"A village in spirit," he said. "All people here are Wa. All coming from the same place."

I pointed at the mountains in the distance. He laughed. "Yes, from that direction but more far than you can see. There was trouble in an old Wa village called Pang Wai. They had to flee here and start over. It happened before I was born."

The largest home, squatting atop the hill's summit, was painted sea-foam green and defended by heavy steel gates. Security cameras peered down from the awnings. "The home of our village leader," Jacob said. "A very important man." I was surprised to see an old red-brick chapel right across from the very important leader's home. A crimson cross painted on its wooden doors removed any doubt: this was a church. Out front, there were two wooden beams jutting upward from the dirt, and strung between them with a heavy chain was an ancient-looking bombshell. Jacob parked next to it, engine idling.

"Patrick, what is your religion?"

I'd expected this. Race and religion undergird every social interaction in Burma. They predetermine your allies and rivals, your career prospects, whether you are merely neglected by the state or targeted by its attack choppers. The stakes for me, a foreign visitor, were obviously far lower, but the wrong answer could close doors. I wasn't sure how to respond. I knew the UWSA was a strictly areligious organization. I knew that the Wa traditionally worshipped a multitude of spirits in nature. But atheist still felt like the wrong answer.

"I was raised going to church."

"Yes, but what kind? RC or Baptist?" RC meaning Roman Catholic.

"Baptist."

Jacob perked up. "This is our Baptist church!" He hopped out of the car, shuffled over to the dangling bombshell, and rapped it with his knuckles. It groaned like a Tibetan gong. A makeshift church bell, he explained. Hung by the village leader after he established this village, long ago, in the wake of a terrible exodus from their Wa homeland.

"Your people here were pushed out because they were Christian?"

"Something like that. Very few Wa are Christian, and the rest view us with suspicion." Jacob said the Christian Wa had been seen as judgmental by the other Wa going back a hundred years, when the former urged the latter to quit planting human skulls on sticks.

Last stop on the tour: a cobbled-together house, half brick, half wood, roof of crinkle-cut tin. It looked a touch shabbier than the other homes. "This is where I live with my wife and children. I hope you will come to dinner sometime. How about tonight?"

It was decided. Jacob would drop me back at the hotel while he and his wife prepared a Wa feast. He would then retrieve me at 17:20 for our 17:30 meal.

JACOB'S LIMP DID NOT owe to some old battle injury. I realized this on the way into his house as I knelt by the stoop to unlace my shoes. I got a close look at his right foot, wrapped in fresh gauze. A minor infection, he said, catching me staring.

"I just need to buy some pills. I will take care of it after your trip."

I felt a twinge of guilt. My imagination had superimposed a grim backstory on Jacob just because he was Wa. I also worried he needed my payment for his translation services to afford antibiotics. That guilt surged when I saw the dinner table. His wife, Grace, was laying out a fantastic spread: fatty cubes of pork, a big golden-fried fish, and a Wa staple called *moik*, a risotto-like rice dish flecked with herbs. So much for stereotypes about unwelcoming Wa. For many in Burma, meat is a once-a-week luxury. They were splurging on my behalf.

They asked me to bless the food, Baptist style. We held hands, and I bumbled through. Then we dined al fresco on a concrete patio by their back garden. Over dinner, I confessed that I was not a churchgoer. That's fine, Jacob said. Not long ago, his life had been devoted more to the UWSA than to Jesus Christ.

"So you *were* a soldier."

"An officer," he said. "But never fighting. I don't like fighting."

"What did you do?"

"Mostly education. I started by teaching small soldiers." I asked if he meant soldiers with low rank. "No," he said, standing up and holding his hand at rib height to indicate a short person. "Ten years old. Eleven, twelve."

As we talked about the UWSA, Jacob slipped into the tone of a man recounting a tragic divorce. "It is a lot to explain, Patrick. There are good people in the UWSA wanting to make our government better. But some leaders, they are not so good. Inside our society there is . . ."

Fumbling for the right word, he beat his fists together.

"A war?"

"Not that strong. But OK. Like a war. Between people who are striving and people who only care about money." *Striving* was one of Jacob's favorite English words. He believed all of humanity was divided between the selfish and the strivers, the latter pursuing some cause bigger than themselves.

His wife spooned more *moik* onto my plate. "Imagine you want to set up a dirty business deal," Jacob said. "The UWSA officers will run to meet you. But if you want to discuss doing good, like building a school, they will arrive two hours late or not at all."

"You like people to be on time."

"Yes," he said. "Wa people are far behind. We cannot waste time."

I sensed an opening. My obsession with the UWSA centered on two leaders. One was Chairman Bao Youxiang, the face of the Wa nation. Like Fidel Castro, he appears to own only one set of clothes: olive-green fatigues, occasionally accented with an Hermès belt. His resting expression is grumpy: lips downturned, eyebrows slanted in a V of vexation.

"What about Chairman Bao? Have you met him?"

"Many times."

"Is he good or bad?"

"Pretty good. A very striving man."

The Drug Enforcement Administration has a different take on Bao. It identifies him as a "drug lord." But in the DEA hierarchy, drug lord is a rung below the more treacherous "kingpin," a title for narco-moguls so paramount that, were they killed, a huge part of the global drug trade would instantly collapse. So goes the DEA theory.

The leader on whom I was truly fixated was the UWSA's so-called kingpin: Wei Xuegang, the organization's finance czar and the DEA's most wanted man in Asia. Whether the UWSA is itself a drug cartel—or a government financed by an in-house drug cartel—is a matter of semantics. Either way, Wei masterminds its drug trafficking, and he is as mysterious as he is powerful. In one of the only known photos of Wei, a grainy mugshot from the late 1980s, he is scowling. He may be 5'6", but to the DEA he is Sasquatch.

I started to ask Jacob about Wei but didn't want to spook him. Better to stick to Bao for now. "Jacob, what do you think? Am I crazy to ask for an interview with Chairman Bao?"

Jacob pushed his glasses back up his nose and sighed. He translated my question to his wife. Grace said nothing but studied my face carefully. Jacob asked what I wanted to know exactly. Everything, I said. Opium. Heroin. Crystal meth. How the whole operation started. What it all looked like from the inside. What the outside world got wrong. And I wanted it from someone with gravitas.

Jacob muttered something to his wife. Both of them seemed to be thinking hard. Grace abruptly scooted her chair back, legs screeching on the concrete. She went into a back garden and rang someone on her mobile phone. I could see her pacing under a canopy of banana trees, talking in a deferential voice. Jacob's ears were cocked to his wife's conversation. The energy felt odd, and I was beginning to regret bringing up Schedule II narcotics during an otherwise lovely dinner.

When she returned to the table smiling, I could not have felt more relieved.

"OK!"

"OK what, Jacob?"

"The village leader will meet you. An important man like Chairman Bao. His name is Saw Lu. He is the father of my wife. He is . . ."

Jacob was grasping for the word.

"Father-in-law?"

"Yes, Patrick. Saw Lu is my father-in-law."

WE WERE IMMEDIATELY up and moving, trying to catch Saw Lu before bedtime. Jacob talked fast. He had only five minutes to brief me on our walk. Saw Lu was once the UWSA's top statesman, his ranking equal to that of Chairman Bao. Jacob struggled to convey the totality of his eminence. He'd been a warrior, a diplomat, and an inspiration, but most of all Saw Lu was a founding father—an architect of Wa nationhood. There was little about the UWSA he did not know. Whether he would indulge my questions would depend on his mood.

A servant girl unlocked the gates to Saw Lu's compound and led us into a living room. The man of the house would be down in a moment. His home's decor looked very 1970s: the walls were painted teal and splotched with condensation stains too deep to scrub off; the furniture looked straight out of a Sears catalog. There were tables topped with doilies and, in one corner, a clunky electrical converter. Everyone in Burma has one, lest power surges fry your electronics, but this model was prehistoric. It wasn't a poor home but one in which the owner did not believe in extravagance.

I deduced the family's prestige by looking up. As in many Southeast Asian homes, photos of kids and grandkids who've gone to college are mounted high on the wall, mortarboards and tassels on their heads, staring down at guests. You usually see one or two at most. Saw Lu's exhibition of university graduates ran wall to wall. In the center of it all, in pride of place, was a portrait of the patriarch: Saw Lu in full regalia, emerald-colored uniform with brass buttons, a peaked cap and a crimson breast tag reading "UWSA." It was a novel sight for me at least—a Wa leader presented not as a fugitive glowering in a mugshot but as a hero worthy of a gilt frame.

This young Saw Lu in the portrait looked debonair with his bright black eyes and service pistol jutting from his leather belt. Though clearly Christian to the core—the opposite wall was graced with a painting of white Jesus—Saw Lu had a face like the Buddha: broad nose, full lips, imperturbable confidence.

The door creaked, and I turned to see a grayer, heavier Saw Lu. He wore slacks and a plaid shirt. Jacob offered an arm to steady the old man's walk, but he waved him off and plopped down in a chair.

I introduced myself as a journalist. Saw Lu asked in his sandpaper rasp if I was American. I thought the answer would make him tense up. Instead his shoulders relaxed. He murmured a question to Jacob in the Wa language, and I caught the letters "D-E-A." Jacob stole a glance at me, looked back at his father-in-law, and shrugged, as if to say he had no idea.

"Like I said, Saw Lu, it's an honor to meet you. Is it alright if I take notes?"

Go ahead, he said. I'd expected an interrogation or long preamble, but it seemed like he'd done this before—played man with the answers for a foreigner scribbling on a notepad. Scoring an interview like this should have taken months. Here I was, on day one, sitting across from the Wa nation's answer to Ben Franklin, apparently, and despite years of research, I felt utterly unprepared. All I could manage was a run-on question about how the Wa started their nation and got mixed up in narcotics.

"No," he said.

No?

The opium came first. Then the nation. And before both, an epoch of self-annihilating blood feuds that stretched back before recorded history. Skull collecting. The tribe's original sin. A ritual that left the Wa weak and disunited, unable to come together as one powerful race.

Saw Lu sent the servant girl to fetch tea.

"Let's start at the beginning. Would you like to hear about the headhunters?"

STRANGER IN THE PEAKS

WINTER, LATE 1966.

Saw Lu plodded uphill on feet numb with cold. At his back were Burma's nubby hills, rounded like molars. He was advancing into the Wa highlands where mountains take the shape of fangs. As he ascended, the whine of insects dimmed. The trees grew stunted, and the air went thin, quickening his breath.

Beside the pebbly trails were skulls mounted on sticks. Crania were arranged in neat rows with eye cavities facing west: the direction of setting suns, the direction of death. That is how the Wa conveyed "no trespassing" without words.

Two or three skulls posted by the trail warned that a small Wa hamlet was nearby. A midsize Wa village might declare itself with twenty heads. But Saw Lu's destination was Pang Wai, a larger settlement worthy of many dozens of skulls glaring at intruders from hollow sockets, some splotched green-black with lichen, fresher kills gleaming white. Headhunters always arrayed skulls at a fair distance from any settlement's entrance—as if to offer uninvited visitors one last chance to heed their squirming bowels and turn back.

Saw Lu saw this grim menagerie and trudged onward. Call it courage if you like. Anyone who knew the Wa by reputation would think him insane. You simply did not enter the realm of headhunters, not without an army. Saw Lu wasn't even carrying a rifle. Worse yet, he'd brought his new wife, Mary, baby-faced, barely out of her teenage years, and wed to a man dragging her through a forest of horrors.[1]

Saw Lu was only twenty-two himself, and once he got an idea in his head, he would not let it go, even if it could get him decapitated. This was not just some facet of youth. Stubbornness was coded into his very being.

At the time, Saw Lu's notion was this: I am going to get inside Pang Wai, this bastion of headhunters. And I will not leave until its inhabitants, my ethnic kinfolk, are civilized Wa like me.

As an agent of Burma's military regime, Saw Lu had orders. He was sent to assimilate among the headhunters, then somehow persuade them to hone their killing prowess against Chinese communists. High peaks form a natural buffer between Burma and China, but at the time China's government was plotting to come over those mountains and spread communism to Burma's indigenous peoples, starting with the Wa.

Though their land technically fell on the Burma side, the headhunters felt no loyalty to Burma or any nation at all. So if he managed to gain their trust, Saw Lu would present the pitch: defend the status quo, for the Burmese will never try to dominate your ancestral lands—unlike Chinese communists, fervid under Mao Zedong's leadership, who hope to erase your unique tribal identity and extinguish your way of life.

Saw Lu intended to follow orders, but only because they aligned with his own personal agenda. As a self-proclaimed "civilized" Wa, educated since childhood by American missionaries, he hoped to enlighten his race in every single way. As Burma's junta instructed, Saw Lu would unite them against communism, but then go further: abolishing their head-hunting ritual, teaching them to read, and perhaps even converting a few to Christianity. It was a near-impossible feat, and Saw Lu didn't have much of a plan. But he felt confident that, in time, he'd find a way to succeed and all Wa would hail him as their savior.

As Saw Lu and Mary reached the outskirts of Pang Wai, they realized the town was larger than they'd imagined. Its outer defensive walls rose high as the trees. At a distance they could see these ramparts were made of packed mud and thick logs, and upon those walls, the Wa had planted *hrax*, a shrub with lacerating thorns, a living form of barbed wire.

They could not walk toward the fortress town from any which way. The Wa were known to surround settlements with traps: moats filled not with water (for water was scarce in the highlands) but with wooden spikes, each sharp point lathered with poison milked from amphibian glands. There was only one proper way to approach the town: a trench path. Entrants had to climb down into a dirt rut and proceed forward. With each step, the trench deepened, gradually forming a mini-canyon that blocked out the sun. This dark corridor snaked at odd angles, shortening lines of sight. Navigating that black gauntlet, Saw Lu and Mary feared swordsmen would lunge from blind corners. But none emerged as they pushed ahead. After a few minutes, the tunnel disgorged them into the sunlight, and they stood before two wooden doors, tall as giants, set into the fortress walls.

Pang Wai's doors were ajar. Within minutes the couple was spotted.

Soon they stood half encircled by Wa men and women, nude except for cloth scraps hanging over their genitals, their bodies plastered with dust the color of yellowed bone.

Saw Lu told Mary to keep quiet. He stepped forward to let the people assess him. He was doe-eyed, thin but sturdy, and richly melanated like most Wa, more so than the Chinese to the east or the Burmese to the west. But the similarities between his appearance and that of his onlookers ended there. Saw Lu was dressed like a lowlander: plaid sarong, shirt with buttons, leather shoes. His panther-black hair was combed to the side. The barefoot observers were unsure what to make of him. It did not seem this man could belong to their race until Wa words spilled from his mouth.

We want to live among you, Saw Lu said. My wife and I. We have come to seek permission.

Permission? From whom? There was no one to give it, they said. Anyone who was truly Wa ought to know that.

THE WA DID NOT obey any man with a golden crown or some council of priests. The fortress town of Pang Wai didn't have jailers or shopkeepers either. With few exceptions, there was only one class of person: the warrior-farmer, an anarchist who did as he or she pleased.[2]

The few outsiders who'd encountered the Wa in the past always struggled to believe people could be so free. In the late 1800s, British colonizers—intent on adding the Wa highlands to Burma, their colony—marched in with a similar request: take me to your leader. Surely, the explorers wrote, this "race of ogres . . . dark-skinned, dirty, poor and savage" must kneel to a great Wa chieftain whom the British Crown could manipulate.[3] But they were wrong. The tribe was scattered into a constellation of many fortresses, each thoroughly independent and often estranged from the others.

How to subjugate a people with no leader? The British were flummoxed. Still they persisted in encroaching upon Wa lands, even after receiving a warning, in 1897, from a village: "Please return by the route you came. Ours is a wild country and the people devour rats and squirrels raw. Our people and yours have nothing in common."[4] Only after losing a few of their own heads did the would-be colonizers get the message. They slunk away in defeat but added the Wa highlands to paper maps of Burma anyway—as if the peaks had been conquered. This was pure fiction. Privately the Brits groused that the Wa were "notoriously subject to nobody."[5]

That remained true in Pang Wai well into the mid-1960s when Saw Lu and Mary showed up at the town gates. All the better, for there was no ruler who could make them leave. Had they come as gun-toting colonizers or warriors from a rival clan, the locals might have chopped them down on the spot. But the couple was deemed harmless, led inside the town walls, and shown a patch of land where they might build a home.

Not a home, Saw Lu said, correcting his hosts. A school. We've come to build a school for you.

Saw Lu and Mary explored the cloistered interior of Pang Wai. Within its walls were hundreds of wooden dwellings with bristly thatch roofs and spacious interiors, big enough to light a cooking fire inside. The town was well populated with more than five hundred denizens and alive with singing children, groaning buffalo, and the clink of ironwork. A painted drum carved from a log occupied its center. This was their public broadcasting system. Morse code–like rhythms could signal danger (enemies incoming) or joy (a successful hunt). Pang Wai even had aqueducts: bamboo piping snaked over the walls and up to a gurgling stream on the mountainside. Fresh water on demand was a great convenience, the locals explained, because they hated traveling beyond the front gates. They would only do so in groups lest they fall victim to enemy clans. Women hardly ever left the walls except to till nearby poppy or corn fields. The men only left to farm, hunt, or slay rivals. They always hurried back.

The locals were kind to Saw Lu and Mary, helping them gather bamboo to build their house. Actually, we're building a school, they repeated. Within days, the couple's novelty wore off. Saw Lu kept repeating that he was ethnically Wa just like them. No one argued, even though his incessant questions revealed an ignorance about the simplest facts of life in the highlands.

Saw Lu and Mary felt hopeful. Though they'd feared living among crazed headhunters, there was little sadism on display. Perhaps the skull-gathering ritual was only perpetrated by a vicious few. Surely most of these softhearted villagers would recoil at such violence. But this naïveté would not survive the month of March—when they witnessed neighbors cheering in front of a newly severed head.

Head-hunting season was beginning.

Half a dozen Pang Wai men had just returned from the wilderness, and they nestled the human head in the crook of a tree, right at eye level. It had a ferrous stink, like rusty nails. Everyone in Pang Wai crowded around, eager for face time with the year's first kill. At these spectacles, aunties would shoulder their way to the front of the throng to gently tease the head: Oh, dear, why did you walk through the forest alone, presenting such a gift to our warriors? They'd crack an egg on its teeth and dribble yolk into its mouth: a final snack for the dead, whose sacrifice would bless them with good fortune.

What had the victim done to anger the headhunters? Another one of Saw Lu's obtuse questions. It wasn't personal, the killers explained. Wrong clan, wrong place, wrong time. The headhunters said they'd crept toward an enemy fortress and laid an ambush on the approaching trail. Some guy happened to walk past. They sprang from the bramble, jostling to sever his spinal cord, and left the body twitching on the trail. They stuffed the head into a wicker basket and hoofed it back to Pang Wai with blood crusting on their chests.

That was the how of the killing. As for the why, Saw Lu knew the gist. Though not raised among headhunters, he was Wa enough to know the tribe's guiding belief—that every human head was suffused with a mystical force. Only the Wa race could extract its power and manipulate it for their own needs.

The procedure was simple: plant the head on a pole, let the flesh decompose and drip onto the soil below. The warrior-farmers would scoop up that gore-sopped dirt and scatter it among seedlings in the fields. Its death force acted as supernatural pesticide, scaring off vermin and insects.[6] Failure to uphold the ritual would result in pests eating your crops and starvation in your village. Per local custom, this newly cleaved head would remain inside Pang Wai's walls until every bit of tissue had sloughed off. Only when the skull was sun blanched and smooth would the warriors add it to their exhibition by the trail—the one Saw Lu and Mary had passed on their way into the fortress town.

Saw Lu was repulsed. But the locals were joyful, as if the home team had just pulled off a victory. Their joy had a sharp edge, though, especially among men who'd failed to join the hunt. They were possessed by a restless feeling that found its release with the favored sport of the highlands. Someone trotted a hulking black buffalo into a dirt arena next to the drum. Men clutching blades encircled the beast. One of them hacked off its tail and flung it skyward; like the firing of a starter pistol, this signaled the game's start. They pounced on the buffalo, swords rising and falling, misting the air red. Whoever sheared off the biggest flanks would be declared victor and enjoy honor second only to that of the headhunters. Competitors often lost fingers in the frenzy, Saw Lu was told. Sometimes ears.

The game was over in minutes. But celebrations carried on into the evening. When the sun fell behind the peaks, they replaced its warmth with a bonfire. The Wa skewered buffalo meat and glugged rice wine from communal bamboo jugs. The drum was rhythmically thwacked. Young and old alike twirled around the flames and collapsed in fits of glee.

But Saw Lu was not in a twirling mood. Their fun was obscene to him. He stood with Mary at the edge of the circle, in the flickering orange light, pitying the revelers for falling under a demonic trance. Some old-timers gathered around them, hoping to impress the newcomers with big-fish tales. One elder, bent with age, boasted that he'd once lopped off the head of a man sprinting at full speed. Nudging Saw Lu in the ribs, he asked, How far do you think a man can run without his head attached?

I wouldn't know, Saw Lu said.

Farther than you think! His body kept running down the trail as I held his head in my hands.

Lord, give me strength, Saw Lu thought. How will I ever make such people decent? He breathed in deeply and reminded himself it was possible—for he was Wa, after all, and the Americans had civilized him.

SAW LU WAS born in 1944 amid the last days of an unusual sect. His people were Wa, but not noticeably so, for they covered their bodies in scratchy black tunics and believed that decapitation angered God.

That is what their oracle had taught them.

The oracle's name was William Marcus Young, an American Baptist missionary from Nebraska. He had a walrus mustache and a conviction that his fiery gospel could refine any nonbeliever, even people from forsaken tribes. Young longed to test his skills in remote parts of Asia, and at the beginning of the twentieth century, in his early thirties, Young sailed with his wife to Burma. It was then a colony ruled by the British Empire, which encouraged missionaries to roam its fringes as "civilizing agents."

The Youngs made their way to the colony's northern environs: a rolling hill country known as Shan State, home to many ethnic groups. At first they focused on converting the Shan, Burma's largest minority group and the most populous race in its north. Most Shan dwelled in fertile valleys, congregating in small, upcountry kingdoms with glittering temples and lively bazaars. Like the Thais, their ethnic cousins, Shan people nurtured a rich faith in Buddhism.[7] They were painfully disinterested in diatribes about Jesus. William Marcus Young lurked around a town called Kengtung, attempting to convert the locals, but he was mocked and occasionally robbed. He achieved little during his first two decades in Burma apart from fathering two sons.[8]

Then came a miracle on four hooves: an alpine-white pony ambling toward the preacher one afternoon. Trailing it were three tribesmen from some faraway place. This creature is enchanted, the bare-chested strangers told Young. We have chased it for weeks down forbidding mountain paths. It leads us to a "great white teacher," an oracle bearing the "true religion."[9]

Me?

Indeed. Our tribe is called the Wa, the men said. And you, sir, must be the "bearer of the white book and white law of God." The trio implored William Marcus Young to pack up his belongings and venture east— beyond the reaches of the British Empire. Follow us to a desperate place where wickedness reigns. Your arrival will fulfill a prophecy that a white man shall someday come to teach our tribe to live in piety.

So goes the Young family lore. Apocryphal would be putting it politely. But this is how the Youngs always explained why they moved to the Wa ancestral lands—or rather to their outlying edges. The tribesmen would not lead the Youngs directly into the Wa peaks where headhunters ruled. Even we cannot go there safely, they said. We are a peace-loving offshoot of Wa who've abandoned our violent heartland to settle nearby, in lower-lying green knolls close to the peaks—an area called Banna.[10]

Banna fell on the Chinese side of the border, inasmuch as there was any recognized border at the time. It was a remote hideaway for Chinese frontier folk: poppy planters, opium smugglers, outlaws, and others brave enough to settle in the shadow of the feared Wa peaks—a place where headhunters sometimes came down to raid villages. The offshoot band of Wa that beseeched Young lived among these gritty lowlanders. They'd laid down their head-hunting swords and, in doing so, lost much of their dignity. To survive, they hired themselves out to Chinese settlers who worked them like oxen. Many were hooked on opium, smoking themselves into a daily stupor. William Marcus Young was keen to save them from depravity. With his wife and sons, he relocated to Banna in hopes of carving out a little Christian utopia—and finally fulfilling his evangelical quest.[11]

Soon after arriving, to the family's delight, they amassed dozens of acolytes. The bedraggled Wa who flocked to their side made easy pickings for missionaries promising a better life, if not now then in heaven. Other disaffected local minorities joined the sect too, namely the Lahu, a long-persecuted, migratory tribe—also native to the China-Burma border—whose name means "tiger hunters." The Wa and Lahu disciples called Young "the Man-God."

By the 1920s, the Man-God and his followers, now numbering in the hundreds, lived together in a large commune. He imposed a lifestyle of militant Christianity. No booze or opium. No nudity. Literacy was mandatory—how else to read the Bible?—yet neither the Wa nor the Lahu had a written language. So the Young family invented one using the English alphabet and translated the New Testament into this original script. There was only one path to redemption: obey the Man-God and the Sons of the Man-God, Harold and Vincent, then in their early twenties. When preaching to their acolytes, the Youngs spoke of love and salvation. Privately, however, they said there was a "strangeness about the Wa nature that few can understand."[12]

The Chinese frontiersmen, observing from a distance, believed the Young family were the truly strange ones: a pale family in safari hats running a teetotaler tribal cult. Babies born into the sect were given odd names such as Jeremiah, Moses, and Peter. Though William Marcus

Young's flock kept growing, he was never satisfied. He gazed longingly up at the fog-shrouded peaks—the terrain of headhunters.

Again, his followers cautioned him. That way lay certain death.

The Wa highlanders, they said, clung to folk stories about mankind's origins, and there was no knocking these ideas out of their heads. Many head-hunting Wa believed humans originated from a hole located in their peaks. The first people to crawl above ground were industrious, inventing tools, farming, and speech. They called themselves Wa. Unfortunately, the hole kept spewing out more people: ill-mannered latecomers who stole knowledge from the Wa and scuttled down the mountains toward warmer, flatter places. Soon enough, these lowlanders made up their own funny languages, and eventually they bowed to emperors and holy men. Today they are the Burmese, the Chinese, the Indians, the Europeans, and other races who've rejected the way of the first humans and their life of undistilled freedom.[13]

Young's flock kept warning him: these head-hunting Wa will never bow before any pallid prophet such as yourself. But the Youngs wouldn't let the idea go. Trying to convert actual headhunters was the ultimate trial of their faith. The white heat of Baptist gospel, they said, could burn away this occultism and fuse all the squabbling head-hunting clans into a single glorious polity under Christ. A Son of the Man-God wrote, "It is impossible to watch this appalling annual waste of human life, or even know about it, and remain unmoved. . . . Christianity is the only remedy."[14]

The Youngs' disciples paid for this obsession with their own blood. Of a failed evangelical foray in 1931, William Marcus Young said, "Four of my boy converts lost their heads. A fifth was brought back in serious condition with a spear through his back." The dead were buried, he said, "with their arms pressed over the neck where their heads should have been." Growing desperate, the Youngs imagined madcap solutions, such as asking the US government to fly airplanes over the highlands and shock the head-hunting Wa into submission. "It would help them to realize, without bloodshed, the overwhelming resources of Western civilization," Harold Young said, "for even their devil doctors do not claim to be able to fly."

William Marcus Young's fantasy of converting headhunters en masse was never realized. By the time Saw Lu was born—in late 1944—Young had been dead for nearly a decade. A Son of the Man-God, Vincent, was running the Banna mission alongside his disciples, including Saw Lu's parents. The couple named their son after Saul, the first king of Israel, who united scattered Israelite tribesmen under an organized state. They dreamed he could one day achieve the same outcome for the Wa.

Though Saw Lu never met the Man-God himself, he was deeply indoctrinated with his dogma. Its key tenets: most Wa were trapped in darkness; Americans were bringers of light; and blessed were the Wa who risked death to civilize their unenlightened kin.

But Saw Lu never got a chance to join one of those "civilizing" forays into the peaks. He was still a little boy in 1949 when his sect had to flee Banna, leaving everything behind. In one of his earliest memories, Saw Lu is five years old. He grips his mother's tunic in his tiny hand. They are walking in a procession: hundreds of black-clad Wa Baptists, miserably trudging toward Burma, escaping only with the clothes they wore, taking neither livestock nor gold. At their backs, the only home he'd ever known—their bamboo-built compound in Banna—grew smaller with every step.

Mother, he asked, from whom are we running?

Communists, she said. Now try to keep up.

STILL A BOY, Saw Lu didn't know much about the Chinese communist soldiers in beige garb and steel helmets spotted marching toward Banna. His parents explained that these men would burn down their mission compound, shoot any white foreigners, then corral every Wa and Lahu disciple into labor camps. The Baptists didn't intend to stick around and give them the pleasure.

Communists despise our kind, his mother said, and that's all you need to know. Saw Lu, toddling behind her, decided to hate them in return. In truth, he was scared witless—as were many others along China's frontiers.

No event in modern Asian history was more monumental than China's takeover, in 1949, by the Chinese Communist Party—an upheaval whose ripples shook every neighboring country and altered innumerable lives. Led by Mao Zedong, the communists won a civil war for control of the country. They'd trounced their enemy: a US-backed regime called the Kuomintang, which had ruled China for two decades after helping chuck the last dynastic emperor off his throne. The Kuomintang were avowed nationalists, "fascist in every quality except efficiency," as one scholar put it.[15] So rotten was the Kuomintang that China's peasantry, riled by Mao, were willing to battle its troops with farm tools, hacking them down in "human wave" attacks and snatching their guns. The overwhelmed Kuomintang government—along with shopkeepers, landlords, and other capitalists—escaped to Taiwan, an island off China's coast.

Mao was triumphant, but his revolution was incomplete. He needed to ensure that all of China, even the farthest borderlands, fell under his iron-hard communist monoculture. China's distant reaches were inhabited by Mongols, Uyghurs, Tibetans, and other minorities committed to their own traditions and faiths. This was intolerable. Every ethnic minority needed taming, including the Wa, reputedly the most untamable tribe of all.

Numbering roughly half a million at the time, the Wa people respected no government and cared little about borders. Their walled settlements dotted both sides of the China-Burma line. For centuries, Chinese dynasts kept their distance, believing the Wa "ugly in appearance and evil in nature," a warrior tribe best left alone.[16] Mao thought differently. No previous Chinese leader had possessed the People's Liberation Army, five million soldiers strong, and this heavily armed goliath would not shrink from headhunters gripping crude swords.

Mao ordered battalions to subdue every Wa living on the Chinese side of the border.[17] This amounted to roughly half the total Wa population and half of Wa ancestral lands. Communist soldiers gunned down Wa warriors, torched their fortresses, kicked over skull posts, and smashed the crania under their boots. Adults were herded onto communal farms, children shunted into Chinese-language schools. This was the terror that Saw Lu's sect fled.

Mao's subjugation campaign lasted more than ten brutal years. By the mid-1960s, all the Wa on the Chinese side had been colonized. Meanwhile the other half, on the Burma side, lived as they had in ancient times. Inhabiting a super-rugged stretch of highlands, about sixty-five hundred square miles all together, were Wa clans who still decorated settlements with rivals' skulls, as did their forebears.[18] They had no rulers, save for a few Wa warlord clans staking claim to slopes and valleys here and there. It was the last refuge of Wa civilization.

According to international law, this untouched zone belonged to Burma's government, but this was a joke. After the British Empire relinquished

Burma following World War II, control of the colony—reborn as a nation-state—fell to a native-born military junta. These Burmese rulers inherited all that the British once claimed, including their lies.[19] No one had ever conquered that part of Wa country except on paper. And unlike Mao, Burma's leaders did not possess an army that could subjugate the Wa highlands and make the lie true.

In the 1960s, Burma was fracturing. The junta could barely keep the country whole. Hills seethed with rebellion. The Shan wanted their own country. The Kachin, the Karen, the Mon, and other indigenous high-landers also wanted to govern themselves, as they had for eons before colonization. Burma's troops struggled to suppress each new ethnic uprising, lest one country split into many. Their army was spread thin, broke, and far too exhausted to take on Wa warriors.

The frazzled Burmese generals would've preferred to forget the Wa existed. But they couldn't. Not with Mao's revolution at their backdoor. Having already colonized roughly half of the Wa tribe—the Wa living on the China side of the border—Maoists had erased much of the human buffer that, for centuries, separated the Burmese and Chinese civilizations. People's Liberation Army troops were now amassed along the border, in prime position to roll across and capture what remained of Wa lands. They could easily claim that the territory was there for the taking—since the Burmese government didn't control the area anyway.

The Burmese junta had good reason to panic. At the time, communism seemed poised to engulf much of humanity. Communists controlled Russia, the world's largest country, as well as China, the most populous. The eastern half of Europe was communist, and Marxist rebellions burned across Africa and Latin America. Worse yet, Maoists were among the most evangelistic type of communist, especially keen to spread their doctrine through brute force.

Burma, teetering on collapse, presented a tantalizing target. If Mao's army wanted to invade the Wa lands inside Burma's borders, the junta couldn't do much to stop them. The Maoists might then decide to keep pushing, swarming the rest of the country, "liberating" its masses from a feckless regime and planting red flags from the misty mountains to the shimmering coast. The threat was real. Burma's generals needed a miracle.

What they got was Saw Lu.

Saw Lu never figured out how the Burmese military discovered him. He knew only that he was exactly what they sought. Someone Wa but not wild. Book smart but brave. Naive enough to take on an extremely dangerous mission.

In late 1966, Saw Lu was twenty-two, all lean muscle and bravado. He'd grown up rough, as a refugee kid in the Burmese foothills, alongside other Wa and Lahu Baptists who'd escaped Mao's China. They'd settled around the city of Kengtung. In boyhood, Saw Lu adapted to his new country quickly, learning the Burmese language, then bouncing around to various Christian boarding schools, always wowing teachers with his smarts. Burmese intelligence officers fished him out of a missionary-run academy outside Yangon, the capital. He was a plucky young man who'd just married his sweetheart, Mary, a Lahu girl also raised under the Man-God's sect. She was studying at the same academy.

The Burmese spies invited Saw Lu to tea. Your Wa race is under threat by communists, they said. The same Maoist army that cruelly banished you from your childhood home now fixes its hungry eye on the Wa living inside our borders. Wouldn't you like to save them?

Under their plan, Saw Lu would deploy into the peaks as a covert agent. He'd infiltrate the fortress town of Pang Wai, presenting himself as a harmless teacher sent by Burma's government to open a free school. Mary could come along, helping teach the Wa to read Burmese.

Teaching would provide cover for his real assignments. Wa country was terra incognita to the junta, so Saw Lu would serve as its eyes and ears, reporting back whatever he witnessed. But his ultimate mission—if he accepted it—would go far beyond scouting. Pang Wai was only a day's walk to China's border, and from there the Maoist empire began, stretching some one thousand miles eastward to the sea. Saw Lu's job would be somehow stopping this colossus from lumbering out of its pen. The junta's idea, ill-defined, was for Saw Lu to get cozy with the Wa, urge them to quit killing each other—at least temporarily—and organize them to fight intruding Chinese communists. Burma's cash-strapped military had few spare guns with which to arm the highlanders, so Saw Lu would have to think creatively, fortifying Wa clans for the looming invasion by any means necessary.

It was a half-baked, desperate mess of a plan, likely to end with a young couple's heads on two pikes.

Saw Lu signed on at once.

Here was his chance to exact revenge upon the godless communists who'd marred his childhood and scattered his sect. Though Banna was lost forever, this fortress town called Pang Wai might be spared. Saw Lu had never heard of Pang Wai—it was some one hundred miles from his birthplace—but he was keen to protect any patch of Wa land from Mao's hordes, however possible.

That night, after accepting the mission, Saw Lu went to his wife and said, Mary, God has laid a divine task before us. The Burmese know not the magnitude of their request. We can go far beyond defending the Wa peaks from communists. We can also revive William Marcus Young's crusade to civilize the Wa highlanders, possibly succeeding where the Man-God faltered.

Saw Lu proposed that he and Mary take the junta's cover story seriously, doing their utmost to teach headhunters to read. The Youngs had taught that literacy was the first stepping-stone toward enlightenment. But Mary, he said, we must show the highlanders "not just how to read but how to live." Saw Lu aspired to end their head-hunting ritual altogether. He believed this would prove essential to uniting them against the Maoists, who longed to swallow their land, their very essence, and prevent them from ever knowing God.

Mary asked, Will you Christianize these headhunters—as the Youngs longed to do?

Saw Lu had his answer ready. He did not want to repeat the Man-God's mistake, needling the highlanders with talk of Jesus from the very first encounter. That had proven fatal. He'd instead focus on the most urgent priority: mustering the Wa against communist invasion. To do this, Saw Lu said, he and Mary would gently ingratiate themselves into their world and discover what motivated the Wa highlanders, so as to sway them in the right direction.

Saw Lu imagined himself as a shaft of light penetrating an abyss dark with ignorance. That grand sense of purpose swept him up into the treacherous peaks, through Pang Wai's gates, into the heart of the town, where he and Mary built a schoolhouse from bamboo, mud, and thatched grass. Assimilating among the Wa was easier than he'd imagined.

Only months later, in the spring of 1967, did Saw Lu fully comprehend the difficulty of his task. It wasn't just the head-cleaving episode that rattled him. It was what followed: an understanding that Wa highlanders only respected raw strength—and that he was just some outsider in funny clothes, armed with nothing more than a savior complex.

SPRINGTIME, 1967.

About three months into Saw Lu's mission in Pang Wai.

It was not in the nature of warrior-farmers to sit quietly and regurgitate rote lessons. The children and teenagers who attended Saw Lu and Mary's classes talked back—or just ambled off once they got bored. Lessons often ended in mutiny.

Inside the bamboo schoolhouse, Saw Lu and Mary would chalk out the Burmese alphabet on a blackboard, its letters whorling and looping in globular shapes. There were no books. The students held their own little black slates, some etching out letters with pointed rocks instead of chalk.

When the teachers' backs turned, the class devolved into gossip. Unable to control their students, Saw Lu and Mary would put down the chalk and listen. They learned about courtship rituals and regional clan feuds, a tangle of grievances as complex as geopolitics writ large. It was sometimes hard to tell who was teaching whom. The kids' parents often dropped by too, chiming in with their own stories. At least Saw Lu was learning, bit by bit, how this society functioned.

Though Saw Lu was ethnically Wa, just like his pupils, a vast cultural chasm stretched between them. Saw Lu was the rarest of Wa and not just because he was raised by nonheadhunters. Few Wa had ever seen electric lights or automobiles, but Saw Lu had. As refugees in Burma, his family had settled down in Kengtung, a bustling town, and as boarding students, he and Mary lived in Yangon—a sprawling metropolis left behind by the Brits, now the capital of an independent Burma.

Occasionally Saw Lu's students, such as they were, wanted to hear about city life: brick buildings, raucous streets, record players. They were curious about modernity but not dumbstruck by its existence. The Young family once believed the mere sight of a flying machine would drop the Wa to their knees, but that was clearly not the case. As it turned out, the kids already knew about aircraft.

The students said silvery propeller planes had once buzzed over Pang Wai, disgorging wooden boxes fixed to "big blankets" that caught the wind and drifted to the forest floor. Each crate contained exotic-looking weaponry. Ask the elders, the students said. They remember it well.

Weapons? What kind?

Metal guns. Heavy and long. What an odd tale, but the highlanders were full of bizarre talk. Saw Lu's pupils also told him to watch out for giant wolf-men stalking the forest.

In interacting with his students and their families, Saw Lu made a few futile attempts to bring up Jesus, just to test their interest, but he wisely gave up. Talk of religion made him seem even stranger, and to properly gather intelligence, he needed to build rapport with the locals. He instead probed their thoughts about communism, discovering that only a few understood it and only in an abstract way. Most were wary of the Chinese in a general sense—the border was only ten miles away—but invasion was a secondary worry, drowned out by fear of rival Wa clans, a constant terror. They also fretted over food. Their soil, tan in color, was a crunchy grit that frosted over for much of the winter. It was so lacking in nutrients that corn and rice sprouted weakly from the earth. Only one crop truly thrived in this alkaline dirt: opium poppies.

School attendance was always spotty, but when poppy harvesting season came, it plummeted to almost zero. Parents needed children working in the fields. Twice a year, slopes bloomed with ivory and scarlet petals, which fell away to reveal little green pods underneath. These pods, when sliced, oozed a milk-colored goop that turned molasses-brown in the air. The Wa would scrape the opium into big clay pots. Next to farming rice and corn, this was the activity around which they organized their days.

At dusk, when parents returned from the poppy fields, Saw Lu would harangue them about their kids' truancy. The looks on their faces said, You are wearing out your welcome. The Burmese language lessons Saw Lu taught were nearly useless. The people of Pang Wai had never met a Burmese person and did not expect to. His lessons brought little utility to their lives.

I'm here to help, Saw Lu said. They told him that if he wished to help, he could pick up an opium-scraping knife and join them at sunrise.

Saw Lu's mission was fizzling. His Burmese junta minders had cautioned him to stay limber, adjusting course when necessary. Saw Lu decided to clear away his preconceptions and focus on what made his subjects tick.

Opium.

They were obsessed with it. No one watching the Wa cultivate it could call them lazy. Saw Lu marveled at their work ethic, but he couldn't fathom their motive.[20] Opium was magical stuff—smoking it could make the pebbly ground feel like a bed of cotton—and yet no one partook unless severely ill. They believed lolling around in a drugged-up stupor was a dereliction of warriordom, practically inviting enemies to an easy beheading. So for whom was all this opium harvested?

Little made sense until the caravan showed up.

One afternoon, a drumbeat signaled that visitors approached Pang Wai. Saw Lu joined a throng of warriors heading out to greet them. Through the dark maze they went, emerging into sunlight. On a nearby ridge stood a brigade of men with Chinese faces, each holding an assault rifle, all dressed in identical khaki uniforms.

Saw Lu froze. The communists are upon us, he thought. But the other Wa explained that these men were noncommunist Chinese: traders who'd come to buy their opium. Wa families poured out of the fortress with clay pots, merrily walking toward the visitors to lay opium at their feet. The Chinese trader brigade had arrived on a long column of donkeys and mules, all strung together, known as a caravan. They pulled sacks off the beasts' backs and dumped the contents onto the ground. Saw Lu saw treasures from the industrial world: Gold ingots, moldable into ornaments. Flintlock rifles and gunpowder, useful for hunting deer or bear. Blocks of salt, invaluable for preserving meat through cruel winters. Fat sacks bursting with rice grains. The traders only accepted one form of payment for these goods: opium, the currency of the highlands. Saw Lu realized why no one smoked it. That would've been like lighting cash on fire.

Unable to speak much Chinese, Saw Lu did not approach the traders. He just watched them pack the opium into canvas sacks, load it all onto the mules' backs, and clomp away. Later, when his students returned to class, he asked about these men, learning that they were truly the opposite of communists: hard-nosed Chinese capitalists, hated in Mao's China. They'd fled into Burma in 1949—just like Saw Lu's sect, back when he was a little boy. These merchants now dwelled in a jungle hideout somewhere on this side of the border. As for the exact location, no one in Pang Wai had a clue or even cared. They just knew that, twice a year, the caravan would show up and trade precious items for opium.

Saw Lu asked how these Chinese outsiders ventured into the peaks, up serpentine paths with slow-moving donkeys, without the Wa snatching their wares and their heads. The men traveled as if they had a permit to enter headhunter country. They basically did, the students explained. Everyone knew starting trouble with a Chinese merchant caravan would incur wrath from their main trading partners: the warlords, leaders of the most powerful Wa clans around.

Not far away, to the south of Pang Wai, there were mountains where poppies grew with greater vigor. That was where these warlords roosted. There were three of them, each dominating his own patch. They weren't rulers or chieftains, the students explained, and the warlords issued no laws other than to stay away from their poppies. But they were unusually domineering, an aberration to the egalitarian nature of Wa life. Each led his own armed posse: a private security force, drawn from the toughest headhunters, protecting poppies and slaying trespassers.

The typical Wa warrior-farmer might own a black-powder gun at best. But the warlord clans? Their fighters, in addition to swords, carried fancy rifles bought off the Chinese traders. As the caravans' VIP customers, the warlords were privy to a menu of high-end weaponry. Most coveted among their wares were metallic autoloading rifles, black magazines jutting underneath, some stamped with the letters "USA." Chinese traders toted the same guns. But they did not sell them to the denizens of Pang Wai, which was only a minor stop on the opium-collecting route.

Saw Lu asked his pupils what the warlords were like. Each is unique, they said. One is flamboyant. He wears gold watches, an ostentatious device in a place where people know no other clock than the sun. Another is cruel. He leads the most prodigious skull-collecting clan in the highlands. The third is a sorcerer. He sculpts little animals out of mud, waves his hand, and makes them dance. When angry, he morphs into a tiger.

So said the rumor mill. Again, Saw Lu wasn't sure what to believe. But in the ensuing months, he endeavored to learn everything he could about these warlords. He did not care for their reputed head chopping and black magic, but he envied their strength. These murderous strongmen might prove useful, he thought, if China's Maoist army—lurking on the other side of the border—ever stormed into the peaks.

IN THE SUMMER of 1967, Saw Lu entered his sixth month in the highlands. At first he'd dismissed that bizarre story about airplanes raining weapons from the sky. Now he thought of it constantly, daydreaming about what he'd do with those guns—if they were even real. It pecked at his consciousness day and night. Determined to figure out if the tale was true, he canvassed Pang Wai's elders.

When exactly did this cargo fall from the clouds?

Years ago, they said. Maybe fifteen.

And what happened after the boxes hit the ground?

We tracked them down in the forest. They were filled with guns but no ammunition. We put the weapons back in their crates and buried them close to where they fell.

Why?

They did not belong to us.

To whom did they belong?

We had no idea. But we didn't want the intended recipients, whoever they were, to find the guns and use them against us.

Why not use the weapons on enemy clans?

Each head we take is a response to some injustice: one of our men slain, one of our women violated. Anyone from the offending clan can pay the head price. But we are not like lowlanders, seeking to totally exterminate our rivals.

Would it be alright, Saw Lu asked, if he dug up a few of the boxes just to have a look? The elders stared blankly. Any Wa was free to do as he or she pleased. To Saw Lu, that was close enough to a yes.

One morning, Saw Lu told his teenage pupils that language classes were postponed. Go home and scour your parents' and grandparents' memories, the schoolmaster said. Ask them where the fallen boxes are hidden. Soon students were leading him into caves and helping him dig beneath buffalo pens. He would forever remember the moment he first plunged his hand into dirt and felt the top of a wooden crate. How he wrested it from the earth and pried back its lid, sticking his arm inside, his fingers brushing against something hard in a nest of fragrant sawdust. The euphoria that washed over him as he pulled out a submachine gun and cradled that black metal in his arms.

It took weeks to find all the boxes. They contained several varieties of weapon. Some of the guns were small, the length of Saw Lu's forearm. Engraved with the letters "STEN," they resembled lengths of pipe with stocks that folded out to brace against your shoulder. Others were like miniature cannons with retractable tripods. There were even some M1 Garand semiautomatics, America's standard World War II–era rifle.[21]

At Saw Lu's request, his students lugged the weapons through Pang Wai's gates and piled them up inside his schoolhouse. It soon resembled an armory. They'd dug up eight boxes, a dozen guns per box, nearly one hundred firearms total.

Saw Lu had no doubt that God was delivering the weapons into his hands, pulling him toward some pivotal moment. It was time to draw upon his evangelical powers of persuasion, bred into him by his Baptist sect, but he would not pressure the Wa to accept Christ. Instead Saw Lu would urge them to accept him as their protector, almost like a warlord—one possessed not by wicked traits but by virtue.

Before his death, the Man-God once predicted that the Wa, who "fight like cats and dogs among themselves," could pause their clan feuds and come together when facing some existential threat. So that is what Saw Lu conjured to the villagers of Pang Wai. He whacked their wooden drum, summoned them to the center of the fortress town, and declared, The communists are coming!

Saw Lu revealed himself as a Burmese agent. Our military analysts, he said, are certain the Maoists will invade—perhaps as soon as this year. Every Wa should've already started preparing for war. Instead, your head-hunters hack each other apart. Disunity will be your downfall. Do not underestimate the communists' cruelty, he told the crowd, for I speak from experience as a refugee from a world they have destroyed. They will snuff out your entire way of life, even eradicating your opium poppies.

That got the crowd's attention.

I may be an outsider, Saw Lu said, but deep down I am Wa, like you, and ready to mount a resistance. You can start by taking up these weapons. Saw Lu held aloft a machine gun like the Sword in the Stone, a great weapon wielded by an unlikely leader.

He thanked the Lord for this windfall—but it wasn't God who dropped these guns from the heavens. It was the Central Intelligence Agency of the United States of America.

GUNS, DRUGS, AND ESPIONAGE

Become the warlord of Pang Wai.

Meet the other warlords and earn their respect.

Unite them against the red menace and save the Wa race.

That was Saw Lu's new plan, more or less. But the young man was profoundly naive about the men with whom he hoped to collaborate. He'd rightly ascertained that the opium-rich Wa warlords could prove useful in subverting communist China's expansionist fervor. He was wrong in believing this idea was original. The Central Intelligence Agency beat him to it.

There was plenty else Saw Lu didn't know. He was clueless to the fact that America, the country he revered from afar, was already a hidden force in the Wa peaks—its clandestine services overseeing an operation run on guns, drugs, and espionage. The warlords were essential to this operation. And those enigmatic Chinese opium collectors armed with American rifles? They were at its very center. So if Saw Lu wanted to become an effective warlord in the Wa peaks, he'd have to first come to grips with this CIA-run enterprise and find his own role to play in it.

THE CIA NEVER set out to entangle itself in Asia's drug trade. This was an unintended consequence of a badly conceived plot—one that involved dropping machine guns from airplanes.

Here's the backstory. In the early 1950s, Mao Zedong's army didn't just flush Saw Lu's sect out of China's borderlands. It purged all manner of undesirables, including Chinese enemies of communism: frontier opium traders, rich landowners, marooned Kuomintang soldiers. These targeted

Chinese groups clung together, escaping death by fleeing into the wilds of Burma.

At first the Chinese exiles wandered, eating lizards and roots to survive, a rabble turning more skeletal by the day. Some got lost in Wa country, doing their best to evade headhunters, while others drifted into foothills dotted with isolated Shan villages. Many expected to starve in this unfamiliar land. But then salvation arrived: propeller planes whirring into view, swooping low, dropping crates hitched to parachutes. The floating boxes contained rice, bullets, and firearms. Each was a care package from the CIA. The newly created spy agency was embarking on its most ambitious mission in Asia to date.

In coordination with the Kuomintang government, displaced to the island of Taiwan, the CIA wanted to arm these communist-hating stragglers in Burma and fuse them into a mighty armed force. Then they'd send them back to China to seize the country from Mao and reestablish Kuomintang rule—so that China would, once again, belong to a US-friendly regime. This clandestine armed group in Burma, created by the CIA and the Kuomintang, went by several names, so for simplicity's sake, I'll call them the Exiles.[1]

The airdrops kept coming. CIA planes stripped of all markings delivered a mishmash of firearms to the Exiles: British-made Sten submachine pistols, M1 rifles, even Thompsons, the machine gun made famous by Chicago gangsters.[2] Many guns were pulled from old US stockpiles, their serial numbers scratched off. The operation was top secret: only the US president and a small CIA clique knew of it.

By the spring of 1951, the Exiles were ready to cross back into their native China. They gathered along the China-Burma border and awaited a fresh round of weapons. Most crates hit their drop zones accurately, but a CIA air crew must have goofed one of the deliveries—because at least eight boxes also fell near the fortress town of Pang Wai, more than ten miles from the nearest drop site.[3] The Wa buried these strange crates and got on with their lives. (Not until Saw Lu showed up sixteen years later were the weapons pulled out of the ground.)

The Exiles, meanwhile, shrugged off the waylaid airdrops and focused on the mission at hand: retaking China. They loaded their weapons and prepared for combat. Numbering in the mere thousands, they were about to face more than three hundred thousand communist troops glued to the border. The CIA naively believed the Exiles would push through and triumph. They were certain the Chinese masses, surely growing sick of Maoism, would rise up and join this fight for freedom.[4] This didn't happen. When the Exile fighters rushed into China, the People's Liberation Army shot them to bits. They ran back into Burma's jungles, wounded and demoralized.

Over the next few years, America goaded the Exiles into several more incursions into China. Each ended catastrophically. But instead of ditching its plans, the CIA concocted ever-stranger solutions, even wondering if it could recruit the legendary Wa warrior tribe to join the cause. CIA officers actually thought Wa highlanders would drool at the chance to serve any campaign led by Caucasians—an idea put into their heads by the Young missionary family. A CIA memo, drafted after consultation with the Youngs, stated, "The Wa have a special feeling of affection and respect for white men—and are unanimous in their desire to have the white man assist them and even rule them."[5]

This was deranged, and the Exiles knew it. Many were Chinese frontier folk who'd grown up near the border—in striking distance of Wa headhunter raiding parties. They were well aware that attempting to "rule" Wa highlanders could result in your brains fertilizing their fields.

The CIA couldn't accept that China was forever lost to communism, but the Exiles had to face reality: they were permanently stuck in Burma. They made the best of it, drifting back to what many knew best: commerce. Though the Exiles continued amassing American supplies—weapons, food, medicine—as if still intending to reclaim China, they treated it as seed capital for a business venture: transforming their guerrilla force into an opium-trafficking syndicate.

Burma's mountains contained Asia's finest soil for poppies, but as the Exiles saw it, indigenous tribes squandered their potential by only churning out a few dozen tons of opium per year. To increase output, the Exiles turned their superior firepower on upcountry peasants. As conquerors on horseback, with new-model American machine guns, they easily strong-armed locals into farming as many poppies as the land could bear. They mostly left the Wa alone—too hard to subjugate—so the Shan people, being most plentiful in Burma's hills, bore the brunt of this coercion. The Exiles bought their crops for a pittance, turning them into serfs living hand to mouth.

This business expansion proved wildly successful. The Exiles boosted Burma's opium production to five hundred tons per year: "almost a third of the world's opium supply," according to the CIA.[6] Drugs were clearly the Exiles' new raison d'être, not vanquishing communists. Yet the CIA still wouldn't abandon them. In fact, when the Exiles needed help moving their opium to buyers in the cities, the CIA lent its airplanes to the task.[7] Agency-hired pilots would skitter down on dirt runways in Burma, offload guns to the Exiles, then onboard bundles of their opium. Then they'd fly to Bangkok, where purchasers, mostly CIA-supported Thai police officials, picked up bulk drug shipments right at the airport. The proceeds of these sales supercharged the Exiles' growth. It was the first instance of CIA-contracted planes running drugs for an armed group—but hardly the last.

Over the next decade or so, the Exiles perfected their business model, assembling an opium-trading behemoth greater than their ancestors could've imagined. Almost all of Burma's opium supply fell under their monopolistic control. Burma's junta wasn't thrilled that a US-armed drug cartel marauded through its country, but the Exiles mostly stuck to mountains beyond the military's control. Occasional shootouts between the Exiles and Burmese patrols often ended poorly for the latter, so junta regiments tried to stay out of their path.

The Exiles even managed to extract the coveted Wa poppy crop, more potent than any other in Southeast Asia. The Wa, unlike other indigenous peoples, were too intimidating to bully, so the Exiles had to acquire their opium by trading fairly. In Pang Wai, for instance, they proffered gold nuggets and black-powder rifles, while the Shan farmers got bolts of cloth and axe heads. In the most luscious Wa poppy-growing areas, the Exiles sought out the toughest head-hunting clans and plied them with finer gifts: US-made assault rifles. From these clans rose the infamous warlords, the very three that Saw Lu hoped to meet.

These warlords were vital opium suppliers. Under the Exiles' guidance, each Wa warlord grew organized enough to consistently supply premium opium—and well armed enough to guarantee the caravans' safe travel into their lands.

By the mid-1960s, the Exiles ran vast trade routes snaking through Burma's upcountry, an area larger than Portugal. The Wa peaks, luxuriant with poppies, marked the far end of their supply chain. Pang Wai, where Saw Lu watched Exiles collect opium near the fortress gates, was one of the northernmost collection points. The caravan he witnessed would have also picked up opium from the Wa warlords, then traveled south to load up in various Shan villages, before lugging it all back to the Exiles' headquarters—a network of camps some two hundred miles south of Wa country, located along Burma's border with Thailand.

The Exiles had come a long way from their scrappy origins. As they evolved, morphing into Asia's largest opium syndicate, so too did their relationship with the CIA.

BY 1967, THE EXILES cartel numbered some three thousand armed men, their calves diamond hard from tromping up and down Burma's slopes. When they weren't on months-long smuggling runs, the men and their mules rested in secret camps strewn along the Thai-Burma border. Business was splendid overall, though the rank and file didn't live in opulence. Sustaining all those armed personnel, plus their wives and children, ate up much of the profits.

Several men led the Exiles, but Lee Wen-huan—General Lee, he called himself—was the most influential.[8] Unlike other Chinese men of stature, he wore no gold or jade. His command center was a stone dwelling with scalloped roof tiles, styled like homes in rural China, even though the structure sat atop a mountain in Thailand's Chiang Mai province. It was located just a few miles from the Burmese border.

General Lee's flinty personality was typical of the Exiles. They were cowboy types, hailing from China's dusty Yunnan frontier province. Almost Texan in their mores, they loved horses and rifles but didn't readily trust outsiders. Lee came across rough—a heavyset man, he often spoke in grunts—but his cunning was incredible. After years of floating around Burma's hinterlands, building the Exiles into a mighty but transient cartel, he'd permanently planted his syndicate in a part of Thailand that most considered semi-inhabitable. As mountain environments went, it wasn't as raw as the Wa peaks—with their cusped slopes and winds that cut you in two—but the Thai-Burma border was still a gnarled and dry place.

Mountains dividing the two countries formed a wall of stone, and Lee was wise enough to see the potential in this bleak geography. On one side of this natural wall were Burma's poppy lands, locked away in a place where only the brave dared venture. And on the other? Thailand, a modernizing country connected to the rest of the world—a portal to millions of potential customers, many longing to melt away their hurt with opiates.

The only way to pass from one side to the other was by navigating slender mountain gaps, some barely wide enough for mules to pass single file. All opium flowing south out of Burma would hit these choke points, little Suez Canals. On Lee's instructions, the Exiles seized these passes, installed checkpoints, and settled in.

They held Southeast Asia's drug trade in their fists.[9]

The CIA called it "ideal smuggling territory" and likened the area to America's own bootlegging heartland: Appalachia. Classified reports describe limestone hills "honeycombed with caves" where the Exiles could stash "illicit cargoes smuggled across the border."[10] But American spies did more than praise Lee's choice of location. They also encouraged the government of Thailand, then a US client state, to let the Exiles unofficially control that border.[11]

Asking Thailand to effectively cede territory to a drug cartel was an unusual request, but times were tumultuous, and this was no ordinary cartel. Its ranks were filled with men who reviled communism, an ideology sweeping across Southeast Asia. The United States had already invaded Vietnam to stop its spread. It wasn't working out too well. In the countries sandwiched between Thailand and Vietnam—Laos and Cambodia—smaller communist insurgencies were heating up fast. America treated Thailand, right-wing and military run, as a firewall through which communism must never pass, lest it keep burning all the way to Burma, India, and beyond.

The United States convinced Thai leaders to let the Exiles dig in and protect that northern border.[12] The idea was that, if communist guerrillas of any stripe dared come near it—or even popped up along dope-smuggling trails in Burma—the Exiles would crush them. They were hardy fighters with rocket-propelled grenades and .50-caliber machine guns, enough US weaponry to hold their own. Best of all, the Exiles would provide this service for free. Drug cartels don't require outside financial backing. As for their criminality, this was something both the CIA and Thai leaders could overlook. Running drugs was unseemly, sure, but nothing was more important than containing communism.

To further ingratiate the Exiles with Thai authorities, the United States nudged them into profitable partnerships. By the late 1960s, the Exiles had progressed far beyond simply peddling raw opium. They now focused on a value-added product: heroin. Hired chemists ran more than a dozen bamboo-walled refineries around their camps. The profit margins were incredible. For an outlay of $300, the Exiles could acquire ten kilos of Wa opium and synthesize it into one powdery kilo of heroin.[13] Wrapped in cellophane, that brick would sell for $1,000 in Bangkok. But the Thai capital was very far away, and the Exiles could hardly march heroin across the country on its mules. Once again, the Exiles needed assistance moving their wares out of the hinterlands.[14]

Thailand's Border Patrol Police—a CIA-created organization—stepped in to help. It owned US-supplied trucks and armored vehicles, rugged enough to drive up steep slopes. For a cut of the sale price, Thai border cops would load their trucks with Exile heroin and drive it down to Bangkok, a fourteen-hour journey. Much of the ride was made smoother by sleek highways, built by the United States to develop the country.[15] Thanks to corrupt Thai police, the Exiles could deliver their product without fearing arrests or seizures.

Piece by piece, the infrastructure of the Golden Triangle narcotics trade clicked into place. America hadn't planned to help construct a 650-mile-long opium pipeline, but that's what it was. At the far end were the opium suppliers: Wa warlords. In the middle, mule caravans, drug labs, and shady cops. And at the terminus, wholesale buyers in Bangkok.

The Exiles exclusively sold heroin to one type of customer: Bangkok's ethnic Chinese, a community that had migrated long before, establishing themselves as urban merchants. They were high-society types, "respected members of their communities," according to CIA files, viewing themselves as "businessmen first and criminals second, if at all." Chinese-Thai families ran export businesses, shipping everything from pineapples to car parts, so they already owned warehouses, trucks, and boats—everything needed to smuggle a kilo or ten to whichever market fetched the best price.

And in the late 1960s, the hottest market for heroin was South Vietnam.

As the US-Vietnam War intensified, draftees kept flooding in, until half a million young men from the world's most prosperous country were plopped down in a jungle nightmare. Terror and trauma ran rampant. Many troops craved chemical escape. Without intending to, the Pentagon created the perfect customers for heroin produced in the nearby Golden

Triangle—all while the CIA helped sustain supply chains that fed soldiers' addictions.

GIs didn't think they were rich, but on an $80 monthly salary, they were far wealthier than the region's peasants, who ate whatever they grew and could never afford a drug habit. As the war dragged on, according to the highest estimates, as many as one in six US troops in Vietnam were using heroin.[16] Americans back home had no idea they were subsidizing Southeast Asia's dope trade. US citizens' salaries got taxed to pay soldiers' wages. GIs took that money and paid Vietnamese dealers. The Vietnamese dealers in turn paid the ethnic Thai-Chinese distributors in Bangkok. And they told the Exiles to keep the product coming.[17]

The CIA coldly observed this flux of dollars and heroin, in which it was complicit, but did nothing to stop it. The agency could hardly claim ignorance. In secret memos, it noted that the Exiles were building new drug labs for a specific purpose: meeting a "sharp increase in demand for heroin by US forces in South Vietnam."[18]

What on earth could justify the CIA propping up a cartel whose heroin shot into American soldiers' veins?

Behind every CIA scandal, there is always some big-picture justification. In this case, it was communism—specifically communist China. The CIA didn't just want the Exiles watching out for communist uprisings in the Golden Triangle. That was only one of their responsibilities. The agency also needed them to go much deeper, probing their native homeland: China, a country controlling nearly 20 percent of all human life, plus a growing arsenal of nuclear bombs.

To America, Mao's kingdom was frighteningly inscrutable, and the CIA was obsessed with peering inside—a highly difficult task. Putting spies on Chinese soil was nearly impossible. China's borders were mostly fronted by countries hostile to the United States—Mongolia, North Korea, North Vietnam—or seawater. But there was one backdoor: the Wa peaks, looming over China's southwestern fringe.

The CIA had finally accepted that Caucasian men were not welcome there. But its drug-trafficking assets, the Exiles, had permission from Wa headhunters to come and go. To enjoy the perks of CIA protection, the cartel would have to collect more than opium. It would also need to help gather intelligence along that border, by any means necessary, even if that meant roping the Wa warlords into CIA operations.

THE EXILES, SECRETIVE as they were, went by various names. If asked, most smugglers would simply say, "We're Yunnanese," referring to their home region in China. The CIA settled on calling them Chinese Irregular Forces (CIF). But one of the Exiles' leaders once suggested a more poetic description for his group: "watchdogs at the gates."[19]

Watchdogs sounded a lot nobler than *drug traffickers*. It evoked courageous sentinels, ready to alert the so-called "free world" if communists stirred in the distance. This description was also fairly accurate. Throughout the 1960s, the Exiles ran surveillance operations on behalf of two spy agencies: the CIA and Taiwan's military intelligence division, practically a subsidiary of the CIA. Taiwan's spy division was "dependent on the United States for [its] very existence," as one high-ranking CIA official put it.[20]

Working in tandem, the CIA and Taiwan helped establish more than a dozen radio outposts across Burma's hills—a string of bases running between the borders of Thailand and China. The Exiles defended and staffed each base. Their brightest soldiers were trained to operate US-made receivers and relay coded messages. These radio outposts kept in close touch with the Exiles' caravans, which roved far and wide on their opium-collecting routes. Embedded in each caravan were radiomen who wore clunky transmitters strapped to their backs: heavy devices, painted pond-scum green and poky with antennae. If a radioman spotted something suspicious along the trails, he'd zap that intel to the nearest base, and the base could beam it all the way back to the Exile camps in Thailand.

This technology was a godsend. Running drugs is mostly a logistics game—moving stuff from A to B without incident—and airwaves held their operation taut. Had warm weather worsened the poppy yield that season? The Exiles knew. Were bandits laying an ambush up the trail? The Exiles knew. And whatever the Exiles knew, the CIA knew as well.[21]

The CIA kept meticulous data on the organization's drug trafficking—down to the average foot speed of its mules: two miles per day with 150 pounds of opium on the animal's back—but that was not the main purpose of this surveillance web. This technological gift was contingent on the Exiles helping the CIA pull intel out of China. They were instructed to extend this radio matrix all the way into Wa warlord territory, right on the Chinese border. Luckily for the CIA, the Wa warlords didn't object

to this; they proved gracious in letting the Exiles, trusted business partners, plant electronic gadgets on their turf. One warlord welcomed the
construction of a permanent radio shack in his territory: in spy parlance,
a "listening post," soaking up People's Liberation Army transmissions
bleeding over the mountains. Another warlord offered to go even further.
For bonus payments in gold, he'd send Wa headhunter teams into China
to slay communist officers and steal documents out of their hands.

The CIA got exactly what it desired: probes into China, courtesy
of what one agency official called "a bunch of dope runners" and other
"strange bedfellows." [22] Strange it most certainly was, this system of
narco-espionage. What kept every player under the covers—the CIA, the
Exiles, the Wa warlords—was a common desire to stop China's Maoists
from expanding even one inch into the Wa peaks. Every group involved
believed this threat to be existential. But each had its own motives.

The CIA viewed communism as a virus threatening US supremacy
and would do anything to stop the contagion, anywhere on earth—even
get cozy with a drug cartel and a head-hunting tribe. Beyond using the
Exiles and their Wa suppliers to collect information, the United States
needed them to keep the Golden Triangle communist-free, denying its
opium profits to enemies. As one CIA secret memo put it, without US
covert action, all Asian people "can be plucked by the Communists like
ripe fruit." [23] A lawless place such as Burma's mountainous north—which
even the country's own junta couldn't control—was the sort of place
where communism could take root. Other members of Team America,
Thailand and Taiwan, harbored similar fears.

The Exiles' motivations were a bit more complex. They genuinely
despised Maoists for driving them from their homeland. But they also
understood that, without a role to play in the Cold War, they were just
a crime syndicate. Belonging to Team America conferred privileges—a
place to hunker down in Thailand, access to weapons and radio tech,
immunity to arrest—that guaranteed their supremacy over the Golden
Triangle region's drug trade.

As for the Wa warlords? They just wanted to keep warlording. And
they knew that if the Maoists conquered their land, they'd go from boss-
ing around their clans to shoveling chicken shit on a communal farm.
Simple as that.

And then there was young Saw Lu—traipsing into this murky situation with big dreams and not much of a clue.

Saw Lu was an agent of Burma's junta—Burma being the only country that, under international law, actually had a rightful claim to those Wa peaks. According to any classroom globe, that land was squarely inside Burma's borders. But neither the CIA nor the Maoists cared much about that. Burma's ruling generals were virtually friendless. Terrified of Chinese invasion, they might have made natural clients for the US empire, but after suffering more than a century of colonial rule, they refused to grovel before anyone—certainly not another Caucasian empire. As a result, Burma's leaders were isolated, and their army was too weak to scare either the CIA or the Maoists away from the Wa peaks. The best they could do was send in the likes of Saw Lu and pray for the best.

Even Saw Lu, after months in Pang Wai, would momentarily forget who'd sent him there. He had his own personal quest, which just happened to overlap with that of his junta handlers. He too was fanatically driven to keep the communists out—but not because of some hyperpatriotic desire to uphold Burma's territorial integrity. Saw Lu just wanted to preserve the last Wa refuge on earth so that he could have a shot at civilizing them: cleansing them of their wicked head-hunting, unifying them as one, and perhaps—when they were ready—leading them toward Christ. Only then would he fulfill the dream prophesized by the Man-God.

Become a warlord. Meet the other warlords and earn their respect. Unite them all against the red menace and save the Wa race.

That was his plan. It was time to get started.

THE LEAGUE OF WARLORDS

There are no official prerequisites for becoming a warlord, but a track record of slaying enemies helps. In that regard, Saw Lu's résumé was lacking. In all his years, he'd killed nothing larger than a monkey.

At least the twenty-two-year-old had connections, which he flaunted to gloss over his lack of experience. Pang Wai's villagers pointed out that, without bullets, the schoolteacher's arsenal was a heap of useless steel. Just wait, he told them. Burma's army will provide for me. Soon it did, sending boxes of ammo on horseback.

Mary continued teaching grammar inside the schoolhouse. But the staccato of gunfire interrupted her lessons. Saw Lu was running combat drills out back, his teenage male students forming the nucleus of a nascent militia. Having never raised a fighting unit, Saw Lu improvised, drawing on what he'd gleaned from hunting macaques.

As a teenage refugee, growing up around the Burmese city of Kengtung, Saw Lu had sometimes borrowed a black-powder rifle, slipped into the forest, and shot monkeys out of the trees. His family was poor and needed the protein. Hunting primates can't be that different from bushwhacking men, he thought, for stealth is paramount—macaques have excellent hearing—and so is frugality with bullets. Accustomed to rifles that took forty-five seconds to load, Saw Lu believed in carefully considering each shot, even though the guns he'd unearthed were automatics.

He requested a showpiece weapon from his Burmese handlers, something highly lethal to impress the villagers. They delivered a .50-caliber machine gun with an ammo belt that he slung over his shoulder. Each bullet looked like a brass carrot, powerful enough to punch through an anvil. The weapon turned heads. Even the headhunters wanted to test it out. Back when Saw Lu first showed up, they'd regarded him as an eccentric—sometimes a pest—but now that image was melting down and reforming into something new. Each day, fresh volunteers came knocking at his schoolhouse turned command post.

Telling people what to do and preparing for a showdown with evil? For Saw Lu, this was a taste of heaven. But his militia's chain of command was droopy. It was more like running a volunteer fire department than a company of Green Berets. Trainees showed up tinged scarlet from boozing, or bare chested, disinterested in the straw-beige uniforms Saw Lu procured from Burma's army. As an outsider, he could command only so much authority.

An area tough guy named Rang noticed the young man struggling. Rang headed a clan that dominated a large tract of poppy fields nearby. He was no warlord—just a minor strongman, protecting his crops with a small band of poorly armed fighters—but Rang and Saw Lu each possessed something the other desired. Rang had good-old-boy legitimacy and local know-how. Saw Lu had the charisma of a warlord in the making, plus a stash of guns, and a steady ammo supply. They joined forces. Rang served as the militia's deputy, helping close the cultural gap between Saw Lu and the native-born highlanders. He often cautioned Saw Lu to temper his idealism.

Take opium, for example. Saw Lu was raised to fear the drug. His sect warned that it could render anyone pathetic, even a strapping headhunter.[1] Though almost no one in Pang Wai was hooked on it—there was a fierce taboo against addiction in the highlands—Saw Lu believed opium was generally bad for humanity. He told Rang that after the communist threat was quelled, the Wa must stop producing it.

Get over yourself, Rang said. Opium is the lifeblood of the Wa and always will be. Our militia must demand a share of the local farmers' crops, like a tax, and sell it in high volume to the Exiles for guns—just like the other warlords. Their militia couldn't solely rely on sporadic deliveries from Burma's army. But don't worry, Rang said. I'll handle the opium: collecting it, storing it, selling it to the Exiles. Saw Lu was relieved to put distance between himself and the drug, for that allowed him to focus on what he loved most: recruitment.

Flanked by rifle-gripping students turned militiamen, Saw Lu took his show on the road. He traveled to smaller Wa hamlets orbiting Pang

Wai with which the fortress town kept friendly ties. (The Wa typically
cultivated rivalries with settlements more than a day's walk away, not close
neighbors.) He'd march past their skull groves, through the village gates,
and up to the communal drum, summoning everyone with a few good
whacks.

Saw Lu's speeches veered from darkness to light. Armageddon looms,
he'd tell the assembled villagers, and it shall come in the form of screaming Chinese stormtroopers. He scared them to death and then, like a good
pitchman, dangled a lifeline. We can repel this menace, but only if you
join my militia and stop decapitating your fellow Wa, for this act tears
us apart at our most precarious moment. No more head-hunting. This
was Saw Lu's most radical demand, and Rang couldn't talk him out of
it. He gave off a whiff of John Brown—the rifle-gripping, Bible-quoting
American abolitionist. "I would preach to them," Saw Lu said, "patiently
breaking through their skepticism. But I would not take no for answer." If
any headhunters sneered, he warned them, "Listen to me. From now on,
if anyone here cuts off the head of another man, we will personally shoot
him dead."

And with that, a centuries-old practice—so ancient no one knew
when it started—started to fizzle away, at least in the vicinity of Pang Wai.
Saw Lu grew cocky. "William Marcus Young [the Man-God] only tried to
bring religion to the Wa," he said. "But me? I was going to change everything about them."

After Saw Lu's speeches, Rang would force villagers to cough up an
opium tax. Call it extortion, call it passing the collection plate: either way,
the militia expanded its turf and revenue. Proceeds were put aside to buy
weapons from the Exiles. As the militia co-opted more and more villages,
Rang also started collecting servants: teenage boys and young men, most
disheveled, some orphaned by clan feuds. For steady meals, they'd fetch
hot tea or wash the leaders' underwear. Of this rotating cast of minions,
the only one Saw Lu remembers is Lai.

Lai was a sulky dude, built like a praying mantis, all bones and inso-
lence. "He would just sit on a log, staring into space," Saw Lu said. "He
never had a worthwhile thing to say. I wouldn't even trust him with a
gun." Lai would drift in and out, playing servant boy for a spell and then
vanish from the militia. Not that Saw Lu cared if he returned. "I thought
he was dumb," he said. "An absolute idiot."

But Lai wasn't foolish, just holding his tongue. Inside, he was seething, fed up with opium-rich strongmen treating poor kids like slaves. Only later would Saw Lu realize how much rage burned inside this sullen young man.

BURMA'S MILITARY GOVERNMENT rejoiced over Saw Lu's warp-speed progress. In letters, they told him, Forget the schoolmaster job; leave the teaching to your wife. You're now our very own warlord. They even gave him an official title. He was anointed the commander of a "self-defense force," an experimental type of paramilitary unit.[2]

A self-defense force was essentially any warlord-run militia loosely allied with Burma's military. This was another junta tactic to keep its upcountry communist-free on the cheap. Mountain warlords could sign up to the program, and if they did, Burma's army would offer perks. We won't micromanage you, junta leaders would say, or impose our laws on your turf. In fact, you'll enjoy an unofficial license to engage in crime. Opium-producing outlaws were the preferred applicants. Once minted as a self-defense force, a warlord and his gang would never have to fear Burmese police or troops. They could safely emerge from their haunts and move drugs along Burma's paved roads, breezing through army checkpoints. Even the Exiles, who dominated Burma's opium trade, couldn't do that; they avoided conflict with Burma's troops by sticking to backwoods donkey trails.

Those were the pros of this arrangement. The cons: Burma's military, forever broke, could provide a self-defense force with little support beyond a bit of ammo now and again or the occasional machine gun. Each gang would need to self-finance. Low on cash? Sell more drugs. Participating warlords also had to pledge that, no matter what, they would never allow any type of rebel—including communists—to take root on their turf. That was the whole purpose of the exercise: outsourcing national security costs to the opium trade. Like the CIA, Burma's junta utilized drug runners to fulfill its political goals.

Burma's generals had already co-opted a few prominent warlords in the Shan hills, though these relationships were shaky and highly transactional. Saw Lu was different though. He was the junta's golden boy—their first self-defense force commander in the mysterious Wa peaks—and they expected him to model the concept for the other Wa warlords. His new orders: track them down, sign them up, convince them to pledge allegiance to Burma and vow to keep Wa country free of Maoist invaders.

That synched with Saw Lu's personal agenda just fine, but he didn't think the other warlords would bite. They already had a good thing going with the Exiles. Besides, offering Burma's seal of approval for their drug trading would just make them laugh. The Wa didn't fear lowlander police or troops—if anything, Burmese security forces feared *them*—and they didn't need any government's permission to do anything.

Despite the poor odds, Saw Lu decided he'd try anyway. Pitching the self-defense force concept would provide an excuse to introduce himself to the warlords. But when he accepted the orders from his Burmese handlers, he cautioned them that his silver tongue would only take him so far. "If you want Wa respect," Saw Lu told them, "you must display strength." To that end, he asked the junta to temporarily loan him two hundred Burmese soldiers, each promising to follow his every command.

SAW LU ONLY knew the warlords by their names and reputations.

One, called Shah, was considered the most ferocious of them all. According to the rumors Saw Lu heard, Shah's clan was "very dirty, eating food off the ground, and only cleaning their bodies a few times a year." Shah's brother Tang was widely known as the most prolific head-hunter in the peaks, reputedly having cleaved off forty-nine heads. Or was it fifty-nine?

There was also Mahasang the Prince, the favored scion of another powerful clan. This warlord dominated an area called Ving Ngun, or Silver Fortress, for its soil was veined with silver ore. Most Wa were averse to pomp, but Mahasang's family didn't care. They mimicked royalty—the only royalty they'd seen. Their closest non-Wa neighbors were the Shan, living in valley kingdoms with the equivalent of princes and dukes, brandishing ornate umbrellas and riding primped horses.[3] Mahasang's clan was no proper monarchy—the Wa warrior-farmers would never bow to them—but they were certainly rich. Of the three warlords, Mahasang earned the highest opium profits, and this allowed him to sustain hundreds of loyal fighters.

The most peculiar warlord called himself Master of Creation. His followers worshipped him as a god, and according to Saw Lu's militiamen, he could levitate. About this man, Saw Lu knew very little.

Saw Lu sent three messengers on foot into the warlords' three territories, each spread along the Chinese border. He invited each one to meet on neutral ground: a Wa valley slightly west of Pang Wai. Burma's army had once ventured to build a little wooden guard post in that valley, but it was seldom manned and could serve as a meeting house. Saw Lu waited a long time before receiving any replies. Master of Creation was the first to respond. His message: Whoever you are, I don't trust you. Go to hell. Saw Lu paced his command post in Pang Wai, wondering how to lure the warlord from his sanctuary. As legend had it, Master of Creation spent his leisure time communing with serpents. It was hard to guess what motivated a person like that.

Saw Lu penned a letter to an uncle living in Kengtung, the Burmese city where he'd spent his adolescence. The letter conveyed an extraordinary request. Saw Lu wanted his uncle to trek into Master of Creation's territory and present himself as human collateral. He'd invite the sorcerer's swordsmen to hold the uncle hostage while Saw Lu and Master of Creation met, only freeing him once both were safely back in their respective areas. Surely this would ease the warlord's suspicions.

While Saw Lu awaited his uncle's response, good news arrived. Shah was willing to talk. Mustering courage, Saw Lu traveled to the appointed valley and prepared the meeting house, telling his servant boys to fill vessels with *blai*, a buzz-inducing rice "beer" essential to Wa socializing. In the surrounding hillocks, visible to anyone approaching, Saw Lu positioned the two hundred soldiers loaned from Burma's army. He wanted Shah to see them: a testament to his authority and an insurance policy in case the meeting went sideways.

On arrival, Shah strode in confidently. He was short but brawny, square faced, backed by two dozen rough-looking gunmen. He and Saw Lu sat across from one another, knocked bamboo cups, and got down to business. Saw Lu launched into a harangue against communism, but Shah waved his hand, cutting him off. Save it, he said. I've heard it before.

Shah explained that he was a freelance commando, hired by foreigners to cross into China and harass communists. For the first time, Saw Lu heard about a ghostly, many-tentacled American organization called the

Central Intelligence Agency. This CIA would send its colleagues, Taiwanese spies, up into the Wa peaks—always by hitching rides on Exile caravans. Shah, who spoke Chinese, would meet with these Taiwanese spies. They'd present him with missions. He was free to say no but seldom did.

Shah's stories made Saw Lu's neck sweat. The warlord said he'd once abducted a high-value target: some communist officer traveling with several hundred People's Liberation Army soldiers. Shah snuck over with a crew of five Wa warriors, all disguised as peasants. They blew up a bridge to create a diversion and, amid smoke and bedlam, snatched their target, dragging him across the border and dumping him at the feet of their Taiwanese paymasters.[4]

Clearly Shah—a contractor working for the CIA-Taiwan intelligence apparatus—did not require a lecture from Saw Lu on communism. His bona fides were beyond question. However, Saw Lu detected zero ideology in Shah. At his core, the man was a true mercenary: bored by politics, enthralled by adventure. The things he revealed threw Saw Lu off balance. Until that day, he'd never imagined that America—a wholesome Christian country—would have anything to do with such a heathen as Shah, even if he was only a hired saboteur.

The reason I've called this meeting, Saw Lu said, is to enlist your service to yet another government: the Republic of Burma. Only this relationship wouldn't be clandestine at all. It would require Shah to loudly assert that his soil sat inside Burma—and that his fighters would defend it from Maoist aggression. Saw Lu explained the self-defense force concept, confirming that he was the commander—warlord, if you like—of Pang Wai. He freely admitted that if Shah became a commander of his own self-defense force, he wouldn't get richer or boost his arsenal of weapons. He instead emphasized that by declaring an affiliation with Burma's military, Shah might deter Mao Zedong from invading in the first place.

I know how lowlanders think, Saw Lu told Shah. They see our homeland as a wild and unclaimed place, up for grabs. Proclaiming that your land belongs to Burma signals that our Wa will fight hard to preserve the status quo. The Wa are squeezed between two nation-states, Burma and China, and it is time to pick sides. Choose the country whose soldiers are too weak to bother you, not the one that will march over and burn your poppies to cinder. It was well known that Maoists despised opium, believing it dulled revolutionary zeal, and hated anyone who sold it.

To Saw Lu's surprise, getting Shah to agree didn't take much *blai*. If Burma's government keeps its distance, he said, I'm in. He asked only that the distant junta never meddle with his opium sales or his espionage side gigs or pitch a fit about his business relationship with the Exiles.

Feeling ambitious, Saw Lu decided to push further. He said that if the other warlords were similarly amenable, they could use this self-defense force framework as a foundation on which to create something more profound: a self-governing league of Wa warlords, nominally pledged to Burma but ideologically devoted to their race's advancement. Knit together by ethnic solidarity, they could enforce their own codes in the Wa peaks—such as a prohibition on head-hunting. Saw Lu told Shah that until all the Wa clans abolished this horrid practice, they would never evolve as a people.

Shah rose to leave. Saw Lu wasn't sure what he'd thought of the anti-head-hunting tirade. But several months later, Shah responded in his own way—with action, not words—fortifying their relationship with a gift. Having learned that Saw Lu was a devout Christian, he offered up the soul of a wretched headhunter. His own brother, Tang, was willing to get baptized.[5]

This elated Saw Lu. He helped bring in a minister from another part of Burma, and soon Tang was standing thigh-deep in a mountain stream. A crowd of onlookers gathered to watch the killer receive the god called Jesus. The minister gripped Tang's shoulders and guided his body backward, dipping his head underwater. But when he tried to bring Tang back up, the warrior resisted. No matter how hard the minister tugged at his body, he wouldn't resurface. Was he trying to drown himself?

After what felt like an eternity, Tang jolted up from the water, gasping for oxygen. Why in God's name, the minister asked, had he stayed under for so long?

"Because I've cut off fifty-nine heads, sir. That much sin doesn't wash off easily."

SEDUCING MASTER OF Creation wouldn't prove so easy. Saw Lu's uncle, good sport that he was, had trekked into Master of Creation's territory—just as his nephew asked. The uncle had since gone incommunicado. Saw Lu wasn't sure if he was dead or alive.

More good news though. Mahasang the Prince was game to meet. Again, Saw Lu made arrangements: same wooden meeting house, two hundred Burmese soldiers standing watch in the distance, endless pitchers of *blai* at the ready. Mahasang swaggered into the room, filling it with henchmen and acrid smoke. He constantly puffed cigarettes, a luxury in the highlands. In his mid-twenties, Mahasang was as ostentatious as Saw Lu expected. He boasted of clan wealth: herds of buffalo, multitudes of servants (slaves, really), and troves of buried silver.

"Whenever Mahasang spoke, his people went silent, like they were anxious he would lash out at them," Saw Lu said. "He talked tough. But I suspected that when fighting broke out, he was the type who hid while others did the killing."[6] That was fine, so long as the Prince signed up as a self-defense force commander and brought his eight hundred fighters with him.

Saw Lu fired up his anti-Maoist diatribe, but Mahasang cut him short. You're wasting your breath, he said. Mahasang explained that he already had a radio base full of exotic electronics hidden on his territory, with Taiwanese officers sitting inside, sponging up intercepts from China around the clock, and sharing their discoveries with America.

Here again Saw Lu heard the letters "C-I-A" and inklings of its vast apparatus. He'd yet to come across any of its spies in the flesh. Not that they'd stand out. The CIA, instead of sending white men, only deployed spies that could blend in: ethnic Chinese (recruited from the Exiles or Taiwan's military) or indigenous people, such as the Lahu. The Exiles provided transport, depositing CIA-trained spy teams in the Wa peaks. Clad in tribal attire, the spies would duck in and out of China: tapping phone lines, monitoring troop movements, and collecting all kinds of intel. According to Mahasang, they used the base in his Silver Fortress territory to beam their transmissions all the way to Thailand, home to high-powered CIA receivers.

Mahasang had every incentive to assist CIA-Taiwan operations. Like Shah, Mahasang feared Maoism down in his guts, and he knew the threat it posed to his life of leisure. But he turned reticent when Saw Lu nudged him to label his militia a self-defense force and declare, once and for all, that the Wa peaks belonged to Burma. As Mahasang saw it, Wa country belonged to no nation.

As Saw Lu pressed his case, the warlord smoked and pontificated and drank. Fine, Mahasang eventually said. If it helps to scare off Maoists, I'll join. But you handle the politicking and tell the Burmese generals to keep their distance. This is Wa country and always will be, no matter what their maps say.

Saw Lu ventured further, soliciting Mahasang's thoughts on abrogating head-hunting. To his relief, he found little resistance. Mahasang was already weary of clan quarrels. Wealth had turned him into a practical man who understood violence was bad for business. As he saw it, this league of warlords, proposed by Saw Lu, could have two benefits: putting up a united front against the communists, while also helping the warlords negotiate opium sale prices as a group. A trading bloc could ensure they always extracted the most generous terms from the Exiles or any other buyers.

Saw Lu's league was taking shape. There was only one more warlord to convince.[7]

SAW LU KNEW something had gone terribly wrong. He'd instructed his uncle to remain in Master of Creation's lair as a willing hostage—refusing to leave until the sorcerous warlord concluded a sit-down with Saw Lu. Now his uncle was walking back into Pang Wai. Alone.

"My heart sank," Saw Lu said. "But my uncle was smiling, telling me to calm down. He told me, 'Master of Creation is ready to meet. He's convinced you won't hurt him.'"

"Why is that?" Saw Lu asked.

"'Because we're all family now.'"

To Saw Lu's astonishment, his uncle was a newlywed. Master of Creation had forced him to marry his sister in an impromptu ceremony. The uncle, a devout Christian, already had a wife back home, but this meant nothing to the warlord. He only cut deals with family. Join or get lost.

Master of Creation boasted at least five wives and roughly three dozen children. As he was barely literate, marriage was the contract he knew best. He even officiated the wedding himself, telling Saw Lu's uncle, "I welcome you into my clan. But if you deceive me, I'll kill you and your nephew." He's really not as bad as he sounds, said the uncle, seeming oddly enchanted by the warlord, even after the man had threatened his life. Once you meet him, nephew, you'll understand too.

Same set up: wooden meeting house, jugs of *blai*, two hundred Burmese troops planted nearby. Master of Creation approached on foot, walking up a dirt road with one hundred gunmen trailing silently behind. When Master of Creation entered the room, Saw Lu was drawn into his liquid eyes. There was no denying his magnetism. When the whiskery mystic spoke, the world around him dimmed. Master of Creation was in his fifties, and when he beheld Saw Lu's young face, he softened, treating him like extended family. He was earthy and warm—the opposite of Mahasang, always straining to be cool.

Again, Saw Lu's anticommunist spiel was unnecessary. Master of Creation wasn't directly involved in CIA espionage, but always meshing business with family, he'd forced a son to join the Exiles. He hated Maoism, fearing provocateurs would sneak over from China and undermine his cult. So if it pleased Saw Lu, his new nephew, Master of Creation, would call himself a self-defense force commander and make common cause with the other warlords. Saw Lu was doubly thrilled to learn that the warlord already forbade head-hunting in his territory. Master of Creation would not abide ancient beliefs about life force swirling inside human heads, for this undermined his position as the world's ultimate spiritual authority. He only condoned rituals of his own design.

A sorcerer, a mercenary, a prince, and a Baptist: the League of Wa Warlords was complete. Saw Lu had to admit it had all snapped together more easily than he'd expected. The warlords already had much in common, thanks to the Exiles—who'd built them into organized opium suppliers—as well as the CIA-Taiwan spying operation, which had turned them into anticommunist assets. Others had inked the dots. Saw Lu just had to come along to connect them.

For the first time in history, a conclave of Wa highlanders willingly acknowledged their soil belonged to a nation-state: Burma. They'd reached this point on their own terms, not through the brutal colonization Maoist forces unleashed upon the Wa in China. The League of Warlords was not an organization acknowledged by the Burmese junta, which only recognized each warlord's individual status as an official militia commander. But the League came to resemble a proto-government in an embryonic state. It collected taxes and issued simple edicts, such as a ban on head-hunting inside its collective territory. It traded with the largest corporate entity in Burma's north: the Exiles drug cartel. And it maintained relations with multiple countries: Burma, the United States, and Taiwan. Junta officials were not thrilled about the League's ties to the Exiles—an intrusive, America-backed narco-army—but they didn't raise a fuss. Preventing imminent Maoist incursion overrode every other concern.

The League was not what Saw Lu had envisioned when he set out to unite the Wa. That opium fueled his alliance was hardly ideal. But Rang, his deputy, had been right all along. Because the Wa used opium as currency and rarely imbibed it, the drug's deleterious effects fell upon faceless lowlanders—whoever bought it as heroin at the far end of the supply chain.

In Pang Wai, Saw Lu built a simple church. He now possessed enough gravitas to convert the fortress town's inhabitants. Many accepted Jesus. The baptism of Tang, the most notorious skull collector in the peaks, inoculated other ex-headhunters against fears that Christ would dull their ferocity.

Saw Lu's arguments against head-hunting went viral, spreading into villages he'd never even visited. A spirit of oneness coursed through the highlands. Saw Lu even saw women and children walking out on the trails, traveling between fortresses to visit estranged kin. Before his arrival, every venture outside the fortress town's gates risked death.

But this harmonious chapter would not last.

THE LEAGUE WAS formidable, and the Chinese communists surely knew it. If Saw Lu had any doubts about that, a strange encounter with a Marxist erased them.

Down in Burma's lowlands, communist cells had existed for decades, even during British colonial rule. Yangon was a hive of Marxist thought, at least in certain tea shops and cafés. Most Burmese who'd turned red revered Chairman Mao, the most successful communist in Asia, if not the world. They had their own underground organization—the Communist Party of Burma—and, by the late 1960s, its leaders were taking direct guidance from China. In imitation of Mao, they plotted to liberate Burma's hinterlands first, then its cities. They believed Burma's Wa territory would make a perfect stronghold from which to wage this crusade—if only it weren't filled with so many Wa, a people who by their very nature abhorred outsiders telling them what to do.

Around this time, a studious-looking Burmese man sauntered into Pang Wai. The locals, who still didn't speak Burmese, could not understand a word he said. Flummoxed, they took him to the schoolhouse turned command post and plopped him down in front of their warlord: Saw Lu. You're just the gentleman I've come to meet, the stranger said. Saw Lu, you've built an impressive league up here, only you've erred in aligning it with Burma's fascist regime. There is still time to correct your mistake.

The Burmese man said he was a Marxist representing the Communist Party of Burma. He said they were brains in need of fists. If the League of Warlords reversed course and went communist, he said, China would give them bigger guns and finer rations. Any fool could see communism was sweeping across Asia and would eventually cover the entire world. Better that Saw Lu embrace this future now. Besides, the Marxist said, what loyalty did any indigenous tribe owe the junta—which treated most non-Burmese like vermin?

The Communist Party of Burma wanted to base itself in Wa country and adopt the League of Warlords as its vanguard armed force, turning its warriors against the Burmese state, eventually sending them down to the lowlands to seize the entire country. As educated men, the representative said, we will lead you. We will serve as intermediaries to our patron, Mao Zedong, while your Wa do what you do best: fight. Together, we can become strong.

Saw Lu gave him a cold, hard no. The man spoke as if stupid mountain folk were only good for killing and getting killed. He was lucky to leave Pang Wai with his skin attached. The Marxist later had the gall to sneak back into the fortress town, locate Rang, and urge him to depose Saw Lu, snatching the position for himself. Saw Lu smiled when Rang told him the story. The Maoists reveal their jitters, he said. Look at how they slink around, begging us to join them. They're too scared of an honest fight.

But Saw Lu had underestimated his enemies' wiles.

A killing wave came not long afterward. There were unexplained deaths in the forests beyond Pang Wai near the Chinese border. Riflemen from Saw Lu's militia would go on patrol and never come back. Their bodies were found with heads undefiled, leaking blood from small bullet wounds that indicated modern rifles, not the flintlocks favored by hunters. Footprints suggested the murderers wore rubber-soled shoes.

In 1968, these hit-and-run attacks graduated into head-on confrontations. Assailants would spring from the trees, often outnumbering League patrols. When League fighters won a shootout, they'd examine the attackers' corpses, finding Chinese-made AK-47 clones in their hands, Chinese-made sneakers on their feet, and in their pockets, accoutrement such as military-issue sewing kits, all marked with Chinese characters. The dead guys didn't look Chinese though. Or Burmese. They looked Wa, and to Saw Lu's astonishment, he learned they were fighting for the Communist Party of Burma, an organization flush with Chinese supplies.

Maoist invasion was finally upon them, though not as Saw Lu had once imagined. He'd feared People's Liberation Army troops surging into the highlands—but this was worse: a cancer metastasizing from inside the tribe. Someone was hypnotizing young Wa men to lash out at the League while China kitted them out head to toe. Soon bands of communist Wa grew bold enough to attempt raids on Pang Wai itself, and Saw Lu killed a human for the first time. He recalls crouching and sighting a distant figure with his Bren light machine gun, then a body collapsing like a dummy with cut strings. He felt no fear or remorse. Only a deep sense of worthiness.

Blood spattered Saw Lu's vision of Wa unity. He told Mary to quit teaching. She would instead coordinate with Burma's nearest army outpost to oversee supply runs. Tell them we need every bullet they can spare, he said.

Was that slithering Marxist behind this uprising? Impossible. The man could barely communicate with the Wa, let alone rally them to action. Saw Lu asked his inner circle to tap their clan networks, collect every rumor and identify the leader of this rebellion. They came back with an answer: our attackers are loyal to a Wa commander who has joined the Communist Party of Burma. Born in these parts, he inspires fearlessness in his warriors—and he longs to kill you personally.

Commander Long Legs. That's what his followers called him anyway. Saw Lu had known him by a different name.

Lai, the idiot.

ENSLAVED NO MORE

In the very old times, the Wa got their slaves through war. A clan feud would boil over, and dozens or even one hundred Wa would swarm a rival fortress, plundering it for chickens and cows and children. Any young boy could be scooped up, kicking and spitting, by a warrior who fancied hauling a servant back home to his wife. Stolen boys would remain slaves until age eighteen or so and then would be freed, according to tribal custom.

But opium warped the nature of Wa slavery. In the eighteenth century, little black poppy seeds filtered into the Wa peaks from China, and eventually the slopes turned lurid with blood-red flowers and green pods bobbing in the wind. Back then, the Wa carried opium to Chinese frontier folk, living in ragged settlements beyond the peaks—such as Banna—and traded the drug for salt, cheap flintlocks, and sundries. Among themselves, they treated it like tender. That gunk was valuable and easily divisible, unlike a living buffalo or a thick chunk of silver ore. Pack it into a clay pot, and it stayed good for years, like a savings account. Opium was a perfect means of exchange.

With opium-money came haves and have-nots. Then exotic methods of domination: loans and debt and interest. A big-shot Wa poppy planter with lots of extra grain and buffalo could give loans to a starving family, plunging them into debt. If families couldn't square that debt with opium, children would suffice as payment. That is how Lai was enslaved.

Born in 1940, he lived with his clan in a hamlet near Pang Wai—a tiny cluster of huts halfway up a mountainside, surrounded by soil that was especially cruel. Trying to grow rice or poppies in that clay was like coaxing life from stone. Lai's family was often hungry and reduced to borrowing from the nearest opium planter.[1] One day that lender walked from his plantation, located several valleys over. Entering the family's thatch hut, he pointed to two reed-thin boys and asked their names.

One is Lai; the other is Li. They are our sons.

Give them to me and your debt is erased.

The boys were prepubescent and thus very valuable. They wouldn't age out of slavery for another ten years. Lai and his brother said good-bye to their parents and went away with their new master, walking with him outside their hamlet's wooden palisade—beyond which the boys had seldom ventured for fear of losing their heads.

They arrived at their master's log house, which sat on stilts. It was the biggest thing they'd ever seen. Underneath there was a buffalo pen fouled with dung. That is where the boys would sleep. Years of toil followed, working grime into their skin. They were always last to eat, surviving on the master's scraps. The humiliation would haunt Lai for the rest of his life. So would awe for the terrible power of opium-money, which could pry sons loose from mothers, transforming little boys into two-legged livestock.

One night, a whisper roused Lai from sleep. It was their father. He'd crept onto the plantation to free Lai and Li—but the boys hesitated to leave with him. To walk away was easy: they wore no chains. But come morning, when the master found them missing, he'd surely hunt down their entire clan.

Lai's father had planned for that. He'd already moved their mother and six siblings to a remote Wa area on the Chinese side of the peaks, beyond the master's reach. This was back in the late 1940s when the Wa still lived freely on the eastern side of the China-Burma line, not long before Mao Zedong's colonization drive.

Lai and Li snuck out of the buffalo pen and followed their father down twisting trails by moonlight. They walked for a long time. The sun was well into the sky when they reached their new home: a farmhouse surrounded by corn and rice stalks. Lai's father said this area was safe—so remote that strangers seldom happened past, serene enough that the farm's inhabitants, a family to whom they were related, did not need to hide behind spiked walls. The host family followed some odd religion, spread around the borderlands by white-skinned missionaries, that abhorred head-hunting. But that was fine by Lai. He didn't like headhunters either.

The soil was much kinder, and so was the company. Lai farmed crops alongside his kin. The host family had a son his age with whom he played games in the fields. Lai finally experienced something like childhood.

Around 1954, when Lai was fourteen, Maoist troops came marching toward the farm. His relatives panicked. Certain of impending slaughter, they fled into the highlands. But Lai's immediate family didn't budge. They were sick of running and willing to take their chances with these Chinese men in metal helmets. When the soldiers reached the front steps of the farmhouse, Lai's family stood there timidly.

Who owns this farm?

Not us. The owners ran away.

Who are you?

We just work here.

The communists looked at the family, limbs daubed in red dirt, and told them to carry on. The farm now belonged to the Chinese Communist Party, just like everything in sight, but as peasants they were free to till it on the party's behalf. Then the troops stalked away.

Lai had a different experience with Maoist China than did Saw Lu. The Chinese troops he met that day were among more than 150,000 sent to colonize the Yunnan borderlands. Where they found Wa fortresses clinging to mountain slopes, they torched them and herded the inhabitants into proper towns where they could be supervised. In the lower-lying foothills and valleys, where they found ethnic Chinese frontier folk, they dispossessed them of their belongings. This was the wave of terror that sent persecuted groups scrambling into Burma. Saw Lu's sect was among them, as were the opium merchants and landowners who'd later comprise the Exiles—all refusing to live under communism: gray, uniform, a weight pulverizing the individual spirit.

But Lai never saw it that way. To a former slave who possessed nothing, equality didn't sound half bad. During the colonization period, running through the 1950s into the early 1960s, China's communist government built roads and hospitals and schools.[2] It forced formerly rich Chinese traders—the ones who didn't manage to flee—to sweat in the fields. It forced the Wa to wear clothing and quit head-hunting. Lai came of age attending state-run primary schools in a nearby town. There he learned the Chinese language and Mao's gospel: Opium is poison. Landowners are wicked. The poor are virtuous. This ideology gave words to the rage that glowed inside him and told him it was righteous.

By the time Lai reached his mid-twenties, in the mid-1960s, the colonization drive was complete. China had transformed its side of the rocky China-Burma border. Maoist officials proclaimed that a once vicious badlands had been put under the benevolent protection of China's Communist Party, with military camps emplaced throughout. Quelling the Wa wasn't easy: the People's Liberation Army had to flood the area with twelve infantry divisions—a permanent occupying force.[3]

There was just one problem left to solve. China had erred in failing to colonize *all* of the Wa ancestral lands, including the still "wild" half across the border in Burma. Chinese commissars called those Wa highlanders "raw," unlike the Wa they'd civilized, or "cooked" to burn out impurities. In Beijing's view, those highlands were like a pustule stuck to China's rear. The local Wa warlord clans were involved in joint Central Intelligence Agency–Taiwan spy operations, and if left unchecked, their imperialist machinations would grow even more brazen. China had to find a way to clear out this infestation of troublemakers.

For the same reason that Burma's junta originally put Saw Lu into the peaks—to sniff around and report back what he saw—China's government wanted to find its own young Wa daredevil to send in from the opposite direction. One day, a Chinese commissar approached Lai and asked if he was interested in a bit of adventure. Though reserved, Lai had proven his intelligence in the classroom—he could even read at a basic level—and he was familiar with the environs of Pang Wai. The commissar presented a mission suited to Lai's unique talents. Perhaps Lai could go back there and conduct some crude counterintelligence—figure out what these corrupt CIA-entangled warlords were up to. The commissar would even loan him a rifle or two, just in case he needed to shoot his way out of a jam.

Lai took those guns with every intention of spying for China. But his activities in the Wa peaks ended up more like banditry. His handlers hadn't given him much in the way of supplies, so he stole. Buffalo and cows belonging to poppy plantations were his favored targets. He'd steal the livestock in one place and sell it in another. Lai was a lone desperado with a Chinese AK-47 knockoff, and as a counterintelligence asset, he was a bust.

Marauding among Wa warrior-farmers is a deadly business. Wa society loathes a thief, its people having so little, so Lai was constantly in scrapes, losing ill-gotten buffalo in the fray. He was routinely hungry and on the run. Having no family left on the Burmese side, Lai sometimes gritted his teeth and hired himself out to one of the only employers around: an anticommunist militia run by a budding warlord named Saw Lu.

This new militia was expanding fast and needed servants to feed horses, brew tea, and fetch water. Lai took the job, handling menial chores for Rang, the warlord's deputy, and the warlord himself. Saw Lu, with his ropy muscles and steely eyes, was several years younger than Lai, but he talked down to him like a boy. Lai found Saw Lu preachy, droning on about Wa racial solidarity, yet clearly acting superior to poor servants. At least Saw Lu wasn't as cruel as Rang and his tax-collecting goons. They treated Lai like a dog.

Lai kept his mouth shut and smoldered. Once again he saw the moral rot that opium-money bred in men. He would toil for Saw Lu's militia in short stints, long enough to hide out, fill his belly, and learn a little something to tell the commissar back in China.

Then he would slip away.

IT BEGAN AS rebellions often do: with a small indignity—a slap in the face that sets loose an earthquake.

At some point in 1968, Lai had fallen back into banditry, roving the highlands around Pang Wai in search of cows to steal. Having nabbed three beauties, he needed a buyer. Any well-off man would do. He thought of Rang, his occasional employer, and led the animals to his door. Rang looked at the unkempt fool standing next to three handsome cows and laughed.

You stole these cows, didn't you?

Lai didn't answer. So Rang seized the animals and offered nothing in return. Now go away, he said. Come back when you want some honest work.

The bandit gulped down his rage and stomped away. Lai trudged east, up and down roller-coaster slopes toward China, through miles of violently sculpted terrain. It was the same route he'd taken as a boy escaping slavery. Rancor crackled inside him. He didn't just crave vengeance upon his tormentors: Rang or Saw Lu or his childhood slavemaster. Lai wanted to burn everything down to black ash.

This walk of fury delivered him to his Chinese commissar. Give me more weapons, and I will find Wa to hold them. Give us training, and we will drown the opium warlords in violence. It was exactly what the commissar wanted to hear. Lai seemed better suited to action than spying. He was ready to form his own militia—a communist guerrilla force, backed by China, that could extend Maoist control into the "raw" peaks over the border. He sent Lai back into Burma's Wa lands to recruit followers.

Traveling on horseback, Lai scoured Wa villages and found people who thought like him. Poppy harvesters who hated paying taxes to the newly founded League of Warlords. Hungry men and women who would benefit from the equity communism promised. Lai discovered that he loved to talk, and for the first time people listened. He felt a proselytizer's zeal welling inside him.

Lai could only quote Mao in fragments, so he improvised the rest. He said slavers and opium lords were a disease infecting Wa culture. That the tribe's warrior spirit had been wasted on internal feuds for too long and must be refocused on their true oppressors. Parts of Lai's spiel were indistinguishable from Saw Lu's sermons. Though one believed in Mao, the other in the Man-God, they'd arrived through convergent evolution at the same prescription: the head-hunting ritual must end. Only in unity could the tribe grow strong enough to strike down evildoers and seize a glorious future. But Lai had a different future in mind than did Saw Lu.

Lai kept accumulating followers. Sometimes whole villages joined his guerrilla cell, eager to receive the Chinese-made rifles that Lai doled out freely. His Chinese advisers told him that instead of circulating Mao's Little Red Book—which hardly any Wa could read—Lai should impose simple commandments on his recruits: Don't drink to excess. Never rape. Don't torture. Never steal from the poor—exalt them instead.

Eventually Lai's Chinese backers revealed their strategy in full. They'd been cultivating others like him: young Wa guerrilla commanders in training, each heading up secret cells. The heartiest was named Bao Youxiang, formerly a teenage headhunter, now a formidable communist warrior in his twenties. Each cell would soon receive even higher-grade weapons and supplies—enough to rise up against the League of Warlords, tear down their flimsy proto-government, and liberate Burma's portion of the Wa peaks.

But there was a catch. Even if these Wa guerrillas achieved victory, they would not govern their own homeland. Neither would the Chinese state—not directly, at least. Beijing had decided that, instead of stealing this chunk of Burma, it would install a puppet group there: the

Communist Party of Burma. Its party members—all lowlanders, far better educated than any Wa—had an advanced understanding of Mao's doctrine. They were fit to rule. The Wa were only fit to fight.

China had high hopes for its ethnic Burmese puppets, far beyond installing them in the remote Wa highlands. That was just the beginning. As Burma's junta feared, Mao hoped the Communist Party of Burma could eventually take over the whole country—recruiting more indigenous peoples in the mountains, later absorbing lowlanders in the plains and cities. The junta would fall. The Communist Party of Burma would reign. Maoists would then dominate a two-thousand-mile-long band of territory, running from China's cold Pacific coastline all the way to Burma's balmy shores along the Indian Ocean. At that point, no foreign power, not even the United States, could stop their spread.

That was China's dream. But it reduced the Wa to battlefield fodder, the chaff to fuel a grand conflagration. Beijing, in prizing book-learned lowlanders over the Wa, was invoking a caste system by another name. If this bothered Lai, he squelched his feelings and readied for battle. He and Bao and the other guerrilla cells had their orders. Wipe out the League of Warlords. Strike down Saw Lu, Shah, Mahasang, and Master of Creation. Hand over the peaks to Beijing's Burmese puppets.

Their uprising commenced in earnest circa 1969. Lai shot from the darkness like lightning: a gangly warrior with a Kalashnikov, galloping into firefights on a cotton-white steed. The highlanders gave him a nom de guerre, shouted whenever he charged forth.

Commander Long Legs is coming!

Commander Long Legs is coming!

Soon word got back to Saw Lu that his former servant was threatening to rip apart everything he'd built.

THE LEAGUE OF Warlords was badly outmatched. Its defeat came down to warm bodies and cold logistics. Altogether, the League controlled fewer than two thousand fighters, and its supply lines amounted to a thin stream from Burma's distant army—and a thinner trickle of ammo and guns bought from Exile mule caravans. The latter, for all its supposed anticommunist credentials, found war unprofitable and kept its distance.

The Communist Party of Burma, meanwhile, was roughly ten thousand men and women strong, a mostly Wa force nourished by a river of bullets, grenades, medicine, food, and guidance coming from China.[4] People's Liberation Army officers embedded in their ranks, beside Lai and Bao, to impart tactics. Red Guards—young Maoist superfanatics from China's cities—heard about the struggle and joined in for kicks. The uprising swept the highlands: rocket-propelled grenades flying, communist Wa barreling into League-run areas in human wave attacks. "There were days," Saw Lu said, "when the mortars fell like rain."

To the League's credit, it held the highlands for several years, surviving until the early 1970s. Master of Creation waved the white flag, and his life was spared. Shah and Mahasang the Prince, having grown brotherly under the League, scurried away in tandem. Rumor had it they fled to the Thai-Burma border and sought shelter with the Exiles, their longtime business partners.

Then there was Saw Lu.

He was driven out of Pang Wai in the spring of 1971. The communist guerrillas toppled the fortress town's walls and pockmarked its poppy fields with bomblets. Dislodged, Saw Lu and his five hundred or so fighters raced west to escape. Enemies at their heels, they sought refuge on an uninhabited mountaintop. Lai's forces lagged by only a day, and Saw Lu told his militiamen, who were by then Christianized, to make peace with God. "I had no hope left, none at all," Saw Lu said. He was certain the communists would track them down and slaughter them to the last man. "All we could do was fire back as they killed us."

It was late in the day when Saw Lu surveyed the place where he expected to die. Their refuge, a mountain summit, was flattish—level enough for a few hundred militiamen to take up positions behind assorted boulders. This summit overlooked a grass-bristled field the size of a soccer pitch. At the far end of that field was the only trail leading up the mountain. To kill us, he thought, the communists will first have to scale the steep mountainside. Then rush the field. Then mount the summit to finish us off.

He had all night to turn the place into a shooting gallery.

Saw Lu positioned three hundred men on the grassy field and told them to dig. Shallow trenches would form their first line of defense. The other two hundred would occupy the summit above, as would Saw Lu.

A precipice up there provided a view of the field below, so he lugged his .50-cal to its edge, unfolded the weapon's tripod, planted the legs. He clicked an ammo belt into its side. Then he laid on his belly and stared through its sights. He waited all night.

As dawn light warmed the dark mountainside, Saw Lu heard gear clanking in the distance: Lai's communists were scrabbling up the first slope. There was a brief hush, and then the battle kicked off in a most unsubtle fashion: a human wave attack, an old-school Maoist tactic, guerrillas howling as they crested into view. Saw Lu's militiamen popped out of their trenches like prairie dogs and fired. Up on the summit, on the lip of a protruding rock shelf, there was a pulsing orange sun: Saw Lu's .50-cal blasting away. He curled his finger, the weapon ka-chunked, the earth quaked. Down below, the communist herd thinned.

They fought the battle in flows and ebbs. The communists didn't run in all at once. They poured in and receded, each new wave littering the field with prone bodies. Some of the dying communists writhed in the grass and used their final breaths to curse Saw Lu by name. They said Commander Lai had marked him for death and they would never stop coming, not until they dragged his corpse off that mountain.

By noon, Saw Lu and his fighters had felled about fifty men, but they could not go on like this for much longer. The communists probably had more fighters than Saw Lu's militia had bullets. Then, strangely, there was a lull. The waves stopped coming. To this day, Saw Lu doesn't understand it. Perhaps the communists felt victory was inevitable and took a breather. Maybe they wanted to starve them out. Either way, Saw Lu took advantage of this pause to take stock, learning that only about two dozen of his militiamen were dead. He rejoiced in God's mercy. Perhaps the Lord wanted them to live after all. But how to save themselves?

The trail running up the mountain was blocked by communists. The far side was steep, with no trail at all, but they could clamber down it to the forest below if they ditched their guns. Saw Lu gave the order to retreat: quietly and not all at once, lest they provoke the enemy's bloodlust, but in twos and threes descending carefully.

By the next morning, their evacuation was complete—and so was their dishonor.

For the second time in his life, Saw Lu was fleeing an ever-expanding communist blob. But this exodus was far more bitter than his first. He was just a boy in 1949 when Mao's army purged his sect, and back then he'd only had to clutch his mother's tunic and put one foot ahead of the other. Now hundreds were clinging to *him* for answers. After their retreat from the mountaintop, Saw Lu's militiamen fanned out to find their wives and children and the elders of Pang Wai all hiding in the forest. Everyone was asking the same question: Where will you take us, Saw Lu, now that our home is rubble and ash?

There was nowhere to go but west toward the lowlands of Burma. A column of somber faces, they put their backs to the peaks. The trek recalled Saw Lu's voyage up into the highlands, some five years prior, only in reverse. As they walked, the slopes became gentler, the air balmier and buzzy with mosquitoes. The toothy Wa skyline receded from view. It killed him inside—to leave that place more godless than he'd found it.

Lai, perhaps not such an idiot after all, had secured the highlands for his communist masters: a cabal of lowlander parasites who answered to Mao's government in Beijing. Saw Lu pondered the consequences of his failure. The Communist Party of Burma, now lording over the Wa masses, would goad them to worship Mao Zedong, Karl Marx, Joseph Stalin. It would capture the spirit of unity Saw Lu inculcated among the tribe but pervert it. It would swiftly abolish opium—and in doing so show principle where Saw Lu had faltered. That his enemy would fulfill elements of his dream was no comfort it all. It only compounded his shame.

Saw Lu led his followers to Lashio, the nearest Burmese city. It was modest in size but, to the highlanders, a whirl of noise and heat. They saw rackety British-built trains, buses retching black clouds, child monks in pomegranate robes chanting Buddhist mantras. Everything about the city was alien.

Not far from downtown Lashio a quiet hill teemed with deer and snakes. This is it, Saw Lu said. Our new home.[5] Using wood scraps and bamboo, they built houses and tried to replicate the old world as best they could. Though converted Christians, some of his followers hung buffalo skulls on posts, a sanitized homage to their head-hunting heritage. Saw Lu scrounged up bricks and constructed a church at the hill's apex. He painted a crimson cross above its doors.

Someone in the village had been lugging around a half-corroded bombshell as a keepsake. Saw Lu requisitioned it and hung the rusty object between two wooden posts. It would serve as their village drum, their church bell.

He struck it.

The bombshell let out a sad, metallic moan.

THAT WAS ALMOST fifty years ago, Saw Lu told me. We were sitting in his living room—Saw Lu, Jacob, and I—not five hundred feet from where the bombshell dangled, out there in the dark, in front of the church across the street.

It had taken him some time to recount the whole story, but Saw Lu seemed satisfied. Now you know all about the head-hunting epoch, he said, and how it came to an end. He told me the communists, for all their wrong thinking, did one thing right. They upheld the ban on head-hunting first enacted by his League of Warlords and enforced it long enough for the Wa to lose interest in the ritual altogether. "As far as I know," he said, "no Wa has decapitated anyone since."

Saw Lu said those godforsaken communists never took over all of Burma, as they'd vowed to do, but did manage to hold on to the Wa highlands for nearly twenty dismal years. Their reign lasted until the spring of 1989, but in that glorious year, courageous Wa highlanders rose up, cast out the communists, and established the United Wa State Army (UWSA), which rules the peaks to this day.

Saw Lu had much to say about that epoch too—the epoch of Wa nationhood—for he joined the UWSA, becoming one of its most venerable leaders. But the hour was very late. It was a story for another time.

BOOK TWO

BOOK TWO

UNSPEAKABLE

My marathon evening with Saw Lu ended with him agreeing to tell me all about the United Wa State Army (UWSA) at some future sit-down. That would have to wait though. He was a busy man, occupied for the rest of the week.

This left me to refocus on the original reason I'd traveled to Lashio: meeting the UWSA's top envoy and securing travel to Wa State. I wanted to request face time with current UWSA leaders—to find out what it was like to govern what the Drug Enforcement Administration called "Southeast Asia's largest narcotics-trafficking organization." The two best-known leaders are Chairman Bao Youxiang, effectively the president, and Wei Xuegang, the chief financial officer. Wei also happened to be the most notorious drug kingpin in the Eastern Hemisphere, and Bao too was wanted by the DEA. If by some miracle I got close to either of them, even speaking to their subordinates, I couldn't imagine anyone proving as forthcoming as Saw Lu. But I was determined to try.

Jacob kept hustling to track down the envoy, and after a few days, he delivered on his word. He'd arranged a meeting inside the UWSA's "external affairs office" in Lashio. It's basically an embassy, but since Wa State isn't recognized by the United Nations, they can't formally call it that. En route to the meeting—Jacob driving his hatchback, me in the passenger seat—he turned solemn and staked out some ground rules. First, he said, no matter what, do not mention to the envoy that you are acquainted with Saw Lu.

This jarred me. Though yet to hear Saw Lu's complete life story, I knew he'd served the UWSA as a statesman of some sort—and a military commander too, judging by the living room portrait of Saw Lu clad in a regal army uniform. I'd even hoped Saw Lu might put in a good word with the current leadership on my behalf. I asked Jacob to explain, but he muttered something about "internal politics," some convoluted drama he lacked the time to recount.

Second, Jacob told me, you cannot reveal any interest in narcotics. You will come off as a spy. "Fine," I said. "I won't ask for Wei Xuegang's whereabouts."

I was being facetious. Obviously, prodding for details about Wei— who has a $2 million head price courtesy of the DEA—would make me sound *exactly* like a spy and instantly doom my travel request. But Jacob bridled at the remark, stiffening in his seat. "Patrick, please. You can never talk about him to any Wa official. Never, never." Wei's name—just his name alone—was even more radioactive than I'd thought. But if I was ever going to grasp the UWSA's inner workings, I couldn't go on forever pretending its narcotics-trafficking mastermind didn't exist. I'd have to find a more opportune time to bring up Wei's name again, perhaps to Saw Lu. Surely they'd crossed paths.

We arrived at the "embassy," a compound located on a Lashio back-street, and parked outside its high concrete walls, topped with metal prongs. The gates were ajar, and looking inside, I saw austere buildings painted powder blue. They framed a cement patio with a wooden table in the center. The envoy was seated at the table. He waved us over and motioned for us to sit down.

"Thanks for finding time to see us," I said. A phone pressed to his ear, the envoy raised an index finger to say just a moment please. Another phone on the table pinged with incoming messages, and I sensed our conversation would take place in the unclaimed air between cell phone bleeps. He was dressed not in his pine-green UWSA uniform but in H&M's fall collection: burgundy hoodie, black polo, casual slacks. Late thirties with a neat haircut and trimmed nails.

"Welcome," the envoy said, finally placing his phone on the table, next to a pot of tea. He filled a ceramic Chinese teacup, waited for me to sip, and asked if it was good. It was, and well suited to such a morning with crisp winds blowing off the bluish peaks in the distance. In a prideful tone he said the tea was grown on Wa slopes that for centuries only sprouted opium poppies. So much for avoiding drug talk: the envoy was broaching the subject himself, firing up a prepared spiel.

The world had it all wrong, he said. Wa State once churned out opium, no denying that, but had since come to reject the manufacture of all illegal drugs. We even have our own UWSA antinarcotics squads, the envoy said. Had I seen his recent Facebook post? I looked it up while he tended to his buzzing phones. It was a photo of a sunlit meadow, satchels full of meth splayed in the grass. Forced onto their knees, behind the satchels, were three young smugglers in denim jackets and tracksuits, handcuffed and terrified. UWSA commandos stood nearby, pointing automatics at their skulls. A recent sting operation, the envoy said, once his call was complete. Non-Wa traffickers often slink through our homeland, but no country, not even your United States, can ever truly rid itself of drug gangs. "We do our best, and still we get blamed for everything. I just want you to see what's really happening in Wa State."

"I'd like to see it myself." He nodded. If it were up to him, I'd get travel clearance right away. "But you are American, correct?" Admitting an American would be rather complicated. "What is it you want to do exactly?"

"To go to Panghsang and interview your leaders. Ideally Chairman Bao."

The envoy smiled in an awkward, tight-lipped way, so I spontaneously downgraded my request. Actually, any high-ranking leader would do. He asked that I submit a formal request in English and Chinese and wait one month for a reply. Then he stood up. Meeting over. I pressed the box of chocolates into his hands and said, "For your children." He laughed and briefly disappeared inside the compound, returning with a canister of Wa tea grown on former poppy fields. "A gift for you." We shook hands.

"A photo before you leave?" The envoy led me to a little reception room off to the side. Emblazoned on a wall was the Wa national seal: a blood-red sun, set against perfect azure skies, glowing above emerald peaks. In imitation of my host, I stood before it and folded my hands as if posing before something sacrosanct. His assistant came out of a back room, snapping pictures with a smartphone, making sure to get a clear shot of my face.

"SO WHAT ARE my odds?"

We were back in Jacob's car. He supposed my request would require approval from the UWSA's central committee, headed by Chairman Bao. They were busy people who would question the benefit of staging a manicured visit for some American.

"Like fifty percent?"

He sighed. "Patrick, if it is really your dream, you will find a way." In the meantime, Jacob offered a consolation prize: a trip to Wa country, if not Wa State.

Wa State is demarcated from Burma proper by a river called the Salween, originating in the distant Himalayas. No one can cross this aquatic border without UWSA permission. Its troops will arrest or terminate trespassers on sight. However, Wa society spills past the river's western banks into Wa-settled villages under the UWSA's sway, if not its direct control.

"I can take you there. I know people. It should be OK."

"Great," I said. "When?"

By noon we were speeding east toward the jagged horizon, the sun a white disc overhead. Out the windows of his hatchback, I saw a slideshow on repeat. Winter rice fields, desiccated and tan. Hairless cows with skin drooping like shaved cats. Country noodle shacks. Families of four impossibly balanced on motorbikes.

About an hour out, we passed a teenager in a lime-green uniform unlike any worn by the Burmese or the Wa, patrolling solo with a fold-stock AK. I asked Jacob to whom this soldier belonged. He shrugged. Some local militant clan, guarding its little patch. There were many in this part of the country, dozens and dozens. Some aligned with the military like modern-day self-defense forces, others totally rogue. The engine whined as we pushed up into the mountains on cracked roads with no stoplights, traveling beyond Burma's terra firma into a liquid place where armed groups bubbled up, burst, and evaporated before you bothered to learn their names.

"What do they do out here? The little armed groups?"

"Same as the big ones. Whatever they want."

"Drug stuff?"

"Of course." Jacob knew for a fact that heroin and ya-ba—slang for meth pills—sold out here for half the city price. He said this with more authority than one would expect from a churchgoer. As the terrain steepened, Jacob shifted into second gear and veered off onto a rutted trail. The car's chassis bucked, axles neighing, back tires whipping up a wake of dust that hung in the air like powdered copper. We came to our destination: a Wa village with wooden homes spaced tightly together. Living in clusters is the way of the Wa, Jacob said. It makes us feel safe.

I felt eyes upon us. Villagers stared at the intruding vehicle from windows and porches, but when Jacob cranked down his tinted window, shouting greetings in Wa, their eyes softened. We parked in front of a bamboo home and stepped out into a weed-choked yard.

"My relatives live here. I don't know if they are home. Please wait."

Jacob stepped through a doorway without a door. He came back outside holding a gun.

With his free hand, he popped the hatchback's trunk, fished out a plastic bottle, and walked over to a fence made of sticks and barbed wire. He planted the bottle upside down on a post, then handed me the weapon: a rifle with a cherrywood stock and a metal scope. The gun's lightness surprised me. It was just an air rifle. We took turns plinking pellets at the bottle, seldom hitting our target. His marksmanship was as horrid as mine.

"Jacob, weren't you in the Wa army?"

"I told you. I wasn't a fighting soldier. I was a teacher-soldier."

When that got boring, we walked through the village to see who was idle. Elders mostly, beckoning us to sit on plastic stools in dirt yards and drink strong tea. We accepted the invitation of a wizened man in his late seventies, wiry but spry, calling out to Jacob by name. A fellow Baptist, Jacob said. They chatted in Wa. The man was soon lamenting, as rural Southeast Asian elders do, that young people kept leaving the village to chase money in the city. Jacob translated so I could chime in.

"Where do they go?" I asked. "Yangon? Bangkok?"

Mostly Panghsang, Wa State's capital, a boomtown thanks to its proximity to China. Jacob explained that most Wa people would rather stick to their own kind, up in the mountains, than settle in the lowlands. "They look down on us. In Yangon, people will ask, 'Oh, you are Wa? I thought you'd have black teeth. Do you still cut off people's heads?'"

Jacob said the elder, born in the Wa peaks, was old enough to have witnessed severed heads on poles back when he was young. The old man seemed to detect my interest because he started orating passionately, making chopping motions with his hands. "He says it was like something from ancient times. His clan was called Leun, and they hated the Braox clan. Back and forth, they killed and killed. He is so grateful those times are over."

Grateful to Saw Lu, as a matter of fact. The old man came of age in the late 1960s, during the League of Warlords' reign, which he recalled nostalgically. He'd known Saw Lu back then, and when I asked for an assessment of his character, he offered an amused grin. Obstinate to the bone, he said, but only a man whose zeal borders on madness would've demanded the Wa quit head-hunting, let alone succeeded.

Saw Lu's contributions to the Wa race are truly manifold, the elder said. He asked if I knew about Saw Lu's time in the UWSA. No other Wa leader had struggled so fervently to wrest the organization away from the drug trade—and a damn shame how that crusade turned out. I wanted to hear more. But our shadows were growing long in the dirt, and Jacob feared driving through the hills after dark. We said our good-byes and God-bless-yous and walked back to the car.

Jacob reckoned we'd get back to Lashio well before Saw Lu's bedtime. Let's see if he's keen to talk, he said. He urged me to ask the man himself all about Wa State's creation—and how he strove from the nation's first years to set it on a virtuous path.

HURTLING OVER BROKEN tarmac toward Lashio, we saw black plumes rising from ochre hills. Families in unseen villages were tending evening fires, boiling rice in metal cauldrons. Jacob and I were both a bit spun up after drinking so much high-octane Wa tea, bitter as kale, and in the intimacy of the car, I ventured the question that was bouncing around my mind all day.

"Jacob," I said. "Can we talk about Wei Xuegang?"

He winced and sucked in air. A pained sound like whistling backward. "That is a not-nice story!"

"I'm sure. But he's the most famous Wa person alive. What do you think of him?"

Long pause. "I think he is a one thousand percent businessman." Contempt seeped into his tone. "There are problems with that man and our family. He is the reason we do not live in Wa State anymore." I noticed he avoided saying Wei's name, as if uttering it would conjure some malignant power.

An uneasy silence followed. I filled it with everything I knew about Wei. That he was once protégé of the infamous Golden Triangle drug lord Khun Sa, helping him build the mightiest heroin-trafficking empire of the 1980s. That he parted with Khun Sa and brought his expertise into the UWSA upon its founding, nourishing the fledgling Wa nation with heroin profits. That his mastery of that forbidden art kept improving and never stopped. Wei is now, to hear the DEA tell it, a drug lord commensurate with El Chapo. A stone-cold genius with the mind of a Fortune 500 CEO. They say harems and cognac do not excite him. That he dresses like a strip mall accountant. That he loves money but hates spending it. Wei would rather pile it up, like amassing tokens in a game—the extremely difficult game of drug trafficking, for he may be the best ever to play it.

When I stopped talking, the silence returned. Just motor hum and darkening scenery. We drove like that for a long time, and when we pulled up to Saw Lu's house, the streetlamps were on, splashing spectral light on the asphalt. Bats circled overhead, softly beating their wings.

Saw Lu awaited us in his living room. He was accompanied by an older woman, her gray hair cinched in a dignified bun. "Are you Mary? Saw Lu's wife?"[1] She smiled. Mary twisted in her chair and ordered a servant girl to fetch a tray of cookies. Saw Lu in his no-nonsense fashion wasted no time. He was already monologuing before we sat down.

The subject that evening: Wa State's genesis and Saw Lu's role in its formation—a magnificent story, he assured me. But he was getting ahead of himself. The Wa nation and its militarized government, the UWSA, were founded in 1989. I reminded him that when our last talk concluded, we were still back in the early 1970s. We'd left off with Saw Lu leading a Moses-like exodus of Wa highlanders out of the peaks, away from the conquering communists, down to the Burmese city of Lashio where they started life anew—right here on this very hilltop.

Right, he said. There was a span of more than fifteen years in which Saw Lu never set foot in the Wa peaks, ruled as they were by Maoists. Those years living in Lashio weren't bad ones—they were among the more peaceful stretches of his life, he said—but he clearly wanted to ramble through them quickly.

So back to Lashio, circa 1973. Saw Lu told the Wa highlanders under his wing, You must acclimate or die. The Burmese city folks assume you are feral. Your survival depends on proving them wrong. Smile, learn their language, feign harmlessness. Do not go outside without clothing.

At the time, Burma's military regime was spiraling deeper into racist paranoia. Ethnic minorities—one in three citizens—were automatically suspected of seditious thought. Saw Lu, a military collaborator since his early twenties, impressed upon Burmese officials that he was one of the good ones, having proven his loyalty by rallying the Wa tribe to fight

Maoist invaders. Even though that mission failed, the junta ought to hold him up as an ethnic leader of impeccable caliber, an example to the other minorities.

The military agreed and found him a new job as a civilian intelligence officer, a position suited to his gifts of persuasion. They sent Saw Lu into the remote hills of Burma's Shan State, where he liaised with all kinds of minority communities. His orders: monitor their activities and gauge their potential to rebel. This wasn't clandestine work. Saw Lu became well known throughout Burma's north as an agent of the regime, but as he tells it, he was usually welcomed into village leaders' homes. Everyone knew that if he marked their area as docile, troops would leave them be.

Saw Lu felt conflicted about the job—surveilling fellow minorities—but he kept at it well into the 1980s. He had his reasons for serving a vicious junta: for as long as it deemed him useful, Burmese soldiers would spare his Wa flock in Lashio from the harassment meted out to other minority settlements. The refugees under his wing, newly citified, had propaganda value to the junta. They played their role as the good and decent Wa, making those Wa communists on the China border seem all the more sinister.

These were quieter years. Saw Lu and Mary raised eight children. They ran their local church, started an orphanage. They built the sea-foam green house in which I now sat. Saw Lu's world grew small. He turned forty. His hairline receded, and so did his visions of greatness.

But then came 1989, a year held sacred by the Wa, just as Americans venerate 1776. In the communist-run peaks, a valorous band of Wa in the town of Panghsang stood up to their overlords, chucked them out, and reclaimed their ancestral lands. Soon afterward, these revolutionaries tracked down Saw Lu and summoned him—for Saw Lu's reputation as a great leader still lingered in the peaks. He joined them in laying the bedrock of the first-ever Wa nation.

Saw Lu's oration was turning grandiose and I sensed the telling of a foundational myth. Every country has one: a glorious account of its birth, scrubbed clean of embarrassing details. It's public knowledge that Wa State funded itself through narcotics from the outset, and that its trafficker in chief was, and still is, a shadowy figure named Wei. So with reluctance, I interrupted.

"Saw Lu? I wanted to ask you about Wei Xuegang."

The name brought him to a shuddering halt. I hated doing this, but what choice did I have? I couldn't fill my notebook with some portrait of Wa State irreconcilable with its reputation. I had to coax out an unvarnished version of the story—or at least try.

"I won't talk about that man."

I had not known Saw Lu could seem nervous. The room fell into an ugly quiet. The ceiling creaked. Outside, insects chittered.

"I just can't."

Jacob tried to revive his mood, asking him to finish the story, but Saw Lu's speech came out clipped and lifeless. He was shrinking into himself, his mind drawn into some dark place where I was not allowed. Mary patted her husband's arm and told us it was getting late. Time for the patriarch to go to bed.

I left his house that night fearing he'd never speak to me again—and that I would never decipher his connection to the DEA's biggest target in Asia.

THE PRODIGY

W̲ei Xuegang is without question the greatest Golden Triangle narcotics trafficker of all time. The story of how he rose to such heights,
however, has never been told in full—in large part because Wei so
doggedly clings to secrecy, preserving even pedestrian details of his life
from public scrutiny.

That's not the only reason though. With other narco-lords—Pablo
Escobar or Wei's former mentor, Khun Sa—the United States has built up
their legends, making giants of these outlaws, so that when felled they'll
make a huge splash. But drawing attention to Wei is riskier. His biography
is littered with inconvenient facts. More than once, his life has intersected
with clandestine US programs in ways that do not flatter the American
government or its allies. He is among the infamous figures, such as Iraq's
Saddam Hussein or Panama's Manuel Noriega, who once assisted the
American intelligence apparatus but later became enemies of the state.

Understanding Wei—and the US interventions that shaped his
rise—requires looking at the Golden Triangle with clear eyes. American
officials depict the region as a maelstrom of quarreling nations, tribes, and
cartels—Chinese, Shan, Wa, Thai, Burmese, and others—forging alliances and breaking them, exchanging bullets and territory ad infinitum.
That's not entirely wrong. But often the roles of two particular tribes are
sanitized.

I'm referring to the Central Intelligence Agency and the Drug
Enforcement Administration.

These bureaucratic tribes share certain qualities with Wa headhunters. They hail from the same homeland but squabble, not for skulls, but
for influence, budgets, and prestige. To make sense of Wei's career, and
thus the United Wa State Army (UWSA), you must first grasp that there

is not one American strategy in the Golden Triangle but two, executed by separate wings of the US government. Sometimes these agencies see eye to eye, but when the DEA and CIA clash, everything in the Golden Triangle quakes. The cleverest traffickers use these disruptions to their advantage—and Wei is nothing if not clever.

A quick ethnography of these two American tribes will clarify why they often feud. Though DEA and CIA personnel serve the same government, they usually come from different family backgrounds, and this was especially true in the 1970s and 1980s. Many DEA agents are former cops or soldiers, sons (and sometimes daughters) of working-class stock. Straight shooters by nature, they never smoked pot in high school. Their worldview skews monochrome: we're the good guys; drug dealers are "scumbags." These narcotics agents ("narcs" for short) court scumbags, pumping them for dirt on other criminals, in hopes of stopping drug shipments. They believe seizing a ton of heroin can save a thousand lives. Locking up drug lords can save even more. Justice must be wrought. The law is the law.

For CIA officers, the law is not the law.[1] Their job is to ensure that America remains the most powerful country on earth, by any means necessary. CIA officers are more often plucked from the Ivy League or other distinguished universities. During training, they're made to feel the empire is on the brink of peril. They must do whatever it takes to save it—including lie. That's what spies do. A CIA officer can lie to anyone, even fellow American officials.

When you imagine a CIA officer, don't picture someone parachuting into hostile territory clenching a knife in their teeth. Picture someone with coffee breath at a desk inside a US embassy. They might be listed in the staff directory under a drab title such as second secretary of agricultural affairs. That's a cover. They'll actually spend their days managing a stable of informants or intercepting communications. Their job is to gather information and, from time to time, use it to sabotage rivals. The last thing they want is another federal agent coming along to crimp the flow of intelligence.[2]

And there's the rub. The DEA would like to lock up every last drug trafficker, even ones providing the CIA with intel. As a former CIA station chief in Burma told me, DEA agents view their "primary job as putting bad guys in jail. In contrast, the CIA prefers to recruit bad guys to provide intelligence on more important bad guys."[3] Like the DEA, the CIA cares deeply about narcotics, but not necessarily for the same reasons. CIA officers understand that heroin and meth, like oil, can give life to new nations or destabilize existing ones. That's all fine and good as long as America manages this dark power. If the CIA has to canoodle with a drug cartel to "defend the national interest" (how they adore this phrase), then so be it. The agency doesn't owe anyone an explanation, certainly not the DEA.

This isn't to say narcs and spies must always despise each other. "I worked around the DEA for a long time," the former CIA station chief told me. "I like the DEA. But there's that culture problem, see? They're cops. They put lawbreakers away. We break laws. Not American laws but any number of foreign laws, sure. That's how we operate."

In the Golden Triangle, conflict between these two tribes was inevitable. The CIA got there first. The DEA came later, in the early 1970s, threatening the CIA's narco-espionage system. Ever since then, their feuding has injected chaos into the underworld—an unpredictability that has baffled local traffickers, many of them viewing the Americans as a confounding people, so warlike they'd fly across the world just to tussle with their own kind.

Not Wei Xuegang though. Wei was different. He *is* different—for his career has yet to end.

A man of uncommon intelligence, Wei has repeatedly peered into the chaos created by CIA-DEA infighting and gleaned opportunity. Wei can discern the plans of spies and the dreams of narcs. He predicts how their interventions might make winners and losers of various drug lords, creating power vacuums he can swoop in to fill. His decades-long reign is defined by how he's exploited various DEA or CIA operations to his own benefit.

Along the way, Wei did not always play this game perfectly. But when he failed, he got smarter—ultimately bringing his accrued wisdom to Wa State upon its formation. It was there that Wei and Saw Lu would clash in a struggle for the young nation's soul.

That tale will come a bit later. What follows directly is the origin story of Wei Xuegang, a drug trafficker whose career ups and downs reveal the madness of America's War on Drugs. It begins in the Wa peaks—in a wooden shack filled with CIA surveillance equipment.[4]

BORN IN THE mid-1940s, Wei grew up in Ving Ngun, or Silver Fortress, a corner of Wa country stuck to the Chinese border. Little about Wei's teenage years hinted at great power to come. He was gawky and shy, a misfit among other Wa boys, mostly sons of warrior-farmers.

Although born to a Wa mother, Wei isn't fully Wa: his father was a Chinese frontiersman who'd assimilated among the tribe. The couple raised three sons, and Wei was the middle child. His dad taught him to read and write Chinese, and that helped Wei land his first job. In the early 1960s, while other Wa teenagers tended poppies, Wei reported to work at a CIA-linked "listening post," set up on the territory of Mahasang the Prince. The listening post's supervisor was an ethnic Chinese officer in Taiwan's military intelligence division.

The radio base was filled with electronic eavesdropping gear powered by hand-crank generators. Wei would sit inside that shack, sponging up Chinese communist radio chatter. He'd siphon out interesting bits and convert them into Morse code for transmission to larger radio bases, manned by the Exiles. His direct employer, Taiwan's military intelligence division, was a junior partner of the CIA, so American spies could've accessed whatever Wei recorded. He wasn't a CIA asset, per se—more like a subcontractor doing espionage grunt work.[5]

A head for figures and codes held no cachet among other Wa his age. Wei quietly endured their mockery. He kept to himself, only palling around with his two brothers, preferring to speak Chinese instead of Wa. In a place where people seldom bathed, Wei kept fastidiously clean. He was a rare specimen in headhunter country: a nerd.

Wei was likely in his late teens when he first saw him—the outsider who would rescue him from this dreadful place and sweep him into the drug trade.[6] Zhang Qifu was roughly ten years older and a head taller. He was handsome too, a tangle of black hair tousling his forehead. Barely thirty years old, Zhang oozed leadership, even though he only led a militia of modest size.

Mahasang ruled Silver Fortress, and though the Exiles bought up most of his ample opium harvest, he'd also sell to others. This included Zhang, who would ride into the peaks on horseback with his posse of riflemen. He purchased Wa opium to supplement the opium produced in his own little fiefdom—a valley to the west, on the far side of the Salween River, a few days' hard ride away. Zhang had that gift, common to politicians and hustlers, of making any stranger in his gaze feel special. When he bumped into Wei and introduced himself, the awkward teen was enthralled.

Wei and Zhang discovered they had things in common. Zhang was also half Chinese on his father's side. His mother was indigenous as well, though she was Shan, not Wa. Like Wei, Zhang felt more affinity for his Chinese side. Both of his parents died before he turned six, so he was raised by an ethnically Chinese paternal grandfather, the headman of a small but tough mountain clan. This clan dominated a poppy-growing Shan village—and Zhang had recently inherited leadership from his aging grandfather.

Zhang's grandpa had been content to sell opium, harvested by local peasants, to the Exiles' roving caravans. But Zhang, ambitious down to his DNA, wanted to level up and traffic it himself. He understood that the poor produced opium, village middlemen like his grandfather collected and sold it, but traffickers—moving the product over mountains—reigned supreme and reaped the greatest profits. So he'd rallied a few hundred Shan militiamen to transport sacks of opium down to the Thai-Burma border: the gateway to international markets. Zhang was a warlord on the ascent, and he believed himself destined to rise far above his benighted birthplace. That was a feeling Wei understood well.

Zhang had been searching for an apprentice, and he offered to mentor Wei, who accepted without hesitation. Wei's job—stenography for the Taiwan-CIA spying apparatus—was dull work and, worse yet, not very profitable. Come to my fiefdom, Zhang said, where I have my own little radio base to guide my smugglers along trails. You can run dispatch and soak up the ins-and-outs of trafficking opium.

They made a perfect pair. Zhang was cocky and loud, a born front man. Wei was demure, comfortable in his new boss's shadow. Money captivated them both. Zhang promised to make Wei rich. Soon enough, he said, they would graduate beyond trafficking minor amounts of opium down trails mottled with donkey shit. All you have to do, Zhang told Wei, is stick by my side and never betray me.

WEI WAS A star protégé. After joining Zhang's crew, he took on responsibilities well beyond radio communications. He tried his hand at managing the militia's budget and proved himself a financial prodigy. By streamlining the militia's operations, Wei made Zhang richer.

Handling the boss's money gave Wei a sense of purpose. As a child, his bookishness drew taunts from the other Wa kids, but where were those bullies now? Barefoot and unwashed in some poppy field. His brains trumped their brute strength every time—for as long as his intellect could generate wealth, he was valuable, and some formidable leader such as Zhang would protect him from harm. Zhang doted on Wei, treating him like a little brother. Wei knew his place: never talking back, always submitting to the boss's demands. Zhang couldn't have it any other way. He needed to play the alpha in every relationship.

In Burma, minor-league mountain warlords, weak as they are, usually have to forge ties with a more powerful armed group to ensure their survival.[7] But Zhang was allergic to authority. Though he'd formed alliances, they seldom lasted. The Exiles had once recruited him as a field commander, tasked with securing trails in the Shan hills, until he cut loose and started trafficking opium himself. After that, Zhang fell in with a Shan princess who led a rebel movement, but he couldn't stand the kowtowing and ditched her too. He joined Burma's self-defense force scheme in the early 1960s just to gain access to government roads—a boon to his upstart trafficking business. That deal actually stuck, only because the Burmese officers were located too far away to bother him. Behind their backs, he called them buffoons.

Zhang would sidle up to anyone who might benefit his interests in the short term. He told Wei that other drug syndicates draped themselves in ideology: anticommunism, ethnic liberation, whatever. But these were phony flags of convenience, flown to obscure the ruthless game of moving drugs through lawless lands. I don't pretend to be anything I'm not, Zhang said. I'm a businessman. Nothing more.

Zhang's arrogance had undermined his relationship with the Golden Triangle's most powerful figure: Gen. Lee Wen-huan, head honcho of the Exiles. Lee had long tried to mentor Zhang. Ten years prior, Zhang was a nobody—some village tough whose clan sold opium to his caravans—until Lee discovered him, lavishing him with guns, money, and horses: a starter kit for Zhang's transformation into a fledgling warlord. Lee believed Zhang possessed the raw materials for greatness: roughneck charm, unstoppable drive, and Chinese blood. He'd even considered ceding his throne to him in the distant future. Lee couldn't groom his own son for the role—he wanted his kids in college, not the drug trade—so his attention flowed toward Zhang.[8]

But Zhang was a fickle mentee. He was ungrateful, receiving gifts of mules and rifles to scale up his militia but never truly accepting Lee's tutelage, not for long anyway. Still, no matter what, Lee refused to give up on him, always hoping he'd outgrow his ego and come into the fold. Though Zhang didn't always follow his mentor's guidance, the two would meet face-to-face every now and again, for they still had a business relationship to uphold. Zhang's militia had to set aside a share of its profits for the Exiles—as did every other opium-trafficking gang in Burma. Like a kingdom demanding tribute, the Exiles insisted on a cut of every bit of opium produced in Burma, whether they'd collected it or not.

The Exiles monopolized control of the Thai-Burma border, the portal through which Burmese opium flowed to the outside world, and none could cross it without paying the tax: $9 per opium kilo, nonnegotiable. Attempting to sneak drugs past the border was suicidal. Their CIA-built radio network was an all-seeing eye. Tax evaders were tracked down and shot. So when Zhang sent opium to buyers in Thailand, he dutifully paid his toll, though he'd grumble about it to Wei.

One day in the mid-1960s, Zhang told Wei to mount up for a days-long journey. He'd decided his young protégé ought to meet the big shot who dominated the Golden Triangle. Straddling horses, Zhang and Wei rode south to General Lee's headquarters in Chiang Mai province, Thailand, just across the Burma border. Dismounting with thighs aching, they tied up their horses and walked up moss-furred steps toward Lee's home.

General Lee ushered them inside his stone dwelling, planted on a mountaintop like some primeval shrine. He was a stout man, then in his late forties, broad shouldered and dressed in rough khaki. Lee spoke in short, grumbly sentences, and, though stern, he radiated paternal warmth. Lee hailed from Yunnan, China's Wild West, a byword for spicy noodles and strong tea. Wei and Zhang also descended from Yunnanese clans, spoke the same Chinese dialect, and relished the same comfort food.

In Lee's home, inside a cement-walled tea room, Wei watched his boss transform into a meeker figure, as if performing a role. He was stunned at how Zhang's brazenness receded. Out came a doting supplicant who filled

Lee's teacup and would not let it go cold. Zhang even called him "Master Lee." The two behaved like uncle and nephew.

Master Lee, Zhang said, I wanted you to see how far I've come. I have my own mentee now: Wei Xuegang. He's a talented radioman but needs to improve his skills. Might he shadow your dispatchers and pick up a few tricks?

As you wish, Lee said. He told his subordinates to escort Wei into the radio room: the Exiles' communication nerve center. It was right outside, not one hundred feet from the general's front door: a boxy white building filled with American-made radio transmitters. Towering above it was a steel antenna topped with three prongs poking into the mountain mist like a trident. Day and night, inside that radio room, soldiers twisted dials and issued orders, in code, to distant outposts in Burma—including Wei's old listening post in the Wa peaks. The skies over the Golden Triangle crackled with encrypted messages, some concerning espionage against China, others devoted to drug-running logistics, with many transmissions flowing through this dim-lit room, humming with equipment.

Zhang drained his teacup, said good-bye, and rode back to his village, leaving Wei to study at the elbow of General Lee's best intelligence operatives. There was no finer internship in the Golden Triangle. After a week or so, once he'd learned all he could, Wei rode northward back to Zhang's territory. He now possessed a blueprint in his head: a mental map of the strengths and defects of Asia's largest drug cartel.

Good, Zhang said. Because neither he nor his prodigy would ever visit cordially with Master Lee again. With Wei's help, Zhang intended to betray his mentor and end his supremacy. It was an early indication, to Wei, of his boss's sense of loyalty. In short, he had none.

EARLY SUMMER, THE start of monsoon season, 1967.

Zhang had it all planned out. First, he'd buy sixteen tons of Wa opium up in Silver Fortress—the largest single shipment in Golden Triangle history, nearly exhausting his savings. He'd then sneak it out of Burma and sell it without paying a single cent to the Exiles. If successful, he would rake in the modern-day equivalent of $5 million and evade $1 million in taxes.

With the proceeds of this megasale, Zhang would fortify his militia with finer weapons and fresh recruits. His fighters would then choke off every trail leading to the Wa peaks, forcing the Exiles to pay a toll to *him* if they wanted to access the coveted Wa opium crop. He would rule a strategic zone of the poppy lands in mimicry of the Exiles. Their aura of invincibility would fizzle, and everyone in the Golden Triangle would respect Zhang as a drug lord equal to General Lee.

That was the idea, at least. His crew had questions.

Sixteen tons? That would require 250 mules marching in a mile-long train, a thousand-hoofed centipede, discreet as a freight train. Sneaking it across the heavily defended Thai-Burma border would be impossible. I know, Zhang said. That's why we're moving the drugs to Laos.

It was an unorthodox suggestion. Burma and Laos are separated by the Mekong River. Moving opium across its waters would still violate the Exiles' demand for tribute; if opium originated in Burma, they demanded a cut. True, the Mekong's sodden riverbanks were poorly patrolled by Exile troops, but for a good reason: Laos was not a choice destination for Burma-based traffickers. The country was a flaming war zone—like Vietnam in miniature.

Two contestants wrestled for control of Laos: local communist rebels in comradeship with North Vietnam versus a right-wing military government, propped up by the United States. When it wasn't battling the red menace, the Lao military—backed by the CIA—also controlled the country's drug trade.[9] Laos was a mountainous land rife with poppies, and its army generals ran a nose-to-tail operation overseeing opium collection, a complex of heroin refineries, and, finally, transport to the top-selling market: South Vietnam. The Lao military even flew heroin to Saigon on planes bequeathed by the United States. The purpose of this donated fleet was combatting communist guerrillas—namely, bombing the Ho Chi Minh Trail, a supply route snaking through Laos and Vietnam—but American aircraft also proved handy for zipping heroin through the skies.[10]

The Lao military's commander in chief was named Ouan Rattikone, a plump general whose ivory-white military uniform dripped with questionable medals. He was the CIA's main man in the country. Zhang had reached out to Ouan and, with his infinite charm, convinced the chief to buy the opium megaload all in one go. Lao generals typically didn't source from Burma—they had plenty of opium at home—but by 1967, demand for heroin was sky-high, thanks to cashed-up GIs in South Vietnam. Chief Ouan could easily turn sixteen tons of raw Wa opium into white powder and reap a delicious profit. So he agreed to Zhang's offer, telling him to drop the shipment at a lumberyard beside the Mekong—on the Lao side of the river.

In July of that year, Zhang's caravan lurched toward the river, its warm waters brown as Ovaltine. His militiamen and donkeys crossed on wooden barges, but Zhang did not join them; nor did his protégé. He'd ordered his crew to unload the drugs, collect payment from Chief Ouan's people, and hurry back across the river. No dallying. The militia reached the sawmill, a maze of log piles heaped on mud softened by recent rains. They were piling canvas sacks on the ground when metal orbs arced shrilly through the sky.

Mortars, incoming.

Ascending the riverbanks was their worst nightmare: a battalion of more than one thousand Exile fighters, hurling bombs and recoilless rifle shells. Zhang's militiamen scrambled for cover in the pudding-soft mud, ducking behind logs, their mules bawling and crazy eyed. They dug in and returned fire. Man and beast alike flopped dead in the muck.

As the fighting raged, Chief Ouan sent a message to both sides: please cease fire so I can collect my opium. Neither stood down. So he called in American-made T-28 propeller planes, loaded with five-hundred-pound explosives meant for Vietnamese communists, and bombed the sawmill to hell. As both the Exiles and Zhang's militia scuttled away, Lao soldiers rushed in to scoop up the sixteen tons left by the riverbanks. Chief Ouan never paid for it. Soon the Wa-grown opium, in which Zhang had invested dreams of greatness, was swept into labs in Laos. It was no doubt converted to heroin and shipped to Saigon, where it swam in American soldiers' blood.

Reputation is everything in the underworld, and Zhang's was defiled. He looked like a fool for challenging the Exiles—and for getting ripped off by the Lao army chief. He stank of defeat. The ensuing years brought humiliation in waves.

Half his fighters quit. He had to slink around, now that the Exiles wanted him dead. Even Burmese generals grew leery of Zhang, whose militia was still registered as a self-defense force. The last thing they needed was an erratic warlord aligned with their army—however loosely—picking unwinnable fights along their borders, pissing off neighboring countries. They opted to clip his wings while he was down. In the fall of 1969, Burmese officials lured Zhang to a meeting on false pretenses, then dragged him off to a high-security prison in Mandalay, a city in the central plains, far from the borderlands.

The charge: high treason. Zhang, his operation on the skids, had been consorting with Shan rebels, mostly to trade supplies and cut business deals. Few seriously believed Zhang would turn revolutionary—he was a huckster, not a freedom fighter, and he'd do business with anyone—but it was a useful pretext for locking him away. In Burma, simply fraternizing with insurrectionists can result in a life sentence.

Deprived of their leader, Zhang's crew deteriorated.[11] Those who stuck around grew despondent. None possessed the charisma required to lead a narco-militia, certainly not Wei, more comfortable with a pencil and ledger than an AK-47. If they wanted to keep the militia alive, they'd have to find some way to liberate their boss from the clink.

ZHANG WOULD END up spending only five years behind bars. Later in life, after reuniting with Wei and other subordinates, he'd admit the prison stint was a blessing. For starters, it prevented the Exiles from tracking him down in the jungle and putting a bullet in his chest. But this interregnum also forced Zhang, then in his mid-thirties, to take a break from the drug trade. To slow down instead of chasing the next big score—to refine his strategy for dominance. This head clearing would prove beneficial. Because while Zhang was locked up, shock waves hit the Golden Triangle, transforming it into a more complex place.

These shock waves rippled out from America, some eight thousand miles away. In the early 1970s, Vietnam vets returned home in large numbers, and a public unmoored by foreign defeat was doubly disturbed to see sons and brothers coming back with track marks. Their loved ones hooked on heroin, families asked why the US government wasn't doing more to hunt down the producers of this poison, whoever they were. This uproar would incite President Richard M. Nixon to declare a "War on Drugs."

"Back then, I believed all the bullshit," said Mike Levine, then a New York City–based antinarcotics agent. "You know, 'We gotta get the evil foreigners making this white powder.' I was a stone-cold believer in that shit."

Levine worked for US Customs in the Hard Narcotics Smuggling Division. The DEA wasn't yet formed, and thwarting heroin traffic was a scattered effort falling to the Justice Department, state and local police, US Customs, and other agencies. Like most Americans, Levine was clueless about the CIA's ties to Southeast Asian heroin manufacturers such as the Exiles, but that innocence would not last. Levine, a rookie agent, was about to stumble across this dark alliance—by accident.

It was the summer of 1971, and Levine found himself in the bowels of John F. Kennedy International Airport. He was sweating a perp, some ex-GI, in a windowless interrogation room. The man had just arrived from Bangkok with three heroin kilos hidden under false bottoms in his Samsonite luggage. To Levine, the guy looked twerpy: slight build, granny glasses, nervous gray eyes. Under interrogation, the perp folded like a lawn chair, squeaking out the names of his suppliers: Liang and Geh, two ethnic Chinese traffickers in Thailand.

Levine followed the clues east. One month later, he was walking Bangkok's neon-drenched streets for his first overseas undercover assignment. He'd tracked down Liang and Geh and introduced himself as an Italian mobster. Partner with me, Levine told the traffickers, and you won't have to use four-eyed dweebs as drug mules.

At the time, Bangkok's ethnic Chinese smugglers were desperate for a high-volume pipeline funneling the Exiles' heroin into the United States. They knew GIs back in their hometowns still craved Golden Triangle dope but they struggled to traffic the product to America. Along came Levine, posing as a mafia capo—alias: Mike Pagano—offering to set up phony export businesses that could pump loads of their heroin straight to New York City. "I really convinced these guys I was some tutti frutti of the mafia."[12] Levine found it hilarious. He wasn't even Italian. He was a Jewish guy from the South Bronx.

"They wanted to do business with me. Bad!" Liang and Geh drowned him in good booze and pampered him with fancy clothes. Their preferred camaraderie-building exercise was a long evening at a massage parlor, the kind where women in heavy makeup bathe their clients. On wild nights out, the pair would boast about "The Factory," a complex of heroin refineries in provincial Chiang Mai whipping up more than one hundred kilos per week. If what they said was true, it was one of the busiest dope labs on earth.

"The Factory was my Mount Everest," Levine told me. "They said it was run by their uncle. After two weeks, they were ready to take me up north and introduce me." But not long after Levine secured plans to visit the Thai-Burma border with his new pals, he received a call in his room at the Siam Intercontinental, Bangkok's fanciest hotel. It was around 2 or 3 a.m. Come to the US embassy, the voice said. Make sure you're not followed.

Click.

Inside the embassy, Levine was cornered by a CIA officer "who didn't give a name—or if he did, it was fake. And he's dressed like what you'd expect a CIA agent cast in a movie to look like. In a bush jacket. You know, everything but a pith helmet and walking stick."

"This guy says to me, 'You're not going to Chiang Mai. We want you to end this case right here.'" New orders: convince Liang and Geh to cough up a single kilo in Bangkok and then bust them on the spot. Hand the idiots over to Thai police, fly back to New York. Boom, you're the new hot shot in your little customs bureau. Deal?

"No way," Levine shot back. "I'm going to Chiang Mai to meet the uncle. They're going to introduce me to the guys running this shit."

"Well, you can't go," the CIA officer said. "We can't protect you up there."

"I didn't take this job to be protected," Levine said. "I want to go."

The agent invoked Levine's four years in the US Air Force—he knew about his service record somehow—and told him to "act like a good soldier. You're ex-military. Follow orders. He says to me, 'We've got the Vietnam War going, it's complicated and you don't understand the big picture.'"

Levine slunk back to the hotel, despondent. He considered going to The Factory in defiance of the CIA. "I'm glad I didn't do that. I don't think I would've survived. If I got killed up there, no one would even know. Maybe they'd put one of those bullshit stars up on the wall."

In the end, Levine obeyed the CIA's orders. He pinched Liang and Geh and booked a return flight to JFK. A close call for the CIA, deftly averted. But the incident augured a greater internal feud within the US government—one that would disrupt the Exiles' business, providing an opportunity to their rivals: Zhang and Wei.

That same summer, in 1971, President Nixon officially kicked off the War on Drugs: a shiny new war to appease the public and distract from defeat in Vietnam. On national television he warned that "if we cannot destroy the drug menace in America then it will surely, in time, destroy us." Congressional lawmakers channeled fear toward drugged-up "new left radicals" and urban Black communities. But officials at the highest levels knew better. They feared putting a spotlight on the drug trade would lead to a reckoning—for anyone pursuing the root source of heroin production in Asia, as Levine did, would run smack into America's own intelligence assets.

The Justice Department's antidrug organization, the Bureau of Narcotics and Dangerous Drugs—a predecessor of the DEA—had the president's ear. Its officials presented a plan to defuse the situation. They sought White House permission to disentangle the CIA from the Exiles and push the cartel out of the opium business altogether, delicately and in a manner that wouldn't embarrass the spy agency or its drug-running affiliates.

In March 1972—nine months after Levine's misadventure—US narcotics bureau officials flew to Chiang Mai and walked onto a Thai army base. There, piled before them on a dirt field, lay a whopping twenty-six tons of opium packed into burlap sacks. This was supposedly the Exiles' entire stockpile. They'd bought it with $1 million in US taxpayer money— a deal prearranged with the help of Thai military officers cozy with the cartel.[13] It was enough opium to generate $3 billion worth of heroin, half a year's supply on America's streets. The sacks were heaped atop logs: ten funeral pyres, each six feet tall. They'd come to watch it burn—an event "without parallel," they said, since China's Qing dynasty had destroyed one thousand tons of British opium thirteen decades earlier.

Conceived by the Bureau of Narcotics and Dangerous Drugs and brokered through Thailand's army, the deal stipulated that the Exiles' leaders, including General Lee, would quit trafficking opium forever. They would face no charges for past criminality. The Thai military would even adopt the Exiles as a part-time auxiliary unit and bestow citizenship upon its soldiers. The ethnic Chinese fighters would stay put, farming peaches and oolong tea along the border, but retain their weapons to scare communists away from the area. All parties would walk away unscathed. Lee and the other cartel leaders agreed to the terms but declined to attend the burning of their stockpile.

American chemists flown in for the occasion tested the Exiles' opium, deemed it pure, and gave the signal to proceed. Thai soldiers drenched the pyres in jet fuel and set them alight. They hissed and poured black smoke for fifteen hours straight. The antinarcotics bureau, ascendent in the milieu of US federal agencies, was triumphant. With the president's backing, they'd just broken up their first foreign drug cartel—Asia's largest—while also mopping up the CIA's mess.

That's what they thought at the time anyway. Come spring, the Exiles ignored the deal and launched mule caravans into Burma's poppy lands right on schedule. They had no intention of shutting down; nor did the CIA appear to pressure them to honor the deal.[14] The CIA wasn't going to let an upstart US bureau dismantle the Exiles. Some cartel or another was going to dominate the Southeast Asian heroin trade. Better to have it run by a vetted, pro-US syndicate instead of one hostile to American interests or, heaven forbid, communists.

In 1973, Nixon created the Drug Enforcement Administration, a tribe of superpolice fanning out across the globe to root out narcotics producers and wage the War on Drugs. But from the start, more astute narcs realized this war would be fought with a caveat: no targeting traffickers deemed valuable by the CIA. Case in point: that very year, an Exiles lieutenant and his crew got caught smuggling opium directly to the United States. He told DEA agents they were CIA assets, tasked with spying on China, and thus protected from prosecution—and he was right. CIA officials forced the DEA to drop the case. The smugglers walked away free.[15]

Some narcs couldn't make peace with this hypocrisy, including Levine, who joined the DEA at its inception. "Bunch of fraternity boys with guns and no honor," said Levine of the CIA. "The people they were protecting? Their so-called *assets*? They were fucking America and using the CIA as a condom."

The DEA-CIA feud was on. Through the mid-1970s, the DEA built up a major presence in Thailand, and though weaker than the CIA, it was a feisty organization that demanded respect. The Exiles couldn't spit in the faces of American narcotics agents. They had to at least pretend they'd transformed into wholesome tea farmers, as they'd promised, if only to save face for the US government. Getting sucked into another loud, nasty battle—like the clash at the sawmill with Zhang's militia years earlier—would not be wise. That would subvert the big lie, attract nosy reporters, and endanger the status quo, perhaps even forcing the US and Thai intelligence services to rescind legal immunity and let the DEA take the Exiles down.

This presented a dire challenge: any drug cartel unable to throw its full might into defending trafficking routes soon finds its turf challenged. The War on Drugs burdened the Exiles with a terrible weakness—and few could sniff out weakness better than Zhang and Wei.

IN 1974, THREE YEARS into the War on Drugs, Zhang's crew finally freed their boss from prison. Busting him out wasn't possible—the Burmese kept Zhang inside a well-fortified prison in the distant, dusty plains of Mandalay—so they had to get creative. They opted for a hostage swap: kidnapping two Soviet doctors from a remote clinic and threatening to blow their brains out if Zhang wasn't freed. Loathe to upset the Soviet Union—then the world's number two superpower—Burmese officials grudgingly unclasped Zhang's manacles. Once turned loose, he reunited with Wei, his mentee, and the rest of the gang.

Prison changed the boss. Zhang said it gave him time to think about who he'd been and what he wanted to become. He'd spent his confinement pondering the future of his race. The Shan race, he meant—much to Wei's surprise. Before his arrest, Zhang seldom mentioned his Shan blood, acquired from his long-deceased mother. He carried himself, in every respect, like an ethnic Chinese entrepreneur. But now Zhang was asking why the Burmese and Thais had nations of their own but his beautiful Shan people did not.

He told his crew that a people with no nation were doomed to grow rice for oppressors' stomachs, their sons press-ganged and their daughters sold as prostitutes. Were the eight million Shan not beggars sleeping on beds of gold—rich in opium yet deprived of its lucre by outside interlopers, such as General Lee? They would live in squalor until some great leader arose to carve out an independent Shan nation.[16]

I am that leader, he said. Bury the name Zhang Qifu. From now on, I am Khun Sa: "Prince of Prosperity" in the Shan language.[17]

Prison clearly hadn't dulled his ego. Shan scholars still debate whether this transformation was sincere. Either way, Zhang appeared to realize—in contradiction to his earlier views—that a mere hustler could only amass so many followers. Few will fight to make another man rich. Many will sacrifice blood to elevate their race. This truth was vindicated as Khun Sa quickly rallied thousands of Shan fighters to his side, rousing them with promises of impending nationhood. By 1976, Khun Sa, with Wei at his side, had chosen a site for this new Shan nation. It was a valley, belonging to the Exiles, on the Thai side of the border.

Locals called the area Broken Rock, a rare breach in the Thai-Burma mountainscape connecting the two countries. The Exiles used it as a thoroughfare for jumbo-sized caravans. Running through Broken Rock was a wide trail stomped to tawny dust by a million hooves. Non-Exile smugglers could also pass through "but any smuggler who wasn't with us had to pay the tax," said Jao Kai Wa, a former Exile sergeant.[18] "Outsiders always paid. Unless they wanted trouble."

Rawboned and surly, Jao was the Exiles' chief toll collector in Broken Rock. One morning in 1976, he heard over the radio that trouble had come through overnight. A few dozen smugglers had slipped through on foot, dropped off some opium on the Thai side, and crept back to Burma without paying. Probably Khun Sa's guys, according to the radio dispatcher.

Khun Sa. Jao knew the name. The scoundrel Zhang, newly reinvented as a Robin Hood, vowing to liberate the Shan one kilo of opium at a time. "I didn't care about any of that shit," Jao told me. "All I knew is that he didn't pay his taxes." Not that Sergeant Jao could see where those taxes were going. His platoon wore threadbare uniforms and only got pork flecked into their rice bowls once a month. Like most corporations, the Exiles shaved costs to the bone. Jao's rifle was a black-market M-16 that had seen better days. But it did the job, and now they had a job to do: tracking down Khun Sa's border jumpers—thirty of them, if the radio had it right. Jao told his men to gear up. They were going hunting.

His platoon crept into Burma and found the offenders at a small gully. Khun Sa's trespassers were resting, some snoozing, exhausted from their late-night foray. Whispering, Jao told his men to encircle the enemy and wait for his signal. "You never want to get into some long, drawn-out firefight if you can help it," Jao told me. "They'll call reinforcements. We will too. Everyone will get stuck out there all day. You want to kill them all at once. To give them a hug."

A hug?

"Sure. Like closing a fist with the enemy at the center. You surround them and squeeze in. Slowly walk toward the middle, shooting every enemy you see, making sure you don't hit your own people."

The massacre only took a minute or two: thirty Shan men slaughtered for the crime of tax evasion. Jao didn't stick around to search their corpses. They'd made a terrible racket. It was time to leave. Darkness fell before the platoon made it back to headquarters, and the famished soldiers headed straight for the mess hall. One might expect their bravery would merit a bottle of *baijiu*, throat-scorching Chinese rice liquor, or at least a few sausages. "But as I recall," Jao said, "they'd run out of rice by the time we got back. We went to bed hungry."

That was the last time Jao got the jump on Khun Sa's fighters. In the ensuing months, the Shan rebels plowed into Broken Rock with greater ferocity, forcing the Exiles out of the valley. They could not be hugged to death. There were too many of them, eyes alight with a freedom fervor the aging Exiles no longer felt. Khun Sa pried loose Broken Rock and flooded it with two thousand loyal fighters, equal to one-third the Exiles' strength. He concentrated them in that one valley, daring General Lee to take it back.

But he couldn't—not under the new War on Drugs strictures. Khun Sa and Wei had gamed it out perfectly. The Exiles could manage a little skirmish up in Burma. But a larger battle, right on the Thai border, would draw press like mosquitos and reveal they were still a megacartel, not a collective of docile farmers. Farmers don't get sucked into dogfights over dope routes. Their hands tied, the Exiles had to let Broken Rock go.

Khun Sa gave the valley a grander title: Shanland.[19] A micronation, roughly one hundred square miles, the size of Washington, DC. New citizens poured into Shanland, hacking down vine-choked thickets, building homes with bamboo walls and zinc roofs. Khun Sa gave them plumbing, electricity, a hospital, and schools, even ID cards. He commissioned a flag stitched from yellow and green fabric and flew it overhead. At 4 a.m., even before the roosters crowed, Khun Sa would mount a black steed and bolt through his virgin country, shouting into the fog.

Wake up, citizens of Shanland!

We have a nation to build!

"Tell me one country that became independent," Khun Sa would say, "without having to bear hardships, without having to struggle and fight? If the struggle of the Shan people to whom this country legitimately belongs is unfair, so was the American Revolution."[20]

Khun Sa anointed Wei as his nation's treasurer. The protégé got his own office, wired up with telephone lines, and a radio room fit to rival

that of General Lee. Wei summoned his two brothers, Xuelong and Xueyin, to help run the treasury. They worked all hours, ringing clients day
and night, forging relationships with up-and-coming heroin wholesalers
in Bangkok, Taiwan, and Hong Kong.

But the Wei brothers weren't content to sell heroin around Asia. They
set their sights on Americans, the most desirable customers, for they were
plentiful and by global standards rich. Various Southeast Asian syndicates had been trying to smuggle heroin to them across the Pacific, some
using former GIs as mules on commercial airplanes, but only dribs and
drabs made it through. Wei and his brothers, working with Chinese dias-
poras, found a better solution. They managed to put Shanland's product on US-bound container ships and cargo jets. Now the heroin could
move in tremendous volumes. The Wei brothers' drug labs stamped
plastic-wrapped kilos of heroin with a signature crest: two red lions
mounting the planet earth—a brand like the Coca-Cola swirl, assuring
traffickers down the supply chain the dope was pristine.[21]

In 1977, just one year after Shanland's founding, Wei achieved what
many thought impossible. He shattered the Exiles' monopoly. Shanland
now controlled a dominant share of the regional opium trade.[22] But never
did Wei seek credit for this stunning reversal, instead letting the Shan
people believe Khun Sa was the sole source of their prosperity.

That made Khun Sa love his treasurer all the more. He fawned over
Wei, often at the expense of others in his crude cabinet of fellow criminals. Why couldn't the rest of them strive so tirelessly, so selflessly? "I
don't want to tell you again," Khun Sa would tell them. "All of you need
to be more like Wei Xuegang."[23]

VOWING TO WAGE "all-out global war on the drug menace," the DEA
kept expanding across the planet. Offices opened in dozens of countries,
including Italy, Mexico, and Peru. Among its targets: Mediterranean
mafiosi and Latin American border gangs, smuggling cocaine and can-
nabis into the United States. But Thailand was a major priority, worthy
of two DEA offices: one in Bangkok, among its largest hubs in the world,
and, in the late 1970s, another outpost in Chiang Mai.

Chiang Mai was a splash of urbanity in the hills: temple bells sound-
ing by day, discotheques throbbing by night. Half-crumbled walls ringed
its downtown, as did a moat, the ruins of an ancient palace. Though pic-

turesque, the area was also a heroin-trafficking hotbed. General Lee kept an estate in Chiang Mai city, a safe refuge for his wife and children, away from his headquarters on the border.

There was also a small US consulate in Chiang Mai city, ostensibly built to assist American backpackers. Hidden within was a CIA station, created in part to liaise with the Exiles and other Golden Triangle assets.[24] When the DEA had the temerity to put its outpost in the very same consulate, US spies grew enraged, and the two tribes were soon at each other's throats. State Department officials struggled to contain their feuds. As one US diplomat, formerly second in command in Thailand, put it, "We spent a lot of time trying to keep those guys from shooting each other. There were some hot-headed people in those crowds."[25]

Many DEA agents in Chiang Mai, fed up with the CIA dictating which traffickers were off limits, became bitter. Not Angelo Saladino. The agent realized tussling with the CIA was futile. Sicilian by blood, Saladino was a former Peace Corps volunteer in Thailand who spoke the language well, and he'd even adopted Thai sensibilities, favoring face-saving work-arounds over head-on confrontations. "Honestly, I tried to avoid the CIA as much as possible," he said. That required concessions. General Lee? Untouchable. But the emerging drug lord Khun Sa was fair game—if only the DEA could find a way to nab him.

Saladino got his first glimpse of Khun Sa's Shanland through a spool of eight-millimeter film. Thai police had confiscated the reel off some low-level henchman and passed it along. The home video revealed a fine soirée: "Lots of guys in suits with all the trimmings of a banquet—as nice as you could have in a jungle setting," Saladino said. "Khun Sa was clearly the big chieftain, receiving people who'd come to show respect. It looked like a pretty comfortable life."

No wonder Khun Sa looked relaxed. He and his whiz kid treasurer, Wei, were virtually inoculated against arrest. Neutering the DEA was simple. American narcs could not single-handedly bust suspects. They just did the sleuthing, propping up local police who held the actual power to arrest. So Khun Sa showered bribes on Thai officials—from provincial cops to military generals to, reputedly, the prime minister himself.[26] Police might occasionally pick off his lackeys, but Khun Sa and his inner circle were immune.

That was the most irksome bit about working for the DEA. You could learn every detail about the local kingpin, down to his taste in cocktails

(Khun Sa was a scotch man), but you couldn't lay a finger on him unless the host country gave the nod.[27] "There were hardly any big drug seizures because how would you get to it?" Saladino said. "Everyone's making too much money. Up to the highest levels of the army, they all got their envelopes."

Some Thai cops, believers in the War on Drugs, would try to assist the DEA. Others played the Americans for suckers. Saladino remembers one night when, working off a tip, he hunted down a suspicious tanker truck reportedly full of opium. He pursued it to a banana farm, jumped a fence in the pounding rain, located the truck, climbed atop its tanker, and flipped open the porthole. Inside, he found more than a thousand parcels of opium. Thai cops showed up, seized the drugs, and destroyed them. The DEA paid a cash reward to the tipster—only later realizing he was a police colonel, not a civilian.

Worse yet, the "opium" was bogus. "It's not that hard to make fake opium," Saladino said. "You take overly ripened bananas, mix it with pig fat or rendered tallow, add in bits of rice straw, and you have a very close lookalike." Saladino could've raised hell. But he understood Thai culture well enough to know this would hurt him in the long run. Thai Buddhists tend to see red-faced fits of anger as lunacy—and no one wants to cooperate with a lunatic.

Those were the realities of DEA work in Thailand. Invisible guardrails everywhere, some constructed by Thai authorities, others by CIA officers. Challenging either was not just pointless but perilous.

AS A MADE man, Khun Sa grew bold enough to venture from his mountain lair. Local tabloids spotted him dancing at Blue Moon, a swanky Chiang Mai nightclub, or sitting in the front row at a Bangkok pop concert. In his closet, he kept a traditional Shan tunic, a drab-green general's uniform, and a pinstripe business suit with 1980s-style shoulder pads. Khun Sa was a shapeshifter—a man of the people or the penthouse, depending on the occasion.

Much of Shanland was pastoral, and its downtown looked like an Old West trading post: little clapboard shops selling rice and fertilizer, a pawn shop displaying furniture and acoustic guitars behind glass windows. Few citizens beheld the opulence of Khun Sa's private quarters, which were always guarded. The head of state inhabited a posh villa with tennis courts and a jumbo-sized swimming pool. Nighttime gave way to tumblers of whiskey, chilled by cubes from his own ice factory. His entertainment room featured a projector screen where Khun Sa showed Mickey Mouse cartoons, as well as porn films titled *Secrets in a Convent* and *The Nun Gathers Mushrooms*.[28] The splendor even attracted defecting Exile officers, tired of serving a cheapskate organization on the decline, eager to work for a rising star.

Wei was an infrequent presence at these hangouts. He never got drunk or partied, instead preferring the company of his brothers and the bustle of his office. He was not missed. The other Shanland officers found him strange. His incessant hand washing. His quietude and know-it-all demeanor. Wei was a germaphobe in the company of killers. He was so fussy that, before sitting down, whether on a chair or a log, he'd run his hands across his thighs, smoothing out his slacks lest his pants show wrinkles. Most of all they hated the smug look on his face whenever Khun Sa praised him.

But no one could mock the treasurer openly. That would rile the boss, and it was unwise to displease Khun Sa, a vindictive leader whose brush with the good life had not buffed his sharp edges. In Shanland, Khun Sa commissioned a special prison: a cavernous underground chamber more than thirty feet deep.[29] Captives entered through a manhole on the surface, and they were lowered into its dark interior by rope. Once sealed from above, the insides went coffin black. Inmates pulled out of the chamber after many days would blink in the sunlight like gummy-eyed newborns. The Romans could not have designed a more dreadful place.

Khun Sa would sentence disobedient followers to time in this hole. The prison always reminded Shanland's top officers that, for all his high-flying rhetoric, their leader still knew how to be cruel. Khun Sa was obsessed with betrayal, as natural-born backstabbers often are.

SALADINO HAD A new boss: Mike Powers, head DEA agent in Chiang Mai. He was muscular and scruffy, described as a "real He-Man, Incredible Hulk kind of guy."[30] A native New Yorker with the accent to match, Powers had been a marine in Vietnam. He'd served as a "lurp," slang for long-range recon patrollers. Scouting deep inside enemy terrain required otherworldly fearlessness, and the CIA had recruited Powers for special missions, the nature of which he would not discuss.[31] When the war ended, he joined the DEA.

In Chiang Mai, Powers crossed red lines. Determined to carve the rot out of Thailand's police force, he exposed officers' links to drug smugglers, ruining careers left and right. In doing so, Powers also threatened Khun Sa, who relied on dodgy cops to prevent his arrest and even transport his drugs. Senior Thai officials warned Powers to back down. But he just kept carving.

One morning in mid-October 1980, Powers received an unsettling phone call. His wife, Joyce, and their three-year-old daughter were taken hostage. Joyce had been shopping in a Chiang Mai market when a young Thai man stuck a .38 revolver to her head. The gunman dragged Joyce, clinging to her toddler, into the cabin of a pickup truck. He'd started to peel out, but cops arrived quickly, surrounding the vehicle with pistols drawn. Curious onlookers encircled the standoff.

Powers raced to the scene, pushing through the gawking throng, walking straight toward the gunman. He ripped open his shirt to prove he was unarmed. Through a bilingual bystander, the DEA agent pleaded with the kidnapper: at least let my kid go. The man complied, letting the bystander remove the child from the truck, but he kept his revolver barrel pressed to Joyce's face. He chain-smoked furiously. His gun hand would not stop quivering.

As Powers offered vast sums of money to the gunman, the pistol abruptly went off, perhaps by accident. The killer then panicked, firing wildly into the crowd. Thai cops instantly filled his body with bullets and sank a .45 slug into his brain. When the gun smoke cleared, both Joyce and the hostage taker were slumped across the pickup's bench seats.

The couple had three children, and Powers, stricken with grief, took them back to the States. Another married DEA agent also left Chiang Mai, fearing his wife could be next. Only a few agents stuck around: two bachelors and Saladino, now elevated to the role of agent in charge. His own wife, Barbara, was mortified.

"That, well . . . it caused some problems," Saladino told me.

"Yeah," Barbara chimed in. "Marital problems!"

"But look," he said, "if I left and we closed that office, that's a hell of a signal to other traffickers around the world who want to get rid of the DEA." Barbara and the kids relocated to Bangkok while Saladino stayed on. "That's probably the closest we came to getting divorced," she told me. "He felt he had to hold down the fort. Or they would win."

But who was *they* exactly? Who'd ordered Joyce Powers's kidnapping?

Surely the CIA would know—or had the power to find out. The agency had ears in every filthy nook of the narcotics netherworld, even in places the DEA couldn't access. The CIA guarded its intel like a dragon squatting on treasure, but the DEA agents thought the agency would make an exception for Mike Powers, a former CIA operator. Their surveillance matrix could determine who'd ordered Joyce's botched kidnapping. Instead the spies, committed to their turf war, froze out the narcs. DEA agents fumed. Left to hash out their own conclusions, suspicion settled on Khun Sa.

"We'd recently confiscated a big load of acetic anhydride from Khun Sa's guys, drums of it," Saladino said. "It was very valuable. We thought maybe he wanted to use [the kidnapping] as leverage to get his chemicals back."

Acetic anhydride is clear as water and smells like pickles. It is essential to the alchemy that turns opium sludge into heroin. Labs overseen by the Wei brothers in Shanland were acquiring acetic anhydride through shady police figures, some recently exposed by the DEA and tossed in prison. Perhaps the plan was not to kill Joyce Powers but hold her for ransom, trading her freedom for that of the imprisoned cops—or the chemicals— but the kidnapper screwed up the job.

The murder was never formally solved. But to this day, the DEA is certain Joyce Powers was killed to "send a message to Mike, to the DEA, to the Americans: if you cross Khun Sa, there will be no question. You will be killed."[32] The DEA fixated on revenge, guardrails be damned. Narcotics officials went all the way to the White House, asking incoming president Ronald Reagan to make the War on Drugs look more like an actual war, starting with a guns-blazing invasion of Shanland.

UP IN SHANLAND, Khun Sa felt under pressure. His Thai police insiders were warning him that the DEA was growing obsessed with taking him out. Stress always enflamed the boss's paranoia, and his coterie of senior officers seized the moment. They channeled the boss's nervous energy toward the target of their own palace intrigues: Wei Xuegang.

"By that point, resentment toward Wei Xuegang was really building up," said Khuensai Jaiyen, former secretary to Khun Sa. "People turned Khun Sa against Wei by mixing some truth with some falsehoods." They alleged Wei embezzled profits behind Khun Sa's back—a dubious allegation. But this much was true: Wei was an inscrutable oddball who, along with his brothers, had amassed great influence over the future of Shanland, for they controlled its finances.

Khun Sa gave Wei no opportunity to plead innocence for his supposed embezzling.[33] He instead sent Shanland soldiers to yank the treasurer from his office and drag him up a little hill. At the top, on the ground, was a circle made of bricks, not much wider than a man's hips. Resting atop the circle was a wooden manhole cover. The soldiers removed it. They ordered Wei to hold on to a rope and lowered his skinny body into the black maw.

Wei should've seen this coming. Clever as he was, he hadn't anticipated how America's drug war would exacerbate his boss's neuroses. He'd benefited when the DEA showed up to Thailand and hamstrung the Exiles, enabling Khun Sa's rebels to snatch away a chunk of their territory, build Shanland upon it, and provide Wei with a base to start a stupendous heroin-trafficking operation. But now the DEA was breathing down Khun Sa's neck too—and the tension was driving him to make impulsive decisions. Like putting his own prodigy into an underground pit.

Sitting at its bottom, Wei watched the rope ascend and the manhole cover slide back into place. He was trapped in a sightless void: imprisoned in cold dirt among earthworms, excrement accumulating around him as days passed. He could have done little else in that purgatory but sit still and try to fend off madness.

MR. SUCCESS

A mechanized din broke Shanland's serenity. On that brisk morning, roughly eight hundred uniformed Thai riflemen stormed the emerald valley in pickups and armor-plated vehicles, helmeted men on motorbikes zooming alongside.

Inside Shanland's primary school, the day's lessons had just commenced. The proctor, teaching adolescent soldiers to read, was losing his students' attention.[1] The noise drew boys from their seats to a schoolhouse window, all of them jostling to see the ruckus outside. Quiet down and return to your seats, the proctor said. Whatever those soldiers are doing, it poses no threat. If they're wearing Thai uniforms, they've been paid off by Khun Sa. "I thought there must be some other explanation for what was happening," the proctor told me. "Like maybe they were filming a movie."

But the invasion was real—and at the first crack of gunfire, the boy soldiers flung down their books and grabbed their rifles, rushing to find Khun Sa so they could defend him to the death.

Thailand's Border Patrol Police, a paramilitary force, spearheaded the siege. They answered to the kingdom's new prime minister: Prem Tinsulanonda, a strait-laced army general who, unlike his predecessors, did not take bribes from any drug lords.[2] Three months before, Prem had visited the White House to meet President Ronald Reagan, also new in office and cultivating his slay-the-narcos persona. The Thai prime minister presented himself as a drug war ally, and after that meeting, US antinarcotics aid to Thailand shot up, hitting nearly $3 million a year. Joint Thai–Drug Enforcement Administration plans to besiege Shanland took shape.[3] The DEA hoped to retrieve Khun Sa's corpse—or at least extradite him to an

American prison. That suited the Central Intelligence Agency just fine, for the agency preferred that the Exiles dominate the Golden Triangle.

The Thai squadrons fought house to house, shop to shop. Shan guerrillas in their underwear sprung from doorways, firing back with M-16s. The battle had the makings of a long and bloody dance between two evenly matched combatants—until the valley resounded with propeller hum. American-made Broncos, twin-engine combat planes, strafed Shanland with bullets and lobbed bombs, blasting buildings into blackened rubble and splitting trees in half.

It took three days to conquer Shanland. The operation ended with roughly a dozen Thais and more than one hundred Shan troops killed. Poking through the smoking wasteland, Thai police searched the villa, the radio room, and the armory, filled with bazookas and fifty thousand ammo rounds. But they did not find Khun Sa. "Those of you who frequently watch American cowboy movies," wrote a Thai newspaper that week, "will understand that, when the county sheriff tries to catch the criminal, the criminal flees into Mexico. The sheriff can only watch in frustration while the criminal makes faces at him across the border."[4]

Khun Sa did more than make faces. He escaped to hills in Burma just north of Thailand's Mae Hong Son province, more than one hundred miles away, and started over. Three thousand or so fighters and most of his citizens followed him to this backup site. The DEA failed to see that Shanland was never just some criminal hideout. Like every nation, it was an idea. Shanland would follow Khun Sa wherever he went.

Neither the DEA nor the Thai troops could pursue Khun Sa further without invading a sovereign country. Not that any government had true authority over those borderlands—they were fluid, the domain of narcos on horseback—but officially this was Burmese soil, even though Burma's military was nowhere nearby. Khun Sa's citizens poured more cement, raised wooden homes, and constructed new schools and hospitals. Shanland 2.0 was even more ostentatious than the original. One observer said its training facilities were fine as West Point, the vaunted US military academy.[5] There were antiaircraft missiles in the hills, and around the leader's new villa art deco streetlights glowed over paved avenues.

Humiliated US officials went to the media, rebranding the "Prince of Prosperity" as the "King of Heroin." As time passed, the superlatives grew bigger, until one DEA chief proclaimed that Khun Sa conjured "as much evil into this world as any mafia don has done in our history."[6] Reporters lapped it up. Khun Sa was "a cutthroat freebooter from a 'Terry and the Pirates' comic strip," according to *US News & World Report*, and the "spiritual father of narco-terrorism." In Congress, US politicians claimed Khun Sa buried humans alive and once killed a barber over a bad haircut. No rumor was too sensational to repeat.

In turn, Khun Sa blurted out secrets the United States had taken pains to conceal. He said the CIA had long protected heroin traffickers from prosecution, all while it "grabs Bangkok's hair by the head," and ordered Thai leaders to do its bidding. To his Shan citizens, Khun Sa said, "We have been labeled the world's worst criminals . . . but their accusations reflect their own guilt." As his followers saw it, the former Shan orphan was taking on a superpower and winning. On special occasions they would hoist Khun Sa onto their shoulders and parade him around.

Khun Sa asked, Am I really a demon with "fangs, horns and tail?" And if I am the "King of Heroin . . . isn't that just one more reason you should employ my services?" He told the American government there was only one way to win the drug war: pay the king to turn off the tap. Just buy all of my opium and burn it, Khun Sa said. You've done it before. Call me when you're ready to cut a deal.

HAD THEY CAUGHT him, Wei Xuegang would've made a nice runner-up prize for the DEA. But he too was long gone by the time Thai commandos raided Shanland. Its subterranean prison was empty when they shined flashlights into its depths.

At some point before the invasion, a circle of light appeared in the endless black above Wei's head, and a long rope dangled down. He gripped it and ascended through that dank hell's mouth, several Shanland soldiers pulling him to the surface. They handed him to the men who'd bribed them: Wei's two brothers. Once swept to safety, Wei scrubbed himself clean and asked for a plane ticket to Taiwan. He wanted to put an entire sea between himself and Khun Sa.[7]

Wei laid low on the island, weighing options. Perhaps it was time to go legit. Surely the ex-treasurer of Asia's top heroin-producing organization could hack it in the legal business world, selling shoes, car parts, electronics. But what a waste of his talent. Purposeless years passed, and all the while, Wei felt the Golden Triangle's gravitational pull.

He wanted to join an armed group deserving of his genius. But his options were limited. He couldn't go work for the communists who ruled his Wa birthplace because, as Maoists, they abhorred all opium trafficking. He couldn't ask Gen. Lee Wen-huan for a job—not after burning him, back when Wei was Khun Sa's sycophant. Wei was damaged goods. He had no choice but to seek out the most disreputable band of drug runners in the Golden Triangle: the Wa National Army.

The name itself was absurd. They weren't a real army—more like five hundred or so mercenaries skulking around the Thai-Burma border. Nor did they aspire to nationhood. But they were sure as hell Wa: a crew of hardened fighters, some former headhunters, all loyal to Shah, Saw Lu's former partner in the League of Warlords. When the League disintegrated in the early 1970s, Shah led his fighters down to the Thai border to hide out, and they'd lurked there ever since. Shah, retaining none of Saw Lu's idealism, turned his militia into a gang for hire—and for paying clients, including the Exiles, they'd fetch loads of opium from ultradangerous reaches of the Golden Triangle: terrain claimed by the Communist Party of Burma or even Shanland.[8] Fearlessness was their calling card; extreme missions, their forte.

Wei resigned himself to applying for a position with the Wa National Army, figuring no other organization would have him. He flew to Thailand in 1984 and headed to the northern border, just above the province of Chiang Mai, where the landscape rolled: high summits descending into narrow, lizard-green valleys. Shah and his people had built an austere camp atop a peak, as befitted Wa highlanders. They lived simply in bamboo shacks with plastic-sheet roofs, the sort of housing they could abandon at a moment's notice. Wei found the camp and entered it, encountering the sort of rugged Wa men he'd once feared in adolescence. They brought him to meet their leader.

Shah, then in his forties, remained strong, a thick-jawed man at ease in the wilderness. He was welcoming and less callous than Wei expected, more tough old galoot than sadist. Shah neither smoked nor drank, instead nursing an addiction to ready-mix Nescafé. He told his guest to sit down and state his business.

Wei's proposition was simple. The Wa National Army had gunmen. It had a smidgen of territory on the Thai-Burma border. It had a forbidding reputation. These were all excellent qualities for a drug-smuggling gang. What they lacked was business acumen. Wei could fix that. Leveling up in the trafficking game would require connections to Bangkok's Thai-Chinese business elites, exporters who mingled in high society and never actually laid hands on shrink-wrapped heroin parcels—even though their employees, working through various shell companies, smuggled drugs far and wide. By and large, they were esteemed men who mingled with politicians and sent their kids to private schools. A goon with cruddy fingernails could not move in these circles. But Wei, a half-Chinese businessman, could.

The timing of Wei's proposal was propitious. Taiwan, a dictatorship still run by Kuomintang remnants, had for years paid Shah to collect intelligence on communist China—whatever the gang could glean during opium-smuggling runs near the Burma-China border. Taiwan kept up these operations even after the CIA lost interest. But in that very year, 1984, Taiwan decided to cut Shah loose and cancel his retainer. Desperate to make up for lost income, Shah needed Wei, an expert moneymaker, just as much as Wei needed Shah.

So Shah presented Wei to his men. Meet your new treasurer. These Wa fighters did not readily trust the man standing before them in office slacks. That he was half Wa paled before his quirks. When they all sat down for lunch, someone offered chopsticks to Wei, and he requested boiling water to disinfect them. As for lodging, Wei refused to sleep in a hut like the others. If they wanted him as their treasurer, the Wa National Army would have to build a cement home for him. Shah told the mercenaries to do as the man bade.

In the coming months, they would learn to overlook his eccentricities. Wei set up new drug labs, staffing them with ethnic Chinese chemists, and when profits rolled in, he shared the wealth. His two brothers became fixtures at the camp too. The Weis seldom ate with the Wa smugglers, a social bunch who loved strong drink and bawdy campfire tales, but neither did they get in their way. The Wei brothers just poured themselves into their work, and soon enough the Wa National Army came to see Wei Xuegang as a second leader, just as essential as Shah.

Wei quickly overhauled the gang into a proper trafficking syndicate, using it to supply exporters with velvety white heroin that made its way to markets in Hong Kong and even the distant United States. It was a boutique operation compared to that of the Exiles or Shanland, but its future looked promising. The Wa mercenaries only had to keep bringing in raw opium and shoot anyone who dared threaten Wei's heroin labs.

AROUND THAT TIME, in the mid-1980s, General Lee was turning portly with snow-white tufts fringing his ears. He spent most of his time at his estate in Chiang Mai city with his wife and children. Grandkids toddled around the halls. He badly longed to retire from the drug trade, this time for real.

So in early 1984, when his mortal enemy Khun Sa suggested meeting face-to-face to make peace, Lee grudgingly agreed to hear what he had to say. He arranged the meeting on safe ground: Lee's own mountain head-quarters overlooking the fog-swept hills of Burma. Khun Sa came into the room exuding politeness and calling himself Zhang, just like the old days. But he quickly got to the point.

Khun Sa said he was well on his way to fully monopolizing the Thai-Burma border drug trade. The Exiles—a shrinking organization—should go ahead and cede their remaining territory to Shanland.[9] In return, he would happily pay Master Lee a lifetime stipend, ensuring he retired rich. Khun Sa was essentially proposing a corporate buyout. But to secure the deal, Lee would have to tell his Thai and American patrons to accept Khun Sa as the Golden Triangle's rightful custodian: a busi-nessman who, despite his bombastic rhetoric, was reasonable and open to cooperation.

General Lee listened closely. "Father was truly ready to wash his hands of everything," one of Lee's children told me. "But in the end, he couldn't go along with what Khun Sa wanted."

Why not?

"Have you ever seen *The Godfather*? That more or less explains what happened."

In the film, Godfather Vito Corleone is an aging Italian mafia patri-arch, based in New York but born in the old country. He is approached by a brash narco-trafficker named Sollozzo.[10] The trafficker knows Cor-leone has New York officials in his pocket, and if he can partner up with the Godfather, he too might enjoy immunity from arrest. But Corleone knows better. The judges and politicians whose patronage he enjoys would never protect a character as sordid as Sollozzo. Corleone, a Sicilian immi-grant, rejects Sollozzo—for he cannot jeopardize his standing in America, his adopted home.

By the same token, General Lee knew sidling up to Asia's most despised drug lord would enrage his American and Thai allies. Worse yet, his own ethnic Chinese soldiers would think him senile, and nothing mattered more to Lee than respect from the other Yunnanese exiles. He saw them as his children. Lee's answer was no. Khun Sa nodded and slipped away.

Soon after, in March 1984, a truck pulled up to Lee's estate. The driver leaped out and sprinted away. Seconds later, one ton of explosives cratered the pavement, shattering windows in a half-mile radius. The blast left a smoking hole in the mansion's side.

Lee's elderly wife, resting inside, was blown off her bed. Regaining her senses, she rushed to the nursery where her grandchildren, aged one and three, had been sleeping. Paint chips fluttered from the ceiling. The toddler was wailing—alive, thank goodness—but the infant made no sound. A pile of scorched planks covered the baby's bassinet. With a maid's help, Mrs. Lee clawed at the rubble and pulled her grandchild out. She was horrified by the trickle of crimson streaming from the baby's ear.

Miraculously, the children were not seriously hurt, and the blast killed no one. General Lee, by a stroke of luck, was away at a last-minute doctor's appointment. Later on, his children gathered around and asked, "Dad, what are you going to do?" Lee's expression was flat. "Nothing," he said. "Such is life. Such is business." CIA files indicate he was less forgiving: the Exiles killed a few of Khun Sa's Thailand-based brokers as revenge.[11] But ultimately, the bombing marked the end of an era. Lee, nearing his sixties, appeared feeble in the face of Khun Sa's wrath.

Khun Sa's soldiers started grinding down the Exiles, swallowing up even more of their smuggling routes. On a recruitment blitz, Shanland's army absorbed smaller Shan rebel groups and increased troop numbers to twenty thousand. Khun Sa was viewed as a menace not only by the DEA but also by the CIA, loathe to see Asia's heroin trade dominated by a moody, America-hating supervillain. Unlike General Lee, he wasn't the sort of drug lord anyone could control.

The CIA had long counted on the Exiles to halt Khun Sa's expansion, but the cartel had lost its vitality. "Prosperity has made CIF members complacent," wrote the spy agency, using its in-house acronym for the Exiles: Chinese Irregular Forces.[12] The cartel "no longer possesses military cohesion," and its "members are aging rapidly."

Thus did opportunity arise for the Wa National Army, the Golden Triangle's attack dogs of last resort. Perhaps the Exiles were too decrepit to smite Khun Sa's forces on their own. But if paired with fearless Wa guerrillas, they might pose an actual threat.

IT WAS 1986, and the US government's "Just Say No" campaign was ramping up. First Lady Nancy Reagan, wearing gold earrings and a prim red dress, told prime-time TV viewers that "drugs take away the dream from every child's heart and replace it with a nightmare." In the War on Drugs crusade, there was "no moral middle ground," she said. "Be unyielding and inflexible in your opposition to drugs."

But in that very year, along the Thai-Burma border, US intelligence officers were embroiled in a plan that was nothing if not morally muddled—for they were secretly encouraging one heroin-trafficking organization to fight another. The plan, conceived by American and Thai intelligence officers, was simple. Fortify the Wa National Army, jointly run by Shah and Wei, with high-powered weapons. Send them deep into Khun Sa's empire to wreak havoc. In return for their services, the Wa gang would not have to fear arrest on drug-trafficking charges in Thailand—even if they produced heroin for export to America.

Thai military intelligence, a close CIA partner, took the lead in strengthening the Wa National Army. "When I first saw them," said a CIA-trained former Thai intelligence officer, "they were short guys wearing Converse sneakers—not even leather boots—and they had old weapons, even AK-47s, those terrorist guns. The Americans didn't want to send their own advisors so they ran [the program] through us. We provided the training, equipment, even some military uniforms."[13]

According to CIA files, Thailand's army gave the Wa mercenaries "easy access" to stockpiles of guns and ammo—an arsenal supplied by the United States.[14] Thai officers even aided the Wa in "planning operations" against Khun Sa's forces.[15] "Everyone knew our fighters were the toughest," one former Wa National Army member told me. "I don't mean *strong* necessarily. Our guys might not be able to lift one hundred kilos over their heads. But we could endure anything without complaint and master any weapon."[16]

Now the Wa were receiving new-model M-16s and unlimited ammo. Thailand was eager to build the gang into a formidable force—in large part to placate the American government. At the time, the United States grumbled that Thailand did too little to weaken Khun Sa. "Honestly, we were trying to avoid a direct fight with Khun Sa," the former Thai intelligence officer told me. "We'd already lost too many lives at Broken Rock, and we didn't want to cross into Burma." The solution: outsource the mission to Shah and Wei's gang. "People say Wa fighters are not afraid to die, right? So why not have them die instead of us?"

Raised on gruesome headhunter stories, Thai officers believed the Wa were almost superhuman in their killing prowess. But with roughly five hundred guerrillas, the Wa National Army could only dole out so much pain. So under the Thai military's supervision, the Wa National Army was paired with General Lee's Exiles to create an anti–Khun Sa alliance. The CIA praised this alliance's "aggressive hit-and-run tactics," but hitting and running is all they could do. As CIA reports noted, the Wa-Exiles alliance was incapable of "set-piece battles." It comprised only about one thousand fighters altogether. Shanland's army was twenty times bigger. At least the skirmishes, mostly on the Burmese side of the border, were so minor that the press barely noticed.

The key benefactor of this arrangement? Wei. Practically impervious to arrest, he expanded his trafficking network and cozied up to Thai officials. Through bribes, he even acquired a Thai passport with a fake name and a birthdate shaving eight years off his real age. He chose the bogus moniker Prasit Chivinnitipanya. In Thai, this means "Mr. Success, One Who Has Great Wisdom Under the Law."

Wei avoided the battlefield, hanging close to the Wa National Army's main camp. While Wa fighters wore fatigues, he dressed in white-collar attire. "I still think about his hair," the former Wa National Army fighter told me. "It was impeccable, even in the jungle. Not a strand out of place." The Wa guerrillas, aware Wei was useless in an ambush, didn't begrudge their financier. "He did his job. We did ours. Wei was quiet and rarely smiled, but when he did speak, he was very honest. We respected that."

By the late 1980s, it grew obvious that no amount of US weaponry or Thai military guidance could help the Exiles-Wa alliance defeat Khun Sa. They'd barely dented his empire. The conflict just fizzled out. The Exiles effectively collapsed, the group's officers ditching their rifles to start tea plantations—as they'd once promised to do. General Lee slid into a placid retirement. The fatigued Wa mercenaries stuck to their own little patch of the borderlands and stayed out of Khun Sa's way. Shah and Wei kept the syndicate going, aspiring to nothing more than trafficking loads of heroin and piling up cash.

But as the Wa National Army devolved back into a straight-up drug gang, it lost its usefulness to Thai and US intelligence. As shock troops

with a cause—warring against the so-called King of Heroin—they
enjoyed legal immunity. Once that mantle of protection frayed, Wei's
trafficking operation was vulnerable to law enforcement.

Once again, Wei should've seen it coming. Already DEA agents
in Bangkok had files on Wei, described as a supercriminal who, along
with his brothers, used the Wa National Army to export "multi-hundred-
kilogram quantities of heroin into the United States." Without higher
powers holding the narcs on a leash, they could hunt him down and score
a career-making arrest.

A TRAWLER BOBBED five miles off Thailand's coast. It was anchored near
a coral-fringed island, uninhabited if you didn't count the crabs and
macaques. By day, foreigners paid good money to snorkel near this island
and glimpse angel fish beneath glassy blue waves, but night was falling,
the tourists were gone, and a black pall fell over paradise.

That was fine by the Thai men on the trawler. They hadn't come for the
scenery. The two smugglers, Somsak and Damrong, were fidgety, awaiting
a speedboat. Their boss had told them it would show up sometime before
dawn bearing 680 kilos of heroin: premium stuff, soap-white flakes, upward
of 95 percent pure. Triple-wrapped to keep out the ocean damp.

The smugglers were anxious to collect the drugs and pilot the trawler
into international waters. Their boat was not fast—eight knots per hour
max speed—and it would take more than a week to reach their destination: Hong Kong, or rather the scattered islands beyond the glowing
metropolis. There, per their boss's instructions, they would rendezvous
with Chinese traffickers at sea, hand over the dope, and motor back to
Thai shores.

The moon was ascending in the sky, casting shimmers on the ocean's
surface. Where the hell was that speedboat?

Somsak and Damrong had done their best to disguise the trawler's
origins—just in case police spotted it and tried to trace it back to their
boss, in whose name it was registered. Before, the words *Sea-Loving
Heart* were emblazoned on the hull, but they'd painted over that with a
fresh coat.[17] Because Thai captains liked painting boats in loud oranges
and mustard yellows, the smugglers did the same, hoping their vessel
would blend in with legit trawlers dragging the sea for mackerel.

At last, the speedboat revved into view and slid beside the trawler. The men on board, working fast, helped Somsak and Damrong hustle the heroin onto the trawler's deck. They were almost done when a terrible roar on the horizon made everyone look up in unison. A gunmetal-gray ship was speeding in their direction, fast as hell, its bow pointed at them like an arrowhead. "Royal Thai Police" was stenciled in white letters on the vessel's side. Somsak and Damrong scrambled out of sight, seeking cover on their trawler, both awkwardly crouching behind the same water tank.

They heard gunfire popping. Traffickers on the speedboat shooting at the cops, laying down cover fire, trying to get away. Good. Perhaps the cops would forget the heroin-loaded trawler and pursue the speedboat instead.

No such luck. Boots shook the trawler's deck, and seconds later Thai marine police stood over Somsak and Damrong aiming rifles at their chests. The pair squealed. It's our boss you really want, they said. You can find him on the outskirts of Bangkok. Here's the address.

Police tracked down the boss, and he snitched too, telling the cops to look higher up the supply chain. I was hired by some rich Chinese guy named Mr. Prasit, he said. Go find him on the northern border. The man was wise to confess because Thai police already knew all about Mr. Prasit, thanks to the DEA. Prasit—real name Wei Xuegang—was their target all along.

A month prior, the DEA had staked out a Bangkok restaurant, snapping photos of a transaction: Somsak and Damrong's boss receiving cash-stuffed paper bags from Wei himself. This was payment for smuggling nearly seven hundred kilos to Hong Kong gangsters, who'd then traffic it all the way to California—all on Wei's instructions. Thai police and the DEA had successfully intercepted Wei's heroin. Now they needed to nab the man himself.

Wei seldom emerged from his Wa National Army camp, just north of the Thai-Burma border. But in November 1988 he came down to rural Chiang Mai province on a business trip. He was indignant when Thai police walked up to him in public and slapped on handcuffs. I'm just a gem trader, he cried, as they hauled him into the nearest police precinct. DEA agents, waiting inside, slammed him against the wall and snapped his mugshot.

Wei refused to face the camera. In the mugshot, his brow is crunched in anger, lips drooping, eyes narrowed in defiance. Wei, in his striped button-up shirt, looks like an actuary having a wretched afternoon.

The DEA intended to fly "Mr. Success" to the United States. Wei had never seen the country, even though he owed his first job to the CIA and his fortune to America's heroin addicts. Soon he might even get to meet a few of them. It looked like Wei might spend the next decade or three inside a US penitentiary, once the United States processed his extradition.

WEI AWAITED LEGAL proceedings inside Thailand's Chiang Mai prison—a steamy, crowded place where jailers herded dozens of inmates into cells built for only a few. They slept on the floor in tight rows, prisoners' bodies trading sweat when they rolled over in the night. Wei's uniform was a tarnished beige smock. Metal shackles chafed his shins red. He was thoroughly miserable.

Not long into his stay, Wei wondered if a little cash might improve his situation. He sidled up to a guard and inquired, How much to remove these manacles?

The next day, when Chiang Mai's prison warden saw Wei walking unencumbered through the prison yard, he sensed trouble. He knew his own guards lacked integrity—and since this inmate held special interest to the DEA, its narcotics agents might raise a fuss if they discovered Wei enjoyed special treatment. Hoping to shift the problem elsewhere, the warden transferred Wei to a larger complex in Bangkok.

In Bangkok, Wei tested the virtue of his new jailers and found them equally fond of bribes. When he requested a private cell, the guards acquiesced. And how about replacing the cell's stained squat hole with a Western-style commode? Again, the guards complied. Wei kept pushing and prodding until he discovered that, for a large-enough bribe, authorities would open the gates and let him walk out. Soon, embarrassed Thai authorities were explaining to the DEA that Wei Xuegang, held on potential death-penalty trafficking charges, had been released on bail. The narcotics agents seethed. To appease them, Thai judges later sentenced Wei to death in absentia, but by then he was already long gone.

Wei had nowhere else to run but back to the Wa National Army camp, north of the Thai border. He was in his early forties, the ground beneath him crumbling. Pursued by the DEA. Banished from Thailand. Even his birthplace in the Wa peaks was off limits, ruled as it was by communists who would never welcome a black-market capitalist in their midst.

Wei's movements were restricted to the small area in Burma—just a few valleys, maybe one hundred square miles—that his Wa National Army mercenaries could defend. But even this little stronghold was in peril. Shanland forces flanked them from multiple sides, and it seemed only a matter of time before Khun Sa sent in his best troops to wipe out the Wa National Army completely, exacting revenge on the former treasurer who'd slipped his grasp seven years before. Numbering in the low hundreds, the Wa mercenaries sought answers from their leaders, Wei and Shah. They had none to offer. The gang's outlook was bleak.

There was a simple radio receiver in the Wa camp, wires strung up in tree limbs functioning as antennae. The mercenaries used it to communicate with home base when they traveled far afield, but it also picked up chatter between other smuggling syndicates and rebel groups. In the third week of April 1989, the receiver lit up with shocking news about the Wa motherland, the place where Wei, Shah, and the entire gang originated.

A revolt.

The communists who'd long subjugated their homeland, some two hundred miles to the north? Deposed. Expelled by indigenous Wa proclaiming the rise of a new era and a new Wa nation, committed not to some Maoist fantasy but to the betterment of their race. Upon hearing the news, Shah and his mercenaries turned jubilant, for many bore scars from battling communist invaders in the late 1960s and early 1970s, during the League of Warlords era. Their fellow Wa had finally come to their senses and tossed the commies out. Comeuppance at last.

Wei too rejoiced in his own quiet way. A potential lifeline was dropping down when he needed it most. Whatever shape this new Wa nation took, no matter its creed, he was certain it could use the expertise of an accomplished heroin trafficker such as himself.

NATIVITY

WINTER, EARLY 1989, IN THE WA HIGHLANDS.
A FEW MONTHS BEFORE THE REVOLT.

Panghsang was a rogue capital, separated from China by a cold river brown as wilted grass. The little town was cradled in a gully, its dirt avenues lined with shanties. Denizens bartered in a market built of poles and tarps, women in rags weighing produce on rusty scales.

These highlands had never known riches, but under the Communist Party of Burma, the Wa contended with both poverty *and* degradation. They were in thrall to the party's politburo: diehard Maoists, all ethnic Burmese, living atop a Panghsang hill in finer brick dwellings, looking down upon the spartan huts of their inferiors. These twenty-one men, identically dressed in dumpy green suits, were neither Wa nor fluent in the local tongue.

Like some priestly caste, the politburo members spoke in a strange lexicon—dialectics, perpetual revolution—citing incantations of dead prophets. Portraits of Mao, Stalin, and Lenin stared down from their walls like patron saints. They composed diatribes that aired from a radio transmitter donated by China, though few Wa peasants had a receiver with which to listen.

The politburo governed a mountainous zone patrolled by fifteen thousand underfed soldiers, most of them Wa. This was the largest communist rebel enclave on earth.[1] The politburo members seldom ventured into the realm they governed, however, and their orders seeped down to the masses through native intermediaries. Foremost among them was a Wa man named Zhao Nyi Lai—the very same Lai, once known as Commander Long Legs, whose guerrillas had vanquished Saw Lu's anticommunist League of Warlords nearly two decades prior.

In his late forties, Lai was still gangly, a commander whose uniform never quite fit. He'd risen as high in the party hierarchy as his race and third-grade schooling would allow. Though he'd devoted much of his twenties to upholding communism in the Wa motherland, he'd come to quietly loathe it, because for all their talk of class equality, the politburo members treated his ethnicity as inferior—a warrior class that did the soldiering while book-smart Burmese Maoists issued decrees.

Lai never forgot the day his heart first started hardening against the party. More than ten years back, at party headquarters in Panghsang, he'd received a Morse code message from Pang Wai, where his pregnant wife and daughters lived. Congrats, it read. Your wife just gave birth to a boy. Lai rushed outside to requisition a jeep, but every vehicle was out of fuel. So he mounted a bicycle and started pedaling. His house in Pang Wai was fifty miles away.

On his journey, Lai passed shoeless children with distended bellies. Nary a school nor clinic. Rat-nibbled corn fields clinging to dry slopes. And few poppy flowers, for the Maoist politburo restricted the harvesting of opium. No longer did the Wa live in skull-adorned fortresses or feud between clans, but they were as estranged from one another as ever. The party invested little in paved roads, making travel between villages difficult. If arteries connected the tribe, Lai thought, a sense of oneness might course through their homeland.

As light drained from the sky, Lai kept pedaling, his long legs burning. The cliffside trail became nearly impossible to see. Suddenly Lai went airborne, wheels no longer touching the earth, his body sailing into the black.

He regained consciousness at the bottom of a ravine, his thumb twisted sideways at a hideous angle, his face sticky with blood. His ribs hurt with each breath. Lai ditched the bike and dragged himself up the hill, back to the path, walking the rest of the way. He reached his house in the bluish dawn. His newborn son slept inside, but Lai was not ready to face him. He sat in the dirt and wept.

How many fellow Wa had he killed to achieve a Maoist utopia—and what had come of that bloody sacrifice? One of his best comrades, another commander named Bao Youxiang, liked to say with characteristic bluffness that the Wa still "lived like monkeys." Illiterate. Dying from common ailments. Disconnected from one another.[2] This was the society in which his son would grow up.

Since that incident, Lai's faith in communism had eroded a little more each day, bit by bit. By the 1980s, radical thoughts agglomerated in his head, gradually gaining shape. Some days he wanted to reform the system. Other days he wanted to smash it. This inner unrest manifested as a funny habit; when fed up with his Maoist bosses, Commander Lai would abandon his Panghsang headquarters and set off for some random village in the peaks.

He'd summon the locals to an impromptu fireside meeting and preach to them with a tent revivalist's fervor, pacing about like an upright panther. He held the warrior-farmers rapt, not with cold Leninist theories but with his own gospel of ethnic awakening, hot and from the heart. "Wa self-love. Wa self-pride. That was his message," Lai's daughter, Ei Phong Lai, told me. "I think he was still suffering deep down from his childhood," when he had been enslaved. "He wanted the next generation to have a better life and he knew communism could not deliver it."

Lai dared not blaspheme against communism directly, but there was a subversive bite to his preaching. It exalted racial solidarity over Marxist theories. Self-reliance above nursing off the Chinese government's teat. When Lai preached, he drank. Seldom did he put down his *blai*, swigged out of bamboo cups. Lai would grow wobbly on his feet, and though equivalent to a four-star general, he'd pass out on some stranger's floor, wake up foggy brained the next morning, and race back to headquarters. The villagers adored him.

In Panghsang, Lai confided his ideas to Bao, his best pal and a fellow commander. Bao was ultrapragmatic, less of a political thinker, with a hearty laugh coarsened by cigarettes. Both privately derided their leaders for dining on Chinese sausages while the rank and file eked by on rice and salt. The two friends spoke in code, calling the politburo "students," for they were bookish and naive.

Like Lai, Bao had grown up rough.[3] In his head-hunting hamlet, the go-to childhood game was a hyperviolent take on dodgeball. Kids collected a local fruit with stone-like pits, then convened boys and girls in a circle. They'd lob the projectiles at each other's heads until only one child was upright, the others semiconcussed in the dirt. Bao was usually the last boy standing. In his teenage years, he graduated to head-hunting, and as leader of a village gang, Bao fought roving indigenous spies loyal to the apparatus run by Taiwan and the Central Intelligence Agency— and he sometimes separated his enemies' skulls from their necks. His exploits attracted Chinese commissars, who made him a guerrilla squadron chief in the late 1960s and later handed him to the Communist Party of Burma. In the war against Saw Lu's League of Warlords, Bao solidified his reputation for fearlessness—and after victory became a commander who answered directly to the politburo. Bao epitomized Wa warriordom, a weapon valuable to whoever wielded him.

By the mid-1980s, both Bao and Lai could sense it: fissures in the status quo through which shone flashes of a brighter future. Chairman Mao Zedong was long gone, dead since 1976. China, under its new leader, Deng Xiaoping, was unclenching the steel vice that gripped its economy, letting markets breathe a little. It spoke of trading with neighbors, not "liberating" their populations through bloody insurrection. Beijing had been whispering to the Communist Party of Burma politburo: Your mission is over. Come retire in China and live the rest of your lives as farmers.

But the politburo, more Maoist than the Chinese, refused to cooperate. So Beijing weaned the party off vital supplies: rice, fuel, bullets, and equipment. The politburo harrumphed and pouted but did nothing to fix the existential crisis at hand. Without Chinese material support, its communist enclave would plunge even further into horrendous poverty.

Wa villagers came to Commanders Lai and Bao, complaining of hunger. Tell your politburo bosses we must return to producing opium, as did our ancestors, selling the highlands' only exportable resource so we can buy food. Lai relayed the message, but the priggish politburo said no. According to Maoist dogma, narcotics tarnished the revolutionary spirit. The party would only let farmers trade opium in modest amounts; anyone caught trafficking in bulk would face imprisonment, possibly death.

Insubordination mounted in the late 1980s. Wa battalion leaders answering to Lai and Bao said that, with the Chinese lifeline snipped, they were going to churn out opium, lest their troops starve. The politburo could go shove it. These battalions took their drugs to the black market and sold them to the Exiles, an organization then on its last legs. Supposed communists were doing business with supposed anticommunists.[4] The world was upside down.

It was time for Lai and Bao to right it.

ON A COLD spring day, April 17, 1989, Lai and Bao amassed mutineers by the hundreds in Panghsang's outskirts, their AK-47s at the ready. It was Thingyan, a major Burmese holiday marking the Buddhist new year. The Wa did not observe this lowlander holy day, but the Burmese politburo leaders did, typically by gorging on food and alcohol. It was a perfect opportunity for the Wa to march through town, up the hill, and knock the politburo members off their rotten pedestal.

The revolt was scheduled for early evening. By that hour, Lai was inebriated and pacing among the rebels, revving them up with talk of slaughtering the oppressors.[5] He always got feisty after a cup or seven of *blai*. Lai was in no state to lead a coup. Bao pulled his fellow conspirator aside and convinced him to hang back, then returned to the head of the formation and led the rebels into Panghsang. Most marched on foot; others rode in jeeps equipped with machine guns. Night enveloped the peaks, and a full moon lit their way forth. The mutineers tingled with a desire for revenge.

News of the rebellion spread fast. By the time they reached Panghsang's shabby marketplace, every civilian had scattered. The road ahead was blocked by a Communist Party of Burma security squadron, also ethnically Wa, and they were arrayed in a line with rifles braced against their shoulders, ready to protect the politburo on the hill beyond. The mutineers mirrored them, forming their own line and raising their weapons. A standoff. Bao shouted to his men, Hold your fire.

A rifle barked. Someone's finger must have twitched, and it was not clear which side fired until a Wa mutineer keeled over, bleeding in the street. Bao's loyalists itched to shoot back but would not do so until their leader gave the command. Such was his gravitas. Bao instead stepped forward and ordered the opposing communist troops to drop their automatic weapons in the name of racial unity. The men hesitated but then, one by one, lowered their barrels. The politburo's defenses had crumbled at Bao's slightest touch. The path forward was clear.

Bao and his forces ascended the hill, a steep five hundred feet. Up top they found the politburo's retinue, ethnic Burmese cadres, standing frozen and mute. The mutineers ignored them and beelined for the politburo members' dwellings. Boots shattered wooden doors, and from within came indignant cries: Look at all these fucking sausages! Rifle butts smashed clay pots full of *baijiu*. After the mutineers rounded up the politburo, Bao asked them a single question: Burma or China? China, they said. Fine. Gather what your arms can carry and start walking. You will not die today. My men will escort you across the river.

Start to finish, the uprising took only a few hours. Most countries, the United States and China included, were founded after years-long welters of blood; yet the Wa, for all their supposed barbarism, freed themselves without killing a single person.

Lai sobered up, rubbed his eyes, and found himself in charge of the first Wa nation in history. For decades, the Wa had fought in lowlanders' proxy battles—communist versus anticommunist—always spilling their own blood for someone else's ideological crusade. No longer. Lai wanted his people to know serenity. He intended to seek peace with his neighbors. But moving forward, the Wa would also demand dignity, and any outsider attempting to exploit them would find the Wa unified, indivisible, and fanatical about protecting their independence—and their motherland. Bao, the new nation's military chief, would make sure of that.

It was time to burn away the detritus of the past. The Wa wrenched portraits of Stalin and Mao from the walls. They ransacked houses of the elite and torched them to the foundations. Every box stuffed with documents, every communist tome, was heaved onto a bonfire.[6] Someone barged into the radio station and turned on the microphone, and in bunkers and checkpoints across the peaks, Wa troops gathered around receivers to learn of their deliverance. "Never again," said a tinny voice, would they suffer under "racist policies" or "kowtow before any aggressor, local or foreign. We may be poor and backwards in terms of culture and literature. But we are strong in our determination!"[7]

Wa State was born.

Once the bonfires' ashes cooled, Lai sent word to Beijing that his nation desired friendly relations and open trade. He received felicitations in return. China's officials, though still communist themselves, regarded the Communist Party of Burma as old gum stuck to their boots, and they were glad Lai and Bao had chipped it off. The People's Republic of China would be more than happy to trade with the Wa and wished its revolutionary leaders well.

Even higher praise came from Yangon, of all places. Burma's army had long struggled to rid its soil of communists, and Lai had fulfilled their wish. Assuring him they came in peace, the Burmese generals sought permission to land helicopters in Panghsang. They collected Lai and whisked him away to meetings in the Burmese capital. Never before had Lai flown through the sky or seen a proper electrified city such as Yangon, with its labyrinthine brick alleys and avenues glowing after dark. It was one of Southeast Asia's most decrepit capitals, yet to Lai it looked highly advanced. My people, he thought, are even more deprived than we knew.

The Burmese generals hadn't known what to expect from Lai. Many imagined some hillbilly warrior king, "rude or coarse, based on how he grew up," said San Pwint, a top Burmese military intelligence officer. "But Lai was polite and fairly reasonable. Most of all, he just wanted respect." The generals feted Lai with sumptuous buffets and tours through resplendent temples. They tried to hypnotize him with splendor so that Lai, who now led tens of thousands of Wa soldiers, would consent to some degree of supervision over the Wa highlands. Perhaps he'd fancy serving as a regime-approved warlord, commanding a gigantic self-defense force that hailed Burma's military as its ultimate authority.

But in negotiations, Lai held to his convictions. Our state will nest inside yours as a nation within a nation, Lai told them. We need not go to the United Nations to seek recognition on paper as an official country. But know this: we cannot bend to your laws.[8] Nor will we abandon our standing army. Your officials are only welcome on scheduled visits. Intruding soldiers will be shot on sight. Accept these terms, and we will prosper as friends.[9] The Burmese officials nodded along. The regime—still struggling to quell rebel movements throughout Burma—was in no position to war with the Wa.

One more thing, Lai said.

Opium.

Everyone knew the Wa lived upon some of the world's most resplendent poppy lands. The politburo had throttled opium production, believing it anathema to Maoist doctrine, but Lai would have to honor the wishes of his people, letting them blanket the peaks in ivory and scarlet petals, harvest vast quantities of opium, and sell it off to feed their families. Would Burma's officials interfere? Not at all, they said. As long as the Wa kept their promise—never declaring full independence on the world stage and embarrassing the regime—Burma's government would not scrutinize how they made ends meet.

Lai returned to Panghsang in good spirits. In securing harmonious relations with both neighbors, he'd passed his first test as leader. Now came the hard part: building a state, from scratch, that offered a better life to the Wa than they'd ever known.

THERE WERE HOPES, in the days directly following the revolution, of discovering wealth hidden by the politburo. But upon raiding their locked storehouses, Wa soldiers discovered only one hundred thousand kilos of rice, twenty-five hundred ratty uniforms, and, inexplicably, five US dollar bills. The treasury was bare.[10]

Wa State was born into frightening poverty. Lai knew he needed an economic strategy but doubted he could devise one. He lacked any flair for business; his wife handled what little cash they possessed. At the time of the revolt, his family still lived in a dwelling made of straw and packed mud, and for dinner they might share handfuls of rice topped with salt and leafy greens. Lai lived in a world of ideas, up in his head, and hardly noticed when his own boots were falling apart.

Though Lai feared the corrupting influence of opium—childhood memories of enslavement to an opium planter remained vivid—he conceded that Wa State's economy would have to center on the drug. Opium was their only viable export. Most Wa were illiterate farmers living in isolated villages, and almost any crop they produced—whether onions or persimmons—would rot long before reaching buyers in distant cities. Only poppy plants thrived in Wa soil, frigid and alkaline, and unlike most agricultural commodities, opium traveled well. If packed tightly in canvas or clay jars, it even aged nicely, like wine. Lai felt his tribe had little else to offer the world. It was their lifeblood, glutinous and black, and as if subject to some primeval curse, they were born to furnish it to humanity's addicted.

So that was the plan. His roughly three to four hundred thousand Wa citizens would harvest opium. His armed forces, approximately fifteen thousand soldiers, would collect it and deliver it in bulk to wholesale buyers, directing some to China but, to avoid angering Beijing too much, funneling most to brokers around the Thai-Burma border. These were the makings of an economy—and a drug cartel. But Lai had no clue how to run either.

A solution to this problem arrived in Panghsang, just four or five months after the revolt, in the form of a slim businessman lugging several suitcases. His name was Wei Xuegang. A native son of the peaks, he was raised in Silver Fortress, though he'd been away a long time. Wei came seeking a position in the nascent Wa government: finance czar. Sitting down with Lai, he claimed rare and impeccable qualifications. In the mid-1970s, Wei enabled an egomaniac militia boss, Khun Sa, to build up a veritable nation: Shanland, still going strong. He did this by manufacturing heroin and funneling the profits to Khun Sa, whom he'd loyally served as treasurer. After their falling out, Wei joined the Wa National Army; once a third-rate gang, it was soon smuggling tons of dope all the way to the United States, thanks to Wei, the trafficker with the magic touch.

Wei spoke of logistics and international distribution, a language of wealth that mystified Lai. He corroborated his fluency by snapping open suitcases to reveal 40 million Thai baht, worth $1.5 million at the time. A gift for you, he said to Lai—if you'll hire me as chief of financial operations. Lacking any other suitable candidates, Lai gave him the position. Though he hardly knew it at the time, this decision, more than almost any other, would reshape the future of the Golden Triangle, for Wei had much more to offer than luggage stuffed with grubby bills. He had a model, in his head, for the perfect Golden Triangle narcotics cartel.

Wei didn't care how Lai wanted to run Wa State: democratically, tyrannically, whatever. As it happened, Lai favored governing his nation through its armed forces—a militant model that would ensure order, limit chaos, and inspire a healthy fear in his neighbors. Fine. But if this government wanted to start a world-class drug-trafficking operation, it would have to think big.

Wa State, with its coveted poppy lands, already had much in its favor. The problem, Wei pointed out, was geographical in nature. Living in a remote and landlocked state, the Wa lacked a direct portal to the region's key heroin wholesale market: Thailand, replete with ports from which exporters could ship drugs to richer countries overseas. This was a severe hindrance. Lai's troops could traffic opium or heroin south to Thailand's border, no problem, but they couldn't go any further—not without a fight. Khun Sa dominated almost every mountain passage into Thailand. They'd have to sell to Khun Sa, a middleman who'd take a hefty bite out of their profits.

Or would they?

Lai was in luck. Wei and his associate, Shah, just happened to control a smidgen of land on the Thai-Burma border—a rare oasis of real estate outside Khun Sa's control. Their Wa National Army stronghold had everything Wa State needed: heroin labs, backcountry trails winding into Thailand, and battle-tested ethnic Wa mercenaries to defend it all.

Wei proposed discarding the Wa National Army's name and establishing it as a division under Lai's armed forces. More crucially, he suggested anointing its one-hundred-square-mile turf as official Wa State territory—a special economic zone, oriented toward generating cash as quickly as possible. The potential for profit was electrifying. Never before had any armed organization possessed both the poppy-lush Wa peaks and a channel to Thailand.

Again, Lai said yes, and from that moment, the Wa nation became cartographically strange. Its main body, the motherland, was nearly as large as Israel.[11] Its new acquisition—totally detached—was far away and quite tiny, spanning only a few valleys.[12] They called the latter Wa Southern Command, or simply Wa South. Since Wa South's main purpose was producing revenue, that left little to do for the aging warrior Shah—founder of the now dissolved Wa National Army. Shah, nearing sixty, was given a largely ceremonial role in the Wa government (political commissar) and effectively retired. Wa South was Wei's baby, and he was its chief administrator.

During this period, Lai settled on a formal title for his government: the United Wa State Army (UWSA), a hybrid military-political institution.[13] Though created in defiance of communism, its structure would ironically resemble that of a one-party state such as Cuba, North Korea, or China, because this was the type of system the Wa knew best. The citizens even called Lai their chairman. Wei went by financial chief but, in truth, preferred no title at all and no public persona. He was a creature of the shadows.

Chairman Lai never grew close to Wei, a nondrinker who thought carefully before he spoke.[14] Lai, always refreshed, burst with passion and let his soul do the talking. The two conversed in Chinese, Wei's preferred language, though they seldom met in person. As financial czar, Wei stayed in the profit-focused southern node, while Lai ruled from Panghsang. Though each had something to offer the other, the two were driven by wildly different motives. Lai was a hard-line patriot who wanted to see his ethnostate grow strong. Wei's ambitions were strictly personal. He wanted to assemble an armed cartel under UWSA auspices, one so daunting that no one—neither his two-faced former boss Khun Sa nor the snooping Drug Enforcement Administration—could ever threaten him again. To keep Wei safe, Lai transferred hardened soldiers from the motherland down to Wa South, fortifying it in case Khun Sa's assassins or American narcs dared to encroach.

Wei got to work, proving he hadn't lost his flair. Opium from the Wa peaks soon flowed to his jungle refineries on the Thai-Burma border.[15] Once he was sitting on a mountain of heroin, Wei reached out to ethnic Chinese contacts in Bangkok and Hong Kong, readying international traffickers to move his product abroad in enormous volumes. Success came very fast. By 1990, within a year of its creation, he'd turned the UWSA into a heroin-producing leviathan, nearly on a par with Khun Sa's Shanland. Combined, the two organizations processed nearly two thousand tons of opium that year, four times the Golden Triangle's output just one decade prior.[16]

Wei's moves shook the planet. The world's other great poppy-growing region—South-Central Asia, the so-called Golden Crescent—was dwarfed in output. In that same year, 1990, Afghanistan and Pakistan produced one thousand tons, supplying 30 percent of America's heroin demand. Burma, meanwhile, supplied 60 percent.[17] Mexican syndicates produced the rest, a comparable pittance. The UWSA and Shanland were the world's largest heroin exporters—and their prime customers, at the far end of the supply chain, were Americans: a people whose appetites proved plenty big enough to handle the production glut.

Golden Triangle dope hit the United States like a hurricane.[18] On American streets, purity shot up, and prices shot down.[19] Never great with geography, Americans called the Southeast Asian product "China White."[20] Unlike Mexican black tar heroin, a sticky substance that must be heated into liquid and injected, China White was clean enough to snort right out of the baggie. Heroin's ethereal warmth was now available to everyone, even people afraid of needles.

The snowy flakes melted into pop culture. Models turned waifish; the media called it "heroin chic." Kurt Cobain and other grunge idols fell under the drug's spell. As A-listers and suburbanites alike dropped dead, drug war rhetoric grew even more sadistic. On the floor of Congress, the Los Angeles police chief opined that casual drug users "ought to be taken out and shot."[21]

Khun Sa, already established as a megavillain, soaked up most of the blame. He did himself no favors by giving interviews to American TV crews, telling *ABC News*, "President George Bush may have the button for nuclear weapons. But I have the button for opium, stronger and more potent than nuclear bombs. I should feed you poison. Why do anything else?" Khun Sa's braggadocio benefited Lai—who was still unknown to global media and hoped to stay that way. But how long could he evade scrutiny? Surely the DEA would, at some point, turn America's attention to Wa State: a renegade narco-nation, run by ex-headhunters and a fugitive financier who'd recently slipped the DEA's clutches. The headlines would write themselves.

Lai's grasp of international-drug-trade economics was weak, but he possessed an acute sense of politics and power. Mollifying Burma and China had proven easy enough. But he faced a much more vexing challenge. With heroin as his nation's primary export, Lai had good reason to fear the Americans' rampaging War on Drugs; yet he wasn't sure how to ward off this threat. Lai could not fathom the minds of white people— but he knew one Wa person, and one person only, who could.

Lai needed this man's advice. Problem was, the two of them had a history of trying to murder each other.

NOT LONG AFTER hiring Wei as finance chief, as Chairman Lai continued filling out his cabinet, he asked his assistants to contact Saw Lu. Find out if my former enemy is open to a face-to-face chat. Tell him I mean no harm. Soon the answer came back: Saw Lu was willing to meet—if Lai would travel to his home in Lashio.

On the morning of the meeting, as Saw Lu awaited his visitor, he struggled to remember exactly what Lai looked like. He could only recall the winnowed face of a young servant in the late 1960s—the kid who'd hand-washed his undershirts and strained his tea. Back when Saw Lu was a warlord, Lai barely spoke a word, other than to mutter, "Yes, sir." Once Lai transformed into a Maoist guerrilla, the two sworn rivals never saw each other, only communicating at a distance through gunfire.

Saw Lu was in his mid-forties, creases marking his face and a U-shaped bald spot hidden underneath his cap. When Lai appeared on his stoop, he saw a matured gentleman of similar age, tall as the doorframe, extending his hand in greeting. Lai's comportment bore no traces of his ill-tempered youth. He was even smiling. Lai clasped Saw Lu's hand, hard, and if any resentment lingered in either man's heart, it was squeezed out then and there.

It was the first of many sit-downs. Their rapport came easier than expected—for the passage of time revealed they were alike in many ways. When they were both bravehearted young men, Lai and Saw Lu wanted the same thing: a unified Wa society. Yet by choosing different ideologies—one communist, the other anticommunist—they'd feuded bloodily, just like the headhunters they scorned. In Lashio, Lai spent long nights inside Saw Lu's home, swilling beer and dreaming out loud. Never much of a boozer, Saw Lu sipped juice and sucked on a bamboo tobacco bong. That they'd once tried to shoot each other seemed absurd.

Chairman Lai treated Saw Lu as an informal advisor. He never demanded that Saw Lu assume a subordinate role, but he didn't have to: Saw Lu voluntarily acknowledged Lai as his superior. His day-to-day occupation—keeping tabs on fellow minorities for Burma's despotic regime—had eaten away at his conscience, and here was a chance, through Lai, for Saw Lu to redeem himself by shaping the future of a fledgling Wa nation. "What else was there to say to him?" Saw Lu said. "Other than, by God, it seems I was not the leader I thought I was. I told him, 'Lai, you've done it. You are our true leader. Tell me how I can serve you.'"

What Lai needed was good counsel from a man who never bit his tongue. Like other revolutionaries before him, from Mahatma Gandhi to Mao Zedong to George Washington, Lai was discovering that governance is rife with ugly compromise—and he'd already made one concession that troubled his soul. He told Saw Lu about the half-Chinese businessman named Wei Xuegang, fast assembling a heroin-trafficking enterprise for the UWSA. This was Wa State's economic engine—paying for food, oil, bullets, vehicles, everything—and Lai feared his citizens would eventually see themselves as mere personnel for a narco-corporation.

You are right to fear this man, Saw Lu said. In fact, you do not fear him nearly enough. Everything you build with Wei's drug money rests on quicksand. As Wa poison flows into American cities, we make enemies of the strongest country on earth.

Lai was, at heart, an isolationist. He preferred minimal contact with neighboring countries and zero contact with Western countries, which, to his mind, had no business on his side of the world. But Saw Lu advised him against this instinct. For too long, Saw Lu said, the Wa have cherished isolation as a virtue, ignoring the world's scorn. But are we not a lonely people, starved for respect? We need things drug money cannot buy: foreign expertise in practicing proper medicine, developing decent schools, building modern roads. Like it or not, he said, the Wa nation will never develop without foreigners' help. And as long as Wei floods the world with heroin, no developed nation will assist us—for we will appear to be a drug cartel masquerading as a country.

As months dragged on, Saw Lu and Lai had many conversations along these lines. Lai hadn't introduced Saw Lu and Wei; nor did he intend to. But each took residence on his figurative shoulders—the devil in one ear, the angel in the other—presenting starkly opposing visions for Wa State. Lai was torn between a dreamer and a cynic.

Suppose Saw Lu got his way and the Wa stopped producing heroin. How would they feed themselves—or even afford weapons to defend their motherland?

Suppose Wei's rise went unchallenged. Would the Wa nation not wither in ignorance, turning ever more decadent, all while the American superpower threw endless resources at its destruction?

Chairman Lai smoked and pondered and drank. As he saw it, both visions led to ruin. Until one day, Saw Lu came to him and said, Lai, I've got it. A plan.

Saw Lu revealed that he was lightly acquainted with the DEA, America's global antinarcotics police. The DEA had a tiny office in Yangon, and its agents sporadically contacted him. Saw Lu, as a civilian intelligence collector for Burma's regime, often traveled to minority villages in the hills—a hotbed of opium production—and the DEA agents sometimes picked his brain, prodding for information gleaned from the poppy lands. He wouldn't tell them much, just enough to earn an envelope of cash. Saw Lu hadn't bothered to inform his Burmese military minders about these DEA confabs: unauthorized contact with foreign powers was prohibited. But the meetings were so infrequent that Saw Lu barely gave them much thought.

Saw Lu wanted permission, from Lai, to upgrade his relationship with the DEA. To speak to them as a secret representative of the Wa government. To propose that America, the country most contaminated with Wa heroin, forgive the tribe and help them go clean. Supplant our heroin profits with US aid, he'd say to the DEA. Assist us in becoming a wiser, more virtuous nation. Both of our populations will benefit.

The concept was outrageously optimistic if not half crazy. But Lai had to admit that—if successful—it might allow his nation to prosper without opium and heroin. The chairman gave his blessing for Saw Lu to reach out to the DEA and explore the possibility. But then, contemplating the thunderous potential for conflict, he added, Saw Lu, for God's sake, do not tell anyone what you are doing, and do not get caught.

More likely than not, Saw Lu's idea would come to nothing. But if the dreamer somehow pulled it off, the cynic would lose everything.

Wa highlander and Wa village
photographed in 1890s by
British explorers.
(Credit: J. G. Scott Collection)

UWSA child soldier
in 1991.
(Credit: Angelo Saladino)

Below: Super-pure "China
White" heroin: produced by
the UWSA, sold in the USA.
(Credit: Angelo Saladino)

DEA agent John Whalen awkwardly sidles up to UWSA leader Bao Youxiang on a Burmese helicopter in 2002. *(Courtesy of John Whalen)*

The Exiles: anti-communist Chinese gifted weapons by the CIA. The progenitors of the Golden Triangle narcotics trade. *(Archival photo obtained by Patrick Winn)*

General Lee Wen-huan: anti-communist, opium trafficker, protected by the CIA. *(Archival photo obtained by Patrick Winn)*

Where meth is made: a makeshift lab located in Burma near the Chinese border.
(Credit: Myanmar police)

The UWSA's signature drug in the twenty-first century: methamphetamine-spiked pills, Asia's best-selling illegal product. *(Credit: Mark Oltmanns)*

Below: Wa opium, bundled in banana leaves and twine, en route to a heroin lab for processing. *(Credit: Angelo Saladino)*

Saw Lu as the Wa nation's foreign minister circa 1993 with Mary, his wife.
(Credit: Patrick Winn)

Saw Lu, DEA asset, sits in a field of opium poppies in 1993.
(Credit: Getty Images)

UWSA commandos capture unauthorized meth traffickers near the Thai-Burma border in 2019. *(Credit: UWSA)*

A Wa heroin refinery torched in 1991 with the DEA's help.
(Credit: Angelo Saladino)

The Wa nation's founding father, Zhao Nyi Lai, with Special Agent Angelo Saladino of the DEA in 1992. *(Courtesy of Angelo Saladino)*

Wei Xuegang, Asia's drug lord supremo and the UWSA's longtime financier. *(Credit: DEA)*

BOOK THREE

CONFIDENTIAL INFORMANT

Jacob drove me to the hotel, windows down in his hatchback. We passed golden stupas shimmering with moon gleam. Street dogs prowled Lashio on the midnight shift.

We'd just left Saw Lu's house, somewhat abruptly, after my bungling attempt to ask about Wei Xuegang. Jacob said I couldn't have known what that man had done to Saw Lu or that simply uttering his name would reanimate trauma. Saw Lu and Wei are "the worst enemies in the world," he said, implying that Saw Lu still bore physical scars from their rivalry. I felt too contrite to ask for details. I'd already probed too deep, hitting pain whose depths I didn't yet understand.

Jacob took a deep breath.

"You have to understand about Wei Xuegang. His name makes everybody uncomfortable. Even inside Wa State." Everyone knows that Wei is Wa State's finance chief, he said, and that the United Wa State Army (UWSA) relies on his fortunes. Yet in public at least, most Wa instinctively lower their voices when speaking about him. Wei is a wraithlike figure. He does not appear at ceremonial events. He avoids daylight. Wa State's central committee has removed Wei's name from its roster. The current party line is that Wei vanished years ago, even though everyone knows where he resides: in a fortresslike compound, outside Panghsang, guarded by a praetorian guard loyal to Wei alone.

"Have you ever seen it? The compound?"

"Yes. From a distance."

Jacob changed the subject as we neared the hotel. "Patrick, do you like music?"

"Sure."

"Can you play music?"

"Guitar, yes. Drums if I have to. I was in a band."

"What kind of band?"

Don't say punk rock, I thought. They're Baptist. "Just a rock band. It was a long time ago."

"Maybe you would like to play music together?"

"Yeah, why not?"

"Very good. Tomorrow, I will ask the assistant pastor to unlock the church. I will pick you up at 4 p.m."

THE GENRE WAS gospel rock, and the chord changes were simple enough for me to follow even though I'd never heard the songs. It was Jacob on keyboard (quite good), myself on guitar (quite mediocre), and his wife on vocals. The drummer couldn't make it, so Jacob ran a syncopated beat on his Yamaha synthesizer. A few sullen Wa teens sang backup. The only words I made out were "Jesus" and "Hallelujah," which always appeared in the chorus, no matter the song.

A massive copper cross hung above our heads. The church walls were freshly painted white, and purple irises adorned a wooden pulpit. The only detail out of place was an industrial rubber trashcan by the lectern.

Our jam session ended around dusk. I needed to get rid of my gum and headed for the trashcan. Thankfully, I looked inside before spitting. The bottom was lined with uncooked rice.

"Patrick, sorry! It is not for rubbish." Jacob was forever apologizing for my mistakes.

"Oh, sorry. What is it for?"

"Our tradition. Everyone who comes to this church should throw a handful of rice inside."

"Who eats it?"

"We do. Me and other staff. I am a music teacher here, one of my jobs. The rice is part of our pay."

The other band members were standing in a circle, waiting for me to join. I knew the routine. We clasped hands, closed our eyes, and bowed our heads. Jacob spoke in a mix of Wa and Burmese. Switching to English, he asked, "Patrick, do you have any praying?" I did. Thank you, God, for letting me play rhythm guitar for Jesus. Please steady my fumbling journey to understand the UWSA's inner workings. Forgive me for being so nosy.

"Our heavenly father," I said, "accept our thanks for these and all blessings. Please bless all of the Wa people and bring them happiness. In Christ's name, amen."

"Amen," they said in unison.

The churchgoers filed out into the dark. It was my last evening in Lashio, and I'd planned on eating something greasy at the hotel and turning in early. I was helping tidy up instruments when Jacob touched my shoulder and invited me to eat at his house instead.

"I'd be honored, ah-ko." Big brother in Burmese. "You're sure it's not too much trouble?"

"It's fine, Patrick. Actually Saw Lu will be there. He has asked to speak with you."

WE HAD *MOIK* again, plus Burmese-style curried pork. Jacob and his wife, Saw Lu and Mary, and I all crowded around a wooden table on the patio. A black dog named Rambo loitered at our feet. Moths the size of jetliners careened into an overhead lightbulb. Saw Lu said grace. I tried to keep the conversation light this time. Kids, food, church. But Saw Lu wasn't much for small talk. He finally warmed up when I asked about past hunting exploits.

"I killed a tiger with a shotgun once," he told me. "When I was young."

"How did it taste?"

"Like beef if you can get past the sour smell," he said. "Tiger meat stinks. But anything tastes good when you're starving."

"Saw Lu, you weren't scared to confront a tiger?" I was trying to flatter my host.

"No, tigers don't scare me. People do. They can lie and play tricks. Tigers can't."

I laughed. He didn't.

Saw Lu barely ate. Mary volunteered that diabetes and a bad stomach constrained his diet. His ailments were mounting in advanced age. He has good days, she said, but on bad days Saw Lu suffered fits of paralysis—a consequence of torture. I dared not ask. Saw Lu then turned to me and with zero abashment asked for a favor. I could use your help, he said, in reconnecting with the Drug Enforcement Administration.

"D-E-A?" I pronounced the letters slowly. "You worked for them?"

"Tell them I have medical bills."

"And the DEA will know what that means?"

"Of course." He alluded to injuries, suffered in the line of duty, that still plagued him. At the very least, the DEA ought to fly him to a decent hospital in Bangkok. "I lost touch with them. I don't know how to get through. You're American. They'll listen to you."

I wasn't so sure. Whatever Saw Lu once was to the DEA, the organization probably wouldn't acknowledge him—least of all to a prying journalist. It was an impossible request. And yet I said none of this out loud. Saw Lu held me in his gaze, pupils unblinking obsidian.

"Yes, sir. You have my word." I plopped my notebook on the table. "I'll need a name though. The DEA is a huge agency."

That was the problem. Saw Lu's most recent handler was dead.

"Can you tell me his name?"

"Bill Young."

"OK. Bill Young. Who is dead. Was there any other agent you worked with?"

Saw Lu leaned back and tugged on his earlobe as if to yank loose some calcified memory. Bruce. But that was a very long time ago.

"Bruce who?"

"I'm not good with white people's names. Just Bruce."

BACK IN BANGKOK, my hunt commenced. I discovered a Bruce who'd served the DEA for three decades with long stints in Thailand and Burma. Bruce Paul Stubbs. Known for his terrific sense of humor and ready smile. Survived by his wife, Su Yon, and daughter, Alana. In lieu of flowers, send donations to the Fred Hutchinson Cancer Research Center in Seattle. So read his 2006 obituary.

More hunting turned up the name of Bruce's former boss: Angelo Saladino, former DEA country attaché in Burma. They'd served together in Yangon in the early 1990s. Saladino would be in his late seventies at least—if he was still around. An online phone directory listed Angelo Saladinos in Florida, Illinois, Colorado, and New York. I carpet-bombed their answering machines. No responses. I waited one week before pestering all of the Angelos again. While leaving a message on one of their machines, there was a click and then, "Patrick?"

"Hello, yes. Patrick Winn. Calling you from Thailand."

"Winn! Hi! You're on speakerphone." A woman's voice this time. "This is Barbara, Angelo's wife. I've advised Angelo to avoid you."

"Oh."

"That was not a happy period in our life. There were physical threats. Internal government rivalries. I'm not sure we should talk about it."

But Mr. Saladino couldn't resist sharing a few old drug war stories while I was on the line. He told me about chasing Thai dope trawlers in the 1970s. The tragic death of Joyce Powers in the 1980s. Adventures with the Wa tribe in the 1990s. Soon enough, Barbara was chiming in too; they'd been married more than fifty years. Each tale was punctuated with "I sure wish it was Bruce telling you this" because Bruce was the better storyteller, able to wring hilarity out of any story no matter how dark.

But who was it that I was calling about? Saul somebody?

"Saw Lu." I ventured a description. Wa man, medium build. Room-filling presence. Recovering warlord. Extremely Baptist. Gifted at recruiting people into precarious ventures, myself included.

"Oh, Superstar! That's what we called him." Hard to forget someone like that. Superstar, he said, was the finest confidential informant (CI) to ever come out of Burma. Hell of a CI. No small wonder a man like that was still breathing.

They'd last seen each other in late 1991, just before their secret relationship came to light. That was the worst episode of my career, Saladino told me. The memory still haunted him—the way the DEA failed to protect his source, and as a result Saw Lu, the Superstar, ended up trussed by his feet and hung upside down from a tree.

KICK THE CAT

Special Agent Angelo Saladino had just moved to Burma with his wife, Barbara, and their two teenage kids. They'd settled into Yangon's diplomatic quarter—British colonial manors stately in their decline, ringing the picturesque Inya Lake. Their appointed home was almost regal, graced with a portico, black-and-white tile floors, a second-floor balcony overlooking a jacaranda tree that dripped purple petals on their lawn. A bit further was the lake's edge, bobbing with lotus leaves.

Saladino was just shy of fifty, silver streaking his dark hair and mustache. On his résumé: stints in Miami, Bangkok, Chiang Mai, and Denver—and now the Drug Enforcement Administration wanted him heading up its Burma office. It should have been their most vital outpost in Asia. Burma was the main source of heroin smuggled into the United States, and as President George H. W. Bush said himself, the drug was "the greatest domestic threat facing the nation today." No narcotic killed more Americans. According to the DEA playbook, Saladino should've teamed up with Burmese cops and troops to lock up narcos, seize dope, and destroy labs, just like agents in Colombia or Mexico. But this was Burma. The rules were very different.

Saladino was the sole DEA agent in the country.[1] His office, hidden inside the US embassy, did not officially exist. The State Department—America's diplomatic wing, which hosts DEA offices in its embassies and lays down house rules—had forbidden him to reveal its existence in public. The US ambassador to Burma, Burt Levin, warned Saladino, Never speak to the junta. He did this knowing the agent needed to fraternize with Burmese police to do his job. Clearly the State Department, a far more powerful institution than the DEA, wanted the Saladinos to turn around and go home. It wasn't personal. The Saladinos were perfectly nice and always welcome at the American Club, a lakeside sanctuary for diplomats' families, with baseball games and cheeseburgers by the pool. But as embassy personnel saw it, the DEA simply didn't belong in Burma.

This attitude had everything to do with a junta atrocity eleven months earlier.

The previous summer, Burma's masses had revolted, protesting for an end to tyranny. Though minorities in the hills had long demanded the same and endured torture for speaking out, this time Burmese lowlanders in the cities were rising up. They simply couldn't take it anymore. Burma was totalitarian to the core. The junta owned almost everything in sight, hoarding the country's wealth. Its police state was pervasive, even listening to whispers in tea shops. Its generals were venal as the worst kings, with at least one of them rumored to bathe in dolphin blood, believing it conferred youth.[2]

All walks of life joined the protest movement: shopkeepers, farmers, students, monks in wine-colored robes. They rallied around Aung San Suu Kyi, daughter of a Burmese martyr credited with driving out the Brits four decades prior. Hair decorated with lavender flowers, Suu Kyi rallied half a million people: a sea of humanity in sarongs and sandals.

The junta locked up Suu Kyi and slaughtered her followers. Infantry went block to block, shooting between three and ten thousand people—a massacre more lethal than Tiananmen Square.[3] Monks were not spared; nor were teenagers. When carnage spilled toward the US embassy, a three-story edifice in downtown Yangon, diplomats looked down from their windows and saw murder in the streets. The ambassador watched students cower behind trees, and when they fled, the "army ran after them and shot them as if they were hunting rabbits." Another State Department official said the "staff witnessed people literally being beheaded. It was a very searing experience for people there."[4]

Before that day, Burma was just another awful regime with which the United States maintained ties. This changed almost overnight. The junta became a sponge for American condemnation. "We were to use Burma to soak up Washington's human rights initiatives that might otherwise be directed toward important countries," said Franklin "Pancho" Huddle, the embassy's second in command.[5] The State Department believed that, in Burma, the United States had "the luxury of [upholding its] ideals," he said. Burma was neither huge, nor armed with nukes, nor a vital supplier of oil. No consequence would come from bashing its junta in the name of promoting freedom and democracy. "Everyone needs a cat to kick," Huddle said, characterizing the new policy, "and Burma fulfilled the role admirably." The junta's villainy was note perfect. It called itself the State Law and Order Restoration Council (SLORC), an acronym so ugly it makes your mouth feel unclean.

In the view of the State Department and the Central Intelligence Agency, which operate in sync, isolating the junta was paramount. Saladino could forget about playing commando with the SLORC—not after its soldiers gunned down monks and college kids. If he had any questions about the "no contact" rule, he could ring his predecessor. The last DEA agent in Burma was caught talking to the junta behind the ambassador's back. He got forty-eight hours to pack his bags.[6] Ambassadors don't micromanage agents' operations, but they can shitcan narcs who break house rules, forcing DEA headquarters to send a replacement. Saladino was that replacement.

Each day, he'd come home from the embassy groaning about another purposeless day. "I remember him saying, 'They've put every obstruction in my way with no other justification than 'This is a bad regime,'" Barbara said. "It was a very political atmosphere. Which was unfortunate because Angelo doesn't like to play politics. Honestly, he isn't very good at it when he tries."

Saladino was excellent, however, at working drug cases. And he was determined to find some way to eradicate heroin in Burma—no matter what the ambassador said.

THOUGH SALADINO WAS the sole US narcotics agent in Burma, he wasn't the only DEA staffer. A colleague lived up the lake's shoreline in an equally charming home. I'll call her Bian. Late forties, smartly dressed, black hair in a bun, Bian was a DEA intelligence analyst.

"In the DEA," she told me, "agents are king. Analysts are second-class citizens." Analysts can't carry pistols. They rarely go into the field. They sit at their desks, sifting through transcripts of whatever confidential informants blab to agents, hunting for clues. They write lots of reports. "Most agents hate writing reports," Bian said. "They just want to catch criminals."

Bian had come to the DEA's Burma office the year before, just in time to witness the 1988 massacre. "I felt sorry for those student revolutionaries. They faced soldiers in boots but showed up in flip-flops. They weren't real killers, not like Vietnamese. We know how to fight!" Born in Vietnam, Bian didn't shrink from much. She'd muscled her way into the DEA, a notorious boys' club, becoming the rarest of its employees: an Asian female immigrant. Before Burma, Bian worked in the Bangkok office, dominated by macho agents who chain-smoked in the halls and held briefings in go-go bars. Bian applied for Burma hoping to make her mark in a country others avoided. "Most DEA agents didn't want to come to Burma because their wives were too scared. Not a problem for me."

Saladino and Bian got along great. He was a family man, not a boor, and he treated her as an equal. Each weekday morning, they'd carpool in Saladino's government-issued sedan, leaving their lakeside idyll and driving into Yangon's downtown—a kaleidoscopic racket. Lining the capital's narrow lanes were brick facades painted apricot, mint green, and butterscotch and often marred by colonies of black mold. Up above, songbirds tightroped across clotheslines. A few blocks from the embassy was a gold-plated stupa, Sule Pagoda, rising magnificently from a traffic circle, slowly orbited by rusty cars.

Saladino would park, and they'd walk into the embassy—through the same portico where protesters had bled out the year before. The basement contained a shop selling cheap liquor and Spam. The CIA occupied the second floor. The DEA's office was hidden on the third. Its furniture was chipped, its carpet cruddy. Saladino had a decent-sized corner office, Bian a smaller one nearby. Seven or eight Diebold safes lined the wall: fireproof, drillproof, impenetrable if you didn't know the combination. Inside one safe was a disassembled AK-47, unregistered, in case the embassy fell under siege. This was Burma. Anything could happen.

The only other DEA "staffer" was a Burmese national, John Tin Aung, paid off the books. He hailed from a high-born Burmese family and spoke regal British English. Officially, John was just a paper pusher inside the embassy, but in truth he was the DEA's superfixer: an interpreter and expert CI wrangler. It was John who approached Saladino one day and told him an occasional informant from Lashio wanted to meet—in a secluded location in Yangon.

Saladino doesn't recall much about his first sit-down with Saw Lu, only that he grasped, over a series of meetings, that this man was no ordinary CI. Saw Lu was potentially a secret weapon who could enable Saladino's scrappy DEA outpost to defy all expectations and pull off something big.

THEY NEVER SAID Saw Lu's real name. In written reports, he was a string of numbers and letters: SWQ-86-0005. In hushed conversation, they used his code name: Superstar.

They never rang him on the phone either. The lines might be bugged. In fact, they couldn't reach out to him at all. Superstar had to contact *them*, often through a messenger carrying a note: here's a date and time, see you at the usual rendezvous spot in Yangon. "We had to be extra careful," Saladino said. "Superstar wasn't some nobody. Burmese military intelligence knew exactly who he was."

And who was Superstar? Saw Lu, a civilian agent of Burma's military. His job: monitoring the hinterlands for the junta. He regularly visited the Shan hills, part of Burma's poppy-growing heartland, a region where many villages harvested opium for rebel groups, criminal clans, and other middlemen, many selling in bulk to Khun Sa's people or lesser drug lords.

But Saw Lu wasn't just collecting information for the junta.

He'd been very busy. Before reaching out to Saladino, Saw Lu had tirelessly mobilized drug-trade informants in the Shan hills—a network unknown to his regime handlers. His moles were indigenous Baptists whose forebears belonged to William Marcus Young's sect. The descendants of these converts still felt a sense of kinship, even though the white missionaries were long gone. Some of these folks had strayed into the drug trade. More literate than most, they'd scored high positions in trafficking organizations large and small. Saw Lu recruited them—more than one hundred men and women—to pilfer intel, and he kept files on his discoveries. It was his own secret spy web, run on Baptist whispers, and all the more ingenious because he had the perfect cover story. His job, after all, was to keep tabs on minorities in the hinterlands.[7]

The point of this enterprise was to impress the hell out of the DEA—and he did. "Amazing stuff," Saladino told me. "You wouldn't think it. But villagers from mountaintop to mountaintop keep great records on how many hectares are cultivated. We had access to all of that."

But this was a highly dangerous relationship. Because Saw Lu lacked approval to speak with US agents, the junta could charge him with subversion. Or just shoot him. Though Saw Lu was a trusted asset, going back to his warlord days, he was still a minority—and Burma's gestapo-like police state watched minorities closely. They were highly sensitive to citizens confabbing behind their backs with the United States. To avoid detection, Saw Lu only met the DEA infrequently. He'd usually wait for his junta bosses to summon him to Yangon for some meeting and use the opportunity to slip away for a quick rendezvous.

Saladino's Burmese sidekick, John, set up a safe house in Yangon just for Saw Lu. It was "something like a middle-class Burmese couple would live in," Saladino said.[8] Bian would come along too, even though in most countries agents never brought analysts into the field. To evade the junta's police state, they'd drive to the safe house using circuitous routes, just in case they were tailed. Once parked outside the house, John would scan the street; after he'd given the all clear, they'd slip through the door. Often Superstar was already seated inside, handwritten reports arrayed on the table.

The typical CI is allergic to paperwork. They just yammer away: embellishing here, obfuscating there, groaning for more cigarettes. But Superstar was a straight-A student: always putting his information in writing, always anticipating the DEA's needs. Collecting tidbits from dozens of moles in Shan State, he provided a real-time portrait of the drug trade: smuggling routes, refinery locations, the status of gang feuds—everything a narc could want to know. Saw Lu hadn't mentioned his affiliation with the United Wa State Army (UWSA) just yet. He was still reeling in the DEA, making himself indispensable. But as the DEA relationship deepened, he'd slip in proprietary documents from the UWSA, Asia's biggest cartel after Shanland. These were real files—straight from UWSA headquarters, not mere gossip—and they indicated how many poppy fields the Wa controlled, down to the hectare. Saladino and Bian, elated to receive next-level insight into Burma's narco-trade, told Superstar to keep up the good work.

Each secret meeting ended the same way. Saladino would produce a receipt for "purchase of evidence."[9] Saw Lu received roughly $1,000 for each report, sometimes more, but to get the cash, he had to sign a receipt. He hesitated to write his name on any document proving illegal cooperation with the United States, but Saladino assured him the receipts were "above top secret," among the DEA's most closely guarded documents.

Fine, Saw Lu said, but he'd take an extra step to obscure his identity. Sometimes he'd scribble his name in Burmese, other times in Chinese or in Wa, which uses the same alphabet as English. On the off chance regime spies intercepted the files, they might get confused, thinking Saw Lu was multiple people instead of one. It was just a little trick to help mask his scent.[10] Back at the embassy, Saladino was always careful to store Saw Lu's receipts in one of the Diebold office safes. Only he and Bian had the combinations.

Saladino and Bian took pains to hide their relationship with Superstar from the ambassador. But as months unfolded, the embassy staff realized this mysterious DEA duo had stumbled onto an intel jackpot. They just weren't sure how.

Every US embassy in a major drug-producing country must furnish, to the White House, estimates of how much cocaine or heroin is generated inside that country's borders. This was the DEA's remit. But by 1990, the CIA—keen to compete with the DEA—had its own counternarcotics wing, and the spy agency produced its own figure. In most countries, DEA and CIA estimates matched up, more or less. But in Burma, they didn't, and the DEA wouldn't explain why.

"Our figures were right," Bian told me.[11] "Theirs were wrong. We had ground truth"—Saw Lu's reports—"and they didn't. Just their eyes in the sky, going round and round."[12] The CIA relied on satellite photos of Burma's hills. They'd analyze the images to identify where the soil sprouted poppies and estimate how much opium all those poppies could produce. Then they'd divide by ten. According to conventional wisdom, it takes ten kilos of opium to produce one kilo of heroin.[13] That was the CIA's formula.

"But it's never that simple, OK?" Bian said. "Depending on the weather and soil, it might take an average of, say, thirteen kilos of opium to make a kilo of heroin. It changes every season, just like any vegetable garden. But oh gee, you can't challenge the CIA! Well, you can. It just takes guts."[14]

Bian had guts. "I tried to tell them. Your formula? It's wrong." The CIA had the technological edge, she said, but "we had something better. Nitty, gritty details," courtesy of Saw Lu. "It was pure ground truth. That was probably the beginning of the CIA hating us. But I won't apologize for being right."

SPRING 1990.

The supreme ruler of Burma's Orwellian state was not a president or a premier but, fittingly, the military's spymaster, Khin Nyunt. The dictator wore oversized golden wire-frame glasses and a thick gold ring. His black hair, parted to the right, looked hard as varnished wood. He was quick to smirk, yet known for his mood swings, and he insisted that everyone call him Secretary One.

America scared the hell out of Secretary One. Following the massacre, the White House blocked US aid to the country. The State Department was urging the president and Congress to go much further, enacting sweeping, shattering sanctions—the sort of economic warfare that could result in even worse poverty, possibly sparking another revolt. Though the United States harbored no plans to strike Burma militarily, Secretary One didn't know that. He'd seen what the United States did to other reviled regimes: Libya, bombed in 1986, and Panama, invaded in 1989. The dictator had to give America some reason to back off, short of relinquishing power. His junta's survival depended on softening Burma's image. Secretary One spoke of rebooting his regime: less dolphin blood, more market reforms. He even promised a transition to electoral "democracy"—a very, very slow one.

The State Department wasn't buying it. No institution hated the junta more. So Secretary One focused on the DEA instead. With America's War on Drugs in full swing, Burma could promise to help US narcs hunt down narco-traffickers inside its borders. Secretary One knew he couldn't *actually* decimate Burma's drug trade: the big whales, Khun Sa's Shanland and Wa State, were too tough to topple. As for middle-tier traffickers and middlemen, junta officers were in bed with them, taking kickbacks, letting smugglers pass through military checkpoints. But a few of these traffickers could be sacrificed—if that's what it took to get the United States off Burma's neck. Big seizures, executed in tandem with the DEA, might win favor with the White House, maybe even get the president to rein in that feisty State Department.

Secretary One told his top deputy, Col. Kyaw Thein, to cultivate a relationship with Agent Saladino. The colonel spoke superb English, and with his gentle face and pomaded hair, he looked like a doo-wop singer. He started regularly inviting Saladino to his office for chats. The US ambassador's term was winding down later that year, and his hard-line communication blockade, barring US officials from talking to the junta, proved difficult to enforce.

The colonel told Saladino, Just call me KT. They got along nicely. "Most guys in the military were like third graders with guns," Saladino told me. "KT was well educated. SLORC was a very bad word at that time, and for good reason, but KT saw a better way to do things. He wasn't so insular." Over the course of long talks, KT, in his lilting voice, would admit to the regime's awful behavior. Such thought crimes would land a civilian in prison. That the dictator's deputy uttered them out loud made Saladino feel there might be hope for Burma yet.

But he hadn't come to turn despots into democrats. That was the State Department's job. Saladino's mission was to shut off the firehose of heroin aimed at America's cities, and he figured the SLORC had every reason to help him out. "I knew this was a horrible regime. I had no delusions. I just wanted to do some good for the American people."

Saladino suggested baby steps. Burmese troops already seize heroin here and there, he said, but everyone assumes you resell it on the sly. Why not burn the drugs in public, KT? Show the world you're serious. The colonel promised to relay the idea upstairs.

In late April 1990, while Ambassador Levin was briefly out of the country, Secretary One seized the moment. He summoned Western diplomats to a dirt field in Yangon. At its center was a metal plinth, piled high with white sacks, each plump with heroin. Foreign media, typically barred from Burma, were allowed to fly in for the spectacle; the scrum included reporters from *Time* magazine and *CBS News*.

Cameras rolled as Burmese soldiers doused the pile with gasoline. Secretary One stood nearby, face half in shadow under a peaked cap too big for his head. The dictator picked up a flaming wand. He was about to ignite a half-billion dollars' worth of heroin, the largest eradication in Burmese history. But he paused, scanned the spectators seated in wicker chairs, and located Saladino in the crowd. He gestured, and the agent, right on cue, strode forth in short sleeves and aviator shades. "He handed me the torch to light this huge pile of drugs. At that moment, the status of DEA in Burma went from covert to operational." A *CBS Evening News* segment anchored by Dan Rather identified the torch-wielding American: Angelo Saladino, Drug Enforcement Administration.

Saladino hadn't sought State Department permission to publicly acknowledge the DEA's presence in Burma. Nor would they have given it. At a televised conference in Washington, DC, following the drug burn, the assistant secretary of state warned that the United States would not "get [itself] into the business of helping [Burma] whitewash its record."[15] The diplomatic corps seethed. As they saw it, Saladino wasn't kicking the cat.

He was making it purr.

THROUGH EARLY SUMMER Saladino continued meeting with Saw Lu at the safe house, sometimes with Bian and sometimes not. Their camaraderie grew warmer with every rendezvous. As CIs went, Saw Lu was one of a kind. Not a rat or a slimeball but a true professional.

By that point, Saw Lu was providing UWSA documents of the highest caliber, including profit-and-loss sheets taken directly from Wa State's Panghsang headquarters. But he needed Saladino to understand he wasn't snitching on the Wa. Saw Lu revealed that he was an advisor to Wa State's leader—Chairman Zhao Nyi Lai—who'd approved every meeting with the DEA. He also insisted that his noble UWSA was nothing like Burma's largest cartel: Shanland. Khun Sa is a callous businessman posing as a revolutionary, Saw Lu said. We're just an impoverished mountain tribe in a bad spot. Producing heroin was but a temporary embarrassment for the Wa, a way to get their nation up and running. We want to go clean. And we need America's help.

Saw Lu revealed the plan he'd carefully crafted in his head. He envisioned the United States building schools, hospitals, and paved roads in the Wa peaks—sending American teachers, doctors, engineers to lay the foundations of a modern state. In exchange, the UWSA would incinerate its poppies and shut down its labs whipping up heroin for export to US cities. Under this plan, both of our civilizations will grow healthier, he said. We're ready to ally with a Christian nation that believes in the power of redemption.

So this was the CI's long game. This whole time, he'd been angling not for a fat Swiss bank account but for a humanitarian outcome: literate kids, decent medicine, Uncle Sam's largesse. It would've been simpler if Saw Lu just wanted a pile of cash. Saladino instantly imagined all the hurdles standing between this dream and reality—and each looked more daunting than the next. Were he crazy enough to endorse Saw Lu's plan, Saladino could expect resistance from the following institutions.

BURMA'S JUNTA

Not in a thousand years would the junta let the US government directly collaborate with the Wa government. An unmitigated alliance between a hostile superpower and a fearsome mountain tribe? Not happening. America was notorious for sneaking into rival countries, riling up minorities, and pitting them against the regime in charge. There was a reason Saladino and Saw Lu had to meet in secret: any contact between the United States and an armed ethnic group, especially the mighty Wa, would trigger Secretary One's paranoia, possibly causing him to boot the DEA out of the country.

But Saladino didn't dismiss Saw Lu's idea straightaway. There might be a way to finesse it—by letting the junta closely mediate an American-Wa project. After all, the junta was looking for ways to take its DEA relationship to the next level. Perhaps the Burmese regime and the DEA could team up, go to Wa State with its leader's permission, and jointly eradicate loads of heroin. Saw Lu indicated that his Wa superiors would allow that, so long as they got schools and hospitals in exchange for their precious narcotics. The trick would be giving junta officials the power to supervise every little interaction between DEA and UWSA representatives. At each step, they'd need to feel totally in control.

To make this work, Saw Lu would need to consider certain concessions. Any hypothetical US aid to the Wa would have to flow through the junta first so the generals could take a cut for themselves. Secretary One would also demand most of the credit for this altruistic project. The dictator was desperate for international acclaim—headlines screaming "Burma Eradicates Drugs"—to redeem the government's loathsome image and achieve his larger goal: warding off the threat of extreme Western sanctions. Bottom line: if Saw Lu was willing to include the junta in his plan, Saladino thought it might have a future. A few drug-burning spectacles in Wa State could even acclimate the Burmese military to the sight of Americans on Wa soil, and eventually perhaps the junta would—under close supervision—allow the United States to send teachers, doctors, and engineers.

THE US STATE DEPARTMENT

A much bigger obstacle to Saw Lu's dream. Its diplomats sought maximum pressure against Burma. If any DEA project flattered the junta, they'd try to thwart it, no matter how much dope hit the bonfire. Worse yet, Saladino was already on their shit list. He couldn't imagine how they'd react if he suggested the United States pump aid, through the junta, to a drug cartel.

Overriding the diplomats' objections would be difficult. In terms of power and influence within the US government, the DEA was a scrappy bulldog, but the State Department was a saber-toothed tiger. Saladino would need DEA headquarters to fall in love with the plan, then convince America's supreme wings of government—Congress and the White House—to endorse the experiment. Only then would the diplomats back off.

THE CIA

Same antijunta agenda as the State Department, only seasoned at getting its way through covert tricks. The institutions were cross-fertilized. Of the fifty or so US personnel rotating through the Yangon embassy, more than a dozen belonged to the local CIA station, though most posed as diplomatic staff.[16] The CIA station in Burma was known for its brazenness. At the time, mid-1990, as Ambassador Levin was preparing to depart, the CIA was trying to install one of its own—a spy embedded in the State Department—as the new US ambassador.[17] The junta got wise to this play and blocked it. Point being, the CIA would go to extreme lengths to get its way, and if Saladino proposed Saw Lu's plan, his own country's spies might cook up ways to sabotage it.

THE DEA

You couldn't miss the irony: Saladino, a veteran DEA agent, proposing a harmonious relationship with a drug cartel. But he believed DEA headquarters would give Saw Lu's plan a fair hearing. Saladino liked it, and his track record was strong. Besides, if this long-shot idea worked, the United States would neutralize Asia's second-largest heroin-trafficking syndicate without drawing a single drop of blood. The UWSA controlled some seventy thousand acres of poppy fields. Burning them down would crater the opium supply and save many American lives, and that was a noble goal, even if pursuing it required cooperating with a murderous junta and a heroin cartel.

"You have to understand," Saladino told me. "Wa heroin was very, very pure. A single kilo, smuggled to the states, was potent enough to adulterate with filler and make four street-ready kilos . . . and the Wa were pushing out thousands of kilos a year. Now if you have an opportunity to stop that, don't you have to take it?

"Honestly, I could see it. His dream," Saladino said. "Hell, it was worth a shot."

Saladino told Saw Lu he'd run it up the flagpole, see how his DEA bosses at headquarters responded. Their interest would determine whether they could even begin to discuss it with other wings of the US government. More thorny still was thinking up a way to suggest the idea to Burma's government without revealing that the DEA and UWSA, through Saladino and Saw Lu, had conspired in its creation.

There were many obstacles ahead. So don't get your hopes up, Superstar. In the meantime, Saladino said, "You be careful coming in to see us. We'll be careful too.'" If Burma's junta discovered the two were meeting secretly, this little dream would die a quick death—and Saw Lu wouldn't fare too well either.

TO SALADINO'S SURPRISE, DEA headquarters didn't just give him the green light. It transferred another special agent to Burma to help explore the potential of Saw Lu's plan. A real second agent, unlike Bian, a mere analyst.

Bian couldn't help but feel threatened. In July 1990, she watched with great annoyance as moving trucks pulled into Yangon's diplomatic quarter. Agent Bruce Stubbs, transferred over from Thailand, was taking up residence next door. "I already knew Bruce from my time in Bangkok. Never liked him. But you know what? He got a modest ranch home in Burma while I had the more beautiful two-story house. His house normally went to embassy secretaries. Ha!"

Stubbs, nearing fifty, was a Southeast Asia longtimer. He'd even helped investigate the Joyce Powers murder back in 1980. Built like John Goodman, he smoked Winstons and a tobacco pipe. His sandy-brown mustache was thick as a painter's brush, and when deep in thought, he rubbed it flat with his fingers.

Bian wasn't the only person dreading Stubbs's move to Yangon. His own wife, Su Yon, wasn't thrilled either. Bruce and Su Yon Stubbs had been together since the 1970s when Stubbs, then a young US military intelligence officer, met her in South Korea. After he joined the DEA, they moved to Bangkok and lived there for nearly a decade. To the couple,

Thailand was familiar and cozy. "We Koreans don't smile all the time, but Thais do and so did Bruce," she said. "He was like a Thai in that way. People said he'd become more Asian than American." She believed Stubbs was the "most gentle person you could ever meet, full of empathy for all types of people," and Su Yon would follow him anywhere—even Yangon, a place she hated at first sight.

All that barbed wire and poverty. The junta's 10 p.m. curfew. The checkpoint in front of their neighborhood, manned by underfed soldiers with dead eyes. On move-in day, approaching her new home for the first time, Su Yon froze by the entrance. An iguana-sized lizard was squatting on the front door frame. At first, it was still as a gargoyle. Then it slowly tilted its head toward her, opened its pink mouth, and screamed, "TO-KAY!"

Tokays are big geckoes, common in Burma, and apparently this one was going to be her housemate. Su Yon was still processing that unappealing fact hours later, while eating dinner at their kitchen table, when the lights sputtered out, plunging the couple into darkness. "Bruce," she said, "how often does the electricity go out around here?"

He laughed. "Often!" Especially during monsoon season, which raged in mid-summer. She'd never experienced anything like it: thunder bellowing like war drums, palm trees bent sideways, black skies sobbing, and the next day storm drains gurgling like drowning animals. "On top of that, it was a prison. The government telling you: don't do this, don't do that. If I left the neighborhood, just to visit the market, military guards asked where I was going."

At least her husband enjoyed his new assignment. Stubbs started working long hours at the DEA office, and he'd come home giddy. Seldom did he discuss drug cases with his wife, but he'd stumbled into something spectacular at work, and it showed on his face. He couldn't tell her much, only that it involved a tribe of former headhunters.

"Bruce! Headhunters!?"

"Yes. I want to go visit them. I think they eat black snakes."

"Bruce! Snakes!?"

"Yes. I'm going to eat snakes with them. I'll do whatever they say, as long as they don't eat me."

As for Bian, her fear of Stubbs was soon vindicated.

He upstaged her in every way. He took over her little office, displacing her to a dinged-up desk on the open floor. His smoke wafted everywhere, seeping into her hair and pastel blouses. Bian had taken pride in joining secret meetups with Saw Lu—few analysts ever laid eyes on informants—but that privilege went away too. Running the CI became Stubbs's job and his alone. He'd float out of the office in the mornings, come back afternoons, and deposit his Glock with a metallic thunk in the desk that used to be hers. He'd gush over Superstar's latest safe house revelations. Soon he was fantasizing about helping Superstar send his sons to college in America. The two were fast friends, apparently, and Bian, the "second agent" no more, was left to analyze Superstar's reports in the office.

It was as if she'd painstakingly watered a tree only to watch Stubbs barrel over at harvest time, plucking away the choicest fruit.

LATE OCTOBER 1990.

Overcast dawn skies, sunbeams cooking away the fog over Inya Lake. A typical weekday morning in Yangon's diplomatic quarter, which in most homes entailed live-in Burmese maids cooking breakfast for their employers and gardeners sweeping leaves off driveways.

Saladino idled his sedan in front of Bian's home.

He was puzzling out how to deliver the news.

Saw Lu's plan was actually starting to unfurl—at least an amended version. "Superstar" had convinced Lai, Wa State's leader, to contact Secretary One and offer up one of the UWSA's heroin labs, along with a large batch of narcotics. You're welcome to come up here and burn it down, Lai told the dictator. And if you like, bring the DEA along to snap photos and show the world what they've seen. When Secretary One asked what the Wa wanted in return, Lai requested one single medical clinic, built and staffed by competent professionals. Whether they were Burmese or American or any other nationality, Lai said he didn't care, so long as they could stop his people from dying of common diseases.

Secretary One agreed. My army will provide your clinic, he told Lai. As for the DEA agents, Burma's military would shuttle them to Wa State on helicopters, allowing them to not just witness the refinery's burning but participate in its destruction.

Saladino was impressed with the way Superstar masterminded the whole affair from the shadows. He'd figured out how to send his DEA handlers, Saladino and Stubbs, up to Wa State—with Burma's regime playing chauffeur. Clearly the junta had no idea one of its low-level agents in Lashio was the brainchild of this endeavor. The Wa would watch how the regime handled it and—if all went smoothly—try to gradually scale it up. Suggest, down the line, that the United States pick up the tab and fund more development in Wa State, saving the junta a boatload of cash. Eventually get the Burmese comfortable enough to let in American experts who'd modernize the Wa nation. And all to the junta leaders' benefit, Saladino thought, because if they didn't bungle this opportunity laid at their feet, they'd come out of this smelling better than ever.

All that was theoretical, contingent on this initial trip going well. Saladino hadn't briefed the State Department yet, but he'd have to do that before the trip, scheduled to take place in a few weeks. The diplomats would balk, but he hoped they wouldn't balk too hard. He wasn't proposing that the United States spend a single cent—not yet, at least—only that the embassy stand aside and let him go to Wa State and help the junta incinerate a heroin lab. The grand stuff about deploying teachers and physicians and technicians could come later. For now, baby steps. Saladino hadn't even briefed his own analyst.

Bian was coming down the walk now. She hopped into the passenger seat, and Saladino began to drive. Bian, it's happening, he said. The DEA is going to the Burma-China border. Up to Wa State. He explained everything, reminding her that no American had ever officially stepped on Wa soil. DEA agents would be the first—a narc's version of the moon landing.

Eyes on the road, Saladino could feel Bian radiating excitement. "She was really happy," he said. "She says, 'Oh, when I get there, I'm gonna do this. I'm gonna do that.' That's when I had to tell her. You're not going. Just me and Bruce are going."

Her mood went black. It darkened with each new sentence coming out of his mouth. It's too dangerous, Bian. We'll be in Wa hands, you know. Even the Burmese can't bring their rifles. We'll just have pistols: my Sig Sauer, Bruce's Glock. Besides, there's not enough space in the junta's helicopters for extra passengers.

But I deserve to go. I've been here longer than Bruce.

Bruce is an *agent*, he said. You know that.

"I was trying to reason with her," Saladino said. "She's acting like it's a trip to Disneyland. She'd be unarmed, and I couldn't protect her. I mean, I knew she'd be disappointed. But I didn't expect her to go bonkers."

Bian exhausted herself with rage. Anger gave way to tears. Then wounded silence.

In the coming months, that morning drive would replay itself over and over in Saladino's mind. He would come to know what it was like to be hated by Bian, whose refusal to accept the word *no* had propelled her far in life, to places few people from her background had ever reached.

In taking up this quixotic venture with Superstar, he'd braced himself for resistance from neurotic Burmese generals and contemptuous American diplomats. But never from his own analyst. "One ripple in time," Saladino said. "You never know the damage it can cause. She just came at me like a freaking meteor."

THE BURN

My first contact with Bian was a cold call. I caught her behind the wheel of her Tesla, killing time at a charging station on the West Coast. Though initially suspicious—"I'm retired. Who gave you this number?"—she warmed up quick. Especially when I asked her to elucidate the unsung role of the narcotics intelligence analyst.

We are keepers of deep knowledge in the Drug Enforcement Administration, she said. "These agents, many can barely pronounce the traffickers' names. We want to know their life stories. Their routes, their methods, the whole shebang. Agents will say, 'All you analysts do is write reports.' They make fun of us! But I always respected intelligence—having started off with the CIA."

No kidding, I said. Tell me more.

"That's secret information. I probably can't divulge it." Then silence.

"You know, Patrick? I don't think anyone has had a more interesting career than me. And I don't regret a thing."

I eventually got Bian to share an edited version of her backstory. It helped me understand why Angelo Saladino's decision enraged her so much. Bian had traveled a long, hard road in life, too far to tolerate anyone sidelining her on a pretext of keeping her "safe." She'd been born in North Vietnam in the 1940s to a family deemed "bourgeoisie" by the local communists, and in her youth they fled to South Vietnam. But Bian wanted to go further. As a young woman, she made it to California, where she applied to the US military's Defense Language Institute. The Vietnam War was raging, and she taught US officers Vietnamese so they could read intercepts or interrogate prisoners of war.

One day, some official-looking men came around and tapped her on the shoulder. They claimed to represent a governmental division outside

Washington, DC, one of the boring ones. They offered a better-paying job, and she accepted. They flew her out to Dulles Airport, picked her up at baggage claim, and led her to a car. "That's when they told me who I was really going to work for."

The Central Intelligence Agency. Bian freaked out. She hadn't signed up for this. "But I'd already packed up and moved all my earthly belongings. I decided to go with the wind. That was the beginning of my career in intelligence. They taught me a lot." The CIA sent her to wartime Saigon. She doesn't talk about these years. When the conflict ended, her position did too, so Bian decamped to Bangkok and found a job with the DEA.

In 1988, when a spot opened up at the DEA's Burma office, she took it. Saladino arrived the following year, and for a while life in Yangon was "hunky dory." She fondly remembers lakeside dinners with Angelo and Barbara Saladino. "We got along fabulously. At first."

So.

About that morning in Angelo Saladino's car.

"I think it all was Bruce's idea." Freezing her out of the trip, she meant. Imitating Bruce Stubbs, she said, "'Oh, it's too dangerous to let her go up there. She's an analyst, she can't carry a gun.' Bullshit. He manipulated Angelo's thinking. Pardon me, Patrick. You've got me worked up!"

Bian recollects the episode differently than Saladino. First of all, I never cried in his passenger seat, she told me. She also contends that "Superstar" Saw Lu had Saladino and Stubbs eating out of his palm. Saw Lu was a decent man but too much of a dreamer, she said, and Stubbs in particular grew infatuated with him, willing to cross any line to bring to life his unrealistic vision—even teaming up with the junta. Any plan that required nuzzling up to an evil regime, she said, was not a good one. Lapsing into her Stubbs imitation, she said, "'Who are we to criticize? We're just as corrupt back home.' I mean, come on. Is your loyalty to America or some junta?"

"The whole plan was fantastical," she told me. "A stupid white guy's illusion."

That's her story anyway. Saladino doesn't recall Bian ever taking a principled stand on Burma's junta—not before he barred her from the trip. But after that morning, her attitude changed. Bian would undermine the upcoming trip with "anyone in the expatriate community who would listen," he said. She coined a phrase that went viral inside the embassy: "Hollywood refinery." That's what Saladino and Stubbs were going to help the junta burn down, she claimed. A "sham drug lab," slapped together by the scheming junta, who were probably in cahoots with the Wa.

"She told everyone it was a total setup," Saladino said. It drove him mad. Bian had no evidence to back this up. "But people in the State Department and, you know, *the agency*," he said, "were just waiting to glom onto something like that." The future of the entire Wa race hung on this trip going well; yet she'd reduced it to hot gossip. He asked her to stop.

Bian, Saladino said, if you think the trip is pointless, why do you want to go so badly?

I just want to document the sham, she said.

In November 1990, as the trip neared, State Department headquarters in Washington weighed in, sending a "cable" (diplomatic jargon for a confidential message) asking why the DEA was playing along with the junta's cheap drug war theatrics. Bian's campaign to discredit her boss was spreading far and wide. Yet the State Department still hadn't blocked the trip from going ahead. Maybe the diplomatic corps wanted Saladino and Stubbs to go to Wa State, realize they'd been duped, and return in disgrace.

Inside the DEA office in Yangon, Saladino grumbled about the State Department cable. Bian shrugged and said, you know, they've got a point. Stubbs snapped, "Looks like someone should go work for the State Department and not the DEA!" There was only one way to silence her and all the skeptics she'd created: fly into the Wa peaks praying the United Wa State Army (UWSA) would offer up a real-deal narcotics lab—just as Superstar promised.

ONE GLANCE TOLD them the Wa refinery was real. All they had to do was look down.

Its packed-mud floor was scalded white, discolored by years of toxic chemicals accidentally splashing over the rims of steel drums. Parts of the floor were caked up with spilled product. "You could've taken the first two inches off that floor and made a fortune," Saladino said. "It was pure heroin."

The interior roof thatch was singed with smoke. Hydraulic jacks, used to compress powdery heroin into tight bricks, were creaky with use.

Stacked in the corner were containers of ammonium chloride, lime, acetic anhydride. Saladino snapped photos. This was no Hollywood refinery.

Saladino and Stubbs emerged from the dark interior into cold sunlight. From the outside, it looked like a buffalo barn. On the ground nearby, piled up in mounds, were basketball-sized orbs swaddled in brown leaves. The Wa had laid them out for the agents to inspect. Saladino picked one at random from the pile, flicked open his Swiss Army knife, and slashed it. Opium oozed out, black as blood pudding.

Their Wa hosts had arrayed more valuable wares nearby: oblong bricks wrapped in manila paper, taped up at the corners, piled in stacks. Saladino examined one. Stabbed it. The blade came back light brown. He scraped the tan-colored heroin powder into a plastic baggie and sealed it tight. He sliced open another brick, took another sample. In total, Saladino collected seven heroin baggies and stuffed them into his satchel.[1]

They'd flown to the Wa mountains in an old Bell—a US-made helicopter—along with their Burmese military escorts, who were milling around and taking their own pictures. Even by Wa standards, the site was remote: some one hundred miles north of Panghsang in a scrub forest along the Chinese border. The UWSA had to scrape a dirt square into the mountainside so the helicopter could land. Wa soldiers were all around, wearing floppy green hats leftover from the communist era, with rifles slung across their backs, steel bayonets poking up behind their heads. Sewn onto their sleeves was the UWSA's battle emblem: two spears crossed like an X against a crimson sky.

The DEA agents were pretty sure their hosts hadn't seen white people before. Stubbs grinned at them, and they smiled back, straining to communicate despite having no common language. Some looked young as twelve. Hard to say if they were prepubescent or malnourished. Maybe both. Once the agents were satisfied, UWSA troops splashed diesel over the narcotics and the refinery too. All helped set it aflame: the Wa troops, the DEA agents, their Burmese junta escorts. The roof crackled. Fire ate the walls, reducing the structure to pillars and joists that smoked like blackened ribs, as ash drifted into the periwinkle sky.

Their mission was complete. Back to the helicopter. They piled into the cabin with the Burmese officers, all hoping the aging machine's engine would sputter to life. The American-made chopper, a 1970s-era relic, suffered for lack of replacement parts, which the United States government would no longer provide. But soon the chopper went vertical, rotors thundering over valleys covered in poppy stalks. The Wa troops, staring upward, became small as toy soldiers.

Stubbs came home smiling that day. He was toting a sword. "A Wa sword," Su Yon said, "with a brightly colored handle. It must have been a gift." But this jolly mood didn't last. Later she found him in the grips of a dark mood, kneeling by their bedroom closet, stuffing clothes into a bag. "Bruce was broken up inside. He said, 'Su Yon, you've never seen that kind of poverty. People with no shoes. Big lumps on their necks. I have to bring them clothes and iodine.'

"'OK, Bruce. Before we give away all of our old clothes, shouldn't we buy some new ones first?'

"He didn't laugh. 'I need to have these ready. For next time.'"

But no future trip was assured. Everything hinged on Saladino's heroin samples, scooped into evidence bags and sent by secure courier to DEA headquarters in the Virginian suburbs outside DC. Scientific analysis would determine if the surrendered narcotics were impure. Or worse yet, fake.

An excerpt from that lab report:

Tan Chunky Powder
Net Weight 7.6 Grams
Found to Contain HCl 65 Percent Heroin Base and Calcium
    Chloride

The agents could exhale. Mexican black tar heroin averaged 20 percent purity. The Wa samples ranged 60 to 80 percent, not quite China White quality but potent enough to prove the Wa weren't jerking them around. This experiment had legs. Saladino and Stubbs knew from Saw Lu that the UWSA was keen to pony up more heroin for eradication.

But to continue, DEA headquarters also needed assurances from Burma's junta that this wasn't just a one-off visit. Recurring DEA trips to Wa State would require deeper cooperation with the military's highest echelons. If the DEA was going to catch hell from the State Department and put its reputation on the line—trusting a loathsome regime's word that it was finally ready to do some good—DEA top brass wanted to look Burmese leaders in the eye and measure their sincerity.

IT WAS THE highest-level contact between Burmese and US officials in a long while. A meeting, held in secret, inside a junta facility. Saladino set it up. Sitting at the agent's side were two high-ranking DEA superiors: the chiefs of the Far East section and global heroin investigations. They'd flown all the way to Yangon to meet someone powerful within the junta, and they got nothing less than the head of counterintelligence, a Burmese military colonel from Secretary One's inner circle.[2]

The State Law and Order Restoration Council (SLORC) colonel, plump and affable, appeared happy to see his American visitors. He told them opium was an "age-old problem in Burma," a scourge whipped up by ill-behaved minorities living in "remote, inaccessible border areas." He meant the Wa. Good news was, this new Wa leader, Chairman Zhao Nyi Lai, seemed keen to slow down his organization's opium-and-heroin production, so long as he received a little aid for his sacrifice. A school here, a clinic there. For the time being Burma's military would oblige— as best it could, given its limited budget. The upshot was that junta officials expected the Wa to cough up more drugs, and they welcomed DEA collaboration in burning them. Implicit was an expectation that the junta would receive US adulation for assisting America's War on Drugs.

The DEA chiefs were game. We're ready, they said, to "work closely with Burmese antinarcotic forces." Wondering what else the DEA could wring from this enhanced relationship, they brought up Khun Sa. He was "basically the ruler of a mini-country inside Burma," and the DEA asked when Burmese troops would get around to snaring this drug lord, "bringing him to justice," and extraditing him to the United States.[3] The junta colonel was frank. No time soon, he said. Burmese troops weren't ready to battle Khun Sa's formidable forces. But the UWSA's fearsome warriors might prove useful in this manhunt.

After all, Shanland and the UWSA were rival cartels, and the Wa surely wouldn't want to divest from the drug trade only to watch Khun Sa gobble up their share, grow even stronger, and eventually come for their poppy-rich homeland. The colonel hinted that, if properly incentivized, the UWSA might fight its way into Shanland, capture Khun Sa, and hand him over to the junta. Whether the junta then passed the drug lord to the DEA would depend on the state of US-Burma relations.

It was all hypothetical but enticing nonetheless. If the DEA partnering with the junta could result in the UWSA shutting down heroin production *and* Khun Sa's downfall, that deal was too good to pass up. Hell, even the State Department itself called Khun Sa "the worst enemy the world has."[4] It wasn't every day that America had the opportunity to neutralize two giant cartels in a country producing half the world's opium.[5] The DEA was confident US citizens cared more about drying up the global heroin supply than isolating some junta in a country hardly any American could find on a map.

Saladino and his DEA bosses left that meeting more determined than ever to expand cooperation with Burma's military—no matter how much the diplomats kicked and screamed. Surely the White House and Congress would see the promise this arrangement held, force the State Department to stand aside, and allow the DEA to make history.

THE DEA'S INTENSIFYING fixation on Burma perturbed the State Department, still committed to its cat-kicking policy. Gossip about the DEA's intimate talks with the junta was swirling around Washington, DC. But actually reining in the narcs was a task that fell most heavily upon one man: Pancho Huddle.

Huddle was number two at the US embassy in Burma, behind Ambassador Burt Levin. By October 1990, Levin's tour was over, and as sometimes happens in countries the State Department despises, the United States declined to designate another ambassador—a way of snubbing the ruling government. That left Huddle running the embassy as de facto ambassador, a role called chargé d'affaires. "I sat in the ambassador's chair," he told me. "I did the ambassador's job."

Huddle was a Harvard man: lean, balding, articulate, and unlike the outgoing ambassador, he wasn't propelled by righteous anger. Saladino clocked him as a cold political climber, someone who cared more about impressing his superiors in DC than any particular agenda. Like most diplomats, Huddle was schmoozy. He talked with his hands, and when he spoke, they sometimes twirled as if possessed of their own mind. He enjoyed attention and loved holding piano recitals for embassy staff. "He'd play these complicated pieces, Bach or whatever," Saladino said. "He was mechanical, hitting all the right notes, but it always sounded weird. Like there was no feeling there."

Huddle found Saladino cordial enough. "Angelo was a nice guy. But the DEA, they were marching to their own drum. DEA had this very close relationship with Burmese military intelligence. And they were explicitly undermining State's position."

Which was?

"Marginalizing Burma," he said. "A hardline human rights agenda."

"If I was a full ambassador," Huddle told me, "it would've been easier to control them. But DEA had their own constituency in Congress, small but strong."[6] Back in Washington, DEA officials were bending politicians' ears, telling them the State Department's fanatical hatred of the junta undermined a drug war breakthrough in Burma. "They put me in a difficult position."

So did the CIA. The embassy's CIA station chief was hounding Huddle. He wanted the chargé d'affaires to invoke his authority and yank Saladino's leash. Hard. Not only were the DEA narcs pursuing their own parallel policy in Burma—which they had no right to do—but they were too cozy with Burma's military, namely the all-powerful intelligence division. Narcs were supposed to pal around with other cops, not ingratiate themselves with foreign spymasters. That was the CIA's job. "CIA wanted [Burma's] military intelligence working with CIA, not DEA," Huddle said. The CIA station chief told the chargé, Kick them out and let us handle drug-trade surveillance in Burma. Whatever the DEA does, we'll do it better. Put them in their place.

Meanwhile, the DEA was trying to scale up in Burma, not down. With all the scintillating possibilities at hand, they wanted a big team in the country, not two agents and an analyst. Huddle felt stuck in the middle, but there was no question which side he'd pick. Displeasing the CIA is never a wise career move. "I'm going to tell you something," Huddle said. "State doesn't have good control over CIA, OK? They have their own classified mechanisms—the need to know—and that keeps us from peeking into their world. The agency can run fairly wild."

Reasoning it was smarter to piss off the narcs than the spies, Huddle went to Saladino and put his foot down. Your DEA office will not expand. You're maxed out at three positions. Deal with it.

At that moment, Bian's position was doomed. If the DEA could have only three personnel in Burma, Saladino wanted three full-fledged special agents: guys who could travel to Wa country, guns on hips. As he saw it, Bian was now more than just a pain in the neck. She was taking up valuable space.

DEA headquarters agreed, and Bian got her marching orders in January 1991. She'd intended to spend at least five years in Burma, but she wouldn't even reach year three. Headquarters gave her a few months to wrap up her work and move stateside, insisting her transfer wasn't punishment for the "Hollywood refinery" comments. Analysts, her bosses said, were free to hold dissenting opinions.

But Bian wasn't buying it. Nor did she intend to go quietly.

MARCH 13, 1991.

The morning started hot, and by noon the city burned. Downtown Yangon was a grid of colonial red-brick buildings holding heat like a kiln. The embassy was located near the Yangon River, and in the shimmering distance, barges churned the silty brown current and hooted their horns. Three floors down from the DEA office, on the baking sidewalk, roving vendors cried out their wares.

The mood inside the DEA office was sour, a funereal silence punctuated by the occasional jangling phone. Three months to go before Bian's departure. Saladino and Stubbs wouldn't say anything of substance within her earshot. She'd sometimes inquire about Superstar. Oh, Superstar? Stubbs would say, fiddling with his mustache. Haven't heard from him in a while. He was lying to her face, freezing her out. Bian was sure of it.

The phone rang. It was Col. Kyaw Thein, deputy to the dictator, Secretary One Khin Nyunt. Requesting a meeting with Saladino.

Urgently.

Saladino met KT in a nondescript café. The look on the colonel's face indicated some terrible disclosure to come. SLORC's good cop had some bad news. It's Secretary One, KT said. He has asked me to convey "extreme displeasure." He is drafting an order to purge the DEA from Burma—all three of you—and once he signs it, you'll have seventy-two hours to leave the country. Saladino was baffled. The DEA and the junta were tighter than ever. What the hell was this about?

KT held in his hands a transcript of a radio story aired days before by Voice of America (VOA), the State Department's in-house broadcaster. As the junta saw it, VOA was a shameless US government mouthpiece. "Very Overtly Aggressive," they called it in junta newspapers because, around the world, VOA set up towers within range of rival countries and bombarded the airwaves with American propaganda. Its most recent lies concerned the UWSA heroin lab torched in front of Saladino and Stubbs, alongside Burmese officers. The VOA insinuated that the lab was fake, and this "news" was being pumped into every Burmese house or hut with a shortwave radio.[7]

Maybe the DEA didn't understand how quid pro quo arrangements worked: the junta helps US narcotics agents eradicate drugs, the US stops villainizing Burma. That was the deal. Or perhaps the DEA was too weak to make the State Department shut up? Either way, KT said, Secretary One felt "cooperation with the DEA has been unrecognized and unrewarded." Colonel KT sent Saladino away with a piece of advice. Tell my boss this will never happen again. Put it in a letter. Do it today. There's a small chance he'll change his mind.

Back at the DEA office, Saladino hunched over his computer terminal, office door shut. Stubbs paced behind him chewing a pipe stem. They had to conjure words that would soothe a dictator—and fast. The screen's cursor blinked green.

To: Major General Khin Nyunt, Secretary Number One. Nothing will please your "naysayers" more, Saladino typed, than expelling the DEA. "Many Myanmar anti-narcotics programs are just now beginning to bear fruit." Myanmar. That was SLORC's new name for the country, signaling a break from the British colonial past. US officials were instructed to keep calling the country Burma—a middle finger to the regime. But Saladino couldn't risk offending Secretary One over semantics.

"As SLORC success in these areas continues, even the most biased critics will be silenced and lose credibility." He wrote that bigger and bolder antidrug projects, executed with DEA guidance, would "painfully wound many of Myanmar's most vociferous critics."

In other words, the State Department.

"Be assured that I, and my staff, will continue to use our own professional credibility—and that of the DEA as the premier narcotics law enforcement agency in the world—to ensure that your anti-narcotics efforts are accurately represented to the world at large." Signed, Angelo M. Saladino, DEA Country Attaché.

It was an obsequious letter, no doubt. If seen by Washington's anti-junta clique—State Department stalwarts, plus a bipartisan congressional club led by Republican Mitch McConnell and Democrat Daniel Patrick

Moynihan—they'd want his head on a platter. Already this clique hoped to snuff out any budding DEA-junta cooperation in Burma. But Saladino didn't intend for them to see the letter. He considered it private correspondence between the DEA and the SLORC.

Printing it on official stationary and laying the letter on his desk, Saladino felt a twinge of hesitation. He couldn't send such a strongly worded memo without DEA headquarters' approval. So he made some calls to the mothership. No one picked up. It was afternoon in Burma, the dead of night on America's East Coast. His superiors were fast asleep some eight thousand miles away. Time was running out.[8]

Saladino stuck the letter in his office safe and closed its steel door. He drove back to KT's office. He explained his predicament. I can't give Secretary One a signed letter, but if I could, here's what it would say. KT nodded and promised to relay his response to the dictator upstairs.

The next forty-eight hours were agony. Saladino and Stubbs could only wait and wonder, Was the dream too good to be true? Over the course of many safe house visits, Saw Lu had woven a beautiful vision for them, indelible in their minds. Most narcs were lucky to bust a heap of coke or smack every so often, maybe make the papers once in their careers, but with Saw Lu's help, Saladino and Stubbs were going to uplift an entire race, all while sparing some unknowable number of Americans from addiction. But how easily this dream could burst like a soap bubble—pricked by something banal as a VOA story. "You know what it felt like?" Saladino said. "You're on an island hauling the treasure back to the boat. And a fucking coconut falls on your head, killing you on the spot. It was not the end I'd hoped for."

KT called. Secretary One's temper was settling. You can remain in Burma, he said. As you were. Such was life under dictatorship, your fate hinging on a tyrant's volcanic moods.

For a while, life went back to normal—as normal as it'd been anyways. Lakeside drinks between the Stubbs and Saladino clans, pig roasts and lobster feasts. Canoe jaunts around Inya Lake. But tension pervaded everything. Funnily enough, Aung San Suu Kyi lived two houses down from the Saladinos; the junta held her under house arrest on her family estate, ringed with palm groves and steel gates. Sometimes the Saladinos would take the boat out, and if it drifted too close to her property, Burmese soldiers would emerge at the shoreline with bullhorns, shouting at them to turn away.

Around this time, Saw Lu convinced Chairman Lai to up the ante. Wa State's leader was prepared to offer more UWSA heroin and more refineries to the junta, all while demanding staffed medical clinics and schools in exchange for this sacrifice. This was all part of Saw Lu's plan. He believed the regime would go along with the drugs-for-aid project for a while but eventually cry broke, claiming it couldn't afford to develop Wa State on its own. The US could then volunteer to pick up the tab—and also offer to send in American teachers and doctors. The junta, desperate for US approval, would allow them to come, and this would crack open the door to a brighter future: his civilizing fantasy realized. Saw Lu thought that if the DEA and UWSA played their role, they could slow-walk the junta into doing exactly what he wanted. He'd gamed the whole thing out in his head like a chess match.

But Saladino didn't want Saw Lu to get ahead of himself. He needed the confidential informant (CI) to understand the precarity of their dream. Any plan reliant on junta leaders was volatile. Sometimes they seemed thirsty for US approval; sometimes they raged over minor slights. Move with extreme caution, Saladino said. Secretary One still believed his junta—and his junta alone—was all that could link the United States to the Wa. If he discovered they were backdooring him, trying to pull his strings like a puppet, he'd erupt. Perhaps violently.

So Saw Lu kept his head down and kept producing intel for the DEA: the amalgamated secrets of many rebel groups and syndicates, not just the UWSA. Sometimes he'd include details of bribe-taking Burmese military bigwigs in his reports, but Saladino and Stubbs warned him that with so much at stake, this was far too risky. Getting caught snooping on regime officers would put the dream in jeopardy. "I didn't want to hear about colonel so-and-so helping someone smuggle drugs," Saladino said. "I needed good cooperation with Burma's government—for his sake and ours."

EARLY SUMMER, 1991.

Saladino and Stubbs had always suspected they were being watched. Even when the DEA and the junta were on harmonious terms, Burmese spies probably trailed them now and again. That's what police states do. But now the two agents felt a sickly premonition that even the US embassy was no sanctuary from surveillance—that the walls of their DEA office had ears. Only it wasn't Burmese spies doing the listening.

"Everything got very weird," Saladino said. "Certain things we discussed in the office would be brought up to us immediately" by State Department personnel, namely Pancho Huddle, the de facto ambassador. He'd come around asking intrusive questions about operations—queries that betrayed a knowledge of private conversations between Saladino and Stubbs. "It was spooky. Obviously, we were being monitored."

Suppose there was a bug in the office. Who'd planted it? The State Department's CIA pals? Saladino considered sweeping the office for wiretaps, looked around at the chipped furniture and the corrugated white ceiling tiles, and figured it was pointless. "There were just so many places to hide a bug. I didn't know where to start. But from that point onward, if Bruce and I discussed something operational, we instinctively put our heads close together and whispered."

Saladino asked himself if John Tin Aung, his Burmese fixer, was involved. He decided that if John wanted to double-cross the DEA, he'd have done it a long time ago. Saladino felt he had no choice but to trust John and enjoin him to help tighten up security. He went to John quietly and asked him to secure a new safe house for their Saw Lu meetups. Do it quick, he said, and no matter what, don't tell Bian.

Saladino then knelt by the steel safes containing his most-sensitive material, including Superstar's reports and receipts, and changed the combination codes. Moving forward, he told John and Stubbs, we must do more to protect our files. Inside the US embassy there was a room containing a gas-fired, potbellied oven and, for nonburnable objects, a fifty-five-gallon barrel of acid. Any nonessential material even hinting at Saw Lu's covert role had to be destroyed. Pronto.

But Saladino worried he was too late in stepping up vigilance. Bian already knew too much, and if she were inclined to blow up his operation—perhaps by sharing delicate information with the DEA's detractors—there wasn't much he could do to stop her. In memos to DEA headquarters, Saladino warned of Bian's "ongoing personal vendetta" against him and Stubbs and possibly Saw Lu. Our "network of CIs in Burma" is known to her, he wrote, including "identities, addresses . . . means and methods of communication." It was "virtually impossible" to gauge how many files she might've already stolen. "You may say I was paranoid," Saladino told me. "No. This was not just paranoia."

To his great relief, Bian finally left Burma in June, moving on to an analyst position in San Francisco. The monsoons started up not long after.

Throughout that drenched summer, Saladino wondered which institution would move against him: the junta or the State Department or the CIA. He lived as if swords were dangling above his head, waiting to drop.

In August, one did.

His private letter to Secretary One was no longer private. Someone must've pilfered it from his safe, duplicated it, and passed it around Washington, DC. Because now a prominent State Department official named Parker Borg had a copy and demanded to know why the DEA's lead agent in Burma had written a love letter to Secretary One—a man known to DC's anti-Burma lawmakers as the "Prince of Darkness."[9]

Hold on, Saladino protested. That's an unsent memo. It was never supposed to leave my safe. How on earth did a copy end up all the way in Washington? Borg wouldn't answer. Saladino cursed himself. He should have changed those safe codes earlier.

Saladino feared the letter would ruin his two-decade career. It was exactly what the State Department desired: written proof that he'd gone far too rogue in undercutting official US policy. He could only hope DEA headquarters would have his back once the diplomats demanded his firing, as they surely would.

Barbara saw it in her husband's red eyes. He was starting to break. Inside their lakefront home, Saladino confessed to hopelessness. Barbara, I can't do it. They won't let me do my job. He asked her over and over, Why am I even here?

Barbara could always fortify her husband before he snapped. It's simple, she said. You're here on the US taxpayer's dollar. That's who you serve, and they want you to stop drugs from coming into America. So you're going to get up and go to work tomorrow—and you'll keep going until our government stops you. "We're just regular Americans," she told me. "In some ways, we were babes in the woods. Not understanding what we'd gotten into."

Not long after, Barbara was sunning by the swimming pool at the American Club. She sensed a figure hovering above her. Some broad-shouldered stranger blocking her light. The man did not introduce himself.

"Hey," he said in a Texas drawl. "Don't be stupid. You tell your husband. Don't be stupid."

Barbara sat up. "Excuse me?"

"Tell him to play golf for the rest of his time here. Tell him to enjoy his time in Burma. Just don't be stupid."

She started to respond, but the stranger was walking away. "I knew it right away. This man was CIA. CIA all the way." Don't be stupid. When Barbara told her husband, he knew exactly what that meant. Stop talking to the junta. Abandon your crazy Wa fantasy. Submit to the State Department and never go against the CIA. From that day onward, the Saladinos knew that no place was sacred, not even their home. It was filled with furniture and appliances provided by the State Department, which furnished the homes of all embassy personnel, including DEA agents.

My house in Yangon, Saladino told me, was almost certainly bugged—"and not by the Burmese." In the living room, in the bedroom, the couple kept conversation light. If they had something delicate to say, they went outside and stood near the jacaranda tree, convening by the lake's edge.

BIAN DOESN'T DENY that she wanted Saladino to take a fall. A hard one.

After leaving Burma, en route to her new post in San Francisco, she stopped by DEA headquarters in the Virginia suburbs outside DC. Bian went straight to the inspections division, headed by a man named Matty Maher, an acquaintance. "I'd known him for years. I trusted him." DEA inspectors are charged with sniffing out agents gone screwy or corrupt—and Bian had plenty to say about Saladino.

"I was a whistle-blower," Bian told me. What she had blown the whistle on, however, she did not seem eager to discuss. "It was a long time ago."

Did she leak Saladino's unsent letter to Secretary One? "A letter?" Bian claimed not to remember it. So I emailed her a copy I'd acquired. She replied as if she'd never seen it: "OMG! I can't believe what I read. It makes me want to throw up." But the letter was referenced in her DEA whistle-blower complaint.[10]

All Bian admitted to sharing at DEA headquarters was this: Saladino and Stubbs were overly smitten with Saw Lu and his grandiose visions—"illusions," she called them—and everyone knows agents and CIs aren't supposed to get that cozy. She had to ring the alarm. "I mean, who the hell did they think they were?"

Thing was, I knew Bian also accused Saladino of something else—something far worse than getting googly-eyed for a hotshot informant. This allegation was so damning that, if proven true, it could've landed her ex-boss in federal prison. Sitting in that inspector's office, she suggested

that Special Agent Angelo Saladino might be fleecing the DEA for tens
of thousands of dollars—and that his "Superstar" informant was possibly
connected to the crime.

I asked Bian about this. Long pause.

"How did you hear that story?"

SEPTEMBER 1991.

By some miracle, Saladino still clung to his job, though he knew the
State Department was pressuring the DEA to fire him, or at least transfer
him out of Burma. He took solace in believing DEA headquarters would
at least put up a fight on his behalf. His superiors seemed to understand
the incredible stress he was under. They'd even offered him a brief respite,
inviting Saladino to Hong Kong for a routine intel-sharing roundtable
with colleagues. A few days away from the Yangon snake pit would serve
him well.

On his way to Hong Kong, on an overnight layover in Bangkok, Saladino caught up with a fellow agent with whom he'd worked in Thailand.
His friend seemed to know something Saladino didn't. Something he
wasn't supposed to share. As the night wound down, he turned abruptly
serious and blurted out, Angelo, I think you should hire a lawyer.

Huh?

A criminal lawyer, his friend added. That's all I can say.

The next day, in Hong Kong, Saladino entered the local DEA office
and found it unnervingly quiet. There was no roundtable. Instead a pair
of inspectors cornered him and said the words enforcers of the law love
to deliver but never expect to receive: You have the right to remain silent.
Anything you say can and will be used against you in a court of law.

Whatever this is, Saladino said, I'll cooperate. Good, they told him.
You're released to fly back to Yangon. We'll travel separately, ahead of you.
Meet us inside your office.

The inspectors awaited him on the embassy's third floor, amid the
curling carpet and nicked chairs. They asked for his safe combinations.
They'd yet to clarify his supposed crimes, but he knew it was bad when he
saw Matty Maher walking in. Maher was the DEA's top-ranking internal
inspector: fast talking, New York Irish, total ballbreaker. He wouldn't fly
all the way to Burma—twenty-four hours minimum in economy seats—
on some minor suspicion.

Inspector Maher was full of questions about Saladino's receipts for payments to CIs. "That's when I understood," Saladino said. "They were accusing me of stealing money." The inspectors splayed out the forms and pointed to the signatures: some in Burmese, some in Chinese, some in Wa. They asked what game Saladino was playing.

Clearly multiple informants signed the forms—or maybe they were bullshit names, invented by Saladino to rack up cash payments that he pocketed himself. Roughly $40,000 had gone out the door to these three signatures. He could either account for each CI, proving they were real people, or face embezzlement charges. "It was insane. I tried to explain." That's a single, highly prolific CI called Superstar, he said, and he likes to sign receipts in different languages. "But everything was cast in a suspicious light. Maher was well prepared. He already had lots of information about the signatures before he'd even arrived." As if he'd already seen photocopies of the receipts, which weren't supposed to leave Saladino's safe.

Again, Saladino winced. The safe codes. If only he'd changed them sooner. Someone must've ransacked his files, made copies, and handed them over. And Saladino was certain who that someone was.

Only one man could clear Saladino's name now, but it just so happened Saw Lu was nearly impossible to summon. What a nicely crafted frame job, he thought. Bian must've assumed "there was no way I could get Superstar to come in on short notice." He only emerged at times of his own choosing, when he could visit Yangon on some official errand and sneak in a DEA tryst. Though Superstar typically went weeks or even a month without contact, Saladino needed him to appear in the flesh within twenty-four hours—or else the agent would face prison time. "I went to John and said, 'Please. Reach out to him.' I was breaking protocol but they were practically ordering me to do it."

Nervous hours passed. John came back to Saladino. Superstar is on his way.

When Saw Lu stepped into the safe house, he found Saladino and three unfamiliar Americans already inside. Inspector Maher sat at a table, yellow legal pad at the ready. Maher behaved like a man in charge, so Saw Lu pulled back the chair across from him and sat down. "I could see it in Matty Maher's face," Saladino said. "He thought he had us."

Maher slid the pad across the table and slapped down a pen. "Do it. Sign your name. Fast!"

Saw Lu's movements were swift but controlled. "I'll never forget it," Saladino said. "Like a freaking Xerox machine. Chinese. Bap, bap, bap! Ten times. Burmese. Bap, bap, bap! Wa. He was completely cool about it." Saw Lu skidded the pad back across the table. Black ink streaked the canary-yellow page in neat columns. His signatures matched the receipts perfectly. He awaited further questions. But there wasn't much else to say.[11] Saladino's reputation was cleared.

The investigators flew back to the States. Saw Lu caught a bus back to Lashio. Saladino, rescued from the abyss, resumed his job and awaited the next crisis.

It didn't take long to manifest.

For two whole years, he'd followed protocol perfectly. Used a code name for Saw Lu. Set up a safe house just for him. Only met Saw Lu when Saw Lu deemed it safe. Anything outside this protocol put his CI at risk, potentially exposing to the Burmese police state that one of their own, a low-level junta asset from Lashio, was engaged in unauthorized communication with a US government agency.

But under pressure, forced to rectify false allegations, Saladino broke the protocol. He'd drawn Saw Lu to the capital on short notice, into a meeting with three DEA officials fresh off a plane. Secretary One's gestapo might not follow Saladino's every move. But Burmese spies would not fail to track the movements of a high-ranking DEA inspector, who'd descended on their country. The junta would want to know what—or whom—he'd come all that way to inspect.

TORPEDO

Father kept secrets.

Where he went. Whom he met. Saw Lu would vanish from their house atop the hill in Lashio for days, and his children weren't allowed to ask questions. "You know he was a guerrilla leader, right? Back in the sixties? Well, he ran our family just like a militia," said one of Saw Lu's eight kids, whom I'll call Isaac. "Dad was a great caregiver. But no jokes, nothing funny. We had to follow his orders."

Isaac was in his early twenties: studious, obedient, in awe of his father. He still cherished the moment when Saw Lu finally confided in hushed tones, *There is an American organization called the D-E-A, sworn to eliminate drugs worldwide, and I am their confidant in Burma. One day, all will behold the greatness that can arise when the American and Wa civilizations unite. Until then, Isaac, no one can know what I am planning. Not your siblings. Not even your mother.*

Isaac felt deeply gratified by his father's trust. "Dad never told me what he discussed with the DEA. But on rare occasions, he'd bring me to their meeting place"—the safe house in Yangon—"and make me wait outside. As a lookout. I think he was grooming me to take over in case something bad happened."

One chill morning in January 1992, two or three soldiers appeared at the concrete porch of their Lashio home. The troops were cordial. *Apologies, Saw Lu, your presence is required inside Northeast Command HQ, but we'd be honored to give you a ride.*

Just a moment, Saw Lu said. *My son will join us.* He shouted inside the house, calling for Isaac. The soldiers went to open the truck doors. When Isaac emerged, Saw Lu shot him a look and whispered, *Stay close.* In quiet they rode down Lashio's cracked streets, past the airport, toward Northeast Command HQ, a complex of hulking gray structures surrounded by iron fencing. The front gates were ajar, and the instant the truck rolled onto the base, black hoods went over both their heads.

Isaac reflexively flailed his arms. Tried to, at least, but felt steel biting into his wrists. Deft as magicians, the soldiers had clapped on handcuffs without him noticing. Thick cloth muffled his shouts and sucked against his lips when he gasped for air.

The soldiers jostled father and son out of the truck cabin and frog-marched them in different directions. Black fabric eliminated all sight. When they dehooded Isaac, he was indoors, standing cuffed and disoriented in a small cell that stank of mildew. He asked where they'd taken his father, but at the first syllable of protest, a soldier punched his jaw. Isaac spun and fell. Heavy boots stomped his chest, and he feared they'd crush his ribs.

Sometime later—minutes, hours, he couldn't say—Isaac regained consciousness with his cheek on the cool cement floor, his tongue tasting copper, his teeth feeling loose. From the next cell over, he heard sharp wailing. Isaac recognized the voice, but he had not known his father could make that sound.

SAW LU'S CELL was an identical black box, roughly ten feet square. Cement floors. Metal door, no windows. No bed. No toilet or drain. Weeks passed as his waste puddled on the floor where he slept. In that nothingness, time stopped. He'd lay supine with eyes open, watching phosphenes float like electric blue amoebas.

Every so often the cell door clattered open, and strong hands would grab him under the armpits and drag him down a corridor, then up some stairs. He wore leg irons, and the limp chain between the two ankle rings drooped behind him, scraping noisily against the ground. The soldiers would carry him into an open courtyard where daylight seared his retinas. There was banyan tree growing there, and they'd deposit him beneath that tree and ply their trade: torture.

They flayed him—flipped Saw Lu on his belly and whipped him with a bicycle chain until the tiny metal teeth had raked his back clean off. One some days, they froze him. Beneath the banyan tree they kept a metal tub filled to the rim with ice water. It was winter in Burma's north with temperatures in the forties; a long soak risked hypothermia. Drop your sarong and get in, they said. The cold blued his lips and slowed his heart. When Saw Lu didn't look miserable enough, a soldier would mash his head underwater until his screams made bubbles.

Supervising the torture was Maj. Than Aye, a Secretary One disciple, Northeast Command HQ's commander. As regional intelligence chief he ruled over the surrounding foothills like some junta liege. Tallish and fair skinned, Than Aye grinned at odd moments, even when threatening murder—and he was seriously inclined to murder Saw Lu.

The junta had discovered Saw Lu's treachery more than a month before. Curious about the visiting Drug Enforcement Administration inspector, Matty Maher, Burmese spies trailed Maher to a nondescript home—the DEA's Yangon safe house—and staked it out. They were startled when, not long after, Saw Lu turned up, walked into the house, discussed something, then walked out. They'd not expected this from their Wa golden boy: a trusted asset for twenty-five years. Clearly Saw Lu had turned traitor, gabbing to US agents behind closed doors. But the junta's spies didn't yet understand what value he held to the DEA. Determining that fell to Maj. Than Aye, spymaster of northern Shan State, the region in which Saw Lu lived.

Once Saw Lu returned to Lashio, Than Aye put tails on him and his associates and probably tapped their phones. He determined that Saw Lu usually conveyed secrets to the DEA through handwritten, hand-delivered reports. Laying hands on one of those reports was the key to discovering the nature of Saw Lu's traitorousness. So Than Aye waited until early January, when Saw Lu completed his next parcel of files, intending to intercept him on his way to Yangon. But some intuition told Saw Lu, Play it safe this time. Don't go yourself. Send the report to the DEA through a trusted messenger.

This was no setback to Than Aye. His men nabbed Saw Lu's messenger en route, ripped the files from his hands, and beat him senseless. They drove to Northeast Command HQ and dropped the report on the major's desk. The contents positively enraged Than Aye: Saw Lu's report was largely about *him*, describing in pristine detail the major's collusion with upcountry drug traffickers.

Angelo Saladino and Bruce Stubbs had cautioned Saw Lu: Don't rat on Burmese officers, it's not worth it. Get caught poking into junta business and our experiment in Wa State goes swirling down the drain. Just stick to reporting on traffickers. But this was a hard rule to follow. In Burma's north, junta officers were entangled with the drug trade, so much so that, for Saw Lu, excluding them from reports proved tricky.

Junta officers weren't drug producers or smugglers. They were toll collectors. Opium transporters affiliated with various drug lords—Khun Sa and another megatrafficker named Lo Hsing Han—needed to move opium from remote mountain villages to heroin refineries, often a long-distance journey. They'd dole out cash to the likes of Maj. Than Aye for the privilege of breezing through military checkpoints. No trafficker could move dope along the region's highways unmolested without paying Northeast Command HQ. And in a stroke of horrid luck, Saw Lu's latest report described Than Aye's kickback system exhaustively.[1]

Had the major intercepted a different report, he might've discovered Saw Lu conveying minutia about the United Wa State Army (UWSA): profit statements, maybe poppy yields in Wa country. Saw Lu still would've suffered punishment for unsanctioned contact with US agents, maybe decades in a cell. But he wouldn't have Than Aye itching to bury him alive.

It wasn't that Than Aye feared his own government discovering his kickbacks; intelligence officers taking bribes was no secret inside the regime. But Saw Lu was detailing this narco-corruption to the American government, and for all Burma's junta knew, the United States had some devastating purpose in mind—like using this dirt to justify heavy US sanctions. This wasn't the case at all—the DEA was desperate to *avoid* upsetting the regime—but this report made Saw Lu look like a garden variety snitch: a junta insider selling secrets to a malevolent foreign power.

Inside Northeast Command HQ, the major's subordinates thrashed Saw Lu bloody for weeks. But they always stopped short of killing him. Saw Lu didn't understand why until Than Aye stood over him holding a sheet of paper. I am not unmerciful, said the grinning major. I can make the pain stop. All you have to do is sign here. Typed upon the page was a confession: I, Saw Lu, traffic heroin for the UWSA. Everything I've told the DEA is untrue. Maj. Than Aye is innocent.

Sign the paper, the major said. Exonerate me and we'll merely imprison you for life. Otherwise, I'll kill you. Do it for your family's sake.

No, Saw Lu said. I can't sign it.

And why not?

Because I don't traffic drugs. And everything I tell the DEA *is* true.

Round and round they went, the major and his men, thinking up increasingly sadistic methods to shatter Saw Lu's spirit. They starved him of food and water and after three days splashed piss in his face. They clipped electrodes to his penis and wired it to a truck battery. Saw Lu would faint from the shocks but wake up with his answer unchanged. Extreme pain wouldn't budge him. So Than Aye tried a different tack.

Bring his wife to me, the major said. Soldiers went into town, grabbed Mary, and hauled her into the military compound. Ma'am, Than Aye said, if your husband does not sign this confession paper, we're going to kill him. Convince him to do it. Tell him to confess.

Confess to what?

You know what he's done.

No, Mary said. I don't know a thing. I'm just a housewife. Let me ask you something, Major. Does your wife know everything you do when she's not around?

They led her by the hair down to Saw Lu's cell. The soldiers flicked a switch, lighting a bare bulb strung from the ceiling. She saw her husband curled on the floor like a prawn. Wake up, Saw Lu. New ultimatum. Sign the papers or the prison guards will take turns on your wife. We'll hold your head and force you to watch. You have twenty-four hours to decide. Nod if you understand. He nodded.

The sun rose and set. The soldiers returned. What's it going to be?

I think you'll do whatever you like, no matter what I say.

So no?

No.[2]

They marched Saw Lu out of his stinking cell, down the corridor, up the stairs. Over to the banyan tree with its marble-smooth bark and limbs thick as pylons. The stars were out, and a noose had been slung from a branch in anticipation of his recalcitrance. They pushed him onto his back and tore off his blood-caked rags. Saw Lu thought the noose would go around his neck, but instead they looped it around his ankles and cinched hard. When soldiers pulled the other end of the rope, Saw Lu's naked body lurched upward, and he swung like a human pendulum.

When the motion settled, Saw Lu dangled upside down a few feet above the earth, his heart in his skull. Last chance, the soldiers said. Half blind with pain, Saw Lu signaled his refusal. The rope slackened. Saw Lu dropped on his neck.

He was still conscious after the fall, just barely, so once again the rope tautened. Saw Lu levitated and again came down hard. It took three drops to knock him out. His body spasmed in the dirt. The soldiers watched until the convulsions stopped, and then they called for a doctor to check the traitor's vitals and confirm he was finally dead.

SALADINO TRIED HIS damnedest to free Saw Lu. Went to Colonel KT and pleaded. If you won't release him, he said, at least put us in a room for five minutes. Prove he's still alive. The answer was always no.

Not that Saladino had much cachet left with the junta. Burma's government could've driven him from the country after they caught Saladino using one of their civilian intelligence agents as a snitch. But Secretary One's moods were hard to predict. A little Voice of America (VOA) broadcast turned him apoplectic; yet the dictator didn't jettison the DEA over the Saw Lu revelation or even threaten to do so. Perhaps the VOA flareup had been a bluff or a bargaining tactic—or just one of the dictator's tantrums.

The truth was, at that moment, Secretary One needed the DEA more than ever. The potential for a War on Drugs breakthrough in Burma was about the only thing stopping the White House from ratcheting up sanctions and making the country's economy scream. The DEA was a lonely voice in Washington urging restraint against Burma. The DC establishment was otherwise full of bluster, seeking new dragons to slay. The Soviet Union had disintegrated the year prior, and as the Pentagon's top-ranking officer, Colin Powell, put it, "I'm running out of demons. . . . I'm down to [Cuba's Fidel] Castro and [North Korea's] Kim Il Sung."[3] Secretary One did not want to join the ranks of irredeemable supervillains with whom no compromise was possible.

The DEA was Secretary One's only hope—and hope was running thin. With congressional approval, President George H. W. Bush had just invoked a new law giving him carte blanche to impose severe sanctions on Burma at his leisure, even blocking loans from international financial institutions. Punishment would not go into effect, however, as long as Burma improved either its "human rights" or its "counternarcotics efforts."[4] The former was a nonstarter: the junta was a machine built to subjugate minorities and dissenters and deny them what the West called "rights." The latter, however, was negotiable. If the DEA wanted to roast more Wa heroin, and the UWSA was still game, Secretary One was inclined to facilitate—so long as his regime truly controlled all contact between the empire and the tribe. With Saw Lu locked up in a military black site, that seemed all the more doable.

But no matter what happened between the DEA and the Wa, Saladino wouldn't get to see it play out. The embassy was blackballing him so badly that he couldn't function in Burma, so the DEA decided to cut its losses and transfer Saladino stateside. By summer, they'd have him running a cocaine task force in Miami's airport. DEA headquarters was ready to reboot its Yangon office. The plan: bring in a new lead agent and tack on a third agent too, with Stubbs remaining in place to maintain a little continuity. The lead agent would arrive in a few months. The junior agent arrived in March 1992. Acclimating him to Burma would be Saladino's last task in country.

Dave Sikorra was the third agent's name, and he was not quite forty. Clean shaven, curly brown mop, Minnesota nice. Sang choir. Stubbs pegged him as a team player, not an obstructionist like Bian. Reaching out to Sikorra before his arrival, Stubbs told him, Dave, Burma's a hidden gem. It's not as chaotic as you might've heard. The living is easy, and you'll never need to pull your gun. Your wife and kid will love it.

But on day one in Yangon, Sikorra second-guessed his decision. His Midwestern wife, whom he'd met at church, wilted in the atomic heat. He fretted over his ten-year-old autistic son, easily unnerved by intense stimulation. Yangon, in all its riotous technicolor beauty, is nothing if not stimulating: ancient buses disgorging black smoke, mosquitoes nipping your neck, cymbals clanging inside Buddhist temples. Sikorra was feeling a bit overwhelmed himself. That night, Angelo and Barbara Saladino had his family over for steaks. Sikorra only got down a few bites before they welled up in his throat. He sprang from the table, ran outside, and retched in the shrubbery. Came back wiping his mouth, mortified and blaming jet lag.

Sorry about the bushes, Angelo.

Don't worry, Dave. The bushes will be fine.

Agent Sikorra had come to Burma seeking exoticism. Devoutly Catholic, he believed "God may have designed me to be sensitive, but he also designed me for the adventure of life."[5] But when Saladino briefed him on the DEA's state of play in Burma, Sikorra shuddered.

The junta—having abducted some confidential informant (CI) extraordinaire called Superstar—had just ripped the heart out of the DEA's intelligence-gathering system. "It seemed like our whole operation pivoted around this one guy," Sikorra told me. "And now he was detained somewhere, basically hanging by his thumbs." Possibly dead. This Superstar, he learned, was also the brains behind a fledgling project with the UWSA cartel: the Wa burn drugs; the junta builds clinics and schools; the DEA praises Burma's regime to the world. Superstar, at the time of his capture, had just convinced the UWSA leadership to pony up fifty-six kilos of China White, worth $120 million.

Now the whole experiment was up in the air. Sikorra's colleagues explained that, on top of all that, the embassy itself was a hive of saboteurs rooting for their failure. They told him to expect the State Department and its Central Intelligence Agency friends to hobble their progress at every opportunity. As Saladino explained the situation, Sikorra's eyes drifted down to the agent's hands. They trembled. "I could see it with my own eyes. This man's nerves were completely trashed."

Sikorra wondered what a few years in Burma would do to *his* nerves. This was way more adventure than he'd bargained for.

SAW LU AWOKE to red blobs obscuring his vision. He was back in that tiny cell—only now the light was on, and Mary was in there with him. He struggled to sit up, but she made him lay still. He rested on his stomach, his back an archipelago of scabs crusting orange. Don't try to talk, his wife said. Just listen.

There's a doctor in this compound: a fellow prisoner. The soldiers force him to treat their victims—like some physician to the damned. They summoned this doctor to confirm your death under the banyan tree, but he told them you were merely concussed. Mary explained that, after the doctor's diagnosis, Maj. Than Aye's soldiers hauled Saw Lu's half-dead body back to the cell. They threw me in here too, she said, and supplied a tin bucket for our waste.

Two weeks passed in that cell, and Saw Lu slowly regained the ability to swallow food and limp around. Isaac was free by that point, and he'd bring plastic bags full of home-cooked meals to the prison each day. Strangely enough, the guards would actually deliver them. That show of generosity roused Mary's suspicions—for it coincided with a shift in their captors' demeanor. The same men who'd electrocuted Saw Lu would now come by to check on his well-being. They'd even send the doctor each evening to disinfect his wounds. They seem anxious, Mary told her husband. Like they're afraid you'll actually die.

Mary's intuitions were correct. Because after all of Saw Lu's wretched luck, he'd finally caught a break. Not long after his near lynching under the banyan tree, Secretary One and Chairman Lai met face-to-face to discuss the aid-for-eradication program's next steps. Lai was normally genial toward the dictator. But on that day he fumed, having just learned about Saw Lu's captivity. That's my man, the Wa leader said. Let him go.

Secretary One informed Lai that Saw Lu was a spy for the Americans. Lai countered that he didn't give a damn. He offered two choices to the State Law and Order Restoration Council (SLORC): release Saw Lu or prepare for war. Wa commandos in plain clothes are already filtering into Lashio, Lai said, and they will raid Northeast Command HQ on my orders. I don't bluff. We will turn your military base into dust.[6]

On the fifty-sixth day of Saw Lu's confinement, on the road leading to the military base, Isaac pedaled his bike through the morning chill, plastic bags full of rice and curry hanging from his bicycle's handlebars. He'd planned on dropping the food off with guards stationed in front of Northeast Command HQ, as usual. But when he arrived, the gates swung open, and Than Aye strode forward, smirking like a jackal. He had the chalky pallor of a man who spent little time in the sun.

"Why'd you come here on a bike?" The major hadn't even said hello. "Doesn't your family have a truck? Go get it. You'll need it to carry your father back home."

Isaac sped home, fired up the family's old truck, and drove it to the military base. He got out, and the soldiers escorted him inside and down to some subterranean corridor. They opened a cell door, and he saw his parents sitting inside on the floor. "My father was not a man who hugged. But I was too happy to control myself." Isaac stooped down to hug him. He was eager to leave quickly in case the major changed his mind.

Father, please get up. Let's go.

But Saw Lu waved him off. He would not be hurried. Guards loitering in the hallway grew audibly annoyed. Isaac was frustrated too but dared not show it. He watched his father force his shaking body into a kneeling position. Mary and Isaac knew what to do. They knelt beside him, and with a voice like palm fronds rasping in the wind, Saw Lu prayed.

He thanked God for His protection during this trial and those to come. Saw Lu asked the Lord to continue wielding him as a divine instrument through which to assert His will on earth. As he prayed, the cell's overhead lightbulb unscrewed itself from the socket as if twisted by unseen fingers, and when it fell, the room blackened instantly. The family heard glass pinging on concrete and winced, expecting shards to shower their bare feet. But the bulb bounced—once, twice—then rolled into a corner.

Behold, Saw Lu said in the darkness. A miracle. A fragile thing flung against concrete by the Lord's own hand, and still it did not break.

JUNE 1992.

The new lead agent in Burma was testosterone personified. Rick Horn was his name, and Sikorra felt the power in his handshake. He stood in awe of the man's size. "Rick Horn was huge," said Sikorra, himself a slender track runner. "I mean, his arms were bigger than my waist. He was a hulk."

Horn was a two-decade DEA veteran, transferred out of Pakistan. He knew the Burma office by reputation, and he knew exactly why they'd sent him. Saladino was a peaceable man by nature, but as DEA headquarters saw it, the US embassy in Yangon needed a lead narcotics agent who'd embrace conflict if necessary. "The DEA had their beef with the CIA," Sikorra said, "and they sent Rick as a torpedo."

In his first week, Horn was settling into Saladino's former office when the phone rang. Pancho Huddle, the chargé d'affaires and de facto ambassador, wanted him to pop down to the second floor. They'd yet to have a proper chat. Horn walked downstairs and found Huddle sitting at the ambassador's desk, its surface covered in papers. They spoke for several minutes. Then Huddle abruptly swiveled around to face the wall: no "see you later," no "have a nice day." Huddle just leafed through diplomatic cables as if the agent did not exist. Horn stared at the chargé's back for a moment, bewildered, and returned to the third floor. Stubbs was waiting by his office door.

So, Stubbs said with a knowing grin. How'd it go?

Horn told him. Stubbs broke out laughing. Welcome to the United States embassy in Burma!

Horn hadn't expected a warm greeting. He was the third DEA country attaché in Burma in nearly four years, and he refused to become the

next casualty. Time to clean house. Horn started digging, discovering that
the local CIA station had rigged the embassy's communication network
so that every DEA teletype (a fax machine precursor) routed to the CIA's
second-floor office.[7] He confronted the station chief, Art Brown, and told
him to knock it off.

To Horn's surprise, he acceded. Station chief Brown was himself a
recent arrival in Burma, and he offered to mend the DEA-CIA rift. He
was frank in articulating the nature of the dispute. CIA headquarters
resented DEA agents' exclusive access to the junta's highest tier: the offices
of Secretary One Khin Nyunt, a spy chief doubling as dictator. Though
the CIA aimed to weaken the Burmese junta, in most countries—even
rival nations—American spies always craved face time with the local
intelligence division, if only to peer into that country's inner workings.
That Burma's intel division talked to America's narcs, and not its spies,
was an anomaly. Officials at CIA headquarters in Langley, Virginia, could
not tolerate the DEA enjoying superior insight into any foreign government, anywhere on earth.

Problem was, Burma's junta despised the CIA and had for decades,
ever since the agency used the Exiles cartel to gather intel on Burmese soil.
That the Exiles were now defunct didn't help much; Burmese officials had
long memories. When the CIA requested meetings with junta VIPs, they
instead got know-nothing lackeys. The DEA, meanwhile, had the dictator's deputy, Colonel KT, on speed dial.

Brown suggested a way to ease this tension. Keep us in the loop, he
told Horn, and fully apprised of your discussions with the regime. No
surprises. If Horn offered more transparency, Brown would keep the
CIA—and the State Department—off his back, enabling the DEA to do
its job in peace. Though guarded, Horn decided to give the station chief a
chance, agreeing to brief him once or twice a week.[8]

In these talks, Brown got pushy, but Horn stood his ground. Nosy
questions abounded—any thoughts on setting up a safe house?—but
Horn said, No, I'll only meet CIs in the privacy of my living room. In
other words: don't bother snooping on me. Horn knew the CIA would
wire up some dinky Burmese safe house in a heartbeat. But bugging a
fellow US official's home without a warrant? That would violate the US
Constitution.

Summer monsoons came and abated, and the weather turned balmy.
It was late in the year, and Horn was finding his rhythm. The embassy

seemed to realize he was no pushover. The CIA was acting "all kumbaya." The State Department allotted him a grand home on Inya Lake all to himself, even though he was a bachelor. A devoted weightlifter, Horn flew in a bench press and installed it inside the house. There were maids to cook his meals and mop the floors. Life was comfortable.

One hazy November evening, a crescent moon glowing above the lake, Horn returned home from work, stepped into his living room, and stopped short. Something was off. The coffee table—the rectangular one he'd seen that morning—had been replaced with a smaller, oval-shaped model. His maid explained that handymen had come by unannounced earlier in the day, and she'd let them in, assuming Horn had requested the table swap. No, he said. I don't know anything about this.[9]

Horn later asked an embassy secretary to explain. Oh right, she said. We needed your rectangular table to complete a sofa set in another employee's house. Is the new one OK? He supposed it was. With everything else going relatively well, the incident was soon forgotten.

CHAIRMAN LAI KEPT a family home in Pang Wai, his ancestral region. It was a simple domicile for his wife and children, amid green peaks and cool mountain air, and he intended for Saw Lu to recuperate there. Insisted upon it, actually, upon learning that, after leaving their prison cell in Lashio, Saw Lu and Mary had come home to find their house emptied of all valuables—looted by junta goons. In a message to Saw Lu, Lai said, You don't belong in Burma anymore. You belong here in Wa State with me.

The chairman awaited Saw Lu's arrival at his mountain home, sitting in the living room, its walls festooned with mounted heads: boar, deer, a solitary tiger, all shot dead by Lai's own hand. Lai winced when his friend walked through the door. The indefatigable Saw Lu was limping, holding Mary's arm to steady himself. The two men shook hands, and then Saw Lu sat down and loosened his shirt so that Lai could see the scarring down his back. The chairman asked Saw Lu's forgiveness for not rescuing him sooner. You did not suffer in vain. I will make it up to you.

Three days later, he did.

It was mid-April 1992, and the nation's leadership had gathered at UWSA headquarters to celebrate Wa State's third anniversary. Finance czar Wei Xuegang was not in attendance—he kept to his enclave on the

Thai-Burma border—but the armed forces chief, Bao Youxiang, was there, along with the rest of Wa State's "central committee." This was the UWSA's rule-making council: one dozen members, structured almost exactly like the communist politburo they'd overthrown. The central committee convened around a long wooden table with Lai at the helm. Saw Lu sat by his side.

Upon the table, Lai laid a peaked cap and a cedar-green uniform. After extolling Saw Lu's sacrifice in a Burmese torture site, the chairman placed the uniform in Saw Lu's hands and inducted him into the UWSA as a full-fledged leader, his rank equal to that of Bao, a founding father. Henceforth Saw Lu would serve as Wa State's foreign minister, a newly created position.[10] The three men would guide the nation as a triumvirate: Lai, the folksy ultranationalist; Bao, the no-nonsense military man; Saw Lu, the visionary, establishing Wa State's place in the wider world.

"I was honored," Saw Lu said. "But among the Wa, respect does not come from titles. It comes from how many people will fight and die for you." If Saw Lu didn't command his own armed unit, no one in the peaks would take him seriously. So the central committee provided a starter batch of weapons and UWSA uniforms, encouraging their foreign minister to go find recruits. For the second time in his life, Saw Lu possessed guns but no followers.

After healing from his torture injuries, he spent months combing the peaks for Wa and Lahu men descended from William Marcus Young's original converts. Hardened by bleak years under communism, which forbade religion, these Baptists hastened to the side of a Wa leader who proclaimed his faith with pride. They formed the core of a new legion under Saw Lu's command. Saw Lu assembled these recruits and their families in Pang Wai. They built a brick compound for their commander, then erected their own wooden homes nearby. They constructed a little church of rough-sawn planks where Saw Lu ministered every Sunday. After each service, they'd fan out into poppy-farming hamlets and ask for tithes, no matter if the inhabitants were Christian or not. Two decades prior, when Saw Lu was a young warlord, Pang Wai was a scene of intense humiliation—at Lai's hands, funnily enough. But soon the Wa would know it as the cradle of a great reformation. Saw Lu was determined to make it so.

By late 1992, as the mountain winds turned icy, Saw Lu still hadn't presented a detailed foreign policy to the other leaders, and Chairman Lai was growing antsy. One Sunday, Lai dropped by Saw Lu's compound unannounced to seek answers. He found his friend clad in black cloth, UWSA coat and hat hung on wall pegs. Saw Lu's loyalists wore plainclothes as well. Chairman, it's the holy day, Saw Lu said. Work here is prohibited. Would you put down your drink and pray with us instead? Lai humored his friend, and the following morning Saw Lu revealed an enhanced version of his dream.

My legion, Saw Lu said, will be a legion like none other. It is an armed wing, within a drug-producing organization, that nevertheless seeks the abolition of all drugs. I call it the United Wa State Anti-Drug Organization, and like the DEA it goes by an acronym: UWADO. Saw Lu said his soldiers were largely Baptists, and in the spirit of the Man-God—the American who'd brought Christ to their forebears—they longed to bring light to the Wa people, especially those who did not wish to receive it.

He'd already corralled nearly one thousand men. Give me a year, he told Lai, and I will raise ten thousand. I intend to reconnect with the DEA, and when I do, the Americans will see that I've fashioned a rod with which to smite the wicked: a fierce antinarcotics organization in imitation of their DEA. This will remove any doubt that our Wa people have the will and means to purge drugs from our nation—and that we are worthy of America's riches and attention.

Lai listened and smoked. Torture clearly hadn't dampened Saw Lu's ambition. But he could see two potential obstacles ahead. One was Burma. Junta leaders were already chagrined that Wa State had named the traitor Saw Lu as its foreign minister.[11] They sure as hell wouldn't like Saw Lu's new creation: the UWADO, a mini-DEA full of militant Baptists, cooperating with the *real* DEA. But Saw Lu didn't care. Let them whine, he said. This is our nation, not theirs, and we have the right to govern it as we see fit. Besides, he said, they'll tolerate our alliance with the United States if that's what the almighty US wants. The junta fears the Americans more than you know.

I hope you're right, Lai said. Because there was another impediment to Saw Lu's vision—and this one was closer to home. Implicit in his plan was the dismantling of Wei's narcotics-trafficking operation, Wa State's economic motor. Lai explained that there was a lot to be said for Wei, unsocial though he may be. Wei never complained or asked for much. His system functioned smoothly. Opium harvested by Wa peasants poured into his little Wa South enclave where Wei's chemists cooked it into heroin blocks, shrink-wrapped it, and sold it to distributors in Bangkok and

Hong Kong. Wei took his cut. He kicked the rest back to the UWSA. The nation met its needs.

But Wa State is not developing, Saw Lu said. This was the crux of his argument. We need foreign expertise to set up an education system, modern infrastructure, proper hospitals—and what country will aid a runt pariah state committed to poisoning the world? Continuing along the same path would ensure the Wa masses remained permanently ignorant, isolated, dying from treatable diseases.

Wa State's economy relied on opium and heroin, and while these drugs were profitable, financing a nation with a half-million population was expensive. Feeding nearly twenty thousand troops, buying weapons, and much else besides chewed through their budget quickly. Ethnic Chinese crime families in the cities, who smuggled Wa-produced heroin to America, were certainly getting rich—narcotics gain value with each border crossed—but the Wa, stuck at a more primitive stage of the supply chain, were just getting by. Our nation, Saw Lu said, can either sacrifice the drug trade or sacrifice everything else.

Lai eventually told Saw Lu he'd endorse his plan, for now, and try to refute any naysayers on the central committee.[12] He'd frame it as a security issue: if we keep pumping out heroin, eventually the United States will come knocking, not as a friend but as a destroyer. Go forth, Lai told Saw Lu, and restore contact with the DEA. See how much money they'll put up. But he warned his foreign minister that US aid would need to reach tens of millions of dollars to compensate for heroin profits.[13] Otherwise, no deal would be possible. Moreover, if the Wa did strike an agreement with the United States, the UWSA would have to unwind its drug business slowly, giving Wei and his cohorts time to transition into legal enterprises. Until that day comes, Saw Lu, leave our financier alone. Let him do his job.

Saw Lu said that he understood. But righteousness has no patience.

SPRING 1993.

After nine months in Burma, Agent Horn's standing with the junta was excellent. This was no fluke. He'd worked overtime to rebuild trust in the DEA, helping Burma's government adopt policies designed to improve its dismal reputation. Horn urged the junta to scrap its archaic antidrug laws—a total scrapping, not a tweak—and adopt a basic version of US drug laws. He assisted with the formation of a new Burmese antinarcotics task force capable of DEA-style investigations, not just seizing dope from bottom-rung traffickers. These were serious recommendations, yet the junta heartily complied.[14] Horn's goal was to put American "fingerprints" all over Burma's justice system, proving the DEA could fight the drug war *and* improve regime behavior, even if the country was never fated to become a flourishing democracy.

At the same time, Horn put his DEA office on a defensive footing. He warned his subordinates, Agents Bruce Stubbs and Dave Sikorra, against indiscreet talk inside embassy walls—not to evade Burmese surveillance but to thwart CIA snooping. Having grown closer to the regime, Horn knew that CIA officers on the second floor would feel justified in spying on his activities. Saladino's mistake had been waiting too long to turn paranoid. Horn would not repeat it.

Horn also ordered, from DEA headquarters, a suite of encrypted communications devices. One high-tech fax machine that transmitted documents securely. Two Inmarsats: briefcase-sized satellite phones, clunky and battery hungry but very hard to tap. And to top it off, one STU-III, a third-generation Secure Telephone Unit. Resembling a standard desk phone, the STU-III had a special feature: insert a key, twist, and communications were scrambled. Only someone with another unit on the other end of the line could hear what Horn was saying; eavesdroppers would hear a storm of garbled static. Horn demanded, from his colleagues, that sensitive communication with DEA headquarters go through those phones. He would only make calls in his living room: his de facto DEA office, a refuge from the prying CIA.

Clearly Horn was strengthening his position in advance of some spectacular move. Sikorra guessed that much. But he had little insight into his boss's intrigues.

One day Horn invited him over to his house and offered to reveal everything—if Sikorra would swear a loyalty oath. Horn was mobilizing a project that, if successful, could devastate the global heroin trade. Yes, it would require cooperating with the junta, but for a project this monumental, he hoped the DC establishment might come to its senses and give the regime a pass. Even if the State Department howled, the White House and Congress would override its objections, and the diplomats would stand down with gritted teeth.

That was Horn's hope anyway. He'd have to set everything in motion quickly, quietly, before the State Department and its CIA buddies found out and strangled the project in its cradle. The road ahead could get bumpy. Horn looked Sikorra dead in his face and asked, Can I trust you?

Sikorra fell mute. The smoldering determination on his boss's face frightened him. "He tried to recruit me as a soldier in this fight. I would only give him a blank stare. I wanted neutrality."

After that encounter, Sikorra tried to keep his head down. "I was left out of the mystery." He "tiptoed on eggshells" around his DEA peers, fearing their schemes would blow up and singe his career. Clearly Stubbs was involved, because he kept disappearing from the office for days at a time on dubious pretexts. Around Sikorra, Stubbs remained genial, still quick with the wisecracks, but when it came to operations talk, he turned "mysterious as the Cheshire Cat." Eventually he pulled Sikorra aside and, in whispers, gave him the gist.

Stubbs said that Superstar was alive. Scathed but dogged as ever—and this time controlling his own DEA-like arm of the UWSA, capable of eradicating drugs on an epic scale. Burma was the largest heroin-producing country on earth, with Wa State controlling 85 percent of its poppies, and Superstar had a plan to destroy them all. Horn thinks he can get Burma's government to play ball, Stubbs said, letting us team up with the Wa to make history. It's all in the works.

Stubbs confided that he'd found a way to meet Superstar face-to-face. Not in some Burmese safe house but in Chiang Mai, Thailand, beyond the reach of the CIA's Burma station. A DEA operative there named Bill arranged a rendezvous with Superstar inside his house. At last, Sikorra knew where Stubbs kept slipping off to—though he didn't want all these details in his head. "Bruce Stubbs was always a big-ideas guy. He was above arresting crackheads, miles above that in his thinking. That's what I liked about him." But no one, Sikorra thought, survives a contest with the CIA. "I knew who would come out on top."

Sikorra believed in divine warnings from God—in angels and demons and an inner voice that guided true believers away from calamity. Now his inner voice was screaming at him to "duck and take cover from the nuclear bomb that might blow up over our heads."

THE SUMMIT

Bill Young had met his grandfather but couldn't remember it. He was just a baby when William Marcus Young, patriarch of his missionary family, held him for the last time. That was in 1936, the old man's final year. On his deathbed he bequeathed to the infant Bill a silver cross, Celtic in design, hanging from a necklace chain.

It was a sacred heirloom. William Marcus Young had worn it among Wa and Lahu disciples in Banna on the China-Burma border. Had it eyes to see, the cross would've witnessed surreal acts of evangelism. The Man-God prevailing upon his flock to go convert headhunters in the high peaks. The flock returning fewer in number, carrying headless bodies of the slain. The stuff of family lore.

Bill's own life turned out no less extraordinary. Raised in Burma's foothills, among his family's proselytes, he spoke Lahu as a mother tongue, only adding English in boyhood. In his adolescence the family moved to Chiang Mai. Bill, a linguistic phenom, picked up Thai, Lao, and Shan. By his twenties, he'd grown to look like a corn-fed quarterback, but he still thought like an indigenous scout. These qualities attracted the Central Intelligence Agency. In the 1960s, the agency employed Bill, then in his thirties, to train his family's acolytes as spies, sending them into China to steal documents and tap phone lines. These missions were highly danger-ous, sometimes fatal. But they'd do anything for Bill Young, grandson of the Man-God.

Grandfather's puritanism didn't pass down. Bill liked his bourbon and smokes; his sexual stamina was legendary. But he did inherit an appe-tite for risk—and whenever the stakes were high, or if certain CIA oper-ations troubled his conscience, Bill would glide his thumb over the silver cross's engraving, asking for divine protection.

Bill eventually fell out with the CIA, deciding its Ivy League geeks didn't give a damn about tribal minorities. On a whim the CIA would send his "assets" on kamikaze missions, hardly caring if they died. To Bill these people were like kin, not "pins to be pushed around on a map." So when the Drug Enforcement Administration came to Chiang Mai in the mid-1970s, Bill switched teams. He became the DEA's secret weapon—this time using indigenous Baptists to spy on smugglers, not communists. Bill held that job for many years, up through the early 1990s, when he was creeping up on sixty.

Around that time, one of his Lahu Baptist contacts told him, Bill, there's a Wa man named Saw Lu who needs to see you. You can trust him. He's one of us.

Bill hadn't met Saw Lu, only heard of him, though they had much in common. Both were undeclared DEA operatives, not on-the-books agents. Both used indigenous Christians—whose parents or grandparents were converted by the Young sect—as sources of drug-trade intelligence. The widely flung Baptists regarded themselves as one big family, even if they'd drifted into smuggling or other unchristian trades. While Saw Lu's network monitored Burma's north, Bill's moles were strewn around the Thai-Burma border; together the two DEA assets had the Golden Triangle covered.

According to what Bill heard, though, this Saw Lu character had wrangled himself a new gig. After running afoul of the Burmese junta and disappearing into its torture cells, he'd somehow resurfaced as a leader in the United Wa State Army (UWSA). Rumor had it the man was unkillable.

Bill put the word out to his contacts: if Saw Lu can find his way to Chiang Mai, he's welcome in my home.

JANUARY 1993.

A good two hundred miles lay between Pang Wai and Chiang Mai, and it was all hardscrabble country: a couple weeks on foot and hoof down pebble-strewn trails. Saw Lu told his fifty best soldiers to load up the horses and pack mules. Their journey to the Thai border would take them south of Wa State through bandit haunts and even near parts of Khun Sa's Shanland. Bring good rifles and ample ammunition, he said. Saw Lu hoped to reach Bill Young with his hide intact.

Southward they marched, his soldiers filing down switchbacks with their bayoneted automatics, some riding horses, others walking, brown mules with push-broom mohawks carrying their gear and leaving half-moon hoof prints in the dirt. It was the first long-range mission of the United Wa State Anti-Drug Organization (UWADO). Saw Lu clad his men in blood-red kerchiefs to distinguish them from everyday Wa grunts. He marched in front: eyes shining, silvering goatee catching the light. His assistant lugged the foreign minister's prized tobacco bong: a bazooka-shaped implement half the man's height.

The weather warmed as they marched closer to the Thai border. No raiders had accosted them; nor did they cross paths with any Shan militants—though they would if they charted the wrong course. Khun Sa's Shanland controlled most of the mountain passes connecting Burma to Thailand. His troops shot intruders on sight.

There was only one place Saw Lu could safely cross the border: Wa South, Wei Xuegang's little enclave of Wa State. By chance its secret trails led right into Chiang Mai province, Saw Lu's destination. Saw Lu hadn't met Wei in the flesh; nor would he seek him out now. That would violate his promise to Chairman Zhao Nyi Lai. He intended to pass through Wa South to reach Thailand, nothing more.

Upon entering Wa South, the UWADO soldiers remarked upon its natural beauty. Here the mountains were less severe than in the Wa motherland, and they sloped down into low-lying pockets, grassed over and luminous green. The soil appeared less hostile to living things. A shame this fertile place was mostly used as a hideaway for Wei's heroin labs. Wei had transplanted Wa troops and their families to perform narco-army grunt labor in Wa South: guarding warehouses, lugging barrels of chemicals, sneaking heroin kilos into Thailand. In a clearing, the UWADO happened upon some of these workers, minding a way station for opium shipments en route to nearby refineries. On the ground, piled on bamboo platforms, Saw Lu saw cloth-covered globes of opium, each tied up in twine like a butcher shop ham. He was supposed to keep walking. But he didn't. He couldn't help himself.

Saw Lu called out to the workers and gathered them close. He bent to pick up an opium bundle, examined it, passed it from hand to hand. Invoking his rank, he told everyone to listen carefully. This livelihood of yours is ending soon, and I'll make sure you're glad to be rid of it. In a coming era graced by God, you will farm rubber or coffee instead. Your children will go to decent schools. Old folks will live long lives thanks to Western medicine. Every heroin refinery nestled in these shadowed groves will go up in flames. Businessmen such as Wei Xuegang will find nobler work, and if they do not, my men in crimson sashes will cast them out.

Saw Lu tossed the opium back on the pile. He asked the crowd to spread the good news. They nodded meekly and got back to work.

At the border, Saw Lu left his UWADO soldiers behind with all their horses and weapons, and he slipped into Thailand along a dope trail. No passport, no stamp. Bill's home near Chiang Mai city was exactly where his Baptist contacts said it would be. Saw Lu was greeted heartily at the door by Bill—a Lahu-speaking white man in a Hawaiian shirt, gray-blond hair swept to the side.

Their rapport came easy. By the mores of the sect, they were brothers in spirit if not in blood. Saw Lu insisted they'd met long ago, as kids at the missionary camp run by the Young family in Kengtung, Burma, where Saw Lu had grown up after fleeing Banna. He claimed to recall Bill— more than ten years older, a strapping teenager at the time—leading posses of Lahu and Wa kids into the forest to shoot deer, a pipsqueak Saw Lu trailing behind.

They conversed in Lahu, which both men spoke fluently. They bonded in a nicotine haze: Bill chain smoking, Saw Lu sucking his three-foot bong. On the wall hung two Lahu swords near a black-and-white daguerreotype of William Marcus Young. Eventually Bill asked in his tobacco-scorched voice why Saw Lu had traveled so far to meet him. Surely this wasn't a social call.

Saw Lu straightened up and said, Brother Bill, I need a favor. You've got to reconnect me with someone in Yangon. A DEA agent who knows me well. His name is Bruce, and we must speak at once. The Wa race's future depends on it.

BRUCE STUBBS FLEW to Thailand as soon as he got the message: Saw Lu is alive and waiting for you in Chiang Mai. He was eager to see Superstar with his own eyes. Stubbs had worked with many confidential informants over the years. Never had one come back from the dead.

Bill assured everyone his house was safe; as a former CIA officer, he was savvy about spy craft and would know if they'd bugged the place. Ashtrays overflowing, the three men sat in Bill's den, brainstorming ways to revive Saw Lu's dream.[1] Much had changed in the past year. Relations between the Burmese and the Wa, never intimate, were strained. The junta was displeased that Saw Lu had been appointed foreign minister—that their official point of contact with Wa State was a traitor to their regime. Since Saw Lu's promotion, junta officers had invited him to meetings in the lowlands, assuring his safety, but he'd refused, fearing it was a trick to lock him up once again. I don't trust the Burmese, he told Stubbs, and neither should you. No more convoluted chess games. No more slowly conditioning the junta to tolerate our alliance. Let's forge ahead and dare them to stop us.

Stubbs told Saw Lu, Sorry, it doesn't work that way. The DEA could only execute projects with host country approval, and under international law, Wa State was a part of Burma. Like it or not, nothing could proceed without Secretary One's consent. The good news was that Stubbs's new boss, Rick Horn, had elevated the DEA-Burma relationship in a major way. Horn could probably convince junta officials to suck it up and approve a DEA eradication project in Wa State, even with Saw Lu involved, if that's what it took to get America on their good side. But Saw Lu would need to swear up and down that he bore the junta no malice, even if this wasn't true. He'd betrayed them, they'd tortured him, score settled. Could he play it that way?

Saw Lu grumbled but said that he could. Soon a plan took shape in the smoky air. Bill suggested that Saw Lu distill his ideas into a master document, something all sides—the Americans, the Wa, the Burmese— could embrace. He put pen to paper and drew up a manifesto.[2]

"The Bondage of Opium"
The Agony of the Wa People: A Proposal and a Plea

Now we want to free ourselves from slavery to an opium economy. This we cannot do by ourselves. Like the heroin addict who wants to kick his addiction, we need outside help to be successful.

Give us the following six offerings, Saw Lu wrote, and the UWSA will reject the drug trade in favor of a "whole new economy." Substitute crops. Expertise in modern agriculture. Paved roads. Hospitals and schools, staffed by foreigners. Western geological teams helping the Wa discover valuable deposits: tin, silver, or gold.

We are not asking for arms. We are not asking the United States to buy our opium crop as Khun Sa does. We do not want to put on a show as the SLORC does for the West. The Wa leadership can stop opium growing and refining at any time. But our people must eat.

You want a better life for your people—which means a life without heroin. It is to our mutual advantage to work together. Please accept our proposal and respond to our plea. Yours truly, Saw Lu

Stubbs loved it, believing it held more promise than any other DEA-backed initiative ever conceived. But there was one glaring problem. Saw Lu littered the manifesto with cheap shots at the junta. He wrote that Burmese officials "systematically threatened, jailed . . . or hunted down" critics. He even accused Burma's military of taking bribes from drug traffickers.

I'll show this to my boss, Stubbs said, but I know what he'll say. We can't bring this to Burma's government. You'd be wise to edit those parts out. Bill chimed in too. Saw Lu, he said, do as the agent asks, or you'll wreck this whole thing. "But I didn't want to change it," Saw Lu told me, "because everything I wrote was true."

On his next rendezvous with Saw Lu, Stubbs brought Rick Horn. The mustachioed hulk insisted that Saw Lu had to tone down "The Bondage of Opium" or the deal was doomed. Convincing the Burmese military to swallow its pride and cut a deal with the UWSA *after* it had made Saw Lu into a national leader? That would be hell enough, but he could manage it, having worked so hard to butter up Burmese officials. However, if the manifesto in its current form ever got out, the junta leaders would blow a fuse.

It took one more lecture from Bill to force Saw Lu into compliance. In the end, he relented, editing "The Bondage of Opium." Horn and Stubbs flew back to Yangon with a sanitized version, something the junta might accept. That was one ego wrangled into submission, more to come. But at least they had a plan—a damn good plan—and they were determined that, this time, they would achieve it no matter what.

DEA HEADQUARTERS DIDN'T need much convincing that the plan was solid or any proof that its Wa mastermind was trustworthy. By extraordinary chance, the DEA's chief of global operations—one of its highest officials—was Matty Maher, newly promoted from lead inspector. He'd recently looked into Saw Lu's eyes to vet his integrity. Though awkward at the time, that encounter in a Yangon safe house left an impression: this man does not wilt under pressure.

"When Rick Horn brought forth the potential for doing this," Maher told me, "I informed the chain of command: memo, chapter, and verse. My thinking was, OK, let's test this out." The DEA had deployed Horn to Burma to achieve big results in the face of State Department and CIA recalcitrance—and now Horn had a proposal to do just that. Though Maher was Horn's boss's boss's boss, they communicated directly. The political sensitivity of Horn's mission demanded close oversight by the DEA leadership.

The two men talked on encrypted channels: Horn sitting in the sanctity of his living room, ear pressed to his Inmarsat phone or STU-III; Maher speaking inside DEA headquarters. Maher's first concern was Burma's government. We need their buy-in, Maher said, on all the terms and conditions. Horn had already seen to that. The junta needed to fix its international reputation with a War on Drugs extravaganza, jointly executed with the DEA, and Saw Lu's plan offered the key ingredient: mountains of opium and heroin to destroy. The junta didn't like Saw Lu, but Horn convinced the Burmese that he no longer harbored any grudge, despite all that had happened. The regime was on board. It had little to lose.

Good work, Maher said. On to the bigger obstacle: the State Department. Seizing the narrative was vital. Once US diplomats saw the proposal, they'd bash the DEA for conniving with a tyrannical regime and a heroin cartel. The DEA had to exploit its first-mover advantage, bringing other influential institutions into the plan, framing it as the world's largest-ever opium eradication—a potential conquest too good to pass up. Maher started working his contacts in Congress. Horn was already courting United Nations agencies. The UN Drug Control Program had offices in Yangon, and its officials loved the idea, even shared it with the World Health Organization and the United Nations Children's Fund, which could help deliver Saw Lu's health care and education requirements. Internationalizing the plan gave it armor. If the diplomats wanted to squash the proposal, they'd have to break hearts at the United Nations, not just the DEA.

"I also told Rick, look, at some point we'll have to discuss this with the chargé d'affaires." Maher was referring to Pancho Huddle, the de facto US ambassador to Burma. Diplomatic protocol demanded that Horn submit the plan to Huddle and seek his approval. Ideally, the embassy would realize that the proposal already had buy-in from other powerful institutions and cooperate—or at least step aside.[3] For a proposal this hefty, Maher said, you want "everyone to pull the rope in the same direction. Because if anyone pulls the opposite way, you have a tug-of-war."

Naturally, Huddle was hip to the plan well before Horn formally presented it to the embassy. It was generating a small buzz in DC among the DEA-friendly congressional lawmakers—and little can stay secret for long in Washington. Though the State Department wielded more power over Congress than the DEA, narcotics officials also held sway, particularly with politicians from crime-plagued districts. "DEA was often flavor of the month in Washington," Huddle told me, "and not much could be done about that."

Now UN antinarcotics officials all the way in Europe were growing excited too.[4] Huddle was pissed. Horn was aiming a flamethrower at his career. Huddle's job was to wave the rights-and-freedom flag in Burma, cowing the junta to make way for democracy.[5] Not to let some muscle-bound narc rehabilitate the junta's image. Never had the DEA come so close to flipping an established State Department policy on its head—and it was happening on Huddle's watch.

Until that point, Huddle told me, "I had a lovely existence in Burma." His staffers basked in the soft workload (there were hardly any programs with Burma's government) and their lakeside homes with live-in maids. They received an "unduly generous hardship allowance," justified in part because Burma led the world in per-capita snakebites, even though they rarely left Yangon's safe (and largely snake-free) expat bubble. Huddle hoped to put in some time and graduate to a full ambassadorship in Asia or Africa.

"The undoing was, well, Horn. A pain in my ass."

Nutcase is actually his preferred honorific for Horn—"and nutcase is putting it mildly." Huddle told me the DEA agent would "go around in an unmuffled Harley Davidson, deliberately not wearing a helmet— which was required—in heavy leathers, in ninety-degree Burmese tropical heat." (Others who knew Horn at the time don't recall him even owning a motorcycle.) Agent Horn found it "exceedingly difficult to recognize the primacy of the State Department," Huddle told me. He and the whole DEA "didn't give a damn about human rights. They just cared about narcotics."

"I'll be straight with you," Huddle said. "Everyone knows the Wa. Can we make a deal with the Wa? That's a Hail Mary. That's a magical solution. Horn's thing was, if you unfetter me, I'll put together a grand coalition to defang the Wa and end the heroin trade. Sure. The check is in the mail."

Huddle needed to squash the proposal fast. He told DEA headquarters that, moving forward, Horn must bring a State Department minder to every meeting with the UWSA liaison, Saw Lu. "And we said, 'Absolutely not,'" Maher recalled. "'This is a law enforcement operation involving a DEA informant. So we're not going to do that.'"

Time was a critical factor. The DEA needed to shift the proposal into motion quickly, arranging a formal summit with the UWSA and Burma's government, for, once the plan gained momentum, it would prove more difficult to impede. Until then, the State Department would seek some way to kill it off—or perhaps let its CIA friends do their worst.

Horn was braced for CIA sabotage. Had been since day one.

But to his surprise, station chief Art Brown told Horn the Wa proposal looked interesting and wished him the best of luck.[6]

SAW LU HAD envisioned it like a prophecy. For months, he'd imagined DEA men descending from the sky, stepping out of helicopters, alighting on a Wa mountaintop. In this vision, Saw Lu, Zhao Nyi Lai, and Bao Youxiang are atop that mountain, welcoming the Americans. Guiding them toward a wooden arch erected for the occasion. Linking arms, the Wa triumvirate and DEA officials walk beneath that arch together—the Americans symbolically guiding the Wa from the past into the future.

So exquisitely laid were Saw Lu's plans that when his assistant received word from the DEA—gather your people, the summit is on—he didn't complain that the date was only three days away.[7] He just hustled to prepare. The location: Mong Mao, not far from Pang Wai. Arrival time: noon sharp. The DEA agents would fly in on Burmese military choppers, junta officials in tow.

As Saw Lu understood it, the DEA would bring memoranda pledging $50 million in aid to the Wa nation, provided by the United States and the United Nations, funneled through Burma's government.[8] Atop that mountain, Wa leaders would pledge to start over as a drug-free nation—a turning point equal in import to the nation's founding. Saw Lu needed to create a setting worthy of his achievement. He ordered his UWADO soldiers to rake a square-shaped helipad into the dirt atop the mountain, then build a stage festooned with bunting. On his instructions, they fashioned a wooden arch so big an elephant could pass underneath.

The morning of the summit arrived. Saw Lu arranged his soldiers in neat lines to impress his incoming American guests. Also in attendance were Wa dignitaries in traditional garb: crimson vests embroidered with silver beads. Sewn over their hearts were black fabric patches shaped like bull heads: an icon of Wa power.

As noon approached, Saw Lu stepped away from the staging area toward a ridge affording a view westward, the direction from which the helicopters would arrive. He sat upon a wind-scoured rock. He squinted at the serrated horizon, its furthest peaks faintly cerulean. He listened for the sound of rotors.

Saw Lu got up and walked back. He reinspected the arch. He checked the signage greeting the delegation in English and Wa and also Burmese, a tactical show of deference to the junta. Then he returned to the ridge and sat some more, wind thrashing his collar. He fidgeted with the knobs on his walkie-talkie. Lai was at the mountain's foot, waiting with Bao. Notify us when you see the helicopters, they'd told him, and we'll join you up top. Lai was planning to read a short speech ghostwritten by Bill Young.

Saw Lu kept squinting and listening. Hours passed. Nothing flew but black birds. No matter how hard he willed them to appear—roaring black specks in the distance—the helicopters would not manifest. Eventually the sun arced low, lacquering the uplands in amber light.

He contemplated his predicament with horror.

Saw Lu waited atop that mountain for two days, long after Lai and Bao got fed up and left. On the third day, he descended to find a phone with which to call Bill Young. Talk to me, Brother Bill. My people doubt me. When will the DEA arrive?

He could hear Bill's breathing through the hiss. Then his voice metallic and distant.

Saw Lu, he said, I think someone set you up.

THE CIA'S SABOTAGE against the DEA and the UWSA has never been revealed in full, until now, even though these events—in the summer of 1993—transformed the fate of the Wa people and the entire Golden Triangle narcotics trade.

Warped too were the lives of Saw Lu and DEA agent Rick Horn, though not in ways anyone would've predicted. One would find himself trapped in a filthy hole—a literal hole in the dirt. The other ended up a millionaire.

I'll start with Horn. According to his claims, the CIA crippled the plan with a one-two punch. The spy agency, posing as the DEA, may have fed a bogus date to Saw Lu, likely through his English-speaking assistant. This would've caused UWSA leaders to gather for a summit that had not yet been agreed on. What better way to humiliate the Wa and poison them against the DEA?

At the time, DEA officials were tinkering with the proposal, making it more palatable to the US government. They were going to propose that UN agencies take the lead in developing Wa State—since that was the UN's specialty—while the DEA only supervised drug eradication.[9] A real summit was in the works, planned for later that summer. But after the snafu on the mountain, the project was dead. Never again would Wa State's leaders trust anything the DEA said.

Horn, through an attorney, also alleged that Brown, the CIA station chief, used another trick to further bury the proposal. He claimed the CIA surreptitiously acquired a copy of "The Bondage of Opium" and slipped it to the Burmese government.[10] Not the sanitized version. The original one rippling with insults toward the junta, signed, "Yours truly, Saw Lu."[11] This would've verified to Burmese officials that Saw Lu, no matter how conciliatory he seemed, would forever try to turn the Americans against their regime.

Combined, these two actions nuked the Wa proposal. That left just one more job to do: booting Horn from Burma. This fell to Huddle, the chargé d'affaires. In the wake of the botched summit, Huddle invoked his powers as the top-ranking US diplomat in Burma.[12] Depicting

Horn as a "nutcase" defying State Department rules left and right, he gave the DEA agent roughly four weeks to settle his affairs and leave the country.

August 12, 1993. Nearly midnight. The sky above Yangon was a vault of storm clouds. A sickle moon glowed dimly behind the pall. Agent Dave Sikorra's phone rang. It was Horn, in an apocalyptic mood, raving about his imminent removal.

I'm bringing the whole DEA operation down, Dave. You'll be leaving with me. We'll all leave together. Understand?

Got it, Rick. Sikorra hung up.

So this was how it would end. Sikorra had told himself, not long after first meeting Rick Horn, that his conflict-prone boss would not reach one year in Burma. He was only a little off. Horn lasted fourteen months.

During the last weeks Horn was allowed inside the embassy, he was pulled aside by a US federal employee with whom he was friendly—an official managing secure communications between the embassy and Washington DC. I think you should see this, his friend said, holding up a printed telefax. Written by Huddle, it was a classified cable sent to the State Department mothership. It read, "Horn shows increasing signs of evident strain. Late last night, for example, he telephoned his junior agent to say that 'I am bringing the whole DEA operation down here. . . . You will be leaving with me. . . . We'll all leave together.'"

Horn was shocked. Strewn through the cable were verbatim quotes from his phone call to Sikorra. Horn's friend said there was only one way someone inside the embassy could've captured that conversation with chilling accuracy.

Rick, he said, I think they've wired you up.[13]

In an ensuing lawsuit, Horn alleged the following. The bug was in his living room, buried inside the oval-shaped coffee table, close enough to hear every phone call he made on his encrypted phones. The CIA probably tracked the Wa proposal's evolution from the very start: listening to Horn's conversations, apparently sharing them with Huddle. Waiting for the perfect time to strike the plan dead. And if it weren't for Huddle's screwup, quoting Horn in a classified memo, they would've gotten away with it.

Horn's case became one of the longest-running suits ever filed against a CIA officer. Along the way, the US government tried to shut it down, once claiming the Constitution's Fourth Amendment (which forbids bugging US citizens' homes) did not apply overseas. Another time, government attorneys complained that the lawsuit, in exposing CIA trade-craft, divulged state secrets.[14] Attorneys for Brown, the former station chief, called the allegations "bizarre," saying that "Art Brown did not do whatever Horn imagines happened back in 1993."[15]

But in 2009, sixteen years after the incident took place, judges finally acknowledged the "seeming impossibility that Huddle would have learned of the conversation by legal means," and the US government, while admitting no wrongdoing, paid Horn $3 million to settle the case.[16]

To this day, Pancho Huddle insists Horn fabricated the whole story. He has an alibi, and it goes like this.[17] On that cloudy evening, Sikorra, fresh off his unhinged call with Horn, picked up the phone once again. He rang his partner, Bruce Stubbs, and described their boss's rant word for word. The next day, Stubbs slipped into Huddle's office, and—according to Huddle—"he says to me, 'You won't believe it. Horn called Sikorra at eleven o'clock last night. To say, "I'm gonna bring the whole place down with me." He'd clearly been drinking. Sikorra laughed and hung up.'" Having acquired these thirdhand quotes, Huddle typed them into a classified cable. But this alibi is flawed. Sikorra says it's nonsense—and testified to that under penalty of perjury. So did Stubbs. More damning still, Stubbs wasn't even in Yangon that day. "My husband hated Pancho," said Su Yon, Stubbs's widow. "Don't believe anything he says."

Institutionally, there were no lessons learned. Even federal courts ruled it "troubling" that the US government found Horn's case "credible enough" to pay him millions but never punished any officials involved in the debacle.[18] Huddle went on to serve as US ambassador to Tajikistan. The CIA promoted Brown to one of its most desirable posts: East Asia division chief.

But whatever the damage done to US integrity, nothing could compare to the suffering CIA sabotage brought upon Saw Lu.

IN THE SUMMER of 1993, as his dream dematerialized, Saw Lu discovered a deeper plane of suffering. He'd known many varieties of pain. Voltage fired into sensitive places. Metal paring flesh down to the white meat. But never before had Saw Lu been rendered so pathetic in the eyes of his own people. It terrified him more than any torture chamber.

At first, he denied his fate, pleading with the other leaders. "I told them, 'Even if the DEA never comes here, even if no one in the world helps us, we have to destroy opium. We can do it by ourselves.'" Lai looked away. Bao stared at Saw Lu disdainfully, saying, You broke your promise, Saw Lu. You and your DEA. It's over.

Saw Lu was further degraded in the months to come. By the year's end, many of his UWADO soldiers defected, handing in their rifles, melting back into their old villages, and tending poppies to survive. By 1994, the legion had all but collapsed. Saw Lu's incongruous creation—an anti-drug unit nested inside a narco-army—seemed suddenly absurd. Why had Wa leaders ever entertained such a thing?

A fellow idealist, Chairman Lai had always protected Saw Lu's ventures. But in 1995, the alcohol caught up to Wa State's leader, nearly killing him. Blood vessels burst in his brain, leaving him half paralyzed and his speech garbled. He could no longer govern. "Under Chairman Lai's rule, my husband was untouchable," Mary said. "The drug traffickers hated Saw Lu, but they dared not harm him. But once Lai fell ill, everything changed."

Bao, an unsentimental realist, assumed the throne. Idealistic thinking fell from favor. Moving forward, the Wa would presume malice from all lowlanders, as had their ancestors. They would run their nation as an isolationist ethnostate, their relations with outsiders reduced to hard transactions. In his pragmatism, Chairman Bao refocused foreign relations on China, the only neighbor that could undoubtedly crush the UWSA in battle. Though wary of China, Bao needed its oil, ammo, machinery, and other supplies. He snatched the foreign minister title away from Saw Lu, ill-suited to a pivot toward Beijing. Saw Lu's spoken Chinese was terrible, and he couldn't hide his adoration of America.

Diplomacy fell to Bao's right-hand man: Deputy Commander Li Ziru, a full-blooded Chinese citizen. He'd come to the Wa peaks in the 1960s as a Maoist Red Guard—helping guide the communist rebellion—and never left. After the 1989 Wa revolution, Li Ziru renounced communism, but as a former card-carrying cadre, he understood China's Communist Party inside and out. He knew its leaders hated that potent Wa opium sometimes seeped across the border, making addicts of Chinese citizens. So he made an offer. We, the UWSA, will prevent any Wa from smuggling drugs into China.[19] You, Chinese officials, will send us road-building crews and discounted heavy weapons. Beijing took the deal. Saw Lu's shame deepened. His promises of American aid hadn't produced any schools or hospitals, but centering foreign relations on China quickly brought material progress: paved streets and cheap arms.

Deputy Commander Li Ziru unnerved Saw Lu to the core. Not only had he stolen Saw Lu's foreign affairs job, but he was also close with Wei Xuegang, the finance czar. Both men shared Chinese heritage and a zeal for entrepreneurship. Li Ziru even owned a stake in Wei's heroin-producing operation—one that benefited from the UWSA's new ban on trafficking to China. After that decree, every single kilo of UWSA heroin, no matter where it was produced, had to flow south into Thailand—directly through Wei's special economic zone.

Li Ziru told the UWSA, Stop treating Wei like a money-printing machine. Before, the central committee was squeamish about even acknowledging the financier, especially during negotiations with the DEA, which still held a warrant for Wei's capture. But their flirtation with America was over. It was time to lavish more respect upon Wei, Li Ziru said, and honor him with a seat on their central committee.

Wei started attending top-level meetings in Panghsang, and for the first time Saw Lu was in the same room with the man he'd only known as an avatar of callous greed.[20] The finance czar would sit with hands folded, listening, in a starched white dress shirt, rejecting glasses of *baijiu* or *blai* pushed in his direction. He seldom spoke—but when he did, the others hushed to hear his quiet voice.

Under the influence of this powerful duo—Li Ziru and Wei—the UWSA peeled away what little authority Saw Lu had left. The UWADO, already gutted, was fully demobilized. The UWSA stripped Saw Lu's military rank too, forcing him to relinquish his uniform and peaked cap. He still lurked around meeting halls like a ghost, but leaders avoided his eyes. His hair fell out in silver tufts. His skin grayed. Mary noticed her husband wincing, talking to himself, muttering about an invisible weight bearing down on his heart.

Saw Lu came home one day from a meeting looking especially ashen. Mary asked what was wrong. He lit a cigarette and explained. Li Ziru was talking nonsense, and I snapped, beating the table until it nearly split in two. Saw Lu knew he'd crossed the line. He would not share exactly what he'd screamed, only that it maligned Wei.

Several nights later, Saw Lu heard hard rapping at his door. Chairman Bao stood on his stoop holding a satchel. The bag looked heavy. When

Saw Lu let him in, Bao sat down and dug red bricks of Chinese yuan from the bag and stacked them on the dining room table.

You need to run, Saw Lu. Tonight. Your life is in danger. They've had enough.

Run where?

Thailand maybe. You can't stay in Wa State. They'll kill you.

Bao laid out thirteen thousand yuan on the table. Worth more than $2,000 at the time. Saw Lu protested, I can't abandon my family—but Bao cut him off. Don't worry about your family. I'll protect them. But you, I can't protect you anymore. Saw Lu sat mutely as Mary listened from a doorway.

After a long silence, Saw Lu shook his head and said, No, I won't leave. So Bao pulled out more money and built bigger towers of yuan on the table. The wooden surface disappeared under notes inscribed with Mao Zedong's face in burgundy ink. The pile added up to fifty thousand yuan, worth more than $8,500. More than most Wa would earn in a lifetime.

Go, Bao said. Tonight.

But my mission, Saw Lu said. It's incomplete.

Mary feared Bao would strike her husband. The chairman stood up, shoveling the money back into the satchel. Why won't you listen to me, Saw Lu? I'm trying to save your life. I never want to see your face again! When soldiers barged into the house and pulled Saw Lu to his feet, Bao turned to Mary and said, This is for his own good. They hauled her husband into the night. He did not resist.

They trucked him to a clearing in the forest and told him to get out. The soldiers turned on flashlights and swept the grass with circles of light until it glinted—a square steel hatch. They lifted it to reveal an underground dirt chamber. A rectangular shaft in the shape of a tall upright casket.

As ordered, Saw Lu lowered himself into the hole. He could not lie down or extend his arms to the side. He just sat, knees folded, the cold earth drinking his body heat. He heard metallic squeaks as the soldiers closed the hatch above his head and slid a lock into place. Entombed in Wa soil, Saw Lu comprehended the thoroughness of his disgrace.

MOST DRUG LORDS would've lashed out long before. Not Wei. Throughout Saw Lu's rise and fall in the UWSA, he kept his cool, even as Saw Lu dared to invite the DEA—which had once put Wei in prison—to come eradicate his precious product. Wei believed in waiting for enemies to stumble, only striking when conditions were advantageous. He hadn't orchestrated Saw Lu's humiliation on that mountaintop—the CIA did—but once Saw Lu started coming undone, Wei hastened his enemy's unraveling.

By the mid-1990s, with Saw Lu's downfall complete, Wei could finally pursue *his* dream. He'd never penned manifestos or spoken of visions, but Wei was no less fixated on his goal. He craved power. Not to be confused with money—power's unit of measurement—or notoriety, which Wei abhorred. Like every CEO, Wei wanted his corporation to grow, to swallow competitors, to monopolize. That required crushing the UWSA's only rival: Shanland, helmed by his backstabbing former mentor, Khun Sa.

Toppling Khun Sa and seizing his territory, all five thousand square miles of it, would require the UWSA's full might. During Saw Lu's time in leadership, the Wa tried to appear decorous, moving away from their ferocious reputation. No longer. It was time for the UWSA to embrace ferocity. It would do what cartels are meant to do: expand through raw violence.

The UWSA wielded twenty thousand soldiers to Khun Sa's fifteen thousand. Wei and Deputy Commander Li Ziru convinced the central committee leaders, including Bao, that eliminating Shanland was essential to Wa State's long-term security. For years, the two cartels had skirmished around the Thai-Burma border, with Khun Sa's forces sporadically raiding Wa South and destroying Wei's refineries. But graduating beyond shootouts to all-out war would demand skillful timing. Wei sought the perfect moment—when Khun Sa was knocked off balance.

By chance, the United States supplied it.

Aged in his sixties, Khun Sa was mouthier than ever. The DEA are "impotent," he'd say, and the CIA want to make "slaves" of Asian people. In Thailand, DEA and CIA officials were on decent terms at the time, despite their colleagues' bitter feuding in Burma, and both agencies wanted to finish off Khun Sa. The CIA crafted a plan to assassinate him but needed a "lethal finding": presidential authority to kill. Bill Clinton wouldn't sign off.[21] So the DEA stepped up, launching "Tiger Trap," an operation wiping out Khun Sa's network in Thailand. It arrested brokers supplying materials to Shanland (fuel, food, cement, bullets) as well as services: money laundering and drug trafficking.[22] Its arteries slit, Shanland withered. Soldiers defected in droves. Wei never missed an opportunity, especially one served up by America. When Khun Sa was at his most vulnerable, the UWSA, under Wei's guidance, dealt the deathblow.

The UWSA surged into Shanland, grinding through its soldiers. The CIA kept tabs on the war, peering down from aircraft, with one officer observing "trench lines everywhere. . . . [I]t looked like the Western Front in 1917."[23] In January 1996, as UWSA troops neared Khun Sa's jungle villa, he waved the white flag, promising Burma's military he'd surrender if the junta saved his life. In a show of magnanimity, the Wa stepped aside and let the junta whisk Khun Sa away. Burma's government put him on house arrest in Yangon, allowing him to bring his mistresses: all four of them.

The DEA and CIA took credit for Khun Sa's defeat, even though neither had laid a finger on the "King of Heroin." Burma's junta said, actually, *we* deserve the acclaim. Meanwhile, the person most deserving of recognition, Wei Xuegang, didn't seek credit at all. He sought something far more substantial: Khun Sa's territory.

The UWSA swallowed Shanland, as conquerors do. Wa South, previously the size of Brooklyn, absorbed Khun Sa's fallen kingdom to become as large as Connecticut. Wa State's total territory, including the motherland, now encompassed twelve thousand square miles, as much soil as the Netherlands. No narcotics cartel had ever ruled so much land outright—an achievement owed in part to the US government, perpetually unable to predict the consequences of its interventions.

Going back decades, American spies sought to influence the Golden Triangle drug trade, denying its awesome power to any group hostile toward the US empire. But under Wei, a single supercartel dominated the region—one led by men with a personal grievance toward America. Wei was the realization of everything the CIA's Cold War–era planners once feared. A tribal group, derided as illiterate barbarians, had outmaneuvered Langley's Ivy League–educated strategists.

And Wei was just getting started.

In the late 1990s, the Wa nation hit a new civilizational marker—though not the kind Saw Lu had prayed for. It became its own sort of imperial power. Historically, the Wa stuck to their own mountains, only attacking intruders and one another. Now they possessed a colony: the ruins of Shanland. Problem was, native Shan peoples populated the choicest areas, so Wei sent UWSA forces to purge some eight thousand unarmed farmers. Resistors were beaten or shot. This was no orgy of

mayhem—that was not Wei's style—but rather a calculated terror campaign, efficient and swift. The UWSA didn't drive out all the Shan, but
those allowed to remain—living on lower-quality plots of land—would
forever suffer the UWSA's menacing supervision.

After ethnically cleansing his new possession, Wei embarked on a
so-called economic recovery plan, entailing the "restoration of the population to normal levels."[24] This meant trucking in Wa highlanders from
the freezing motherland to populate his frontier. They remain there today
in Wa South. It is among the most unique political creations on earth: a
settler colony ruled by a drug lord.

BOOK FOUR

MANIFEST DESTINY

A t last, my pilgrimage to Wa State was imminent.

Stand by, the United Wa State Army (UWSA) envoy texted. The week before Chinese New Year celebrations looks promising for a trip to Panghsang.

There were terms. No soliciting interviews with specific leaders, such as Chairman Bao Youxiang. Nor could I show up solo; they wouldn't waste their time on a single reporter. The envoy told me to bring other journalists of varied nationalities. I assembled a team of six: an Australian, a Swede, a Singaporean-American, a Chinese national, and myself. Jacob, a former UWSA officer, would serve as translator and glorified babysitter.

Our expected entry route: Wa State's semisecret backdoor, a channel that circumvents territory controlled by either Burma or China. We'd start in northern Thailand, cross the Mekong River, and stamp into Laos. We would wait at the King's Roman Casino, a criminally inclined riverside playground. True to the name, its architecture is opulent kitsch: Corinthian pillars and statues of ancient emperors. Beyond baccarat, the casino zone's offerings include ketamine and tiger-bone wine. The entire complex is sanctioned by the US government, which alleges it warehouses crystal meth for the UWSA.

We'd spend a night at the casino, then take a boat up a stretch of the Mekong known for freshwater pirates. Roughly one hundred miles upriver, we'd disembark at a river port administered by the Mong La Army, which is not really an army, rather a warlord-run militia in thrall to the UWSA.[1] A Wa driver would collect us at the pier and chauffeur us to Panghsang—a twelve-hour journey up zigzagging mountain roads.

That was the plan. I'd already packed. In my bag: a phone scrubbed of suspicious contacts, an audio recorder, and twenty-six thousand yuan ($4,000). Plus a jar of peanut butter. I would not starve or lack cash for bribes.

Then came a wild card courtesy of Xi Jinping. That January, the Chinese president announced a surprise visit to Yangon, and the UWSA informed me that under no circumstances would they host Westerners during Xi's trip to the Burmese lowlands. If we created scandal while in Panghsang—by posting salacious tweets or getting injured or even dying—the bad news would leach attention from Xi, a person no one wants to upset. Our trip was put on hold.

While in Burma, Xi glad-handed with military generals, promoted Chinese pipeline and port projects, and then flew away. On the way back to Beijing, he paid homage to the Wa. Xi stopped by a tiny village in China, not far from the Wa State border, where the town's inhabitants are ethnically Wa—highlanders colonized in the 1950s and their descendants. Children in red gowns greeted Xi and escorted him to a wooden drum engraved with images of bull skulls. The premier whacked it with a mallet, thrice, wishing the locals propitious rain and riches. His message was explicit: Asia's most powerful man is not afraid to dignify the Wa people.

Once Xi returned to Beijing, my trip could finally commence—or so I thought. That village photo-op would be one of Xi's last public appearances for a very long time. A mysterious virus emanating from the city of Wuhan was spreading fast, forcing China to quarantine citizens and close airports and land crossings. High-tech fencing and security cameras went up along China's borders with Burma, including Wa State.

The Wa, imitating China's policy, insulated themselves too. Never before had they faced an invader so fearless as Covid-19. UWSA soldiers in white biohazard suits corralled all non-Wa visitors—mostly Chinese traders—and evicted them from the peaks. Aware their health-care system was dreadful, the Wa government hailed stopping the disease as its "most important" mission.

Needless to say, my pilgrimage to the Wa capital was doomed.

EVEN BEFORE THE pandemic, I was devising schemes to enter Wa State without permission, just in case the official route never panned out.

I'd already linked up with a young businessman in Panghsang who offered to sneak me in, or at least try. I'll call him Huli. He was a tour operator who smuggled Chinese thrill seekers into Wa State for profit. He dreamed of diversifying his clientele, providing "adventure tourism experiences" to Westerners, starting with me: a writer whose escapades, once published, would generate wider interest.

As we chatted online, Huli whetted my curiosity with a video he'd filmed atop a Wa mountain. The view was spellbinding. The valleys below his feet were hidden under a carpet of clouds: creamy white, flat as a table, so still they resembled heaven's floor. Huli called this phenomenon "the cloud sea" and wanted to charge rich athletes to bicycle through it. "Words cannot describe how it looks in real life," he told me. "Wa State is brimming with opportunities. Those who cross borders illegally will get the first shot."

Huli's usual customers crossed the Hka River, its green current dividing China from Wa State. Boatmen ferry people across for a small fee, and before the pandemic, the UWSA shrugged off these unlawful passages—but only for Chinese nationals, a special class of visitor. Wa State's economy would shrivel without Chinese traders going back and forth. Any Caucasian trespassers, however, would be interrogated and handed over to Chinese police.

Huli operated under patrons: UWSA officers protecting his business for a 20 percent share of its profits. He was urging them to bend the rules for small groups of well-supervised, non-Asian tourists such as myself. But this was a work in progress. In the meantime, Huli tinkered with his future itinerary and sometimes solicited my advice. "I have a question," he said. "It's about Western people and Chinese people. For the Chinese, we do a four-day trip. Each night we will send someone to their room. Two or three someones."

"Are you talking about women?"

"Yes. We have excellent quality here."

"Right. Well, I think most Westerners would be freaked out by that."

"I see. Strange. We feel this is a sign of a good host."

Huli believed Wa people were curious about international visitors, but in their isolation some had developed unorthodox notions of hospitality. After hearing his questions, I was inclined to agree. By learning which faux pas to avoid, Huli hoped to gain an entrepreneurial edge over other Panghsang hustlers. He'd personally witnessed business

deals ruined by cultural misunderstandings, even between Wa officials and Chinese guests, the foreigners with whom they were most
familiar.

"Imagine a Chinese from an upper-class family comes here to invest,"
Huli said. "He is greeted by a Wa government official." Said official is
flanked on all sides by grimacing troops with Chinese-made Type-97
rifles, perhaps "a few teenage girl soldiers carrying RPGs. Now this guy is
frightened to the bone. But we ourselves do not understand why. We think
this is good. It shows the official is strong and can protect the investment.
As you can see, some behavioral work must be done."

Tourism was just one of Huli's interests. Others included luxury
goods (authentic and otherwise) as well as cryptocurrency. He was certain
that Wa State—above the clouds, beyond the law—could find a unique
role in the twenty-first-century global economy. "It's the most free place in
the world, man. This is not propaganda. It's 100 percent true. There is no
environmental authority. No quality checks. No one asking what you pay
your workers."

One day, Huli sent a message asking if I was in shape. More or less, I
said. "I have a route. No boats involved. But physically it is quite demanding. You'll have to cross a river by jumping rock to rock. Then lift your
body weight with your hands up onto cliff edges. If you can do that, it's
the safest route possible."

I considered Huli's proposal, mindful that Chinese border authorities
had recently nabbed a Chinese-American reverend crossing illegally into
Wa State. They spotted him crossing the Hka, pulled him ashore, and sentenced him to seven years. Visions of joining him in a gulag diminished
my temptation to sneak over from China.[2] So I asked Huli how well he
knew Wa State's other territory: Wa South on the Thai-Burma border.
Very well, he said.

Many Wa officers see their southern territory the way white Americans in the nineteenth century saw the Old West frontier—a harsh land
where tough folks, driven by destiny, go to seek fortune. Not through cattle ranching or gold mining, in this case, but through methamphetamine
production: importing precursor chemicals, protecting labs, guarding
trails leading into Thailand. Securing a job in the booming meth trade is a
short path to relative prosperity.

Intuiting my thoughts, Huli issued a warning. "No. Forget about Wa
South. It's strictly forbidden." Most settlements there amount to a "lab

surrounded by a barracks surrounded by farmland. All Wa must have special permission to go. Even I cannot visit there without certain connections. You would need a phone number that can stop a bullet."

I cited my past crossings from Thailand into other rebel territories in Burma, all of them successful. "No," he told me. "One of two things will happen. At best you will bribe Wa border guards who will take your money and still won't let you in. Because they will be executed for doing so." The other scenario? "You walk through snake-filled jungles for four hours before reaching a UWSA camp." There, he said, you'll be detained or shot on sight. "Please. Don't try."

I tried.

Not by stumbling across the Thai-Burma border alone with a pack full of cash but with the assistance of experienced guides. If visiting Panghsang was impossible, I would instead find a way to peer into Wa South—a realm shaped by none other than Wei Xuegang.

OVER SEVERAL MONTHS, I made repeated forays over the border, each time nipping at Wa South's perimeter. My guides were career people smugglers, charging $300 per crossing, round-trip. They were amiable men and women, all ethnically Shan, with relatives on the other side: a land once ruled by Khun Sa, now ruled by Wei. In 4x4 pickups we rumbled up mountain passages so rutted that I feared the axles would snap. My head bouncing off the cabin's ceiling, I understood why the Exiles cartel once plied these same passages with mules instead of trucks.

They brought me near hills topped with concrete structures: UWSA camps. The slopes below were shorn of trees so that Wa troops could spot intruders. My guides explained: our indigenous Shan are valley people, but these Wa invaders take comfort in altitude. They prefer living as high up as possible. One excursion brought us within one thousand feet of a UWSA outpost: a cement cube with no roof but a tarp. Late-afternoon sunlight painted its gray walls bronze. Two UWSA soldiers stood guard, with rifles at hand, but we did not fear them. At our feet yawned a chasm separating our hilltop from theirs. The pair stood at the rim gazing back: human-shaped green specks, faceless in the distance. I needed to get closer.

In time, I found guides willing to sneak me into a tiny village under Wa South's control. The dirt path snaking across the borderline was unguarded at the time, but a misspelled sign posted beside the trail read "Illegel Crossing." I recalled Huli's warnings with a shiver.

We came to a cluster of huts fashioned from the forest's meager offerings: walls made of overlapping husk, drooping roofs of sunbaked grass. Chickens scratched at the red dirt. Rubber flip-flops strewn near open doorways told me we were not alone. The people who emerged were Shan, not Wa. Children relieved me of the gift I carried: a cardboard box full of Mama-brand instant noodles. A delicacy, suggested by my guides. The locals would prepare it with water scooped from rain barrels and heated over charcoal fires.

I pulled out my audio recorder, but they made me put it away. Too black, oblong, gun-like. They hurried me under a wooden shelter where I could not be spotted from a distance. Hunkering atop a nearby hill was a UWSA fortress: metal-roofed buildings, ringed by a wooden stockade, with Wa sentries vigilant against mischief at the far end of their binoculars.

You don't want them to see you, said a gray-haired man in a white tunic sitting across from me under the shelter. They have 120s, he said. I must have scrunched my face dumbly. He explained: 120-millimeter mortar shells; if fired, they would land here in seconds. Yanda was his name, and he spoke in the high timbre of a woodwind instrument. He wore no jewelry, only a bracelet of cotton twine.

Where was he from? Originally, valleys nearby. He'd lived in a basin of fertile land, as did his grandparents before him, until the Wa soldiers came, forcing Yanda and everyone he knew to this place—this bald hill— where the soil was lifeless as chalk.

That was almost twenty years ago. Living up here, he said, was like living with a gun in your face twenty-four hours a day. This was no ordinary corner of Wa State. It was a fresh-air ghetto: a reservation for indigenous Shan, trapped under the gaze of their conquerors.

I asked Yanda to tell me the story of his dispossession.

WHEN YANDA WAS a young man, he went to the local temple and beseeched the monks for tattoos. His back became their canvas. The monks inked his flesh using wands of bamboo with brass needles welded to the tips. His skin came alive with mythical creatures and proverbs in Pali-Sanskrit, a language known to Buddhist monks and few others. "Some of my tattoos prevent poisoning," he told me. "Others protect me from blades and bullets. Or snakes. A dog could bite me and its teeth would not pierce my skin."

Yanda lived in the Mong Kan valleys, just north of Thailand, home to about ten villages. It was always an unstable place, but Yanda knew his homeland was very special. Why else would so many outsiders desire it? He'd seen marauders passing through his whole life. The Exiles' caravans in the 1960s and 1970s. Burmese infantry, struggling to control lands that technically belonged to their country. In the early 1980s, Khun Sa's forces took over, Yanda said, but they were at least Shan, the same race as the valley's native people.

Yanda married. Raised children. Later became a grandfather. His tattoos grew runny with age, but he still credited his longevity to their protective powers. Yanda owned little but never felt poor. How could he with such wealth at his feet: a backyard electric green with rice stalks and gardens rich with pumpkins, melons, tomatoes. The valleys fed several thousand Shan, nourished by their ancestral soil. He pitied city people toiling for some boss's handouts.

The Wa showed up in 2001. Yanda lived in a teakwood house on stilts and saw them coming from his elevated porch: a few men in pickle-green uniforms with red emblems on the sleeve. They craned their necks up at him, AK-47s strapped to their backs. Come down here, they said. So he did. One of the UWSA soldiers spoke halting Shan. You need to leave, he said. You and the whole village. Now.

Why? What did we do wrong?

It's not about right or wrong. Just leave.

Yanda asked to speak to their commander. You're not listening, the soldier said. Look around. From the sky to the dirt, everything here belongs to the Wa now. So gather up your family and go. Bring any possessions, and we'll shoot you in the back.

"I'd never heard anything like that in my life," Yanda told me. "Even my great-grandparents never heard a thing like that. That soldier said, 'Nothing belongs to you anymore.' I couldn't believe it." The soldiers threatening him belonged to Wa Southern Command, helmed by Wei. Victorious in their war against Khun Sa, they were going valley to valley, evicting Shan families at gunpoint.

Yanda called his wife and children to come outside. He could see other villagers gathering beside a trail leading south, readying their exodus. The day prior they'd finished communally harvesting the rice fields, and Yanda realized none of them would taste the grains they'd spent months farming.

Did anyone from the village resist?

Yes, Yanda told me. The headman.

Almost everyone evacuated, but in one of their last glimpses of home, the villagers turned back to see their headman berating the Wa soldiers. He owned a rice-milling machine of which he was very proud, and he refused to leave without it. Only two Shan men stuck around to defend the headman. Yanda and the rest trudged away.

The evacuees moved southward, chattering anxiously, wondering where they'd lay their heads come nightfall. They came upon an uninhabited hilltop covered in briery shrubs. There they stopped, collecting branches and leaves to make crude shelters. There was talk around the fire that night of gathering crude weapons and returning to retake their land. But then two villagers—the men who'd hung back with the headman—wandered into the makeshift camp and sat down with horror written into their faces.

The men recounted what they'd seen back in the village: Wa troops dragging the headman to a wooden hitching post and binding him to the post with rope. The soldiers unsheathed knives, first severing the headman's left ear, then his right. They dismembered him as if dressing an animal. They cut off his hands and his feet. Finally the Wa drove a blade into his neck to silence the screaming. You two, the soldiers said, leave this place. Go tell your people what you've witnessed. "A very effective method," Yanda said. "Not once did we consider fighting them after hearing that story and we have not contemplated it since."

Other villages all around the Mong Kan valleys were also purged, and soon thousands of Shan people joined the first arrivals on that rugged hill—the very hill where I now sat with Yanda. The hill and its environs were mostly sterile, unsuited to growing rice. To beat back starvation, able-bodied Shan refugees snuck into Thailand, labored illegally on tea plantations for horrid wages, bought rice, and smuggled it back to their families.

In time the refugees grew bold enough to come down from the hill and sow rice in a ribbon of decent land unused by the Wa invaders. They worked this land with halting footsteps, fearing landmines underfoot. The Wa monitored them, glaring down from an elevated fortress in the distance. For many years, they let them be. The Shan refugees survived like this for nearly two decades—a people displaced only miles from home yet totally immiserated. Eventually the UWSA's tolerance expired. In 2019 Wa officers came down to the fields and told the refugees they lacked permission to farm rice in Wa South. From that moment on, entering the paddies was punishable by arrest.

On cloudless days, Yanda can see it from the hill's apex: a section of the valley stolen from his people. "It makes me sick," he said, imagining colonizers drinking his water, lazing on his soil. Instead of pumpkins or tomatoes, the Wa grow rubber trees: a cash crop shipped to China. Soil his ancestors once tilled now nurtures a commodity used by Chinese factories to make running shoes and car tires and other products exported to shopping malls around the world. "They took everything from us. All for money," Yanda said. "Money and power. That's all the UWSA believes in. They hate justice and invent laws to satisfy their desires."

It was time for me to go. Before bidding good-bye to Yanda, I delicately brought up the name Wei Xuegang. I wanted to know how he felt about the ruler of Wa South and the architect of his dispossession.

Yanda started to speak but stopped himself and fidgeted with the loop of twine around his wrist.

It's OK, I said. You don't have to answer.

THE GREAT MIGRATION

Growing up Wa among lowlanders in Burma meant knowing your place.

Raised in Lashio, Jacob was taught to mute his ethnicity. In the early 1990s, as a young teen, he did not speak Wa in the market or at school, where the curriculum painted minorities as unruly simpletons. He knew the Burmese locals would never embrace his Wa community. The Wa were merely tolerated, so long as they behaved like an underclass: domesticated skull collectors, lucky to mingle with the townsfolk.

Within his community, though, Jacob and his family members could be themselves. They spoke their mother tongue, ate *moik*, and hung monochrome portraits of their forebears: wrinkled Wa couples in black robes, the original converts of William Marcus Young. Come Sunday mornings, the church bell—that old bombshell—would toll, its metallic clang summoning families to the chapel. Inside they'd see Saw Lu standing behind a lacquered pulpit, leading the community in prayer. To the hundreds of Wa adults in Lashio, he was a living legend—the man who, in the early 1970s, led them from the peaks, vile communists at their heels, down to Lashio, where they built this community from scraps. To Jacob and other kids, listening rapt on splintery pews, Saw Lu was like some Old Testament prophet: all-knowing, unassailable, with molten eyes and a voice like thunder.

No one questioned his authority. Only under Saw Lu's majesty, and through his connections to the regime, was their community able to live in relative peace, spared the persecution—night raids, extortion, random beatings—that Burmese soldiers visited upon other minorities. He was their shepherd. They were his flock.

Saw Lu's house contained the neighborhood's only television: a black-and-white set with rabbit ears. Jacob would while away afternoons watching tacky Burmese soap operas with Grace, Saw Lu's daughter. Two years younger than Jacob, she was, like him, both brainy and churchy, and he felt the stirrings of a crush. But Jacob couldn't divulge his feelings. "Are you kidding? No way. Like every kid, I was terrified of her dad."

Tragedy provided an opening for romance. In 1992, following Saw Lu's torture by the junta, the shepherd escaped Lashio, slipping off to Wa State with Mary to escape further torment. But Saw Lu did not bring his children because the highlands had hardly any schools. So Grace and her siblings stayed behind under the care of an aunt. "She was orphaned, sort of," Jacob said. "In a sense, we all were."

Deprived of their protector, Lashio's Wa community fell victim to prowling Burmese agents: police and soldiers menacing the Wa, falsely accusing them of crimes, demanding cash to make charges go away. "That's how we grew up—in fear," Jacob told me. "As we got older, I saw that Grace really suffered without her parents around. I wanted to step in and soothe her. My heart went beat, beat, beat, and I was, you know, falling in love."

By 1995, Jacob was eighteen years old, enrolled in a local university (his major: geography), and coming into his own. Built like a match-stick, he grew black hair past his ears and traded his sarong for ripped jeans, seeking to imitate grunge rockers glimpsed in uncensored Western magazines, which his buddies passed around like contraband. He finally screwed up his courage and proposed to Grace when she was a high school senior. She said yes. But after her graduation, the young fiancés looked around Burma and saw nothing in their future but endless harassment.

They felt the call of the peaks: their ethnic motherland. But as town dwellers, neither knew much about Wa State. They imagined it as a utopia under construction: poor but wondrous, improving bit by bit. Saw Lu had abandoned his flock for a higher calling—building up the Wa nation—and the couple wanted to see what he'd achieved. Let's go, Grace said. You can finish your degree through distance learning. My parents will house us. We'll finally feel free.

In 1997, Jacob found a pickup truck driver willing to drive them into the peaks: a twelve-hour journey up corkscrew trails. Jacob had vague notions about Saw Lu's progress in Wa State over the previous five years, hearing only that the United Wa State Army (UWSA) had declared him a great leader. So he couldn't fathom why the truck driver, following written directions to Saw Lu's home, dropped the couple off in front of a hovel. There must've been some mistake.

Stepping inside, Jacob and Grace looked down at the dirt floor, then up at the thatch roof. Daylight glowed through fissures in the ceiling. The walls, made of plaited bamboo, wobbled at each gust of cold wind. The place was a dump. Confusion turned to shock when their eyes fell on the patriarch himself.

Out shuffled a gaunt and broken-down man who looked much older than his mid-fifties. What remained of Saw Lu's silver-black hair had gone shaggy. His dark skin looked bloodless, and his cheeks were razored down by hunger. Jacob greeted his father-in-law to be, but the reply came back muffled—as if Saw Lu's spirit were trapped behind some invisible membrane.

"Father," Grace said, "we need some money to pay the driver." Saw Lu would not meet her eyes. Mary, shamefaced, slipped outside. The couple heard her pleading with the man in the truck. Give us twenty-four hours, she said, so we can scrounge up cash from the neighbors.

In the coming days, Jacob worked up the nerve to ask what had gone so horribly wrong. Saw Lu explained that this hovel doubled as his personal prison. The government forbade him from walking more than three hundred meters from the front door. Old friends kept them alive by leaving buckets of rice and cooking oil by the door. Saw Lu wasn't a leader at all. He was a beggar.

Honestly, son, I am lucky to be alive, he said. Certain influential people had wanted him dead. Chairman Bao Youxiang had to hide him in a rathole for weeks, waiting for his enemies' fury to wane. He eventually convinced them to let Saw Lu continue drawing breath, but only if he led a pitiful existence under house arrest. I was on a mission, Saw Lu said, to rid this nation of narcotics. I failed. Chairman Bao is a decent man, but he complies with the traffickers—for their revenues sustain his army. All the while, everyday people live in squalor. Go walk the streets of Panghsang, Jacob. See the society they have wrought.

As instructed, Jacob headed downhill toward the capital's marketplace. He saw mud-brick homes alongside shops with stone facades, the odd karaoke joint catering to visiting Chinese traders. Wild-haired children, pantsless, darted past. The ground beneath his sneakers was clay, much harder than the squishy loam of the Burmese lowlands. In the distance, the Hka flowed turgidly, with China's shoreline visible through river mist.

Jacob located the market: a shabby bazaar set up along a main avenue. Vendors squatted under canopies, their wares arrayed on mats: rice, tools, onions, and herbs. Opium sellers peddled without shame, weighing fudge-like gobs on antique scales, using AA batteries as counterweights, doling out portions to smokers lining up in ragged queues. Like all sellers in the Wa capital, they only accepted Chinese yuan.

Jacob heard a commotion of smacks and yelps at the far end of the avenue. Stumbling in his direction were a few unkempt men, chanting unintelligibly, with random household items strung around their necks: a plastic stool, a dead chicken. Jacob asked the locals to explain. Thieves, they said. Forced to parade their ill-gotten goods and confess their crimes. As the men grew closer, Jacob heard what they were mumbling: we are thieves, we are thieves. Merchants kicked their shins as they passed. To Jacob, it was like some biblical scene from a pre-Christian, forsaken age.

He'd not expected to experience culture shock among fellow Wa. In the coming weeks, Jacob would witness a far more disturbing scene. One afternoon, UWSA trucks drove through the capital, loudspeakers on their rooves, ordering citizens to gather at a barren knoll on the town's outskirts. Jacob arrived to find a crowd already assembled, jostling to see a clutch of damned men: three criminals standing in a line, hooded, with wrists shackled.

Flanked by uniformed grunts, a UWSA officer shouted out their offenses. All were accused of murder. Behind the convicts, up on the knoll, Jacob saw a rectangular earthen pit four feet deep. "One of the convicts was going insane. He screamed, 'Mother, father, are you there? I can't see anything. Is this real?'" Another prisoner trembled as a wet patch darkened his trousers. When the officer was finished speaking, troops trotted the convicts up to the pit's edge and guided them in, arranging the murderers in a tidy row, so that the rim of the pit was level with their chests. The troops stood overhead, aimed their rifles downward, and shot the convicts in the heart. Jacob jumped at the gunfire. Most of the crowd did not.

Following this public execution, Jacob veered toward an identity crisis. A gentle soul, he disapproved of all killing, but what really disturbed him was the crowd's reaction. Most seemed indifferent, some even amused. This was not the Wa society he'd known back in Lashio. Clearly the intimacy of his old neighborhood didn't scale up to a nation of half a million. He wondered if he'd ever acclimate and second-guessed moving to Wa State. He needed guidance—but the only person who could provide it was Saw Lu, wasting his days squatting on a stool and staring at clouds. In desperation, Jacob came to him and expressed his disillusionment. To his relief, Saw Lu sat up straighter, his dark eyes focusing, as if Jacob's confession had restorative powers. A long time had passed since anyone sought his wisdom.

Saw Lu lit his tobacco bong and nodded and listened. Son, there is little I can achieve now that I am an outcast. But you are a free man. You possess gifts rare among the highlanders—half a college education, Christian values—and you are obligated to share them. There is still some decency in the Wa government. Join the system. Improve it from within.

But how, sir?

Our nation needs teachers. And you're more than qualified.

As his shepherd bade, Jacob enlisted in the UWSA as an instructor, keen to spread literacy among the tribe—just as Saw Lu had three decades earlier, as a young man first entering the Wa peaks. Jacob knew how to write in Wa using the Roman script invented a century ago by the Young family missionaries. The UWSA, though atheistic, was adopting the same script out of expedience rather than inventing a new one. But very few officers could read it. Nine in ten could not read at all, and the literate only knew Chinese characters.

When the UWSA officers who enlisted Jacob realized he was a college student, submitting coursework by mail, they told him to skip basic training. He would report directly to Chairman Bao's compound, which housed a small regiment of future leaders in training. Bao, a hardline nationalist, wanted the next generation to read and write in their mother tongue, and Jacob would fulfill this wish. His proximity to Wa State's supreme leader thrilled him. Back in Burma proper, no Wa stood a chance of climbing society's rungs so high or so quickly.

Jacob expected Bao's cadets would be eighteen to twenty-two years old, roughly his age. But on his first day, the classroom filled with children: the youngest six, the oldest fourteen. The little ones swam in their uniforms, their droopy sleeves rolled up and fastened with safety pins. As weeks passed, Jacob also noticed students coming to class with bloody scrapes and welts. Afternoon drills, they said. "I thought, my God, they train them as brutally as grown men." Even the female cadets were bruised up, but none complained. They always showed up scrubbed clean and ready to learn.

Bao himself would sometimes swing by the classroom, causing students to stiffen in their chairs. "I was nervous too—at first," Jacob said. "I'd just arrived, and now I was in the same room with our leader." But Bao was unpretentious, stern but kind, simply inquiring about the day's lessons. "He'd barely finished fourth grade, but clearly he valued education. I liked that." Encounters with the chairman softened Jacob's skepticism about the Wa government. "Unfortunately, it was a kinglike system"— with King Bao on top of it all, trying to hold his motley court intact— "but at least the king was a good person" and an inspiration to boot. A former teenage headhunter was running a nation larger than many in Europe. How many heads of state had overcome such a gruesome past?

Like many Christianized Wa, Jacob fetishized the West, and he dreamed the nation might one day transition to democracy, or at least a more democratic system. A long shot—but perhaps the next generation of Wa officers, his students, could work toward such lofty goals, if he instilled the desire. At that age, their minds were still supple. "At last, my life had purpose," he said. "This was my destiny."

Despite their initial doubts, Jacob and Grace decided that Wa State, however imperfect, should become their permanent home. The couple married in a ceremony inside the hovel. With dust motes twinkling in the morning light, Saw Lu served as officiant with his worn, leather-bound Bible. Soon enough, Grace was pregnant. Each night before bedtime, sharing a mat on the floor, the newlyweds spoke to God. They promised to strive for the betterment of their nation, asking Him to deliver it from darkness, so their children could one day sit in Grandfather Saw Lu's lap, listening to his stories of bloody turmoil. They would struggle to believe their homeland had ever been so benighted.

CHAIRMAN BAO DIDN'T mind his subordinates getting a little rich. Most had grown up scrappy like him, and they were owed a little luxury. Bao's own ring finger twinkled with sapphires, and a Rolex ticked beneath the sleeve of his fatigues.

But by the late 1990s, the chairman feared greed was out of control. His division commanders officiated the drug trade: taxing poppy farmers, opium transporters, and heroin labs in their respective areas. Tax revenues were meant to flow through the entire state. Instead they congealed around the commanders and their kin. At this rate, the UWSA leadership risked calcifying into an elite, numb to the masses' suffering, just like the communist politburo before them.

Bao put every commander on notice, openly castigating those who'd "forgotten how to contribute to society." He warned that even in the middle ranks, many behaved as "officials in name only, focusing primarily on business."[1] Some interpreted this as a coded warning to officers trying to imitate Wei Xuegang, the wealthiest Wa (or rather half-Wa) person to ever live. But Bao would not dare censure Wei by name.

Officially Chairman Bao was Wei's boss. But as many quipped, Bao was the nation's "muscle," Wei its "brains," and neither could function without the other. Brains referred to Wei's financial brilliance, not his political acuity, but even that distinction was blurring. As governor of Wa South, Wei was not just a drug baron but a leader in his own right. One man ruled the motherland, the other the frontier, and the two seldom met. It was possible to imagine Wei seceding and taking his chunk of the nation with him. Or the entire UWSA, mesmerized by Wei's fortunes, abandoning its state-building ambitions and morphing into a straight-up drug cartel—rather than operating as a nation that, as Bao saw it, just happened to produce narcotics by the ton.

Bao knew he needed to rebalance the economy away from heroin. Saw Lu's diagnosis from years before still held truth. Without outside help, the Wa would never "break the bondage" to opium—and though Bao wasn't one to care what foreigners thought of the Wa, he needed to attract aid and investment, diversifying their revenue streams. That meant scrubbing Wa State's dirty reputation clean.

The chairman set aside a chunk of land near the capital—about five hundred square miles, the size of Los Angeles—for an experiment. He said the United Nations' antidrug agency, if it so chose, could come and improve this special development zone as it saw fit.[2] In return, the UWSA would raze some of its poppy plantations. UN aid experts arrived in 1998. Calling the initiative the Wa Alternative Development Project, they got to work: treating lepers, teaching farmers irrigation techniques, and vaccinating Wa kids by the thousands. Compared to Saw Lu's dream—a $50 million extravaganza, erecting a welfare state overnight—this was a meager operation. The UN project's annual budget hovered at around half a million dollars.[3]

But it was a start. Bao believed foreign aid coming through the United Nations—not the shifty Americans—could prop up the Wa economy as it transitioned away from heroin. He even convinced Burma's junta to let the experiment play out. At the time, Secretary One Khin Nyunt was once again dangling hopes of "reform" to distract the West from Burma's totalitarian misery, and the dictator wanted the United Nations on his side.

From the outset, Bao was clear: foreign aid alone would never replace drug revenues. The UWSA had to build its own agricultural and industrial sector to become self-supporting—and it would direct exports toward China's fast-growing economy. That meant mining, mostly tin, and harvesting rubber, a commodity for which China's factories had a screaming demand. Rubber trees, like poppies, flourish in low temperatures and at high elevation. Wa State would also open factories making liquor and cigarettes for the Chinese consumer market, which, by the late 1990s, was exploding.

There was skepticism, even among the Wa, that the chairman wanted to completely ban all opium and heroin production. So Bao, in his bluff way, attempted to remove all doubt. He started telling anyone who'd listen that if poppies still sprouted in Wa soil after the year 2005, he'd invite the "international community" to "come chop my head off."

This declaration drew laughs from the Drug Enforcement Administration, but the Wa public realized he was serious. After two centuries, they were finally going to forsake the opium poppy for good. The news swirled all around the peaks, from the capital to outlying towns, even reaching isolated mountaintop villages gnawed by cold. Saw Lu learned of Bao's declaration from friends who left rice on his doorstep. They presented it as good tidings. He was inclined to agree.

Saw Lu's dream—pronounced dead, dismembered, and buried in 1993—was reanimating, clawing back to the surface, albeit in a much weaker form. Bao's plan was quite different: slower paced, entangled with the Chinese economy, missing Saw Lu's Baptist fervency. There would be no wave of American doctors and teachers and geologists descending on

Wa State, just a smattering of UN workers, closely monitored, operating on a tiny budget. Yet none could deny that Saw Lu, pariah though he was, was the progenitor of this idea.

When Saw Lu asked the inevitable question—What will the UWSA do about Wei?—his friends' expressions melted and their hands fidgeted.

About that. Apparently Bao, keen to avert an internal schism, had somehow secured the drug lord's participation in this opium-eradication scheme. And in Saw Lu's mind, that confounding and hideous fact corrupted the spirit of his dream beyond all recognition.

SAW LU WASN'T the only person confused. It was inexplicable, if not flat-out bizarre. Why would Southeast Asia's top heroin lord endorse the wholesale extermination of Wa opium poppies—the raw ingredient sustaining his empire? But Wei had his reasons. As it happened, he badly desired something that only Bao could supply.

People.

Having purged so many indigenous villagers from Wa South—Shan villagers like Yanda—Wei needed to populate his territory with servile subjects. A consummate dealmaker, Wei suggested that he and Bao help each other out. The chairman was about to rob many Wa of their livelihood: poppy farming. The United Nations couldn't feed and clothe them all. Nor could Bao employ every highlander in some brand-new factory. So send them to me, Wei said. I'll make use of them along the frontier.

They called it the "great migration," and it was one of the most ambitious social engineering feats in Southeast Asia's modern history.[4] The UWSA would round up more than one in four Wa, totaling 120,000 people, and transplant them to Wei's territory along the Thai-Burma border. Every highlander chosen for relocation was instructed to show gratitude. UWSA officials told them Wa South was a slice of paradise. No more shivering on the Chinese border. You'll start life anew in green valleys bristling with rice shoots. Go raise pigs, be happy, forget all about the bleak hamlets in which you were born. Transport to the south was free, compliance mandatory.

Most of the migration occurred between 1999 and 2001. Along the border with China, UWSA platoons would enter Wa settlements around sunrise and blow whistles to wake everyone up. Evacuation in thirty minutes, they'd shout. Bring no belongings. Troops would then corral poppy-farming villagers by the thousands and march them to the nearest drivable road. This was often a days-long trek.

One evacuee, a poppy farmer then in his forties, recalled, "After we'd been walking for five days, we heard a sound in the distance—a sound like strong wind. My wife and daughter asked me what the sound was. But I didn't know either."[5] When the villagers rounded a corner, they saw a six-wheeled cargo truck, idling on a muddy slope. They knew motor vehicles existed. But they'd never heard the growl of a big engine. Soldiers packed the villagers onto the open-air truck bed so tight their limbs smushed together. When the truck lurched forward, passengers wailed in horror, and soon vomit pooled at their bare feet. The soldiers parked, got out, and pulled a plastic tarp over their human cargo, as if covering a parrot's cage to silence its squawks. They had nearly two hundred twisty miles ahead. "I felt like I was being punished in hell," the poppy farmer said. "I prayed that, in the next life, I would never ride in a vehicle again. I preferred death to suffering so much."

In this fashion, hundreds of thousands of Wa peasants became involuntary pioneers. Trucks dumped them in depopulated villages in Wa South. The landscape was indeed gentler, comparable to moving from the Rockies to Appalachia. The Wa transplants settled into empty Shan homes, built on stilts, already replete with cooking pots and sleeping mats—as if the previous inhabitants had evaporated. Later arrivals, finding every Shan house claimed, cut down trees to build homes in the Wa style: windowless structures shaped like acorn shells. Such houses are well suited to mountaintops six thousand feet above sea level. But at Wa South's two-thousand-foot elevation, they were sweatboxes trapping in heat and bugs.[6] Thousands of Wa migrants died from malaria, a disease little known in the motherland, which is too frigid for mosquitoes.

As transplants kept coming, Wei divvied them out to trusted subcommanders, each managing a different patch of Wa South's five-thousand-square-mile terrain. To acclimate newcomers, Wei's lieutenants doled out care packages: rice, farm tools, and, for fighting-age Wa (including post-pubescent boys and girls), a UWSA uniform, boots, and an assault rifle. If called upon, they explained, you will defend this land to the death. But your primary duty is simply to farm and occupy these valleys.

With an obedient population under his thumb, along with roughly four thousand of the UWSA's twenty thousand troops, Wei was more formidable than ever. But all that power came with unwanted prominence.

His responsibilities were mounting. He was Wa South's governor, commander of the territory's armed forces, and still the entire nation's finance czar. He loved strategizing over the frontier's development but deplored the schmoozing inherent in politics. To avoid large groups of strangers (and their germs), he kept vampiric hours, preferring to work all night and go to sleep as the sun came up. Face-to-face meetings were often delegated to his two brothers, effectively the territory's deputy governors.

As for public gatherings, the best Wei could manage was the occasional closed-door address to UWSA officers, but even these meetings were infrequent, and photography was forbidden. Targeted by the DEA and still facing the death penalty in Thailand, Wei was loath for anyone to snap his picture.

An existential question hung over the frontier, one Wei needed to step forward and answer. If Bao's poppy-free pledge held true, the Wa opium supply would run dry in a few years, and all of Wei's China White refineries would run out of raw material. Would Wei really walk away from the narcotics-producing behemoth he'd painstakingly built, brick by heroin brick? If so, how would he continue financing Wa State—his primary responsibility?

To clear the air, Wei convened loyalists for a rare address at his Wa South headquarters: a no-frills, one-story complex of buildings painted bone white. One of these Wa officers was perhaps not so loyal, however, because he captured the speech on a tape recorder and, years later, shared it with the DEA. The recording provides a glimpse of Wei's approach to statesmanship.

Like a CEO kicking off an annual stockholders' meeting, he led with positivity: "We have defeated all of our enemies" and now turn to nation building, a task that will "challenge us in new ways." Nasty habits must fall by the wayside. Too many soldiers drink to excess, and gambling is rampant. Poor discipline threatens our efficiency. The Wa cannot simply live to fight, he said. Our southern region must also feed the elderly and educate children. But Wei only gave public service a cursory mention—a throwaway nod to corporate social responsibility—before turning to the subject overshadowing all others.

"You've all heard the UWSA is getting out of the opium business. I know what you're thinking. Sometimes we lay down rules with no intention of enforcement. But this time, it's serious." Wa State will criminalize opium, he said. Not tomorrow. Not in a year. But soon. "Our revenues are going to drop." But Wei promised his followers that if they were patient, the good times would return. Stick with me, he said, and alluded to new revenue sources, including one bristling with potential. Wei did not provide specifics. He only asked for his subordinates' trust. This speech, short and direct, ended on that note of mystery.

Wa South's senior officers—the elite corps allowed to see his face—filed out of the room without solid answers. Most troops in Wa South still didn't know what Wei looked like, only that he was Chinese in appearance and never wore a UWSA uniform. They were in thrall to a shadow.

To this day, there are only two photos of Wei in the public domain. In one, his 1988 DEA mugshot, Wei grimaces; in the other one, of uncertain origin, also taken around that time, his eyes are downcast. But other images do exist. I've seen a few. A former Burmese intelligence colonel who called himself "good friends" with Wei once showed me a private photo of the drug lord taken around the time of this CEO-style address: a snapshot apparently captured without Wei's knowledge. In the photo, Wei looks boyish in his mid-fifties. His fair skin is unlined, his black hair combed forward in a neat bowl cut. Wearing a white polo tucked into high-hitched green trousers, he looks more like an insurance actuary than a kingpin.

Those who've met Wei usually remark that he's quiet, unless the subject turns to business, and that he never laughs. But in one photo I saw, Wei is grinning impishly, teeth showing, as if the shutter snapped mid-snicker. In retrospect, the narco-mogul had every reason to smile. At the time, he was perfecting a corporate strategy that, if executed just right, would deliver unimaginable profits to the UWSA and revolutionize the Asian drug trade—all without lancing a single poppy bulb.

Wei was about to orient his drug-production machine away from heroin and toward methamphetamine. And if his calculations were correct, this overhaul would deter any DEA agent from dragging him out of the Wa frontier, either dead or in cuffs.

VANILLA SPEED

LATE 2001.

The great migration was all but complete. Wa South was developing fast, and Wei Xuegang governed from a hilltop complex in the territory's de facto capital: Mong Yawn, a speedily constructed, heavily militarized zone wired up with electrical cables and phone lines. The Drug Enforcement Administration closely tracked Wei—a laborious task that principally fell to a special agent named John Whalen. He was located far from Wei, some three hundred miles southwest, at the US embassy in Yangon, Burma.

Whalen kept a dossier on Wei. Chronicling the drug lord's success, it grew thicker by the year. "We had files on Wei going way back," he said. "Very smart guy. Savvy businessman. Deep down, an opportunist. And a survivor, certainly that."

Whalen was entering his fifth year in the DEA's Burma office, the longest-ever stint in an outpost marked by quick turnover and tumult. He'd been a Marine Corps captain in his youth and later joined the DEA, making his bones in the 1990s by chasing Asian street gangs around Los Angeles. Dealers in California peddled China White, and in coming to Burma, Whalen hoped to attack the Asia-to-America heroin pipeline at its source.

During his first week at the US embassy, inside that musty third-floor office, Whalen swung open a Diebold safe and squinted in disbelief—just as Saladino had nearly a decade before. "There was an AK-47 in there. Chinese-made. Older model with a nice wooden stock. No one could tell me where it came from." The weapon suggested that Burma held hard-core action in store, but once Whalen settled into the job, he realized it actually favored a patient, methodical approach.

"You'll never go around Burma slapping handcuffs on criminals every day." This wasn't Colombia or Mexico where DEA agents join *federales* in bashing down doors. The State Department wouldn't allow that in Burma, and, frankly, neither would the junta. Attempting to appease the United States via the DEA wasn't working out for the regime. The White House, citing human rights atrocities, had banned all new American investment in the country in 1997; the few US brands producing goods in Burma—PepsiCo, Levi-Strauss, Anheuser-Busch—pulled out. And by the early 2000s, human rights advocates, with the help of a congressional clique headed by Mitch McConnell, had successfully turned *Burma* into a byword for despotism.

It is a credit to Whalen's persistence and good humor that, despite thick tension between Burma's government and his own, he somehow developed a decent relationship with his regime counterparts. Like his predecessors, he grew close to Kyaw Thein, or KT, since promoted from colonel to general. But the Burmese wouldn't bring him along for the rough stuff, like storming traffickers' stash houses. "In Burma," Whalen said, "you're just collecting information in hopes of arresting somewhere way down the line. If you get lucky."

It was a slow-burn job, ill-suited for wannabe Rambos. But Whalen didn't mind. Thrill seeking was behind him. He was content to gather intelligence, work sources, and slowly detangle the web of smugglers, armed clans, and secret investors ensconced around Wei's operation. Tracking a cerebral drug lord would demand a cerebral strategy.

Wei's whereabouts were no mystery. The DEA possessed satellite images of the white-walled hilltop complex where he rested his head. It was roughly ten miles north of Thailand's Mae Ai district in Chiang Mai province. Sometimes, if Whalen felt mischievous, he'd go to his Burmese antinarcotics counterparts and suggest they team up to go nab him.

"Sorry, John. We don't know where Wei Xuegang is."

"I'd say, 'Oh really? Here are the coordinates.'" Whalen knew they'd squirm. The regime wanted no beef with Wei or the United Wa State Army (UWSA), a rogue state too mighty to confront.

Under Whalen, the DEA's Burma office—seen as cursed following the Angelo Saladino and Rick Horn episodes—finally lost its reputation for chaos. Like a good marine, Whalen didn't buck the system. He kept the State Department in the loop. As for the Central Intelligence Agency, their partnership was strained but manageable. The agency constantly tried to turn Whalen's best contact, KT, into an "agent." That's spy talk for an informant betraying his or her governments' secrets. In US embassies around the world, this is a frequent source of DEA-CIA friction: spies poaching narcs' contacts, muddying their relationships. But Whalen, a no-drama sort of guy, avoided open conflict with the agency.

When it came to the Wa, Whalen and the CIA were mostly simpatico, thanks to a policy shift at DEA headquarters. The top brass had ditched any hope of collaborating with the UWSA, now viewed as a straight-up drug cartel, not a charity case. Whalen and his superiors wanted Wei in a concrete cell—and so did the CIA.

The CIA had its own motives to seek Wei's downfall. Despite spending his formative years at a CIA-linked radio base, Wei deeply despised the United States, and in establishing Wa South, he'd brought the UWSA—a China-friendly narco-army—down to the doorstep of Thailand, one of America's oldest Asian allies. For decades, this was the sort of scenario CIA officers had struggled to prevent. A former CIA officer active in Southeast Asia at the time confirmed to me that "Wei and his brothers were targets—big targets. We didn't have a lethal finding. But we hoped to put 'em out of business" and, in turn, bring about the UWSA's collapse.

DEA headquarters sought the same outcome. Their thinking on the UWSA and all other narco-armies was colored by the September 11 attacks, which threw the entire US government into a belligerent mood. Among US officials, it became fashionable to rebrand everything as a terror threat, including drug cartels. Even before the rubble had been swept up in Manhattan, President George W. Bush's DEA chief, Asa Hutchinson, publicly decried the specter of "narco-terrorism" on the floor of Congress, where he condemned the Wa alongside cocaine-smuggling Peruvian leftists and the opium-taxing Taliban.[1] The Wa, said the DEA administrator, are a "tribal violent group" that must be stopped. Wei Xuegang was labeled a threat to "the security and freedom of all Americans," alongside other designated "kingpins" such as dons running the Tijuana and Juarez cartels in Mexico.

Because the CIA had its hands full in the Middle East, Whalen, perhaps more than any other official, was responsible for putting Wei out of commission—an impossible-seeming task. Wei was far too clever to ever leave Wa State, so unless the United States wanted to invade—which it didn't—"the chances looked pretty much nil," Whalen said. Still he kept collecting facts, adding them to Wei's dossier, trying to conjure a breakthrough.

His intel suggested that paranoia devoured Wei's mind. Fearing US satellites tracked his every move, Wei often donned a bulky jacket and hiked up its collar to shroud his face. He even wore it indoors while sitting on his sofa watching Hollywood DVDs, a favorite pastime. He'd learned to cook so that no traitor could poison his meals. He trusted no one. This pathological condition prevented Wei from forming intimate friendships with other leaders, namely Chairman Bao Youxiang. According to Whalen's analysis, the chairman and the financier were trapped in a cold marriage of necessity.

Perhaps he could find a way to drive a wedge between them.

ALONG WITH PRACTICALLY every other Western antinarcotics agent, Whalen initially laughed off Bao's vow to eliminate opium from Wa State. But by the early 2000s, all intelligence indicated the Wa leader was trying his damnedest to deliver. As promised, Bao sent UWSA squads to hack down poppies. Month by month, the fields were disappearing—and fast.

So too were many of the labs rendering opium into China White. The typical Wa heroin refinery, whether on the China or the Thai border, was essentially a big wooden barn filled with metal drums, sacks of lime and charcoal, jugs of vinegar-smelling acetic anhydride, and, of course, putty-thick opium. A goat napping in the corner would look right at home. But as these old-school heroin labs shut down, Wei replaced them with a different style of lab.

His new facilities were sturdier and built of cement. Inside, brand-new equipment glinted with an industrial sheen. Each contained stainless-steel vats that sprouted squid-like tangles of tubing. Rubber hoses linked the vats to glass bulbs, big as volleyballs. Also on hand: barrels of sodium cyanide—a potent insecticide—as well as hydrochloric acid, a solvent used to make everything from car batteries to ketchup. The new labs' most essential component, however, was pseudoephedrine.

A few drops of "pseudo" will clear up your sinuses. Wei bought the chemical in fifty-five-gallon plastic barrels smuggled out of China, home to a growing pharmaceutical sector. He then hired whiz-kid chemists from

Taiwan and Hong Kong. Their instructions: synthesize crystal methamphetamine. Tons of it. "Clearly that was Wei's strategy all along," Whalen
told me. "Let the UWSA do away with poppy cultivation, sure. But supplant it all with methamphetamine. He had no intention of getting out of
the drug business."

At the time, crystal meth was somewhat rare in Southeast Asia,
and a less savvy mogul might've simply flooded the market and profited
greatly. Crystal meth sells itself: those who smoke it enjoy a shimmering, hours-long delusion that they are vitally important to the universe.
But Wei had a grander vision. As instructed, his chemists cooked crystal
meth, but then pulverized the glassy shards into a powder and used it as
the key ingredient in a value-added product: speed pills.

This idea wasn't entirely novel. Starting in the 1950s, the pharmaceutical giant Burroughs Wellcome, founded by two Americans, sold
amphetamine tablets around the world, including in Thailand. The company's logo, a unicorn, was stamped into each tablet. Thai people mistook
the unicorn for a mere stallion and called the tablets *ya-ma*. Horse pills.
For decades, Thai pharmacies sold the pills as freely as cough drops—
until the 1970s, when the DEA brought its War on Drugs dogma into
Thailand, nudging the country to criminalize amphetamine.

This prohibition didn't work. Underground entrepreneurs stepped
into the void, whipping up copycat horse pills in Bangkok kitchens.
Through the 1980s and mid-1990s, bootleg horse pills sold in Thailand's
back alleys, and rackets vying for repeat customers would press symbols
into their pills. Some opted for "9," an auspicious number in Thailand.
Others went with the majestic Thai character ฬ or its close lookalike: the
letter *W.* The drug was mostly popular with the working class: truckers
and stevedores, not students or office workers.

Starting in the late 1990s, Wei pumped out his own special speed
tablets. He co-opted the "horse pills" concept and improved it. Just as
Apple took an existing device, the smartphone, and created a superior
iteration, Wei oversaw the rollout of an enhanced pill—one that would
transform how Asians get high as much as the iPhone changed how we all
communicate.

Wei spiked his pills with meth, a more potent drug than its weaker
sibling: amphetamine. His chemists dyed the tablets hot pink and infused
them with a chemical fragrance that smells like Oreo vanilla creme filling.
Meth constituted roughly 20 percent of each speed pill's makeup, along

with an ample pinch of caffeine. Made with thicker binding agents, the pills also could withstand flame. A traditional horse pill, if exposed to fire, would instantly burn to black char; Wei's tablets melted slowly. Customers could either gulp them down or, for a more scintillating high, freebase them. Remove the foil from a cigarette pack, plop a pink pill on that silvery strip, heat it from underneath with a lighter, and a tendril of white smoke lifts from the pill. Inhale that smoke through a straw, and a blast of euphoria ensues, much brighter than if users soak up the magic through their stomachs.

This was no ordinary horse pill. Thailand's old-school ya-ma makers couldn't compete. Not only was their product weaker, but they had to work nervously in makeshift kitchens, cooking small batches, scurrying away if Thai police came knocking. Wei suffered no such restrictions. As Wa South's governor, he could open meth labs there with abandon and run them around the clock. His pills were stamped "WY," distinguishing his merchandise from "W" tablets, an already popular line of ya-ma. In the underworld, unlike the corporate world, copyright protections don't apply.

Wei forecast that his pills would make up for lost heroin revenue and then some. Bao and the UWSA central committee members were convinced. They didn't seem to think this new profit engine would undermine their looming achievement—the elimination of all opium poppies—or jeopardize the international recognition they were due. Most viewed meth pills as a modest vice: a naughtier alternative to Red Bull. After all, hadn't a US conglomerate sold "alertness" pills just a generation prior? The UWSA was so unabashed that in 1998, when Wei oversaw soft launches of his product, the Wa government listed $960,000 in meth-based revenue on a government document.[2] They thought horse pills were hardly worth hiding—at least initially.

Wei was a trailblazer, wholly shifting to synthetics while top Mexican cartels still focused on plant-based drugs: cocaine, heroin, and marijuana. Going 100 percent chemical brought extraordinary benefits. No longer would Wei depend on hundreds of thousands of farmers or fret over the weather. Winter cold spells could enfeeble poppies, causing them to produce low quantities of opium sap, but meth labs are impervious to nature's moods.

They're also hard to detect from space. Previously, the CIA could spy on Wa State's poppy fields and estimate its potential opium yield. But a meth lab, from above, looks like any car garage or warehouse. In a sense, Wei was poking the US government's eyes out. And if his strategy played out as he hoped, the United States might even lose interest in him altogether, because Wei didn't intend for Americans to buy his new product. His target consumers were Southeast Asians.

Since the days of the Exiles and Khun Sa, Golden Triangle drug lords had sold heroin to networks of globe-spanning, ethnic Chinese traffickers who, in turn, smuggled to whichever country offered the highest profits. That was usually America, a voracious narcotics consumer. Though concealing dope on cargo ships chugging eight thousand miles eastward was a logistical chore, traffickers had no other choice.[3] Southeast Asians, by and large, lacked enough money to get high routinely.

But by the early twenty-first century, that was changing. The Southeast Asian economy was sizzling. Farming hamlets had emptied out. Former villagers wanted wage-paying jobs in cities. Workers drove taxis, mopped shopping mall floors, constructed condos, and twisted rivets in Ford factories. They canned tuna fish and pineapples to fill American supermarket shelves. They stitched Nikes for foreign feet. They finally had a little cash to play with. Their jobs were monotonous, but nothing makes tedium enjoyable quite like meth. On speed pills, repetitive action produces pleasure rather than boredom.

It was the perfect drug for Asia's modern workforce. Heroin's voluptuous torpor held no appeal. Laborers wanted vanilla-scented speed, priced at just $2 or $3 per pill. They could smoke one, pull a double shift, collect extra pay, and go buy more. Heavy users might develop psychological problems—exacerbated by lack of sleep—but unlike heroin and other opioids, ya-ma seldom killed customers, even if it derailed their lives. There were enough potential meth pill buyers in Thailand alone (population: seventy million) to fill the UWSA's treasury, and the rising economies of Vietnam, Bangladesh, and Malaysia looked ripe for conquest too. Southeast Asia's population was half a billion strong and growing. To Wei, American consumers were no longer relevant.

His pink pills proved a rollicking success. Speed became a mainstay on the assembly line, then in nightclubs and college dorms. Flustered Thai officials, hoping to scare citizens, rebranded the pills from *ya-ma* to *ya-ba*: insanity pills. But meth users adopted the phrase ironically, rushing to their dealers to ask for insanity pills by name. Ya-ba was the UWSA's North Star: unlimited promise packed into a little disc the size of a baby aspirin. As Wa leaders saw it, Americans ought to commend them. No longer would addicts in New York City keel over from their China White. That product was discontinued.

Decoupling from the US market also brought potential security benefits. How could US narcs ever justify a big-budget assault on Wa State if not a single American citizen OD'd on Wa drugs? Though the UWSA didn't control global supply chains, international traffickers wouldn't buy ya-ba in bulk and smuggle it to the United States; the American appetite for speed was already well sated by Mexican cartels and biker gangs. Wei's shift to speed even called into question the DEA's huge footprint in Southeast Asia: many dozens of agents and analysts protecting American citizens from—what exactly? The heroin pipeline to the United States was shutting down, thanks to the UWSA.

Wei still faced outstanding DEA charges, but he was probably safe from arrest, so long as he never stepped outside Wa State. A lone agent such as Whalen might buzz around Wa State's perimeter, but he'd struggle to crack the UWSA's protective shell. Threats to the mogul would have to emerge from within—and Wei had already proven he could vanquish any Wa who dared imperil his rising empire.

AS WEI CONTINUED lining the Thai-Burma border with ya-ba factories, the first warm breaths of spring wafted over Wa highlands to the north. Around Panghsang, frost-furred pine branches began to drip, drip, drip, and for the first time in a long while, Saw Lu was upbeat. It was 2001, and his purgatory was ending. Chairman Bao had decreed it himself, confident that more than five years of penury could grind down any man's ego—even Saw Lu's. The former leader could rejoin society, this time as a commoner, set free under the condition that he never again seek rank or power. Saw Lu gave the chairman his word. I'm past all that, Bao. My heart isn't so strong anymore, and I've turned diabetic. My only dream is to till soil in the fresh air, living the rest of my days as a simple farmer.

In his first week of freedom, Saw Lu sought old friends in high places, asking for help securing a patch of farmland. Panghsang sits in a basin, ringed by hills more verdant than most in Wa country, and Saw Lu hoped to start a farm overlooking the capital. To get the ex-leader back on his feet, the government allotted a plot in the town's outskirts—one untouched by others because it neighbored the dusty knoll where the UWSA executed and buried criminals.

Saw Lu didn't mind. The soil there was decent, and so was the vista, peering down on an emerald band of the Hka River. He kept pressing government contacts for more cash so he could build a concrete farmhouse, purchase two hundred pigs, and plant one thousand lychee trees. They gave him the money. Saw Lu's powers of persuasion had not atrophied.

The plantation Saw Lu constructed was more grandiose than that of a "simple farmer," but at least he appeared to take agriculture seriously, dampening any lingering concern that he might slide back into politicking. No one, not even his sympathizers, wanted that headache. When officials checked up on him, they found him sweating in the lychee groves, dust caking his forearms. Closer friends noticed that Saw Lu lived vicariously through his do-gooder son-in-law, Jacob, a teacher fervently trying to shape the minds of Wa State's future leaders. But that was a forgivable indulgence. By all appearances, the most stubborn man on earth was rehabilitated and content with obscurity.

Saw Lu's reentry to polite society was smoothed by another man's misfortune. Bao's portly, hard-drinking deputy Li Ziru—Wei's closest ally in the capital—had suffered a stroke two years prior. Though coherent, he was weakened and frequently away in China for health checkups. This allowed the ascent of a different deputy: Xiao Minliang, Bao's top political strategist. Rawboned and fiercely intelligent, Xiao was—like Saw Lu—an ultranationalist at heart, believing the UWSA must first and foremost provide sanctuary to the beleaguered Wa race and treat business as a secondary concern. He was also the point man for the UWSA's poppy-eradication drive. Xiao viewed Saw Lu as a well-meaning fellow who'd flown too close to the sun. He saw little harm in keeping him abreast of the central committee's inner workings, even soliciting the odd bit of advice, now that Saw Lu was cured of his zealotry.

That summer, Saw Lu tested the length of his leash. He asked for permission to venture outside the capital. His ailments—high blood pressure, low blood sugar—deserved proper medical attention. Wa leaders always sought treatment in nearby China, but for Saw Lu this was not ideal: China's intelligence services regarded him as a US-crazed mischiefmaker, and even a quick trip over the border could stir a fuss. Burmese cities were off limits for similar reasons. So he floated the idea of seeking a good doctor in Thailand. The UWSA leadership wished him a safe journey.

Jacob offered to accompany his father-in-law. No, Saw Lu said, I need you here, overseeing the farm. Jacob thought this odd: a man with shaky health eager for rough travel all on his own. The trip to Thailand entailed riding southward in a series of pickup trucks, bouncing along potted dirt roads, then illegally crossing the border on foot—swollen feet at that. "Saw Lu had his own way of doing things," Jacob told me. "His wife and daughter never questioned him. So neither did I."

But Jacob suspected his father-in-law was up to something.

Though Saw Lu wouldn't admit it to his family, the dream still glowed inside him—an ember he'd secretly tended throughout cold years of isolation. He held tight to his unadulterated dream of a drug-free Wa nation embraced by America. He abhorred this mutant parody of his vision, supported by Wei, with its cheap sleight of hand: swapping heroin for speed, trading one poison for another. If the Wa leaders believed this would improve their loathsome image, he thought, they were delusional. In time, his family might understand what he was about to do. For now, Saw Lu just needed to reach Chiang Mai.

After a long, bone-rattling ride, Saw Lu reached the Thai border and slipped across without incident. He found a taxi by the roadside, but instead of going directly to the hospital, he headed toward Bill Young's house. The man Bill saw standing on his stoop was not the Saw Lu of the early 1990s who, even after months in a Burmese torture cell, looked hale and spry. This Saw Lu was bent, eyes sunken, haggard from his journey. They'd not seen each other in seven years. A mere intermission, Saw Lu said. He kicked off his sandals, stepped inside, and asked Bill for a cigarette.

In his mid-sixties, Bill was little changed: same florid Hawaiian shirts, same biting wit and love of daredevil schemes, though his chronic cough had worsened. Bill confirmed that he still served as a DEA operative: off the books, plausibly deniable. Saw Lu and Bill bantered in Lahu, their shared tongue, two old friends catching up. But soon talk turned serious, and the jagged contours of a plot emerged.

It was nothing short of a coup d'état. Conceived with hopes of deposing the UWSA's leadership, aligning Wa civilization with the "Free World," and delivering Wei to his rightful place: a prison cell.

They called it the Whiskey Alpha rebellion.

WHISKEY ALPHA

With more than fifty billion pills produced so far this century—a conservative estimate—ya-ba is among the most popular illegal products ever created.

It's probably the most consequential narcotic innovation in modern times.[1] Cocaine, heroin, and meth were first synthesized in the mid- to late 1800s. These were chemical breakthroughs. Ya-ba is a triumph of design: confectionary, colorful, easy to brand. You can't stamp a logo on white heroin powder or crystalline meth shards, but Wa pills bear a symbol: "WY," as recognizable to Asian drug users as Nike's swoosh. Today, per annual units sold, ya-ba pills outperform Big Macs and Starbucks coffee orders worldwide. Costing roughly $1 to $5 apiece, the pills are priced to move—and move they do, much to authorities' dismay.[2]

Moral panic over ya-ba has washed over Southeast Asia in several waves. The first one hit Thailand circa 2001, when Wei Xuegang had roughly one hundred meth pill factories up and running along the Thai-Burma border. His ya-ba was all the rage: as many as one in twenty Thais had tried it.[3] Thai officials fell into morbid hysteria, similar to the one that had seized American lawmakers in the 1980s crack cocaine era. In their eyes, ya-ba was no mere stimulant. It was a virus infecting the body politic, turning citizens into pepped-up delinquents, if not rapists and murderers.[4]

Thailand's military labeled ya-ba the "nation's foremost security threat"—a peril emanating from the vaporous hills of Wa South.[5] The media wrote screaming headlines—"Meth Menace" or "Ex-Headhunters Guard Burmese Speed Factories"—conjuring images of old-world barbarians unleashing new-wave synthetic terror.

Time to get tough, Thailand's new prime minister, Thaksin Shinawatra, declared early that year. If Burma's junta won't do its job and destroy Wa meth labs inside its own borders, "we'll do it ourselves."[6] That spring, Thailand amassed American-built tanks, Scorpions and Stingrays, along the Thai-Burma border, right across from Wei's frontier. The stage was set for invasion, potentially the largest strike against a Golden Triangle narco-army since the 1982 siege on Khun Sa's Shanland, a joint operation with the United States.

But this time, the Americans weren't so keen to help. "Our relationship with the US was changing fast," said Pittaya Jinawat, then a top official with Thailand's Office of Narcotics Control Board. "They called ya-ba a 'local problem' that didn't really hurt Americans." This was true. Aside from extremely rare mail shipments into Asian American communities, ya-ba wasn't reaching the United States. Both the Drug Enforcement Administration and the Central Intelligence Agency considered the United Wa State Army (UWSA) a menace. But just as Wei predicted, neither could secure US resources to attack an organization that wasn't feeding Americans' addictions.

The United States provided Thailand just a couple Black Hawk helicopters plus twenty Green Berets, none of whom could join antinarcotics operations along the border, certainly not into Wa South, which was technically Burma's sovereign soil. US Special Forces were limited to instruction drills only. A Thai intelligence agent told me, "Some of us were upset. Come on, that's it? After all we did to fight heroin? But the Americans basically said, 'You're all grown up now. Figure it out yourselves.'"

Thailand's army dialed back its ambitions. Instead of blowing up labs, it would hit the UWSA farther down the supply chain, wiping out Wa drug transporters the second they crept across the border. Wei's Wa Southern Command usually trafficked ya-ba into Thailand using ten-man teams: eight Wa soldiers lugging backpacks, each stuffed with one hundred thousand pills, with rifle-toting troops at the front and rear of the column. "Our orders were to find them and shoot them on sight," said a sergeant with the Thai army's premier antinarcotics regiment.[7] I'll call him Jok. "Anyone with a backpack walking through the jungle, we open fire," Jok told me. "We're not cops. We don't do buy-busts. Foreigners invade our homeland, we shoot them. Simple as that."

Only it wasn't so simple. The divide between Thailand and Wa South stretched 150 miles across brambly terrain. The CIA described it as "ideal smuggling territory" in the early 1970s when the Exiles ruled that stretch of border—and it was ideal still. Thai troops tried to block every little dirt footpath leading out of Wa South, but Wa soldiers, aided by Lahu scouts, slashed through snarling curtains of greenery to create new paths. The border was impossible to seal off.

"We started relying heavily on CIs," Sergeant Jok said. Ramshackle villages lined the border, and in each one Thailand's army hired locals to spot ya-ba smugglers. "We told them: call us if you see a group of guys wearing black boots. That was a dead giveaway. The Wa always wore boots and green uniforms with insignia removed."

Jok was a stocky soldier in his late twenties with a black widow's peak. To his unit, the "War on Drugs" was not a euphemism. They confronted well-trained enemies who'd fire back to protect their merchandise. This was a genuine war authenticated by adrenaline and gunpowder. Jok's unit spent nights crouching in jungles screechy with bugs, enveloped in velvety blackness, listening for the rhythmic crunch of rubber soles disturbing the earth. They learned to differentiate the footfall of humans and wild boar. "Everyone knows the Wa reputation. Pure brutality. But I didn't believe in that shit. We think in military terms: numbers, organization, hardware. We Thais outnumbered them. No one was going to come into my country and cut our heads off."

Throughout 2001, Thailand seized a record-breaking ninety million ya-ba pills—enough to theoretically get the country's entire population high for a day and then some. After each successful firefight, Jok's squad would pull backpacks off dead Wa and inspect their bounty right there in the forest. The meth was usually sealed in airtight, plastic-wrapped bundles reinforced with ungodly amounts of brown packing tape. Sergeant Jok, flashlight in hand, would watch his lieutenant slice open the bundles with a pocketknife, loosing that sickly sweet vanilla aroma. Together they'd sift through pink pills in search of the odd lime-green tablet. "Wei's organization had a system," Jok said. "Throw in one green pill for every ten thousand pink pills. It makes the arithmetic easier for dealers down the line. Six green pills, that's a batch of sixty thousand."

Jok's lieutenant received a call, in early 2002, from a confidential informant (CI) in Mae Ai, a rural district in Chiang Mai province that touches Wa South. The village CI specified a date when UWSA smugglers would cross before dawn—and he was certain the Wa would rendezvous with a buyer inside a bamboo shed, just a few hundred meters south of the border. The lieutenant told his unit to gear up. He wanted them to get there first, lay in wait, and intercept the traffickers. A routine job.

Dressed in all black, Jok's squad rolled eight deep to the location in a pickup. It was nearly midnight. Jok sat in the truck bed, rifle jutting between his legs, while his lieutenant rode up front. Straining up a slope, the truck lurched into first gear. The soldiers were leaving behind the luminescence of civilization—streetlamps, electrified villages—revealing an ancient cosmos above.

The soldier at the truck's wheel slowed, parked, and left the engine running. He was supposed to drop everyone off, vanish, and return once the mission concluded. Jok was about to hop from the truck bed when his vision went white: a blinding, cornea-searing flash.

Grenade.

Detonating under the truck, bucking the chassis, deafening the squad. Glass bits sleeted over Jok's hands. From that instant, his memories crack into fragments.

In his next remembrance, he was crouching by the truck's tailgate, spotting a bamboo shed in the distance, unloading his M-16-A1 in its direction. If there were Wa inside, they didn't return fire; the grenade tossers were either fleeing or sitting still, letting darkness swallow them whole. Jok's attention swung to a confusion of shouts nearby. His fellow soldiers were pulling the lieutenant out of the truck cabin, laying him on his back behind the wheel well. The lieutenant's face shone milk white in the gloom. "The weird thing was . . . he wasn't covered in blood. We ripped off the lieutenant's shirt and saw a little entry wound from shrapnel. It was so tiny, and it didn't bleed unless we pressed on it. I never heard him whimper or cry. He just wouldn't wake up, no matter how much we shook him."

They blamed the lieutenant's death on corrupted intel. Jok believed the Thai CI had been paid by the Wa to send his squad straight into a death trap. The UWSA had been cultivating its own CI network in the Thai villages, outbidding the Thai army and flipping informants to its side. "Wei's people had spotters in the Thai villages, and they always seemed to know where we were. Every night, they'd call plays, like a coach, sending traffickers wherever we weren't. They could also pull us into an ambush."

Khaen-jai directly translated from Thai means "wrath-heart." "It's difficult to explain if you've never felt it—that need for vengeance," Jok said. "After they killed our lieutenant, I was totally *khaen-jai*. Like, fuck the Wa, let's kill them all." Bad news from the Thai army compounded his rage. The borderland seizures weren't working. Ya-ba was still easy to find in the cities, its street price—one hundred baht, or $3—barely budging. Thailand's antinarcotics agency calculated that police and troops caught no more than 10 to 15 percent of the ya-ba cascading out of Wa State. Moving forward, instead of just blasting away at traffickers, Jok's squad was instructed to catch, interrogate, and flip them. Send a few back into Wa South as freshly minted CIs, hoping they'd feed tidbits back to the Thai military from inside Wei's machine.

Sergeant Jok grudgingly obeyed orders. If any Wa survived a firefight, he'd haul them to the base, toss them in a cell, and squeeze them for information. To a man, they were quiet as stones. "They told us nothing. Not their names or rank, not their division number. It was infuriating." Eventually the squad realized that if they left a length of rope in the cell, the Wa captives would sometimes hang themselves. "Geneva applies to state-to-state warfare," Jok told me. "Not to armed criminals."

"I don't like to praise the Wa," Jok said, "but I'll say this. Thais will backstab other Thais, especially for money. But the Wa? Loyal to the death. They never, ever think of turning on their own people."

On that point, Jok was wrong.

Because elsewhere in Chiang Mai province, in the sitting room of an aging American antinarcotics operative, a Wa man named Saw Lu was conspiring to overthrow his own government.

THOUGH ESSENTIAL TO the Whiskey Alpha conspiracy, Saw Lu was not its lead architect. Bill was, and in documents drafted for the DEA, he called it the solution to "virtually uncontrollable trafficking . . . by the current Wa leadership"—a crisis demanding "bold thinking and covert action."

Covert action was Bill's answer to many of the world's problems. Even in grizzled middle age, he still loved a good exploit—the kind ripped out of spy novels. It's easy to understand why. In his younger days as a CIA officer, he'd cooked up madcap schemes—sending indigenous assets into China to sow havoc—that actually worked. A conspiracy that sounded fantastical to the everyman was, to Bill, perfectly achievable with enough pluck, ingenuity, and M-16s. Despite his bitter parting with the Central Intelligence Agency in the late 1960s, Bill's operational thinking still skewed old-school CIA, and Whiskey Alpha was shaping up as a classic of the genre.

The gist? Back a band of dissidents, send 'em into an enemy state to depose the leadership, and hope your rival's armed forces and citizens rejoice in their liberation—or at least fall into line. A method previously seen in China courtesy of the Exiles (1951, failure), then in Iran (1953, success), Guatemala (1954, success), Indonesia (1958, failure), Cuba (1961, failure), South Vietnam (1963, success), and so on. Whiskey Alpha would follow the same well-thumbed playbook. With Saw Lu as his conspirator, Bill wanted to slap together a Wa commando team to seize control of Wa State, pulling off a coup d'état.

Bill crafted a pitch to his employer—only Bill wasn't a DEA employee as such, more of a shadow agent. They paid him as a CI, like he was just another anonymous informant with a code number, but Bill was much more. With few exceptions, DEA agents posted to Southeast Asia were extended visitors, putting in about four years before shuffling onward to Tijuana, Detroit, wherever. Not Bill. Raised in Burma's foothills by his missionary family, he was a Golden Triangle native— an oracle who spoke its obscure tongues, including Shan, Lahu, Lao, and multiple Thai dialects. Bill was a one-man intelligence service with moles among rebels and smugglers. Borderland tribal politics stupefied most agents, but Bill could transmute these enigmas into hard-boiled American English, shaping how the DEA perceived Burma's minority groups.

Take the Wa, for example. They weren't *all* bad, Bill would say. Some, such as Saw Lu, were fed up with their tribe's reputation as "the assholes of the world" and deserved American support. Bill believed the UWSA had followed a decent track until its visionary founder, Zhao Nyi Lai, suffered a stroke in 1995. Once Bao Youxiang took over as leader, Bill said, the Wa government became a "Chinese-led dictatorship" powered by Wei Xuegang's "vast business empire." What the Wa people desired, he'd say, were Wa leaders ruling under international (read: Western) principles.

So in the interest of taking down Asia's biggest drug cartel—and ending the meth nightmare in Thailand, a US ally—Bill recommended that the United States secretly aid Wa dissidents in unseating the current UWSA leadership. Bao would go unharmed, according to Bill's plan. This was Saw Lu's influence at work; he believed Bao was misguided but good at heart. As for Wei, if the drug lord didn't "escape in advance," he'd get snatched up and extradited to America—an outcome that would "redeem the blemished name of the Wa people in the eyes of the world."

Having established Whiskey Alpha's raison d'être, Bill turned to operations. He needed a force capable of executing this coup. It was time to reassemble Saw Lu's long-defunct League of Warlords, which briefly ruled the Wa peaks in the late 1960s and early 1970s. The goal was to install these aging ex-warlords as a ruling council loyal to the "Free World." This meant pulling the nation away from China's orbit and out of the drug trade.

Not all of the former warlords were available for the conspiracy. Master of Creation was out of the running. Saw Lu said he was far too old, and busy somewhere in the Wa wilderness running a backwoods cult with seven wives and innumerable children. Pass. But Shah? He was a maybe. In his late sixties, Shah had retired in his birthplace, the Wa motherland, where the UWSA ruled supreme.

Creaky with age, Shah was largely overlooked by Wa society despite his contributions to the nation. After all, it was Shah who—after the League's defeat by communists in the early 1970s—first led Wa fighters south to the Thai-Burma border. His armed band, the Wa National Army, established the first Wa toehold there. Wei joined this mercenary gang as its treasurer in the mid-1980s, outmaneuvering Shah and buying his fighters' loyalty with heroin profits. Then, in 1989, Wei became finance czar to the newly established Wa nation. He convinced then chairman Lai to add the Wa National Army territory to Wa State and turn the gang into a UWSA division. After that, Shah was shunted into obscurity. He had every right to feel bitter. If it hadn't been for Shah, Wa South wouldn't exist.

Perhaps he was disgruntled—and if so, the Whiskey Alpha rebellion would offer a shot at retribution. Though no longer physically fit, Shah could lend battlefield expertise and perhaps even scrounge up a few ex-guerrillas formerly under his command (or more likely, given the advancement of age, the ex-guerillas' sons).

Saw Lu agreed to reach out to Shah. As for his own role in the coup, he'd play man on the inside. Well placed in the capital, Saw Lu could keep feigning harmless interest in the UWSA's inner workings while steadily seeking weaknesses to exploit. At the same time, he'd begin secretly recruiting Wa and Lahu Christians to join the plot as combatants. The rebellion would need all the manpower it could muster.

Finally, there was Mahasang the Prince, the only League of War-lords veteran who could still call himself a warlord. He was the plot's lynchpin—for better or worse.

In his mid-fifties, Mahasang roosted in a primitive camp in Burma that clung to the Thai border like a barnacle. Ringed with wooden pali-sades, the camp was a hand-me-down fort built by the Exiles long ago as a pitstop for opium-smuggling mules. The Exiles later abandoned it, and Mahasang moved in—along with several hundred Wa, the last subjects of his faux-royal clan.

Mahasang had joined the League of Warlords in the late 1960s to help protect his clan turf from communist takeover. His family, the richest in the peaks, was haughty and fierce, flaunting shiny bangles on their wrists and ornamenting their territory, Silver Fortress, with human skulls. But when the communists defeated the League, Mahasang—like Shah—fled with his followers. Seeking a place to hide out, they took shelter on the Thai-Burma border inside the deserted Exiles camp. And nearly three decades later, Mahasang and his people remained there, living in gorgeous isolation. Their settlement overlooked a silvery lake and a dusty smug-gling trail—a backdoor connecting Burma to Thailand's Mae Hong Son province.

Even in 2001, Mahasang's followers still called him "Prince." Though bratty in his youth, he'd mellowed with age, evolving into a well-spoken man, crisply dressed despite his austere surroundings, with a full head of black hair gelled to the side—a coif worthy of a game show host. For the right audience, Mahasang could spew mellifluous odes to "democracy" and "human rights." He'd picked up these phrases on trips to Chiang Mai city, home to a feisty diaspora of Burma-born minorities. United in hatred of the Burmese military regime, many worked for Western-funded activist groups established to "Free Burma" from tyranny.[8] Mahasang hovered at the fringes of this scene. He positioned himself as an alternate face of the Wa tribe, more enlightened than the drug-trafficking leaders of the UWSA. "The press always describes Wa people as outcasts, criminals, drug traffickers," he once said.[9] "But not all the Wa are involved in crimi-nal activities. The Wa are peace-loving, hardworking people who, same as other ethnic groups, want to live in a free, democratic country."

Whether the Prince was himself mixed up in narcotics was an open question. ("Mahasang: man of his people or drug runner?" asked one Thai magazine.) But he was certainly a warlord, if only a minor one, squeezing tolls from anyone who passed by his camp. Though the Golden Triangle's prime smuggling trails belonged to Wa South—its vast territory lying thirty miles to the east of Mahasang's patch—some traffickers opted for the long route. They could exit Burma on a footpath near Mahasang's fort, transporting gems or cattle or human beings, sometimes opium and meth. Mahasang insisted he never taxed drug traffickers, and this was technically true: the Prince did not personally collect tolls, suffering as he did from cigarette-induced asthma and often lugging a metal oxygen tank behind him. Fee collection fell to his private militia: 100 to 150 loyalists with automatic rifles, some of them sons and grandsons of headhunters.

Mahasang joined the Whiskey Alpha coup plot at Bill's request. They'd known each other for decades. Bill dreamed up big plans for the Prince's little militia, positioning it as the nucleus of the rebellion—a core fighting force, later taking in any fighters Saw Lu or Shah could rustle up. In memos to the DEA, Bill said that Mahasang "stated his total willingness to work and fully cooperate under any terms and guidance . . . from the Free World side."

And what could the "Free World" offer the Wa coup plotters? Professional soldiers and cutting-edge technology. Bill wanted Thailand's army to covertly beef up the militia with hardened special forces troops—guys like Jok pretending to be Wa. Meanwhile, the United States could supply "Western encrypting and decrypting systems" to help plotters communicate with one another, as well as with any future recruits scattered around Wa State, ready to rise up when given the signal.

According to Bill's plans, once the coup ousted Bao and Wei, Saw Lu and the other plotters could rush to the home of Lai, the Wa nation's founding father. Though wheelchair bound and slurred in his speech, Lai was still the UWSA's "general secretary," a ceremonial position akin to king for life, at least on paper. If successful, the coup leaders—Saw Lu, Mahasang, and Shah—would ask Lai to consecrate their legitimacy as a new ruling council.[10]

That's how everything would play out if the plot succeeded. But this was a gigantic *if*, shot through with assumptions. Bill had inherited, from his missionary grandfather, a capacity for wild hope. William Marcus Young had thought he could save headhunters' souls, and one century later Bill believed some washed-up ex-warlords with failing organs could seize control of Wa State and its army, now nearly twenty-five thousand troops strong.

Saw Lu—listening to Bill, pondering the bad odds—swallowed hard, prayed, and kept plotting by his side. He didn't agree with every detail. But Bill, and Bill alone, dangled the bewitching possibility that, after years of degradation, Saw Lu's sacrifice might end in redemption. That every dark scene from his life—his back lashed bloody at a Burmese black site, the aborted DEA mountaintop summit, his five hungry years in a rickety shack—would serve as prelude to a glorious finale. That Wei Xuegang, whom he hated down to his entrails, would finally suffer God's fury.

These were still early days for Whiskey Alpha. They'd merely fashioned a loose proposal contingent on DEA interest. It could take a year or more to actually execute the coup. For now, Saw Lu needed to return to Wa State, lest the leaders grow suspicious. Bill handed him a handheld Inmarsat satellite phone with a rubber antenna thick as a rifle barrel. Use this to stay in touch with me when you're in Panghsang, he said. When you get there, dig a hole, bury the phone, and tell no one of its existence.

OBLIVIOUS TO SAW LU'S scheming, Wa State's leadership pursued a very different route toward redeeming the blemished Wa name: plowing cash into the legal economy as fast as possible. The UWSA was going corporate.

UWSA elites cumulatively raked in hundreds of millions of dollars per year—a mingling of personal and state revenues—and by the early 2000s, this lucre supported a constellation of businesses.[11] With his brothers, Wei founded his own multinational: Hong Pang, with offices in Panghsang and Yangon, plus shell companies in Thailand, Hong Kong, and Singapore. Its investments were promiscuous: gems, construction, textiles, cement, gas stations, and compact discs. The Bao clan ran a smaller conglomerate, Tet Kham, which managed hotels, logging operations, a Burma-based bank, and, most impressively, a controlling stake in Yangon Airways, one of Burma's few airlines.

UWSA officials hailed this as an achievement. At last the Wa were diversifying beyond narcotics. But the DEA preferred a different phrase: money laundering. "They were turning black money white," Whalen said. "Especially Wei, the chief financial officer. They couldn't have done it without him."

It was March 2002, three years away from the poppy-free deadline, after which—according to Bao's promise to the United Nations—not a single poppy stalk would sprout from Wa soil. In the capital, the Wa government set up factories to employ former poppy farmers after the transition. Bao, keen to show off his progress, invited regional diplomats and UN officials to Panghsang for a briefing.

On the guest list: ambassadors from Singapore, Laos, Pakistan, and even the US chargé d'affaires Priscilla Clapp, Huddle's successor. Burma's junta, always hungry for good PR, agreed to fly in every foreign guest via helicopter. The regime readied its finest fleet, suitable for VIPs, with plush seats arranged inside the cabins in the style of civilian airliners. "It was going to be a total dog and pony show," Agent Whalen told me. But he wouldn't have missed it for the world.

Whalen was also oblivious to Bill Young's coup plot. The DEA agent was fixated on more conventional antinarcotics work: investigating Wei's meth-trafficking network. This trip to Panghsang could bring him face-to-face with Wa leaders—Wei's cohorts—while also inducting Whalen into that rare club of DEA agents (or Westerners period) who'd walked on Wa soil. DEA personnel overseas are technically considered diplomats, so nothing stopped Whalen from tagging along with the American chargé. "We didn't say, 'Hey, the DEA is coming,' just that 'Our diplomats will come see your alternative development projects.'"

The night before flying out, Whalen, a Burmese officer, and an Australian narcotics agent killed off a bottle of cognac. So when Whalen descended over Wa State the next morning, its stony landscape rippling in every direction outside the helicopter's window, he was in no mood to soak in the view. The agent had a hangover—one intensified by the blades roaring overhead.

UWSA officials greeted the delegation on the helipad. Eager to showcase Wa State's first steps toward industrialization, they began the tour at a cigarette-making facility full of clunky Chinese-built machinery. Then over to a distillery producing a clear alcoholic liquid labeled Hong Pang rice wine. "Pure moonshine," Whalen told me. "You could probably run your car on it." Bao's chief political strategist, Xiao Minliang, joined the tour, assuring Whalen and the other visitors that Wa State's antiopium drive was irreversible. Once virtually all Wa villages harvested opium, Xiao said, but now fewer than half do. This has not been easy on our population. Still, we forge ahead for the betterment of our citizens and yours.

Whalen's heartstrings went unplucked. "He starts asking for aid: $11 million from the US government, spread out over the next ten years. 'Our people are so poor' and all that. And I'm thinking, 'Why don't you sell your cars?'" Whalen noticed Xiao and other officials rolling up in midnight-black Land Cruisers. "Or how about selling your watch? There was a $20,000 Rolex on his wrist."

The tour's final stop—a Wa area, fifty miles north, recently cleared of poppies—would require a short helicopter trip. "So we all go back to the helicopters. Keep in mind, I'm still a little hazy from the night before." When Whalen peered into the dark cabin, he saw some Wa guy in a green polo shirt, black hair receding, settling into a comfy window seat. "And I'm like, hold on, who the fuck is this asshole sitting in my seat?"

"Then it hit me. That's Bao Youxiang!"

Whalen jumped in, plopping down next to Bao. The chairman's eyes widened. He knows exactly who I am, Whalen thought, and he is not happy to see me. Soon they had company: a high-ranking Burmese intelligence official sliding into a nearby seat. When the junta official craned his neck to glance at the duo behind him—the leader of a narco-army and a veteran DEA agent strapped in side by side—his face froze.

John, the Burmese agent said in English, please behave. He's terrified of you.

Oh, really? Why's that?

Because you're DEA.

Give me a break, Whalen said. We're in his world. He knows I can't touch him here. As Whalen and the junta official bantered in English, Bao faced the window, listening without comprehension.

Tell you what, Whalen said to the Burmese official. I'd like to make a deal. You tell Bao to turn Wei Xuegang over to the DEA. Turn him over to *me*. Do that and we'll never bother him again.

Blades above their heads revolved. The cabin levitated, and the din of flight drowned out any chance of negotiating further. When the chopper landed twenty minutes later, Bao unbuckled and hastened from his seat.

NOT LONG AFTERWARD, circa 2003, the UWSA leadership started claiming to outsiders that Wei was missing. "He just vanished," Bao told Chinese media.[12] "Everyone knows 'they' are hunting him and, if I knew that,

I'd run away too. We're not going to formally revoke his titles. But Wei Xuegang is no longer a Wa leader."

As Bao made these claims, the hot gossip in Panghsang concerned a magnificent new mansion in the hills outside town. A small army of builders had lathed down the side of a mountain, buzzing down trees and clearing boulders, to accommodate it: a three-level palace colored cream and umber, with east and west wings, flanked by auxiliary buildings big as hotels. The $35 million complex rose from a terraced, manicured lawn, and if the rumors were true, it also sat atop escape tunnels and a steel-reinforced bomb shelter. The property was visible from a nearby road, but if uninvited guests came too close, sentries emerged from the trees with rifles drawn. The Wa had never seen anything like it: a private estate bigger than a village, reputedly the domicile of a single man with no known children.[13]

Wei Xuegang had in fact vanished—into the confines of this mansion. He'd relocated from Wa South to distance himself from Thailand, a hive of US-backed spies and assassins.[14] Wei nominally left his little brother, Wei Xueyin, in charge of the frontier, but everyone knew the younger sibling was just a puppet. Wei still ruled Wa South by remote control, issuing orders over the phone. Seldom did he leave his mansion, defended by a praetorian guard: hundreds of Chinese-speaking soldiers with new-model rifles. They answered to Wei and no one else.

Jacob, still teaching cadets, was as intrigued about Wei as anyone. He knew only one person who'd met the financier face-to-face: his father-in-law. But Saw Lu went oddly silent if anyone mentioned Wei's name. Jacob instead listened to the scuttlebutt inside Bao's compound, where in his downtime he'd pal around with other mid-tier officials.

"Everyone said Wei was a genius," Jacob said, "but so paranoid that he wore rubber masks and wouldn't even pick up a glass of water without gloves, just to avoid leaving fingerprints." What disturbed Jacob was the awe Wei inspired in his peers. Many Wa officers spoke of him as a Robin Hood–like figure, wringing cash out of foreign addicts, diverting it toward the nation's development. This wasn't altogether false. Wei's operations funded construction projects that helped lay nearly two thousand miles of paved roads in Wa State—no small feat for a place craggy as the Alps. But that didn't impress Jacob. Wei was a trafficker. Of course he wanted to interlace the nation with roads, rendering logistical operations more efficient. When might his oceanic drug wealth splash back on schools—the foundation of any modern state?

By that time, Jacob recognized that his cadets, though bruised and battered in training, were the lucky ones: children of elite officers, guaranteed an education. The typical Wa kid never saw the inside of a classroom. Wa State (population: six hundred thousand) had only a few hundred primary schools teaching twenty thousand students. The government ran about ten middle schools, and lacking a Wa-language curriculum for grades seven through nine, they relied on secondhand Chinese textbooks. There were no high schools at all. Little wonder Bao sent his children to a Singaporean boarding academy. "We were killing our own future," Jacob told me. "Killing it off with apathy. Everyone's attitude was business first, education last."

Jacob blamed Wei for stoking this mind-set. To many Wa, his mansion redefined the awesome power of money, serving as a shrine to the fast-spreading religion of profit at all cost. Jacob and his colleagues made only about eighty yuan per month, the equivalent of $12. Many grew obsessed with chasing fortunes. But the quickest route to cash for any mid-level or even high-ranking Wa officer wasn't necessarily through drug trafficking; only UWSA division commanders possessed the capital and manpower to start a meth lab. For the lesser ranks in Panghsang, their best bet was to court starry-eyed Chinese investors and squeeze them for cash.

Among wildcats and hustlers in China, Wa State was increasingly seen as a land of second chances. A down-and-out Chinese businessman, perhaps fleeing loan sharks or a ruined reputation, could slip across the Hka River with a backpack full of yuan and maybe start a fly-by-night factory or a rubber plantation. Wa labor was dirt cheap, regulations nonexistent. But with no real rule of law in Wa State, they needed UWSA officers to take them under their wing—for a protection fee.

Chinese businessmen seeking such relationships buzzed around Panghsang's K-TVs: karaoke lounges, awash in pink light, where hostesses cooed in customers' ears. Many a deal was brokered over shots of rice wine and discordant warbling. Jacob, badgered into joining these soirees by peers, would abstain from booze. "I was a water and coffee man," he told me. He was also shocked when, in some of the grittier K-TVs, he saw Chinese traders passing around pink pills. "The only *really* taboo drug was heroin," he said. Though the UWSA no longer produced its own China White, neighboring armed groups still did, and their product was available on Panghsang's streets. "Heroin was a serious thing. Unless your family name was Bao, you'd go to jail for that. As for other drugs, if a Chinese guest wanted it, they usually got it."

All around Jacob, his fellow Wa State officers went cash crazy, focused on extracting money from Chinese visitors rather than carrying out their duties. Jacob felt that Bao should rein in this mania, stamp out corruption, and only promote high-minded officials—just as he'd once promised. But the chairman seemed more interested in filling out the Wa government with his own relatives and sycophants, no matter their qualifications or ethical pedigree. Bao had become an extreme nepotist, doling out the highest UWSA positions to his three brothers, with legions of Bao nephews, Bao cousins, and Bao war buddies taking the rest. The chairman was building a superdynasty that could stand up to Wei's influence, and apparently that obsession left little time to focus on improving the lot of ordinary people.

So far, Jacob had followed Saw Lu's advice: try to improve the Wa government from within. He still revered his father-in-law as a mentor. But every time Jacob tried to consult with Saw Lu, he seemed distant. Preoccupied by something. Once again, Jacob felt spiritually marooned, deprived of guidance. Jacob sometimes spotted Saw Lu pacing through his farm's lychee groves, jabbering away in Lahu—a language Jacob did not understand—with a funny-looking telephone pressed to his ear. He knew better than to ask questions.

JANUARY 2005.

It was going to be *their* year—a year of change, of rebirth, of sacrifice exchanged for dignity.

Shortly after New Year's Day, the UWSA prepared for another big visit from foreign envoys. Emissaries were inbound to see Wa State's achievement with their own eyes: slopes bristling with rubber trees and tea shrubs, hardly a poppy bulb in sight. In all of Wa country, there remained only a few dozen square miles of poppy fields, and they were slated for razing by summer. Bao wanted every international visitor to behold his progress, then go back and tell their fellow citizens, The Wa are good as their word after all.

The diplomatic trip, arranged through the United Nations Office on Drugs and Crime (UNODC), was scheduled for January 24. Dignitaries from Germany, Japan, the United Kingdom, and six other countries had confirmed attendance. US officials, notoriously unpredictable, had yet to respond. No matter. The UWSA focused on readying for the spectacle at hand.

But about one week before the tour, DEA officials privately warned the United Nations that an American operation against Wa State was imminent—set to commence the very day diplomats were due to land in Panghsang. The DEA couldn't divulge much, only that this "law enforcement action" would enrage Wa leaders, possibly provoking them to harm Western guests.

Scratch the trip, the DEA said. The UNODC, reliant on the US government for much of its funding, had little choice but to comply. It canceled the showcase. The United Nations also advised its small number of staffers resident in Wa State—providing aid to former poppy-farming hamlets—that an American plot was nigh, telling them to desert their posts and slip away quietly.[15]

The operation afoot was not Whiskey Alpha. DEA headquarters ultimately rejected Bill's coup plan and for good reason, Whalen told me. "When you're talking paramilitary operations, that's not really what we do. If we did anything remotely close to that, we'd try to lure Wei to the Thai border and snatch him there. But launching incursions into a sovereign nation"—meaning Burma—"is not going to happen."

Instead, the DEA opted for Operation Warlord: a wave of indictments against the Wa government's executive branch. The DEA declared its intent to capture and extradite all four Baos (the chairman and his three brothers, all top-ranking UWSA officers) and the three Wei brothers. The charges: manufacturing and trafficking massive amounts of narcotics for export, up to $1 billion worth of heroin. The penalty: minimum ten years in a US prison cell, maximum life. Anyone assisting US efforts to apprehend the Wa leaders would receive a $500,000 bounty. The drug lord Wei Xuegang was an exception: his head price stood at $2 million.

Rumors burned through Panghsang like a fever. Word spread that every foreigner in Wa State was suddenly gone, perhaps fleeing in advance of US military air strikes.[16] Citizens stayed indoors. Bao treated it like a war declaration—and it sure sounded like one. In announcing Operation

Warlord, DEA chiefs decried the Wa government as a "grave threat to the safety and security of all Americans."

The United Wa State Army, the DEA said, "purports to be an independence movement" but is nothing more than a "powerful criminal syndicate . . . feeding the addiction that undermines human dignity [as it] spawns crime and violence, decreases productivity and causes a whole host of social problems."[17] America and its allies were duty bound to "disrupt and dismantle" the UWSA, just as they were obligated to destroy other cartels around the world.[18]

To Wa leaders' ears, this announcement heralded an invasion. The United States had zero intention of storming Wa State—the indictments mostly amounted to threats, meant to further criminalize and isolate Wa State—but the UWSA had no way of knowing that. Aware that US regime change operations kick off with jet strikes and helicopter attacks, Wa soldiers shouldered Chinese-made missile launchers, each powerful enough to drop a Black Hawk, and watched the skies. At the time, the United States was pummeling Iraq with bombs, even after dragging deposed dictator Saddam Hussein from a stinking spider hole. "Try invading us like you invaded Iraq," said Bao, taunting the US government in remarks to Chinese media.[19] "See if your tanks can climb our mountains. Every Wa has an education—in fighting. So think carefully before you intrude on this supposed poor and backward place."

Behind the bluster, the chairman was genuinely befuddled. To justify Operation Warlord, the DEA called the UWSA "one of the largest producers of heroin in the world," but this was no longer a fair description, thanks to tremendous feats of social reengineering. The Wa had just pulled off what one UN antinarcotics official called "the most effective and efficient banning of opium in history."[20]

Only one decade prior, Burma's narco-armies (namely the UWSA and Khun Sa's Shanland) were generating half the world's opium. But with Shanland conquered by Wa troops, and the UWSA's in-house eradication more or less complete, Burma now eked out a mere 5 percent of the global opium supply. It was an extraordinary reversal, extolled by the UWSA: "We banned the poppy, we chose the road of peaceful development. . . . [We] stepped into the most glorious period in our region's history."[21] The UWSA—now a meth cartel—had reduced the Golden Triangle to a heroin-producing backwater.

The world's heroin users had to get their fix from somewhere, of course. So which country seized the opium and heroin producer crown?

Afghanistan, a country under US occupation.

Poppies naturally thrive in Afghanistan, the heartland of another great opium-producing region: the Golden Crescent. Through much of the 1990s, the ruling Taliban oversaw Afghanistan's opium trade. But by the year 2000, the Taliban had decided to mow down poppies instead. Like the UWSA, the Taliban naively hoped that eliminating opium production would generate international acceptance. As a result of this eradication campaign, with few exceptions, poppies in Afghanistan only bloomed in a northern part of the country: a mountainous area controlled by autonomous warlords who despised the Taliban. They called themselves the Northern Alliance.

Enter the United States. In late 2001, the CIA, spearheading the US invasion of Afghanistan, provided heavy weapons to the Northern Alliance and built the warlords into a pro-America vanguard that could attack the Taliban alongside incoming US troops. Under siege, the Taliban retreated to the countryside and once again sowed the earth with poppies. Only through selling opium could the Taliban pay fighters, buy weapons, and afford a long resistance. Meanwhile, the Northern Alliance continued aggressively harvesting opium in its territory, as it always had.[22] With all sides in the drug trade, a narco-superstate was born. By 2005, Afghanistan was well on its way to supplying 90 percent of the world's opium, much of it grown by CIA-backed warlords.[23]

Behold the maddening logic of the US government. As the CIA propped up opium-producing warlords in Afghanistan, the DEA mostly kept silent. What did the DEA do instead? It targeted a totally different group of Asian mountain dwellers, the Wa, just as they were *quitting* opium production. And with no apparent irony, the Americans called their anti-Wa offensive Operation *Warlord*.

It was a muddle from which only one lesson emerged: the War on Drugs crusade would never apply to narco-armies favored by the CIA, no matter how much opium and heroin they produced. Chairman Bao could not hide his confusion. "You treat us like terrorists when we don't even know how to make firecrackers," he said. "What do you want from us? To come here and plant more poppies?"

What *did* America want exactly?

The answer depends on how "America" is defined. Those at the very pinnacle of US government—the president, the secretary of state, most congressional lawmakers—were probably unaware that the Wa race existed. As for the DEA's administrator and the CIA's director, they would've known about the UWSA but deemed it a distant concern, far behind Mexican cartels and Islamic terrorists.

Thwarting Wa State was instead the remit of mid-tier DEA officials and, to a lesser extent, CIA officers assigned to Southeast Asia—by then a low-priority region for America. The UWSA ticked their boxes: it was a narco-army; it was friendly with China; it was beyond America's control. But since no one important in Washington cared all that much about the UWSA, the DEA was limited to an offensive on the cheap: no flashy raids, just extradition threats that would sound tough but prove impossible to execute.

As for the American public, they were as oblivious to the Wa then as they are today. Media yawned at the DEA's indictments. News outlets focused on two hot wars and Jennifer Aniston's recent breakup with Brad Pitt. But such is America's power that a peripheral operation—unnoticed by its citizens—can rock a civilization half a world away.

The Wa were indeed rocked. Through Operation Warlord, the United States rendered their government untouchable. The DEA insisted the UWSA owed reparations to the American public: $103 million, acquirable through seizing its companies and assets. Just as corporations are "persons" under US law, the White House designated the entire UWSA government as a "kingpin." Anyone of any nationality consorting with Wa State—by providing loosely defined "goods or services" to any UWSA officer or associate—faced imprisonment or a $10 million fine *if* the perpetrator also held funds in a US bank account, for this meant they'd infected America's financial system with dirty Wa drug profits.

Other than investors from China or Burma with zero exposure to the US economy, hardly any entity, even humanitarian organizations, could risk associating with Wa State after Operation Warlord. The United Nations' Wa Alternative Development Project succumbed to the stigma: donor funding evaporated, and the program collapsed. Only a tiny UN food aid program in Wa State survived.

Packaged with Operation Warlord was an intel dump on UWSA, Inc. The DEA laid bare the structures of Wa leaders' conglomerates, with extra attention paid to Wei, a "plague on the society and economy of Southeast

Asia," according to the US Treasury Department.[24] The United States revealed many of Hong Pang's shell companies, scattered in Thai shopping malls and office parks. Each was publicly named: Nice Fantasy Garments, A-Team Chemicals, Plus Tech Auto Supply. So was the drug lord's wife: Warin Chaichamrunphan, a Thai national in her late forties. Though Wei had hitherto concealed his spouse's existence, the United States splashed her details on the internet: age, passport number, addresses in Thailand, names of siblings who also laundered cash for Hong Pang. Thai police raided their businesses, never catching Wei's wife, but the DEA still hit Wei where it hurt. Nothing mattered to the mogul more than his privacy.

The year 2005 marked a new epoch for the Wa nation, albeit not the sort its leaders envisaged. Though robbed of optimism, they at least gained clarity. Now the Wa knew exactly how they appeared to the "international community": as barbarians who could do no right, their sins magnified, their every virtue refuted.

MOUNTAIN FORTRESS CHINA

PANGHSANG, 2010. FIVE LATER.

Take a hard swig of *baijiu*, squint, and you might confuse the Wa capital with a third-tier Chinese metropolis.

In the city center—for it was a real city now, not a rebel trading post built of bamboo and clay—high-rises shot up twelve stories, painting sidewalks with shade. The capital boasted wide avenues plied by new-model Toyota pickups and the odd Land Rover. Looming above intersections were Chinese-language billboards advertising liquor and jewelry, evidence of a Wa consumer class.

Come dusk the silhouette of distant peaks—robin's-egg blue by day—would fade to purple and then black. Streetlights lit up and so would the entertainment district downtown, glowing like a rainbow fireball. With flashing, golden signage, casinos lured in baccarat junkies: rich Wa and Chinese visitors. Violet strip lights prettified rent-by-the-hour hotels. Up the block were lanes incandescent with rosy neon: the universal beacon of anything-goes massage joints. Sitting in front of these parlors: a succession of women dressed identically in black skirts, reeling in male passersby with come-hither greetings in Chinese.

True to its design, Operation Warlord rendered the Wa nation into a pariah state, scaring away UN workers and forcing the Wa into near-total dependence on their one ally: China. And that, as it turned out, was not the end of the world. The more the West scorned the Wa, the more China embraced them.

Before the indictments, Wa State was deeply reliant on China, but afterward it became a full-on Chinese protectorate. This arrangement brought benefits. More assistance flowed to the Wa nation through China's Yunnan provincial government, focusing little on education and health care, but heavily on hard infrastructure: improved roads and bridges, an expanded electrical grid. Via deniable back channels, the People's Liberation Army (PLA) sold a higher class of weaponry to the United Wa State Army (UWSA): antiaircraft cannons, armored vehicles, and artillery, all of it discounted. More Chinese citizens poured into Panghsang to trade—and party. Hot yuan sloshed into new gambling halls and brothels in the Wa capital, with the UWSA taxing the profits. Flush with Chinese cash, Wa State's capital outshined that of Burma. Panghsang had everything Yangon had—supermarkets, bazaars selling electronics, even a bowling alley—plus comforts no Burmese city could claim: good sewers, consistent twenty-four-hour electricity provided by a hydropower dam, even a reliable mobile phone network tapped into China's telecom grid.

Two schools of thought reigned among Wa officialdom. One basked in material progress, holding few qualms about Wa State's dependence on China. Another feared their ancestors, who'd so valiantly resisted colonizers, would lament Wa lands becoming a vassal to their powerful neighbor. Jacob hailed from the second camp. And as a Baptist, he believed Chinese visitors were turning the capital into a high-altitude Sodom. "Why put a casino in the middle of the capital city? Why not make a doing-drugs area, a getting-girls area, and put it outside the city center with a big wall around it—so if other foreigners come, they don't think Wa State is just a big K-TV?"

Linguistically adept, Jacob had picked up some Chinese, enough to eavesdrop on visitors chattering in the city's brand-new hot pot restaurants and karaoke joints. He learned their favorite epithet for Wa State: *Shanzhai Zhongguo*, a nickname both clever and snide.

Zhongguo means "China." *Shanzhai*, meaning "mountain fortress," historically refers to walled barbarian forts beyond the reach of Chinese civilization—with ancient Wa fortress towns being a prime example. But in the 2000s, *shanzhai* took on a slang meaning. On the outskirts of big Chinese cities, illegal factories popped up to make copycat versions of Western goods, and bootleggers concealed their illicit sweatshops behind tall aluminum fencing. People jokingly called them modern-day *shanzhai* forts, and soon enough the word referred to anything bogus: a pair of *shanzhai* "Adidos" sneakers with four stripes, a *shanzhai* "Rolax" watch. Wa State, the Chinese joked, was the biggest *shanzhai* of all. An imitation mini-country, created by Wa bumpkins, as authentic as an Appl Hiphone.

This galled Jacob. Wa State was not a punchline. But he blamed his own leaders more than the Chinese. Over in China, authorities cracked down on gamblers and brothel-goers and drug users—as they should, in his opinion. So why did Wa society provide a refuge for these miscreants? His homeland was a dumping ground for Chinese vice. "If I pointed this out to other officials, some would agree. But most told me, Jacob, you're a nice guy. But you've got to relax."

Jacob was no longer teaching cadets. After a series of promotions, he'd joined Wa State's literacy department, becoming its fourth-highest-ranking official. The department's core duty was devising a curriculum for the nation's primitive education system. On paper this was Jacob's dream job, yet he was miserable. In the twelve-person literacy department, he was the only college-educated official, and his boss treated him like a prize poodle. "He basically made me into his secretary. I had to follow him everywhere." The department boss was lazy, only reporting to the office twice a week, fiddling around, then going home. He spent most days in his living room playing mah-jongg with the other literacy officials, and in lieu of crafting a curriculum, Jacob had to sit by his boss's side, keeping his beer glass full to the rim while the man shuffled ceramic tiles.

A middle-aged ex-guerrilla, the boss had scored his position thanks to Chairman Bao Youxiang. Back in 1989, when Bao needed mutineers to overthrow the communist politburo, this man joined without compunction, thus securing Bao's undying loyalty. But he lacked any other credentials. "My boss could not write A-B-C-D," Jacob told me. "He was totally illiterate. And he's our national leader for literacy!"

The literacy department was an afterthought, its budget minuscule. This was owed to the Wa government's dysfunctional funding mechanism. Each UWSA division received only a slice of its budget from the central state. They had to generate the rest on their own. An armed division with thousands of troops—such as Wei Xuegang's Wa South regiments—could develop high-profit ventures: running drug labs, taxing Chinese-owned plantations and factories, maybe even running a gold or tin mine. Their revenues were assured. But literacy officials, lacking in firepower or manpower, had far fewer means of making money—either for their department or for themselves.

So to the K-TVs they went: green uniforms pressed, service pistols on their hips, sniffing out Chinese businessmen with whom to partner and extract protection money. Despite his unimpressive job title, Jacob's boss could always namedrop Bao, telling potential investors that any project under his aegis was safe—for no one messed with Bao's relatives or old war buddies. Jacob, obligated to join these courting sessions, at first resisted shots of *baijiu* slid across the table, until he tired of his boss's glares and joined in. "The Chinese guys liked to drink until they couldn't walk. *Gambei! Gambei!* over and over." Getting sloshed was an occupational requirement.

The boss's business portfolio included several hotels and rubber farms, nothing too lucrative. Protection payments from these Chinese-funded businesses were supposed to benefit the department, but much of the yuan vanished into the boss's pockets. "He wasn't a stupid person and, to his credit, he never got involved in drug trafficking," Jacob said. "He just couldn't do his actual job. Like I said: business first, education last."

When Jacob prayed at night, God instructed him to forgive his boss, born as he was in an age of violence and ignorance. The Lord told Jacob to buck up and turn the gears of progress with his own hands. So his corrupt colleagues wouldn't perform their duties. Couldn't he do the work of the entire department all by himself? This epiphany jolted him into action. In the farmhouse where he lived with Saw Lu, Mary, Grace, and his sons—they had two now, a preteen and toddler—Jacob secluded himself in his bedroom. At a table by the window, he hunched over piles of paper, analyzing his broken department, determining how best to fix it.

It was a daunting exercise. Most Wa kids didn't go to school at all, and those who did usually just made it through one of Wa State's four hundred primary schools, which taught in Chinese and Wa. The primary schools' syllabus was well established, and Jacob lacked the cachet to alter it. He instead set his sights on middle schools—of which there were few, several dozen or so. The Wa government was starting to build more, even without established lesson plans in place. Unless Jacob intervened, the Wa middle schools would muddle along by hiring Chinese teachers dredged out of poor Yunnan villages, bringing over dusty old Chinese Communist Party–approved textbooks. As Jacob saw it, this was proof positive of his department's failings, a fast track to the death of his mother tongue. He decided to write the entire curriculum for grades seven through nine himself, inculcating Wa youth with his own pure, undiluted vision of progress.

Jacob penned lessons on magnetic fields, algebra, human biology—all in the Wa language. He took special pride in his geography lesson. "Most

Wa kids barely know they're in Burma, let alone where other countries are." So he drew a series of maps: the first depicting Wa State, the next zooming out to show Asia—India, China, Southeast Asia—and the final map revealing the entire world with the Wa motherland right at the center. Jacob would impress upon young minds that the Wa were not peripheral to humanity; nor was their nation some knock-off China.

Once again, his life gained purpose. Before the epiphany, Jacob had started to slip: hanging around hard-partying Wa officials, swilling too much booze, losing sight of his promise—to himself, his family, and his God—to uplift the Wa nation. Though Jacob stuck to beer, his peers sometimes swallowed pink pills or even smoked heroin. Now, when this raucous crowd called him to hang out, Jacob begged off. Can't make it, he'd say. I'm busy.

Jacob was still his boss's lapdog—following him around, keeping his beer cold—but every unclaimed hour went into designing lesson plans. Deep down, Jacob hoped his mentor Saw Lu would notice, maybe dispense rare words of praise. Was he not carrying forth a mission held sacred by their Baptist sect since the days of William Marcus Young: spreading the written word to the Wa people? But Saw Lu still seemed distracted, lost in private thoughts he wouldn't share. So be it. In his early thirties, Jacob felt he was coming into his own, and through this endeavor—however small in the grand scheme—he could create his own legacy.

After drafting lessons for more than a year, Jacob neared completion. He hadn't shown his boss the materials, but he could imagine how it would go down. His boss would take full credit while Jacob kept his mouth shut and plinked more ice into the ex-guerrilla's Tsingtao. Fine, so long as the curriculum went into effect across the Wa nation. He didn't need credit, only the satisfaction of preserving his culture from China's creeping influence.

AGENT JOHN WHALEN called it "going to see Moses on the mountain."

Moses being Bill Young. The mountain being Chiang Mai. Each time Whalen flew into the northern Thai city, he'd clear an entire week from his schedule. A marathon hang in Bill's den could reveal a "wealth of information. You never knew what you'd learn from one of his little tangents. We'd talk for hours and hours until, at some point, you just had to let him rest."

By 2010, Bill was weakened by emphysema, his lung tissue scarred by a lifetime smoking habit. He still held court from a chair in his den, aluminum oxygen tank and respirator mask within reach. "But the disease really pulled him down," Whalen said. "You could tell he wanted to go out there and be active. Since that was impossible, he did the next best thing: acting through other people."

The Drug Enforcement Administration calls those other people *subsources*: human assets managed by a trusted intermediary. Bill had subsources galore. Cell phones scattered around his den ringed and dinged incessantly. "It was incredible," Whalen said. "I remember Bill holding two phones—one at each ear—going back and forth in two different dialects of Lahu."

But Saw Lu remained Bill's crown jewel. His "main man up in Wa land" would whisper into a satellite phone, and Bill would pass his morsels on to the DEA. Occasionally Bill could compel Saw Lu to trek from Panghsang down to Chiang Mai for face-to-face debriefings with Whalen. "Bill Young first introduced me to Saw Lu around 2007," Whalen said. "Those two were close. Close like brothers. Bill used to say he was a Wa prince, Wa royalty, something in that vein." There was nothing royal about Saw Lu, born on a mud-hut floor inside the Baptist mission founded by Bill's grandfather. Yet, for some reason, Bill embellished his buddy's origin story. His efforts were wasted; Whalen didn't need an epic backstory to respect Saw Lu. With access to classified files running back to the early 1990s, the agent knew plenty about Saw Lu and already held him in high regard. For two decades straight, he'd been one of Southeast Asia's gutsiest confidential informants.

But more than ever before, Saw Lu was a CI in the classical sense: someone close enough to a criminal organization to betray its secrets. In the parlance of narco-traffickers: a rat. In his mid-sixties, Saw Lu was putting on weight, his hair reduced to silvery wisps, purple tubular veins rolling under the leathered skin of his hands. To Whalen, the man exuded old-world grit. "I was always impressed by him," he said. "What Saw Lu provided was information on Wei. And his information was *very* good."

Up in Panghsang, UWSA leaders no longer held their tongues around Saw Lu. They let him fraternize at private gatherings where Pu'er tea, *blai*, and shoptalk flowed. This wasn't a decorous bunch; the UWSA's inner circle liked feisty debate, and Saw Lu played the role of principled super-patriot, arguing against overreliance on China. Some would scoff; others

nodded in agreement. Wei was never present—he didn't socialize, preferring the solitude of his mansion—but the other leaders knew Wei's
business and discussed it freely. Saw Lu would memorize bits of useful
information and later mutter them into his satellite phone. If exposed, he
faced a short march up a dusty hill and a bullet in the heart. But until that
day came, Saw Lu would continue risking his life for the DEA. He proved
invaluable to America's understanding of Wei's affairs.

To the DEA's frustration, the drug lord was doing better than ever.
Operation Warlord hadn't obliterated his network, only forced Wei to
learn from his mistakes. He'd erred in branding his ventures under a
common name—Hong Pang, too easy to track—so he ditched the title.
Wei's empire now went by no name other than the Wa State Ministry of
Finance, and though it generated loads of revenue, the other Wa leaders
had almost no say over its operations.

The Ministry of Finance was a many-limbed leviathan. It specialized
in industries US authorities could not easily touch. Jade mines in war-torn
parts of Burma. Construction and real estate firms hidden in a new crop
of better-disguised shell companies in Yangon and Chiang Mai. And of
course, methamphetamine: both ya-ba pills and, for more discriminating
customers, crystal meth, upward of 95 percent pure.

The ministry's structure was part corporate, part mafioso. From his
megapalace, Wei dispensed orders to several caporegime-style lieutenants.
They in turn ran stables of "earners," who seldom, if ever, enjoyed contact
with the chief financial officer himself. Wei was wise to limit his exposure.
One top earner was a Burmese construction magnate who, while adept at
laundering money, had the social media discipline of a Kardashian. He
constantly flaunted his life on Facebook: flashy wardrobe, luxurious vaca-
tions, bottles of Hennessy Paradis (retail price: $1,700). Less conspicuous
earners managed high-end brothels, gambling dens, loan-sharking gangs,
or seemingly aboveboard businesses. All kicked a percentage to the ministry, which provided capital for expansion and armed protection courtesy of UWSA troops. "When I say Wei ran the treasury, I mean that
literally," Whalen told me. "He had vaults full of gold, gems and cash in
multiple currencies. Everything except *kyat*. No one wants to hold *kyat*."
(The *kyat* is Burma's currency, vulnerable to wild swings and erratic junta
policymaking.)

As for his top-grossing trade, narcotics, Wei's strategy was evolving.
Before, his regiments had managed their own labs and trafficked their

own meth. No more. The Ministry of Finance favored a "landlord" model: renting turf to non-Wa crime syndicates, letting them do the dirty work, and taxing their profits.

This was a service in high demand. China had a roaring domestic meth trade centered in the coastal mainland beyond Hong Kong—namely, the Guangzhou area—where crime syndicates concealed crystal meth factories in the industrial sprawl. But circa 2010, police were busting these labs left and right, forcing syndicates to seek a safer haven. Wei's ministry put the word out: you're welcome to set up shop in Wa State, a land beyond the reach of law enforcement. The syndicates were shown plots of Wa land near streams (meth labs require lots of water) and offered long-term leasing agreements, which included 24/7 protection from the UWSA. The main catch was that every Chinese syndicate had to obey Wei's house rule: absolutely no trafficking drugs back to their native China. His guests were required to export their meth to the Southeast Asian market via the Thai-Burma border.

Far from home, the relocated Chinese syndicates didn't know the local terrain and couldn't transport meth from their newly built labs to the border. That job fell to other contractors: trusted Lahu or Shan gangs permitted to traverse Wa State's roads. The most dangerous job—actually trafficking the meth into Thailand—fell to yet another set of specialists: gangs adept at evading (or paying off) Thai security forces. From the chemists to the transporters, everyone shared a taste of their profits with the Ministry of Finance.

Wei was fine-tuning his machine. A consummate capitalist, he shaved internal costs by outsourcing labor and production. He understood that the UWSA's most valuable asset wasn't narcotics. It was real estate. His ministry could simply issue permits to other underworld professionals and watch passive income roll in.

This model was so attractive that it inspired copycats. Circa 2010, new militias sprouted like mushrooms in Burma's northern hills. They were helmed by minor warlords, many of whom aspired to become little Wei Xuegangs. Belonging to various minority groups, the warlords aligned themselves with Burma's junta—which had just dusted off its old self-defense force scheme.[1] As in the past, any armed clan leader or malcontent rebel commander could betray his ethnic kin, establish a pro-junta militia in the mountains, and receive tacit permission from the Burmese regime to manufacture drugs. Dozens took the deal. Some newly minted regime-aligned warlords, imitating Wei, invited Chinese syndicates to open meth refineries on their land. Others started less-sophisticated ventures, such as pill-press factories. They'd buy crystallized meth powder wholesale from labs in Wa State, take it back to their turf, mix it up, and pump out *shanzhai* ya-ba tablets with the symbol "WY."

Though they infringed on Wei's brand, he didn't seem too bothered. Every warlord militia had to ship its merchandise to market—and the best routes into Thailand ran through Wei's domain: Wa South. None could pass without coughing up a toll. All across the Golden Triangle's meth value chain, Wei extracted profit. "When it came to drugs," Whalen told me, "he had a financial stranglehold on the region."

Saw Lu, keeping an eye on the Ministry of Finance for the DEA, confided that Wei's success disturbed the other Wa leaders. They were particularly rattled when Wei used his fortune to double the salaries of every UWSA soldier, from privates to commanders, buying their admiration. Bao's mainline faction was much larger and more muscular—his relatives controlled Wa State's key military divisions—yet he feared Wei's riches and his wiles.

Wei was also a Chinese intelligence asset, liaising with the Ministry of State Security division in Yunnan province. Chinese technicians helped Wei create a surveillance network inside Wa State that tapped landlines, mobile phones, possibly satellite phones too—with all data accessible to Chinese agents upon demand. There wasn't much Bao could do to weaken Wei's links to China—for he served the same master. His UWSA, like a baby receiving nutrients through an umbilical cord, needed Mother China to supply weapons, ammo, and even training. This relationship was hardly secret. By 2010, Chinese Communist Party officials were regulars at UWSA ceremonies, appearing at Bao's elbow in suits and neckties, while the chairman himself wore his signature dark-green fatigues.

In short, China was co-opting the most fearsome drug cartel in Asia. Wei in particular was a godsend to Beijing: absorbing pesky crime syndicates from mainland China, channeling their meth output elsewhere. It was (and is) a highly beneficial arrangement—one far more effective than America's strategy in its own borderlands.

On the US-Mexico border, the United States clings to the same old tactics: try to smash cartels and lock up kingpins. Not only does this aggression come at a heavy price, paid in billions of taxpayer dollars and kiloliters of Mexican blood, but it also doesn't work. Breaking up big cartels creates power vacuums. Smaller cartels rush to fill them. The prize goes to the most sadistic competitor. Murders attributed to Mexico's internecine drug wars since 2005 are pegged at three hundred thousand and counting.[2]

China doesn't have this nightmare on its borders. Instead of breaking up the megacartel next door, China's government befriended the UWSA, recognizing that one big whale is better than a swarm of piranhas. By fortifying the Wa with advanced weapons, China has ensured that no one—not Burma's military, not the DEA—can ever defeat the UWSA and wreak havoc in its backyard. And by making sure both Bao and Wei—the muscle and the brains of Wa State—depended on it for their survival, the Chinese Communist Party guaranteed its sway over the Wa government.

Saw Lu's intel helped explicate this portrait of Chinese dominance over the Wa. In addition to monitoring drug-trade developments, he'd always keep an ear cocked for information on other aspects of the UWSA-China alliance: trade deals, weapons upgrades, and so on. An example of a phone missive to Bill: "Five PLA advisors inbound to train UWSA heavy weapons units. Training on 120mm mortars and SAMs," meaning surface-to-air missiles. After rattling off some new finding, Saw Lu would ring off, power down, return the sat phone to its hole, and bury it under handfuls of dirt. So went the protocol. Lingering on the line risked interception.

Before going to see "Moses on the mountain," Whalen would always buy lots of satellite phone cards, used to top up the Ericsson Inmarsat device hidden on Saw Lu's farm. Bill could refresh the phone's credit from afar. Maintaining fly-on-the-wall access to top-level UWSA conversations was vital. "At the time," Whalen said, "Saw Lu was on good terms with Xiao Minliang and even Bao. He was telling us all about their power struggles with Wei. I respected what he was doing for us. Saw Lu, man. Tough as nails."

But because Saw Lu seldom emoted—because he concealed feelings behind scar tissue thick as granite—Special Agent John Whalen could not sense his CI's malaise. It fermented in Saw Lu's insides: the nauseating feeling that, with so much left to accomplish, the clock was running out.

"Me and Bill, we are history-making men," Saw Lu told me. "We were sent here to change the world." Yet, as a CI, he was merely documenting the doings of other powerful actors, one murmured tidbit at a time. "I told Bill that I was disappointed in my life. I didn't think we were making a difference." Bill would reach for a lighter—he still smoked through his sickness—and blow gray clouds that hung at the ceiling. Then he'd trot out more "crazy schemes," as if the last one—Whiskey Alpha—hadn't been kiboshed by the DEA.

Who was Bill fooling? Everyone from their fraternity of misfits was in some stage of ruin. Shah was ill from natural causes, clinging to life in a hospital. Mahasang was dead; Thai police nabbed him for drug trafficking, and in 2007 the Prince passed away in confinement. Zhao Nyi Lai had suffered a final, fatal stroke in 2009. He was buried up in Pang Wai. "Bill was unwell too," Saw Lu said. "He'd fall asleep in mid-sentence. He wasn't his usual self."

Saw Lu couldn't shake something morose Bill said at one of their rendezvous—in a private moment when Whalen wasn't around. Bill, usually sardonic, was never one to turn maudlin. "But I'll never forget it. He goes, 'Saw Lu, if you can't achieve your dreams, then I don't want to be alive in this world.'"

JACOB'S MIDDLE-SCHOOL CURRICULUM was complete. With his own money he printed prototype textbooks: bound and stapled editions bedecked with original art, all the better to impress his illiterate boss. Each book cover featured a pencil sketch of a solitary human eye gazing at a lit wax candle, its flame symbolizing enlightenment. Inside the literacy department office, Jacob fanned the books across a table and admired his work. The office was quiet. A plastic wall clock's second hand revolved with stuttering clicks.

The day had come. At an appointed sit-down, his boss would finally inspect Jacob's efforts. The department chief only had to grunt approval, slap Jacob on the back, and allot funding for printing and distribution. When his boss finally arrived, late, he was in a mood—like a deadbeat dad inconvenienced by his child's recital. Jacob led him to the table. With nicotine-stained fingers his boss picked up *PHUK LAI GAU 3* (Wa Study Book 3), flipped through the pages, and put it down. Unable to read the title, he glared at the cover art and frowned.

What's this supposed to be? Someone setting fire to their own eyeball?

No, sir. It's a candle lighting the way forward.

The boss nodded, futzed with a few other books, and blandly praised Jacob's efforts. He promised to raise the topic at the next all-department assembly. But when the assembly came and went with no mention of the new curriculum, Jacob had to wonder, Is he snubbing me? Afterward, the ex-guerrilla mumbled something about having too little money to print textbooks and started to walk away.

Though naturally obedient, Jacob could not suppress the indignation welling up inside his chest, practically singeing his tongue. Printing textbooks would cost a pittance. At stake was the future of their native tongue. Was his boss that shortsighted? Lazy? Envious of Jacob's intellect? Fighting every deferential instinct, Jacob rounded on his boss, cornering him.

Stop, he said. Give me a better answer.

His boss just looked at him with contempt and growled. Don't bring this up again, Jacob. Understand? Just drop it.

"Years of my life. Wasted," Jacob told me. "My hope was gone, gone, gone." He saw the cold truth of it: no dream, no matter how small, could withstand the UWSA's crushing apathy. Even educating Wa adolescents in their own language, teaching them to see their people as unique and noble, rather than drilling them with old Chinese textbooks—to hope for that, from a government this myopic, was futile. Jacob felt that, as in ancient times, no Wa highlander could see beyond family and clan or strive to build a better tomorrow as a collective. It was an affliction from which he longed to save his people. But they did not want his salvation.

Months passed in a blur. The prototype books took residence in a cardboard box shoved into a corner. Jacob wasn't home much. When fellow officials called him to go carousing, he couldn't think of a reason to say no. He fell in with a boozy, rascally crew, and they delighted in pouring *baijiu* and Johnny Walker Black down Bible Boy's throat. If he drunkenly groaned about his idiot boss, they asked why the hell he still worked for the dead-end literacy department. A clever guy like Jacob, still young, could quit, go serve a commander with real power, maybe even get rich.

SEPTEMBER 3, 2010, A FRIDAY.

Jacob got home late to the farmhouse. He shuffled up the path under a half-moon just bright enough to make out the gray craters pocking its surface. Nearing the front door, Jacob sensed something amiss. On the patio, loose papers were strewn about, catching the night breeze and scraping across the concrete.

The interior was wrecked. Furniture upside down. Mattresses dragged into the front room and slashed open, cottony guts spilling on the tile.

Books splayed on the floor with pages ripped out, and boxes of papers tipped over. Saw Lu's wife, Mary, her face frozen stoic, attempted to tidy up. Jacob's wife, Grace, emerged from their bedroom with puffy, pink eyes. I've tried to reach you. Seven or eight officers ransacked the house. They were hunting for something but wouldn't say what. They took father with them. Saw Lu is gone.

Jacob asked what their uniforms looked like: black like Panghsang police or dark green like soldiers wore? Grace was too frazzled to recall, only that she'd never seen that kind of uniform. They called themselves "special police," she said. Jacob nodded gravely. That wasn't good. Grace resumed sobbing, moaning the Burmese word for *why* over and over: why, why, why—her vowels elongating sorrowfully. Jacob kept quiet. He didn't know exactly what his father-in-law had done. But he knew why Saw Lu had done it. The old man couldn't help himself.

The next morning, Jacob put on his UWSA fatigues and walked Grace and Mary over to Panghsang's central prison. Guards stopped them at the front gates. You can't go in, they said. Jacob ordered them to call out the warden. The guards refused. So the three made a nuisance of themselves until finally the warden stomped out, shouting that he'd arrest them if they didn't go home.

Just tell us where you're keeping him, Jacob said.

Where who's keeping him? I never even said *he* was here.

Jacob sensed affected drama in the warden's swagger and suspected he was putting on a tough-guy show for the guards. Another bad sign. Saw Lu's charges must've been truly heinous, so bad that no official would want it going around that he'd shown mercy to a traitor's family. Listen, Jacob said to the warden, you can't just feed him prison slop. Saw Lu is diabetic. We're going to come back every day with decent food. Enough for you and the guards. But you'd better give some to Saw Lu so he doesn't fall ill and die.

In the ensuing weeks, they lavished the prison with Mary's cooking, always rotating in Saw Lu's favorite dish—*pe pyote*, fried yellow peas—to send a message: we know you're in there; we're fighting to get you out. But they had no idea if Saw Lu was trapped inside that concrete prison or buried in the forest.

Jacob stopped going to work. He laid around in bed but seldom slept, turning more bilious by the day. The farmhouse, in Saw Lu's absence, felt eerily empty, and it was silent, the air scented with cooking oil. One afternoon, Jacob picked up his mobile phone and rang his most ne'er-do-well acquaintance. He asked what heroin feels like. Comfort, came the reply. You won't care about a thing in the world.

That was all he needed to hear. Because for as long as Jacob could remember, he'd cared until his heart burst, and then cared some more. Trying to be good availed nothing to him or Saw Lu or anyone he'd ever known. It was time to fully immerse himself in being bad.

THE RECKONING

Saw Lu awoke in a small, boxy cell with cinderblock walls. Lying on a cold concrete floor, body thrumming with hurt. He was indoors—so why the sound of birds chirping? But when his eyes adjusted, he realized half the cell's roof was gone. Its missing section framed the porcelain sky in a rectangle.

They'd snatched him up at home and started beating him en route to the prison. The thrashing continued on the inside as Saw Lu's captors shuffled him from room to dark room, erasing any sense of place. He couldn't recall their faces or entering this cell. They'd clasped a rusty iron collar around his neck, and he must've pawed it in the night because his fingertips were stained orange.

After a while, the steel door swung open, and in walked four men, each kempt and ethnically Chinese in appearance. One squatted to remove the collar. He pulled Saw Lu upright, putting his back against the wall.

Where am I?

Maximum security wing.

What are the charges?

Nonconformism. Unauthorized contact with a Western country. Unpatriotic behavior.

You're Wei Xuegang's people?

They ignored the question. We know what *you* are.

What am I?

You're a VIP for the Central Intelligence Agency.

The men had a log of every trip to Chiang Mai going back years. They knew about Bill Young but believed he was an active CIA officer. Saw Lu protested—"My whole life, I never once talked to the CIA"—but this only annoyed his captors. They said the Drug Enforcement Administration and CIA were one and the same, and there was no use pretending otherwise. The interrogation began, and their questions concerned a DEA gambit called Operation Hotspot or, alternately, Spot a Druglord. It had kicked off nine days prior.[1]

Saw Lu said he'd never heard of it. He was telling the truth.

This operation, executed by DEA agents in Thailand, involved printing posters, clothing, matchboxes, coasters, and other tchotchkes featuring Wei's mugshot, two decades out of date. They doled all of it out in tawdry nightlife spots near the Thai-Burma border, as well as in red-light districts in major cities. In Bangkok, Phuket, and Pattaya, go-go bar staff wore T-shirts that read "Wanted: Wei Hseuh Kang—Reward Up to $2 Million." Bartenders served longnecks in foam koozies bearing Wei's face with DEA hotlines underneath in bright-red ink.

The DEA called it "aggressive community outreach," a thrashing of the bushes to shake loose tips. But the whole endeavor hinged on a surreal notion—that Wei might occasionally slip into Thailand to swill beers and ogle bikini girls in clubs catering to Western tourists. Never mind that Wei was a nonboozer who seldom left his Panghsang mansion and, if caught planting a single toe in Thailand, faced death by lethal injection.

In a media blitz coinciding with the operation, DEA officials branded Wei the "financial genius" behind the United Wa State Army (UWSA) and "the CEO of the criminal organization." Maybe the purpose of splashing Wei's photo everywhere was to fluster the drug lord. Perhaps, by citing Wei as the organization's "CEO" instead of Bao Youxiang, the DEA hoped to inflame the Bao-Wei rivalry—a "powder keg," according to classified US documents.[2] But Saw Lu wasn't in any position to explain the DEA's thinking. He had nothing to do with Operation Hotspot, and neither did his handlers, Bill Young and Agent John Whalen. It had been conceived by the DEA's Far East Section, concentrated in Bangkok.

Saw Lu's captors believed otherwise, and they intended to pound the truth out of him with wooden batons. At all hours they'd appear—sometimes two men, sometimes four—to roll him prone, strike his naked back, bruise his internal organs. They were methodical and sober, seldom raising a voice in anger. After a futile month, in which Saw Lu never changed his story, the interrogators tweaked their approach. Sign this, they said, presenting a typed statement: I, Saw Lu, am a CIA spy and international drug trafficker. He shook his head no. The interrogators didn't curse or shout. They just unholstered their batons and got to work.

Saw Lu hardly ever left the cell. Most of the time he was alone, curled up in a ball to preserve warmth. They fed him twice a day: a weak gruel of broken rice and mustard greens, though occasionally a Wa guard snuck in Mary's home-cooked food or some medicine. Saw Lu was always thirsty. His cognition flowed like frozen sludge. December brought light rains that pattered the cement floor through the open roof, but when Saw Lu retreated to a dry corner, the door would fly open, and the interrogators would drag him back into the wet half of the room, forcing him to soak up the cold drizzle.

On cloudless days Saw Lu starfished his aching body on the sun-warmed cement floor. His thoughts drifted back to the winter of 1967. His first months in Pang Wai. Seeing Wa mothers, babies at their breasts, emerging from wooden huts on frigid mornings to locate sunny patches on the ground. Before heading to the poppy fields, they'd plop the naked infants down on sunshiny dirt to warm their bodies. Sister, he'd say, it's cold enough to freeze water! Why don't you swaddle those babies in cotton? They'd stare back blankly. We just don't, young man. We get along just fine.

By his third month in captivity, Saw Lu lost sensation in his lips. His feet went numb as rocks. There was a lesion on his neck that never healed, and if he twisted his head, the iron collar massaged rust into his bloodstream. The beatings increased in intensity. Once a captor whacked Saw Lu so hard that the cudgel snapped in two, the blunt end sailing free and clattering against the wall. They no longer bothered brandishing phony confession papers. They just pummeled Saw Lu and left him groaning on the floor.

Why not a quick bullet to the head?

Why this drawn-out murder in increments? To maximize his suffering?

Saw Lu didn't think so. Wei wasn't one for melodrama. More likely he'd calculated that killing Saw Lu outright would aggravate Bao's mainline faction of the UWSA, known to harbor Saw Lu sympathizers. An "accidental" death under interrogation might go down smoother, causing minimal disruption to his operations. Wei had probably expected him to die in the first few weeks; most sixty-six-year-old diabetics would've. But in his final act of defiance, Saw Lu intended to madden his enemy by dying as slowly as possible.

CHAIRMAN BAO'S INNER circle understood perfectly well that Saw Lu could be a pain in the ass. But he was *their* pain in the ass.

For years, they'd let him hang around because Saw Lu, in his own guileless fashion, exhorted everyone to do the right thing, no matter how inconvenient. His interpretation of the "right thing" was sometimes detached from reality, but they'd always hear him out. As Wei's influence grew, so did Saw Lu's appeal, especially among Wa leaders who regarded Wei as essentially Chinese and an avatar of Chinese overreach into Wa affairs. As they saw it, the UWSA's ruling court needed Saw Lu around— a sayer of discomforting truths, an unapologetic defender of their race.

In a general sense, Saw Lu was guilty of Wei's accusations, even if he had no role in Operation Hot Spot. Nonconformism? Check. Unauthorized contact with a Western country? Classic Saw Lu. But unpatriotic behavior? This was a matter of perspective. Saw Lu loved the Wa nation like a parent loves a wayward child. Wei, on the other hand, did not pretend to love anything but power and money, even though neither brought him discernible joy.

By early 2011, as Saw Lu clung to life, Bao faced two choices. Choice one: allow Wei Xuegang to finish off Saw Lu. After all, he'd exposed Saw Lu as a snitch. Though Bao and the other leaders didn't know how far he'd once gone in betraying the UWSA—they were not cognizant of the Whiskey Alpha coup plot, aborted nine years prior—there was no denying that Saw Lu was ratting out Wei to the United States, a declared enemy of the UWSA. For this "unauthorized contact" offense, Saw Lu certainly deserved punishment. However, to the senior Wa officer corps, America was becoming an abstract, distant threat. They instead fixated on the racial dynamic of this standoff: a poor, pure-blooded former Wa leader, Saw Lu, in the clutches of a half-Chinese drug baron who seldom deigned to show his face.

Choice two for Bao? Pry loose from Wei's grasp the only man brave enough to challenge the narco-mogul. An even more perilous move. An enraged Wei could cut revenues vital to sustaining the Wa government. As Bao deliberated, word of Saw Lu's condition spread, and he became more than a mere prisoner. He was a crucible testing the chairman's capacity to rein in his financier. Saw Lu's fate would reveal which man was really in charge.

"All the officers were talking," Jacob said. "I was pulled aside and told, 'Your father-in-law is in a big political mess. Don't get dragged into it.'"

This warning came straight from Jacob's new commanding officer—one of Bao's nephews. During his depressive episode, he'd taken friends' advice, ditching the literacy department in pursuit of genuine power. Jacob was quickly scooped up by a brigade commander overseeing Naung Khit: UWSA Western Sector, a region fronting Burma proper. The commander hired him as his adjutant. "I wanted to serve someone who could make things happen easily with a quick phone call to his uncle," Jacob told me. "And I was happy he didn't play mah-jongg."

The commander—a thick-set, industrious man in his mid-fifties with close-shaved hair—didn't drink alcohol either. He couldn't afford to dull his wits. The Baos were a prodigious clan with many nephews vying for esteemed posts. This particular nephew clawed to the top through clean living and hard work. He'd transformed the choppy peaks of Naung Khit, once blanketed in poppies, into a profitable source of rubber and rare timber, as well as pink-colored stimulants. "I think you know what I mean," Jacob told me. "There were always trucks coming in and out, late at night, moving things to the border."

As adjutant, Jacob managed the commander's calendar. He scheduled appointments with foreign investors, Chinese and Burmese alike, as well as fellow UWSA officials. The two shuttled back and forth between Naung Khit and the capital, Jacob chauffeuring his commander in a sable-black Toyota Land Cruiser with tinted windows; even the license plate, issued by Wa State's transportation division, was black. Officially Jacob still earned a terrible salary—roughly $20 per month—but this was a fraction of his actual take-home pay. His commander sporadically peeled off one-hundred-yuan notes and stuffed them in Jacob's breast pocket.

For your family, he'd say.

Most of the cash went to Jacob's dealer.

"What can I say? I was a bad guy. Smoking, drinking. Sometimes the pink pill. But mostly using number four." This is narco-trafficker slang. Poppies transform into heroin through four stages. Step one: collect opium. Step two: boil it, add chemicals, and dry it into clumpy morphine powder. Step three: refine it further into injectable, brown-sugar heroin. Step four: purify it into China White. For thirty yuan ($5) Jacob could cop a rock of "number four" similar in size and color to a wisdom tooth. Flick the baggie, powderize the dope, dash it on foil, and suck the smoke through a plastic straw. "After that first time, I never stopped. In a few weeks, I was hooked and needed it to function." But Jacob felt confident he was playing it cool—that his commander was clueless about his near-daily heroin habit.

Using his enhanced status—he was right-hand man to a Bao nephew—Jacob convinced a few prison officials to help keep Saw Lu alive. They'd smuggle in home-cooked food and medication under the nose of the warden. But in early March one of these contacts informed Jacob that his father-in-law was on death's precipice. A Wa guard had found Saw Lu inside his cell, in a blubbering fugue, with the right side of his body offline—as if disconnected from his brain. Saw Lu could not stand or speak coherently. He needed medical attention. Immediately. Urgent inquiries went out. High authorities were roused and consulted.

Bao had no more time to deliberate. His hand was forced. Within hours, instructions came down from the chairman's office: get Saw Lu to a Chinese hospital. Yunnan's provincial security bureau might not appreciate the UWSA sending a half-dead, America-loving spy into their country, but Bao could explain later. The closest decent hospital was in Pu'er, a Chinese city more than one hundred miles to the east. Bao ordered subordinates to rush Saw Lu there as fast as possible.

JACOB GOT THE CALL a few weeks later. Your father-in-law survived. He's on his way back from the hospital in Pu'er. Come collect him at the border in Panghsang.

Jacob drove to a bridge, spanning the Hka River, that served as Wa State's main portal to China. He passed underneath a colossal stone archway ornamented with a black stone bull's head and pulled up to the border checkpoint. Saw Lu was waiting in a wheelchair: alone, gray, wind bitten.

Jacob parked, approached, and recoiled at the thing on Saw Lu's neck: a volcanic wound encrusted white. In a hoarse growl, Saw Lu relayed the Chinese doctors' prognosis. He'd narrowly survived a stroke. Much of the right side of his body would be intermittently paralyzed, likely forever. His blood pressure was frighteningly high, and his kidneys were almost ruined. I might live a while longer, he said. I might not. Though Saw Lu's criminal case was still unresolved, the UWSA central committee had decreed he could recuperate at home—under the close supervision of Wei's "special police."

How about you, son? Are you OK?

Jacob hesitated. He felt the eyes of his erstwhile mentor upon him: scanning, rendering judgment. He tried very hard to hold back tears.

I'm alright, father.

I hope so. I need you to be strong.

They drove to the farmhouse, and Jacob helped his father-in-law into bed. For the first few days, Saw Lu mostly slept. Mary and Grace, aghast at Saw Lu's gauntness, replenished him with vitamin-rich meals: boiled peas, beef soup, greens aplenty. But no one in the house could relax. Not with sour-faced men, handguns and batons affixed to their belts, dropping by unannounced to poke around. Go ahead, Mary said. Look at him. He can't hurt anyone. He can't even walk. Sometimes Wei's men left right away. Sometimes they loitered on the patio and smoked.

Saw Lu waited about a week to make his move. One night he threw off his blanket with his good arm, rolled out of bed, and flopped onto the floor. The paralysis on his right side was not total, and with effort he could crawl. He moved tortoise-like to the bedroom door, through the house, and into the yard. He kept going, inching along all the way to the orchard. Saw Lu found the right spot and clawed at the loose earth with his left hand. Praying they hadn't found it. Praising God when his fingers met hard plastic beneath the soil.

Saw Lu extended the Ericsson sat phone's antenna to its full 6.4 inches and mashed the power button. The screen glowed atomic green. He knew the number by heart.

When Bill answered with a froggy hello, Saw Lu spoke in Lahu as fast as his tongue would allow, afraid the line would cut out before he could divulge everything: the torture, the stroke, the very real possibility that Wei's men could show up any minute. You have to help me, Bill.

Bill?

Through the hiss Saw Lu heard ugly, drenched breathing. I'm sorry, Bill said. You're a good man. The DEA broke its promise to you, Saw Lu. They let you down. I'm so sorry.

It sounded like Bill might be crying. Or drowning. Saw Lu wasn't sure what to say. So he said good-bye. The two men would never speak again. The following week, on April 1, 2011, Bill Young shot himself in the head with a Colt .32 handgun. Chiang Mai police found him dead at his house with the pistol in one hand and, in the other, his grandfather's silver Celtic cross.

DESPITE SAW LU'S lifelong enthrallment with America and its supposed ethic of salvation, no American could save him now. His survival depended entirely upon his own people, namely Bao and his UWSA faction. He laid under a blanket in his farmhouse, awaiting what came, feeling more alone than he'd felt in that cinderblock cell.

He might die from organ failure, or he might be assassinated. Possibly the UWSA would take the formal route: ceding to Wei's wishes, binding Saw Lu's eyes, and executing him atop the dirt knoll. Or maybe—just maybe—his sympathizers among the Wa leadership would prevail in the tug-of-war with Wei, ensuring that Saw Lu remained under house arrest instead of in prison, so he could at least waste away in his own bed.

Unbeknownst to Saw Lu, certain UWSA central committee officials were busy machinating to secure his freedom. They were keen to sweep him out of Wa State: swiftly, silently, before Wei could strike again. For months, they'd negotiated with their military counterparts in Burma—a country in flux. Secretary One Khin Nyunt was no longer dictator, other military generals having usurped him in a 2004 internal putsch. Burma's new administration was intent on a makeover. The junta sought to molt its skin, creating a civilian government stocked with retired generals: lawmakers wearing sarongs instead of army greens and calling themselves democrats. Sanitizing the country's image, they hoped, would convince Western countries to lift crushing sanctions, bring in foreign cash, and reduce Burma's worrisome overreliance on neighboring China.

In March 2011—around the time Saw Lu was stroking out in a prison cell—the Burmese junta officially dissolved itself. It even freed Aung San Suu Kyi from house arrest and, by June, allowed her to meet US Senator John McCain inside her Yangon home. This paved the way for more spectacular visits. Secretary of State Hillary Clinton also dropped by Suu Kyi's lakeside manor and presented a chew toy to her pet dog; President Barack Obama later flew to Burma, lifted sanctions, pecked Suu Kyi on the cheek, and urged US corporations to invest in the once reviled country.

The UWSA central committee members seized upon this unprecedented US-Burma lovefest. They prodded Burmese officials to forgive the old traitor Saw Lu and let him back into Burma proper—without stringing him up from a tree this time. He's harmless now, they said. Too decrepit to make mischief with the Americans. Burma's officials acquiesced and Deputy Xiao Minliang, the UWSA's number two, began planning Saw Lu's evacuation under cover of darkness. "Xiao came to my home to deliver the news," Saw Lu told me. "There were tears running down his face. He said, 'I sure wish it didn't have to be like this, Saw Lu. We'll remember you. You'll stay in our hearts forever.'"

In mid-July, the family slipped out of Panghsang before sunrise: Saw Lu, Mary, Grace, and the grandkids in cars accompanied by Xiao's rifle-bearing escorts—just in case. Dawn broke as they corkscrewed down blacktop roads, and for the last time in his life, Saw Lu gazed across Wa peaks jutting skyward like a dragon's spine. As they descended the pines grew taller. The air thickened and clogged their ears. They cruised through the final UWSA checkpoint near the Burmese city of Tangyan, and everyone admitted that roads on the Burmese side were much shoddier than Wa State roads built by Chinese engineers. By the time they reached the foothills, rain streaked the glass windshield, and the wind smelled like hot mud.

They pulled up to their old house atop the hill in Lashio. Home looked much as they'd left it: sea-foam green with yellowing shutters. Relatives had kept the place up nicely, just as Wa folks in the neighborhood lovingly maintained the red-brick church across the lane. The church's doors gleamed white with a blood-red cross painted on the exterior. The bombshell, oxidized brown-pink, still dangled out front from a thick chain.

But the family was missing someone. Jacob did not join the evacuation to Lashio. He'd elected to stay behind in Wa State, where he could self-destruct in peace.

JACOB WORE HIS depression like a lead cloak. For a while the heroin worked as advertised: lightening his anguish, ushering in blissful indifference—to his people, his family, his own existence. But the longer he smoked it, the briefer the trance, until the heroin just calmed the intestinal cramps and snotty fevers so that he could loathe himself with a clear head.

After his family vacated the Panghsang farmhouse, Jacob moved into his commander's country manor in rural Naung Khit. He lived in the adjutant's quarters: clean and well-appointed with servants underfoot. Parked on the dirt outside were Fords and Toyotas—a whole fleet of trucks and sport utility vehicles—and Jacob held keys to each. As long as you stay with me, Bao's nephew told him, you'll want for nothing.

Jacob just wanted his hope back. He'd sit up late with a Bible in his lap, flipping onionskin pages and whispering to God. What happened to me, Lord? Life feels so heavy. I tried to be a good father, a good husband, a good son-in-law. But the weight grew too heavy to bear. He'd hoped moving to the hinterlands, many miles from his dealers in Panghsang, would force him to detox. Within days he was wheedling UWSA supply-truck drivers to cop baggies in the capital on his behalf and sneak them into Naung Khit. Jacob's weight dropped. Yellow film veneered his eyes. "I don't know how I went four months without the commander catching me. He did, eventually. He was so disappointed. 'A smart guy like you? On *heroin?*'"

The commander told Jacob to hole up in his room and sweat it out. Disappear for months if you have to. Whatever it takes to get clean. Fix it, Jacob. Just fix it. Jacob was back on heroin within a week. So the commander drove Jacob to the local brig, booked him, and said I'll return in six months. The UWSA prison guards swapped Jacob's green uniform for thin pajamas and escorted him to a courtyard full of deserters, thieves, and fellow drug users. Everyone but Jacob wore leg irons; the guards wouldn't clasp manacles onto a high-ranking adjutant's ankles.

His body rioted: spasming, joints howling, fluid spewing from both ends. When the withdrawal symptoms faded, it was waiting for him—a more viscid depression than he'd ever known. Some unholy voice took residence in his soul and beckoned him to end it all. Life was a hellish monotony. Six months passed like a century.

On Jacob's release date, his commander collected him at the brig gates and handed him a black electronic fob—the keys to a Land Cruiser parked nearby. You drive, he said. His commander was in a sparkling mood. Now that you're all better, he said, I can buy you a house and a car of your own. You'll bring your wife down here, and she'll open a country store selling goats. Move your whole family down—everyone except your father-in-law, of course. As Jacob drove, the commander prattled on like this, dictating to Jacob how his future would unfold.

Jacob gripped the wheel. He stared straight ahead at the coiling blacktop crowded on both shoulders by dwarf trees with fingerlike branches. He hadn't spoken to Grace in months. How to explain to the commander that his wife reviled Wa State for the ruin it had brought her father—and reviled Jacob for abandoning their family to suck heroin fumes off hot foil?

Sir, I was thinking. Maybe I could go visit my family for Christmas.

His commander shifted in his seat. No, no, no. I need to keep a close eye on you. Don't make me tell you twice.

The commander had a meeting later that week in the capital, and normally Jacob, as adjutant, would've come along to take notes. His commander struggled to write. But Jacob begged off, requesting more downtime to ease into life after jail. Fine, the commander said. Rest up while I'm gone. See you in a few days.

Jacob rose early the next morning and walked to Naung Khit's marketplace. Hands deep in his pockets, body hunched against the cold. He spotted a pickup idling across a paved lot and started walking over. Two UWSA officers shouted his name—Jacob! Where you been? Hey!—but he didn't turn his head. He rapped on the truck's windshield and held up a roll of cash so the driver could see. A fistful of burgundy and royal-blue bills totaling sixty thousand Burmese kyat. Roughly $70. Drive me to Lashio and it's yours. The driver told him to get in.

The trip took four hours. By afternoon Jacob stood in the driveway of his father-in-law's familiar green house. The same house where, as a lovesick boy, he'd watched awful Burmese propaganda films on a black-and-white television, just to sit next to Grace: the girl he would one day marry with Saw Lu officiating; the mother of his children; the wife he'd neglected for China White.

Jacob walked through the door and found the old man in the sitting room. He stood before him, rakish and disheveled. Spine like a warm noodle and his face hot with shame. He recounted his sins and begged forgiveness. He knew that Saw Lu—however infirm, however scandalized in their motherland—still retained ultimate authority over matters of family. If the patriarch willed it, Jacob the absconding heroin addict would face excommunication, never again sleeping beside his wife or knowing his children's love.

The silence was excruciating. Then Saw Lu spoke. Son, you're broken to pieces. But that's no reason to cry. It just means we'll have to rebuild you.

The family shipped Jacob off to a Baptist rehab: a bamboo-and-thatch camp hidden away in Burma's foothills. He lived in an open-air dorm with fellow recovering addicts. All submitted their minds and bodies to jungle faith healers, fiery-eyed men who cured dope lust with baptismal rites: dunking men backward into cold water, over and over, amid a feverish laying of hands.

The addicts rose early to toil the land. Come languid afternoons they read the Bible. Each night they held hands and praised God in song. Jacob lost himself in the ritual. He became less of a discrete soul with its own yearnings and dissolved into the multitude—becoming a ripple in a stream of humanity. "I learned to let go. There was so much anger underneath my skin. So much thinking about my failure at the literacy department. By letting go—letting go of my desire to control the world—I accepted God's will and finally found peace."

I asked him if Saw Lu ever found that same peace.

"Honestly, Patrick, I don't know. Maybe not. Until the very end he wanted to put his mark on the world."

OCTOBER 31, 2019.

Lashio. A windless night lit by a waning moon.

Saw Lu was upstairs in bed. His phone jangled around 7:30 p.m., Grace's name flashing on the screen. He answered. His daughter was calling from her back garden, pacing under banana trees, talking about a white man at her dinner table. He wants to meet you, father. What do I say?

American?

I think so.

Bring him over. I'll come down. Saw Lu stood up from the bed—his right-side paralysis was semicured by now, only afflicting him sporadically—and retied his sarong. He slapped a blue baseball cap on his bald head and called to the servant girl. A guest is coming. Make tea.

When Saw Lu shuffled down to the sitting room, the stranger was standing there in tan slacks and pastel-blue socks—a man tallish and pale with a pointy nose, gazing up at a photo hanging on the wall in a faux-gold frame. Staring down at the American was Saw Lu circa springtime 1993, his portrait taken in full UWSA regalia. A dashing figure with brass epaulets on his shoulders and a revolver on his waist. Saw Lu was forty-eight at the time. That was one of his life's greatest years. Chairman Zhao Nyi Lai had just anointed him foreign minister. He was poised, through the DEA, to unite the Wa and American civilizations in an everlasting union. The dream radiated inside him bright and hot, and in that photo Saw Lu's pupils shone like black pearls.

That evening, Saw Lu talked to me until nearly midnight. It was the first of many encounters. Years later, I asked Mary what her husband made of the foreigner who materialized one dark night with a notepad and a head full of prying questions. "You certainly gave us a shock. He had to wonder—is he some special agent with DEA? CIA? We discussed it. But he decided you were just a simple man. 'Mary,' he said, 'I think that man is going to write a book about me.'"

I had to laugh. Stumbling backward into Saw Lu's life that night, I could hardly process everything he said—skulls, warlords, heroin—and I barely knew what to believe. Only later, after hunting down people who'd fought or plotted alongside Saw Lu, or even against him—including sources whose names cannot appear in these pages—was I convinced his stories were true, honest failures of memory aside. Saw Lu had regarded himself as a legendary figure, snubbed by history, until I appeared: God's unwitting instrument sent in the eleventh hour to correct the error. But he'll never read the book whose existence he prophesized that October night.

SUMMER OF 2021. Burma. A country roiling from the foothills to the sea.

It took about ten years for the military's dalliance with democracy to run its course. The generals had convinced themselves they were widely beloved—yet to their frustration, the population, through a series of elections, kept voting for Aung San Suu Kyi's party instead of the army's political puppets. So they threw a tantrum. In February of that year, the military rolled tanks through the streets, locked up elected officials, and declared the junta was back.

Having tasted a bit of freedom, the masses revolted harder than ever. Fed up with peace marches, a new generation of lowland dissidents ran to the borderlands and begged ethnic minorities—the Karen, the Kachin, the Chin, and the Karenni—to teach them how to fight. They bought black-market guns and studied bomb making. They shot junta officials dead in their homes and blew up army convoys with roadside detonations. In turn, the regime, venting its rage, incinerated places suspected of harboring revolutionaries: temples and clinics, whole neighborhoods, even schools with children still inside. The junta even beheaded dissidents, leaving their corpses in the street for all the see.[3]

In tandem with this civil war, the Covid-19 virus swept through Burma. The military seized hospitals and hoarded oxygen tanks for its troops, all while many citizens, malnourished from wartime food shortages, died for lack of basic medicine. Everyday families had little choice but to lock themselves in their homes. Jacob's texts to me grew dire. "This country is a bad dream, brother. Everyone has the virus. Please pray for us!"

But Saw Lu—having survived headhunters, communist guerrillas, and exotic varieties of torture—didn't fear the plague. He would not stay indoors despite his family's warnings. "My father-in-law acts like he has magic powers. He wants to be among the people, even though the streets are empty."

On July 28, Jacob sent a photo of Saw Lu via encrypted chat. I saw him laying supine in bed: head on his pillow, Bible resting on a wooden headboard. Waxen in death. A medical worker in a blue biohazard suit sat on the bed beside Saw Lu, pinching his face with a rubber-gloved hand. They'd come to remove his body.

Ping.

Another photo. More shapeless humanoid figures in blue suits, standing above an earthen grave. Red dirt smudging their feet. They gazed down onto a wooden casket.

Saw Lu's ceremony was rushed, attended only by Mary and several others in masks and protective gowns. It was hardly the funeral Saw Lu would've wanted—a great outpouring of admirers commemorating his ascent to heaven. Even his children and grandchildren were absent. Most were sick with the virus or blocked from traveling because of the civil war. "I feel so sad," Jacob told me. "Very few people by his side at the very end. Saw Lu would've hated that."

Above his grave stands a cross made of polished hardwood upon which white letters are painted.

RIP
TAX SAW LU
IT DAO CAO KHRIT

In the Wa language: Sleep in Lord Christ.

EPILOGUE

Every nation has a story. A saga about where you come from and what you've achieved. What is sacred, what was lost. Who you've hurt and why you were right to hurt them. In other nations' stories, the Wa always play the rogue, but I wanted to know the story they told themselves. That was my goal in setting out to write this book.

Meeting Saw Lu early on was a stroke of luck, for he was an author of the Wa nation's story. A "history-making man," as he put it, and he'd earned the claim: advancing head-hunting abolition as a young man, later setting into motion a movement to reject the opium poppy—an effort delayed by the Central Intelligence Agency's sabotage but ultimately fulfilled. Saw Lu portrayed himself as a hero: brave and unrelenting. But along the way, gathering up his memories, I realized that he was a hero of the tragic variety. Authoring history was never good enough for Saw Lu. Deep down, he wanted to be *the* principal author of the Wa story, not just one of many. He sacrificed everything, even his own flesh, to make his nation into something it would never be. To meld its fate with that of America, not the America that was but the divine abstraction of America in his head.

Saw Lu probably believed in the War on Drugs more than most Drug Enforcement Administration agents. In many ways he personified its dogma and shared its flaws. Rarely did he doubt his own righteousness or his enemies' depravity. With an evangelist's fervor, he strove to purify his society—to "break [its] bondage" to narco-traffickers, a class of people President Richard Nixon called the "slave traders of our time." Like a true drug warrior, Saw Lu never quit, even in the face of defeat.

The War on Drugs is America's longest war, ongoing for more than a half century. Because its primary battlefields are in Latin America and the

United States' own cities, most forget where it started: Southeast Asia. It was here that GIs first savored Golden Triangle heroin, much of it refined from poppies grown by Wa peasants. Their addictions sparked panic back home, then a US crusade to challenge narco-armies in foreign lands. And here we are today.

Southeast Asia remains a front in this war, though a quiet one. The DEA is still pursuing the United Wa State Army (UWSA) to little effect. Not a single current official at DEA headquarters would speak to me about the Wa. Can't discuss an "active investigation," they said, despite constantly giving interviews on Mexican cartels. I suppose the DEA lacks anything positive to say about the UWSA. It's hard to champion a battle that the supposed supervillains won. Harder still to confront America's secret history with the Wa—a long, strange chronicle featuring CIA-backed Wa warlords, bugged furniture, broken promises, and vicious internal government feuding.

An honest telling of the Wa story threatens the US government. It damages our national myths. President Ronald Reagan, another drug war icon, called America the world's "mightiest force for good . . . united and committed" against "those who are killing America and terrorizing it with slow but sure chemical destruction."[1] Decades later, US politicians still talk like this. But the Wa experience proves the United States is not always united or an unquestionable force for good. It's mostly just mighty.

Whose story contains more truth? Is America a noble avenger against drugs? Or an insidious empire, condemning traffickers at the podium, conspiring with them in the shadows? In writing this book, I've met my share of good-hearted narcotics agents driven to reduce human suffering, men and women who believed in a cause bigger than themselves. Like most people, I can accept that my government is a convoluted machine, with various wings pursuing different agendas that sometimes clash. "America" isn't one coherent story but a blend of many.

If only we could extend such grace to the Wa—the right to be several things at once.

A persecuted people defending ancestral lands. Conscriptors of children. Survivors of plots concocted by the world's empires. Citizens of a state that is wrapped around a meth cartel. All of the above. The truth is that Wa State is a nation like many others. Its government is run by aging men. Some are ruthless, others selfless. But most are something in between.

IN MY FINAL conversation with Saw Lu, two months before his death, I asked for a prediction about Wa State's future. He recalled a scene he'd witnessed in 1967: nearly nude Wa men and women crowded before a human head wedged in the crook of a tree. He said in his leathery rasp that despite the nation's troubles today, it would never return to such a hideous past. For that he was grateful.

Fair enough. But I was seeking insight into what the future would actually look like for Wa people in a world shaped by technology and emerging geopolitical forces. So I'll take a crack at this question myself, separately examining two strata of Wa society: the narco-elites and everyday people.

Meth producers can expect sunny horizons ahead. The sheer volume of methamphetamine pouring out of Wa State is astounding. The largest drug seizure in Asia's history took place in October 2021 on the Thai-Lao border: 55 million ya-ba pills and 1.5 metric tons of crystal meth, hidden in beer crates. Thailand-based narcotics officers assured me this was "Wa meth" and that similarly huge shipments routinely slip through undetected. This titanic output is owed to a breakthrough. The UWSA and its criminal affiliates have perfected a new skill: synthesizing their own chemical precursors.

Meth superlabs run on a key ingredient: pseudoephedrine, or "pseudo." Making just one kilo of crystal meth requires ten kilos of liquid pseudo. Problem is, it's highly regulated and difficult to obtain. So Wa State operators have started buying drums full of a common and less-regulated chemical, one easily acquired from Chinese factories. Called propionyl chloride, it's a flammable, urine-colored substance used in a range of products from cheap dyes to fungicides. In the hands of good chemists, it's also a *pre-precursor* that can be used to make pseudoephedrine from scratch.

This is new-age alchemy, turning lead into gold. Anyone who can generate pseudo in near-unlimited quantities has a veritable license to print cash. It's tempting to assume this innovation arose in the genius brain of Wei Xuegang. But perhaps not.

"Wei? He's kind of a retired old man now."

So said Huli, the Panghsang businessman who tried to whisk me into Wa State. He would know. I later discovered that, the entire time I was communicating with Huli, he was connected to the Ministry of Finance as an earner, answering to a lieutenant in regular contact with Wei.

Though Wei outlived Saw Lu, he won't live forever.[2] Soon to reach his eighties, Wei is gradually stepping back from the empire he created, according to Huli. Though he hasn't named an heir, at least not publicly, a trusted circle already manages many of the ministry's day-to-day operations.

Wei's lieutenants are modernizing and diversifying its revenue streams. "IT is the future," Huli told me. Information technology. In this context, the term loosely describes everything from cryptocurrency to sex-cam websites to, most lucrative of all, online casinos. As vices go, playing baccarat is far more popular than smoking speed. "Younger IT guys don't really look up to the drug trade," he said. "They'd rather talk about crypto than some lab or stinky plants. The alphabet people"—meaning the CIA and DEA—"still look for drugs while guys make bricks of money doing crypto in our pajamas."

Huli isn't involved in narcotics, and he stays away from IT's most vicious side: extortion rackets. Scammers in Wa State will ring foreigners around the world using spoofed numbers to imitate insurance companies, police, even relatives. They bilk people out of life savings, sometimes resorting to "sextortion": pay up or we'll expose your perverse online escapades to your wife and boss. These call centers are known as pig abattoirs. "The whole process is modeled on a slaughterhouse. Pig feed, butchers, it's all pig terminology. You'll see a guy with $30,000 saying, 'I just slaughtered a big pig.'"

But as with drug refineries, non-Wa civilians do the grunt work in these ventures, not UWSA officers. They don't like to manage any operation outright. "Their goal is always to serve as a shareholder in exchange for 'guaranteeing the security of the operation,'" Huli said. "The officers are dealmaker-rentmasters with little active involvement, unless it's necessary." This hands-off model allows Ministry of Finance officials to focus on building even bigger portfolios. They are the richest in the Wa nation, living in the Hamptons of Panghsang, an area outside the capital lined with "glass-fronted, modernist buildings, looking like they were designed by German or Italian architects," Huli said. "Inside it's all gold, all jade-colored furniture. Fridges filled with Lafite Rothschild," a Bordeaux red selling for $1,500 per bottle.

"They celebrate their investment victories with bear paw soup. Or that anteater thing."

Pangolins?

"Yeah. Then they post it to WeChat. It's pangolins and stuff on there, all day long."

THE TYPICAL WA person will never know such decadence. They're just getting by. Their lives are often entwined with the UWSA, which demands one son from every family. Young women also join, just for steady meals, health care, and a meager paycheck in yuan. Despite Wa soldiers' hardcore reputation, they seldom fight. The UWSA is the apex predator of the Golden Triangle, and no outsiders, not even professional armies, dare challenge their domain. To fill their days, grunt soldiers drive trucks, till fields, or repave roads. Many are becoming more like municipal workers than commandos.

There's hardly a middle class in Wa State, just elites and commoners. More than half of all Wa never go to school.[3] Common illnesses still go untreated. Cancer is a death sentence. In recent years, the Wa government hailed a promising decree—10 percent of all revenue must go toward education and hospitals—but it's badly enforced.[4] This is the true tragedy of Wa State. Its leaders could meld Saw Lu's vision with Wei Xuegang's fortunes, showering citizens with high-quality schooling and health care, as do petrostates such as Norway and the United Arab Emirates—only the Wa could fund their welfare state through meth. But as in most nations, the rich hoard wealth for themselves.

At least Wa State's masses now have a voice. Though the BBC's description of Wa State as "one of the most secretive places on earth" still holds truth, it's less accurate than ever before, thanks to social media. Two China-based phone applications are popular in Wa State: WeChat, a superapp on which users share photos and videos, and Douyin, the Chinese-language version of TikTok.

These apps offer glimpses into Wa people's lives. Some online videos live up to Wa State's ultragritty rep. I've watched competitive slap fights in Panghsang nightclubs. A mob tying a thief to a basketball goal with rope and whacking him with flip-flops. Even a public execution: three Chinese nationals, accused of murdering a Wa gold shop owner, led up a muddy hill and shot.[5] But cheerful scenes outnumber these grim posts. A platoon strumming guitars and crooning the Wa State national anthem. A B-boy crew, in UWSA uniform, breakdancing in the middle of a highway. The most common type of post features a UWSA soldier, male or female, striking a dreamy pose through a gauzy app filter—the ubiquitous mating ritual of Gen Z. It's hard to square this with their reputation as narco-warriors.

As for Wa State's political future, new crises will arise, but the state itself is highly stable. This has much to do with its connection to China. Though the term *Shanzhai China* is demeaning, the Wa government is indeed a client state. The UWSA central committee doesn't have to obey every little request from Beijing, but it does consult with Chinese Communist Party liaisons who effectively hold veto power over major policy change.[6] Wa leaders aren't happy about their subservient role, but as long as China supplies weapons, fuel, equipment, telecom infrastructure, and more, they must bend to their gigantic neighbor's desires.

An up-and-coming nation hitching its star to a rising superpower isn't unprecedented though. Taiwan and Israel have flourished as US client states. So too can Wa State thrive as a Chinese client state, especially if China's power keeps rising in the twenty-first century. All the while, Wa leaders will cleverly maintain the fail-safe policy that all but prevents China from swallowing their land. Because Wa State is nested inside Burma, China can't grab its territory outright—not without invading a sovereign, UN-recognized country.

Existing inside Burma—a country in chaos—actually strengthens Wa State's position. The Burmese military regime can't beat the UWSA on its best day, let alone while insurgencies rage across the country. So it mostly leaves them alone. If the junta wins the ongoing civil war, nothing changes for the Wa. If pro-democracy revolutionaries triumph and a new set of lowlanders takes over, the Wa will demand they honor the state-within-a-state arrangement. Either way, the Wa can't lose.

The biggest threat to Wa State remains internal division, though UWSA leaders have taken steps to prevent it. Chairman Bao Youxiang has a succession plan. When he's too old to rule—which won't be long now—command will fall to his better-educated sons and nephews, groomed from birth like princes. By all accounts, Bao and Wei are on tolerable terms, but Wei will also fade away eventually, and both Wa leaders will take their DEA indictments to the grave. This presents an opportunity—if the West wishes to take it.

The next wave of Wa leaders won't have DEA charges hovering over them. The United Nations could use this turning point to forge better relationships with Wa State—and vice versa. If Wa officials want to diversify aid, instead of relying solely on China, the United Nations might help deliver decent schooling and health care to their people. Moreover, the UWSA will need the UN if it ever attempts, once again, to forsake the drug trade. Current leaders insist they've already renounced narcotics production—a sly claim, resting on the fact that they're mostly hosting and taxing meth labs run by Chinese syndicates, not managing factories directly—but if the UWSA decides to truly go drug-free, it will need UN experts to validate that achievement.

Meanwhile, the "international community" (translation: the West and its allies) needs a real diplomatic channel to the Wa government. The West might not realize the importance of Wa State now, but it will moving forward. With each passing year, it grows harder to deny: in the heart of mainland Southeast Asia sits an unacknowledged nation-state—roughly 137th largest by area, 170th by population—a small-to-medium-sized nation with a formidable army and a say in Asia's future. This is not just some drug cartel to be dismantled.

The struggle for Wa autotomy hasn't been pretty. But through wits and bloodshed and, yes, narcotics, they have achieved a dream that has eluded the Basques, Cherokees, Tibetans, and other minorities the world over: the preservation of their motherland.

ACKNOWLEDGMENTS

This book is filled with secrets and pain. Other people's secrets. Other people's pain.

In the course of writing this book, I've popped up in strangers' lives, asking them to recount harrowing experiences or nudging them for information they perhaps shouldn't share. My deepest gratitude goes out to the dozens of sources who spoke to me, many of whom I cannot name. To those who do appear in these pages, please know that I tried very hard to do right by your stories, elucidating your motives and the complexity of your circumstances. I apologize for any failings. I'm gratified that some sources who began as strangers are now something more.

Special thanks to:

Pailin Wedel, master storyteller and love of my life. Being married to a guy with maddening obsessions isn't always easy. Thank you for gluing me and this book back together when we cracked into pieces. I may be a "southern narrator," as you put it—prone to taking scenic detours en route to the point—but at least you always return me to the right path.

David Lawitts, official biographer of Bill Young and author of the forthcoming book *American Warlord*. You, sir, are a scholar of the Southeast Asian drug trade, and I couldn't have completed this book without your insights and edits. Thanks also to Gabby Paluch, author of *Opium Queen*, for early edits and invaluable sourcing tips.

To Kelly Falconer, agent extraordinaire: thank you for believing in this book when it was half-baked mush and for sticking with me until I got the recipe right. I'm lucky you're in my corner.

To PublicAffairs and Icon Books: what an honor to work with two extraordinary publishers. Thanks to Clive Priddle and Anupama Roy-Chaudhury for seeing this book's potential and guiding it to fruition, and also to Duncan Heath. There wouldn't be a *Narcotopia* without *Hello, Shadowlands*.

To Dan Lothian, Matthew Bell, and the rest of The World team: it's a privilege to work for the best foreign news program on American radio.

To my grandmother, Margie Winn: thank you for nurturing my love of reading as a child and for instilling a moral code in my head—one to which I still aspire.

Thanks to the journalists and researchers who helped line up interviews: Saw Closay in Burma, Cece Geng in Chiang Mai, and Theresa Somsri in Chiang Rai. The brilliant Khuensai Jaiyen, former secretary to Khun Sa and a formidable analyst of Shan affairs, was a priceless resource. So were others in Thailand's Tai (Shan) community as well as northern Thailand's Yunnanese community, especially children of former exiles now flourishing as Thai citizens. My excellent longtime tutor, Pornpatima Yenbut, helped me prepare for Thai-language interviews.

I'm indebted to anthropologists Magnus Fiskesjö, Andrew Ong, and Hans Steinmüller, whose collective work contains more insights into Wa society than superficial media reportage on the Wa.

My greatest thanks go to the family of Saw Lu, especially Jacob, for opening your homes to a hypercurious foreigner and treating me like a long-lost relative. You've taught me volumes about people of faith. May you and all Wa people know contentment, dignity, and freedom.

APPENDIX

SAW LU'S MANIFESTO

Saw Lu provided the following proposal to the Drug Enforcement Administration in early 1993. DEA operative Bill Young helped draft the document.

"THE BONDAGE OF OPIUM"

The Agony of the Wa People: A Proposal and a Plea

We, the leadership of the United Wa State Party (UWSP) and the United Wa State Army (UWSA), propose to anyone who might be interested that we eradicate opium growing and stop the production of heroin in all the territory controlled by the Wa. This we are willing to do. It can be done very quickly. I have full authority to speak for the United Wa State Party and the United Wa State Army, which [have] ample power to carry out this proposal.

The Plea

The plea is a necessary part of the proposal. We need food for our people while we develop substitute crops. Our people are already so poor that to take away opium production without giving them food would mean starvation. Beyond that, we need help of every appropriate kind to make the transition from an opium-based economy to a new agricultural economy. For thirty years the Wa have been trying to eradicate opium growing, but instead we have become continually more dependent on it. Like the heroin addicts that result from the opium we grow, we too are in bondage. We are searching for help to break that bondage.

Currently, the Wa area is one of the heaviest producers of opium in Southeast Asia. The official policy of the Burmese government is to suppress opium growing. This is a "window dressing" policy only to impress the West. In the past, the United States has even given the Burmese aid to carry out the policy. All the while, in fact, the Burmese officials encourage opium growing and enable its marketing for their own benefit. They take their "cut"—the major "cut."

The Wa people have been pawns in the violent, destructive games of others. We have been used as fighters for both the Ne Win government and in the military arm of the Burma Communist Party (BCP). Neither army was under Wa officers. The Wa fought other people's wars in return for food and clothes. Finally, we have come to realize that we were being used to kill each other off.

Ne Win, through the Burma Socialist Program Party, indirectly encouraged the growing of opium, while Ba Thein Tin of the Burma Communist Party urged the Wa people to do so.[1]

When we Wa came to understand that we were being used to kill each other, we decided to revolt. In April 1989 we rejected the BCP leadership and sent the leaders to China. We made a peace agreement with the State Law and Order Restoration Council (SLORC) in October 1989 not because of any sympathy with the Burmese but to preserve what we had left of our people and homes. We were left war weary—twenty-two years war weary—destitute, and opium dependent. We were also left with an army large enough to control our own area and to assure a time of peace.

Since 1989 we have become a unified Wa people with Wa leaders. For the first time ever, we can speak and act as one people. For the first time, we can hope to escape opium dependence. It is now possible to stop opium growing in our area.

Development

Now we want to free ourselves from slavery to an opium economy. It is in our interest and, we think, in the interest of the rest of the world to stop opium growing. This we cannot do by ourselves. Like the heroin addict who wants to "kick" his addiction, we need outside help to be successful. We have the determination; we need the support.

First, and most immediately, we will need food for our people. If we ask them to relinquish their present means of livelihood, we will have to provide subsistence. Our people are so poor that they cannot risk any kind of change in agriculture unless there is assurance that they will not starve.

Also, where they are pressured by outsiders to grow opium, they cannot risk stopping without the protection which assures their safety.

During the twenty-two years of warfare, more than twelve thousand Wa were killed, leaving thousands of orphans and widows and countless wounded/disabled. We struggle to care for these dependent people without any outside agencies to help and with no internal care structure or agencies.

For a transition period we will have to feed our people. We have neither the food to give nor the money to buy it. Food is necessary to start the process of opium eradication and rehabilitation of the Wa country. Relief food is sent all over the world from generous donor countries to starving peoples, some of whom currently are turning back relief convoys for political reasons. We would not be like Bosnia. We would welcome and expedite the distribution of food, but we will not want our people to starve first in order to get it. Food must come along with the cessation of opium growing, not sometime afterward.

In contrast to the usual famine relief, temporary food support for the Wa people would do more than just feed hungry people. Beyond that, it would enable the destruction of the opium economy and be the critical starting place for the recovery of the Wa people and the development of a whole new economy.

Second, beyond subsistence, we want not only to rehabilitate our area but to develop it. The cultivation of opium substitute crops is crucial. Crop substitution has worked in Thailand. It can work in the Wa area. We want the help necessary to make it happen.

We need to diversify our agriculture. We need improvements in seed stock and in breeding livestock. We need to learn more productive agricultural practices. None of the international aid programs that have helped other peoples develop their agriculture have reached us—first due to war and now due to isolation enforced by the Burmese.

Third, we sorely need to construct roads and to develop infrastructure that will support a new economy. At present there are no paved roads in the Wa area, not even any gravel roads. The roads that exist are hand hewn and follow preexisting footpaths or are strategic roads designed only to get artillery to the top of the hill. These are passable only during the dry season. There are no engineered roads designed for vehicular traffic. Roads and other improvements reported in the Burmese press were constructed only in the news media.

Fourth, modern medical care is nonexistent. There are no hospitals, not even any clinics. We need medicines. We need medical treatment facilities. We need medical training facilities. We need rehabilitation for our disabled and care centers for our orphans. We are doing what we can on our own. We will establish sixteen care centers for the blind and the disabled. We have started to level the ground for the first center.

Fifth, we need schools. The vast majority of the Wa have no formal education. There are only a few informal primary schools taught by teachers who themselves have been only to primary schools. These have to be self-supporting. There is no educational system. Few children can attend a school even where there is one. They are needed to work to get food. We want schools to train leaders. We want to make our people literate. We also want to preserve, develop, and spread our culture, our traditions, and our customs. We want to focus [on] and highlight our Wa identity. We want to give our people what is rightfully theirs but what [has] been shattered by constant war.

Sixth, we need help to reforest our denuded hillsides and to find what natural resources are in our area. We desperately need all kinds of developmental help—grants, loans, technical advice, agricultural aid. We welcome it from any source.

Democracy

Our political goal is to restore real democracy for all of Burma, a democracy in which the majority rules, but equally importantly, where minority rights are protected even if the minority is a minority of one person. We will strive for the equality of all citizens.

The democracy we seek is not the sham "democracy" of SLORC. Their bogus election was a charade for the purpose of pleasing the West. It did not result in the transfer of power to those overwhelmingly elected. It did, however, identify the leaders of the political opposition, who were then systematically threatened, jailed, put under house arrest, or hunted down. Aung San Suu Kyi, U Nu, and U Tin Oo are only the most noted examples. Others less well known did not fare so well.

We want the restoration of Wa State within Burma. We are not separatists, but we want some autonomy for our people. Under the British and until 1962, there was a Wa State in the northeastern corner of Burma.[2] After Ne Win's 1962 coup, his government redrew the map. Wa State just disappeared. It was swallowed up in Shan State. We have historic roots in and a historic claim to the area east of the Salween River from Kokang south to the Thai border. We want to administer the area as part of a federal union in Burma.

We are not asking for arms. We are not asking the United States to buy our opium crop, as Khun Sa does. We do not want to put on a show as SLORC does for the West. We are taking the initiative of offering to stop opium growing. The Wa leadership can stop the opium growing and refining at any time. But our people must eat.

Finally, the top priorities of the United Wa State Party and United Wa State Army are

1. eradication of opium in the Wa State,
2. achievement of the Wa Autonomous Region,
3. rehabilitation and development of Wa State, and
4. restoration of real democracy in Burma.

We want a better life for our people, which can only begin by breaking the bondage to an opium-dependent economy. You want a better life for your people, which means a life without heroin. It is to our mutual advantage to work together. Please accept our proposal and respond to our plea.

Yours truly,
Saw Lu

NOTES

AUTHOR'S NOTE

1. According to United Nations Office on Drugs and Crime data from 2019, Southeast Asia's narcotics economy is worth up to $71.7 billion annually: meth accounts for $61.4 billion, and heroin brings in $10.3 billion. Myanmar's GDP was $69.2 billion in 2022, according to the International Monetary Fund.

PROLOGUE

1. Magnus Fiskesjö, *The Fate of Sacrifice and the Making of Wa History* (Chicago: University of Chicago Press, 2000).

2. James George Scott, *Gazetteer of Upper Burma and the Shan States*, Vol. 1 (Rangoon: Superintendent of Government Printing in Burma, United Kingdom, 1899).

3. United Nations Office on Drugs and Crime, "Organized Crime Syndicates Are Targeting Southeast Asia to Expand Operations," press release, July 18, 2019.

FIRST ENCOUNTER

1. Attributed to Alan Winnington, a British journalist aligned with the Chinese Communist Party. He visited Wa villages in 1957.

STRANGER IN THE PEAKS

1. On this particular leg of the journey, Saw Lu and Mary walked east from Mong Mao, a Wa-inhabited area with a tiny Burmese military outpost about twenty miles west of Pang Wai.

2. Magnus Fiskesjö, *Stories from an Ancient Land: Perspectives on Wa History and Culture* (New York: Bergahn Books, 2021), 96: "Every man, and generally also every woman, was regarded as independent and autonomous in themselves, according to an ethos that strongly emphasized equality and was bolstered by codes of honor and moral norms."

3. G. E. Harvey, *Wa Précis: A Précis Made in the Burma Secretariat of All Traceable Records Relating to the Wa States* (Rangoon: Office of the Superintendent, Government Printing, 1932).

4. Scott, *Gazetteer of Upper Burma and the Shan States*. The British explorer describes an 1897 expedition into Wa lands.

5. Attributed to British diplomat G. E. Harvey in documents dated 1933. Harvey, *Wa Précis*.

6. This ephemeral life force is called *si aob* and was also believed to dwell within tigers, but not, say, deer or snails.

7. *Shan* and *Siam* (Thailand's former name under absolute monarchy) are different pronunciations of the name for the same ethnicity. The Shan call themselves *Tai*, starting the word with a harder *t* sound than the pronunciation of *Thai*.

8. William Marcus Young had three sons total, but one was poisoned as an infant, along with his wife, by Chinese agents who loathed his evangelizing on the China-Burma border.

9. Harold Young, *Burma Headhunters* (Bloomington, IN: Xlibris, 2014).

10. Banna was located in what is now called Nuofeng Township in China.

11. David Lawitts, "The Transformation of an American Baptist Missionary Family into Covert Operatives," *Journal of the Siam Society* 106 (2018): 295–308.

12. Young, *Burma Headhunters*.

13. Different Wa clans had their own theories about humanity's origins. One proposes that a gourd cracked open in the middle of a swamp in the peaks. The first people who crawled out were Chinese and Burmese. Then came the Shan, Lahu, and so on. In the sludge at the bottom of the gourd were black tadpoles who slithered out and grew into Wa men.

14. G. E. Barton, *Barton's Wa Diary* (Rangoon: Office of the Superintendent, Government Printing, 1933). Quotes Harold Young speaking in 1932.

15. C. P. Fitzgerald, *The Birth of Communist China* (Harmondsworth, UK: Penguin Books, 1964).

16. The Qing Dynasty's *Yunnan Gazetteer*, 1736, partially quoted in Fiskesjö, *The Fate of Sacrifice*.

17. Fiskesjö, *The Fate of Sacrifice*. Chinese colonization of Wa territory began in the early 1950s, but among the Wa, the year 1958 is a byword for calamity. Fiskesjö writes that this was the year "most of the grand aspects of Wa ritual life came to an end. . . . The skull avenues outside of the villages—once the most powerful, final reminder to any traveler or intruder of the ferocity of the masters of the land—were also destroyed, or left to oblivion."

18. Burma's Wa area, roughly sixty-five hundred square miles, was about the size of Kuwait.

19. The British Empire did not directly pass control of Burma to a dictatorship. Burma was briefly a multiparty democracy after independence in 1948, until a coup in 1962 installed the military junta.

20. The Wa work ethic is embodied in a common Wa saying: "The cock's crowing says 'heave!'; the break of day says 'weave!'" From Justin Watkins, "A Themed Selection of Wa Proverbs and Sayings," *Journal of Burma Studies* 17, no. 1 (2013): 29–60.

21. The larger weapons were Bren machine guns, capable of firing five hundred rounds per minute. The smaller ones were Sten guns, light as seven pounds and better suited for close-range kills.

GUNS, DRUGS, AND ESPIONAGE

1. Some of these titles included the Yunnan Anti-Communist Salvation Army, the "Lost Army" (colloquial), and the Kuomintang 93rd Division.

2. The planes operated under various front companies registered in Thailand and Taiwan. Southeast Asia Supply Company and Civil Air Transport were two of the companies' names. CIA-provided weapons were also smuggled into Burma's jungles across the Thai border.

3. Richard M. Gibson and Wen H. Chen, *The Secret Army: Chiang Kai-shek and the Drug Warlords of the Golden Triangle* (Singapore: Wiley, 2011). In May-June 1951, CIA planes dropped weapons in and around Yungho, a village barely inside Burma and very close to Pang Wai. Even more were dropped around the Wa settlement of Ving Ngun (Silver Fortress).

4. This operation preceded the disastrous Bay of Pigs invasion of Cuba by ten years. The CIA returned to the same blueprint, even though it had failed miserably against China.

5. CIA, "Background Information on the Wa States," information report, March 11, 1953. Accessed from the CIA's Freedom of Information Act Online Reading Room.

6. Opium production figures come from multiple sources. One is Bertil Lintner's "The Golden Triangle Opium Trade," Asia Pacific Media Services, March 2000. Another is Burton Hersh's *The Old Boys: The American Elite and the Origins of the CIA* (Saint Petersburg, FL: Tree Farm Books, 2001). The latter book contains the "one-third" figure, attributed to Richard Stilwell, former chief of the CIA's Far East Division from 1949 to 1952.

7. Allegations of CIA flying opium out of Burma first appear in *Kuomintang Aggression Against Burma*, released by Burma's government in 1953. The practice ended after Burma exposed it to the United Nations.

8. The group referred to as "the Exiles" in this book was a cartel both in the modern sense of the word (a trafficking supergroup) and in the classical sense. It comprised two factions, each run separately, that collaborated and colluded to set prices. They would also unite to attack any aggressors. Lee Wen-huan ran the more powerful faction, based in Tam Ngob, Thailand. He called his group "The Third Army," a title derived from their stint fighting under the Kuomintang in the 1950s. Though in the late 1950s they slowly quit taking directives straight from the Kuomintang in Taiwan, the "Third Army" designation stuck. The other faction—based in Mae Salong, Thailand—was run by a Chinese exile named Tuan Shi-wen. He called his faction "The Fifth Army" for the same reason. Both fell under the protection of the Thai military, which was closely aligned to the CIA.

9. CIA, "Thailand: Military Actions Against Narcotics Traffickers," memorandum, March 23, 1983. Accessed from the CIA's Freedom of Information Act Online Reading Room. This file reported that Chinese exiles "controlled almost all of the smuggling routes" along the Thai-Burma border.

10. CIA, "Northwest Thailand: Geographic Factors Affecting the Illicit Movement of Opium from Burma's Shan State," March 1973. Accessed from the CIA's Freedom of Information Act Online Reading Room.

11. Paul Chambers, *Knights of the Realm: Thailand's Military and Police, Then and Now* (Bangkok: White Lotus, 2013). As Chambers writes, during the Cold War, the United States often supplied a large part, if not most, of Thailand's military budget. For example, Washington supplied 70 percent of Thailand's defense budget in 1953 and 47 percent in 1972.

12. The Thai military's decision to let the Exiles control much of Thailand's northern border was unpopular with many locals. From an anonymous op-ed in *Thin Thai* newspaper, based in Chiang Mai, May 14, 1982: "The [Thai] government has allowed this evil group to enter the country . . . even though they knew it was evil and involved in narcotics trading. The claim that this was done to have them serve as a defense line against communists is not reasonable . . . Thais, the owners of this country, cannot set foot in [that border area]."

13. It takes about ten kilos of opium and an array of chemicals to synthesize a single kilo of heroin.

14. As with any commodity, opium and heroin prices fluctuated by the year. These figures are estimates drawn from CIA memos and former Exile officers. Prices are quoted in CIA, "Narcotics Prices and Composition of Traffic in Southeast Asia," October 1975. Accessed from the CIA's Freedom of Information Act Online Reading Room.

15. CIA, "Opium Production and Movement in Southeast Asia," January 1971. Accessed from the CIA's Freedom of Information Act Online Reading Room. Thai police both trafficked the Exiles' opium directly and took fees from independent truckers. From the report: "Officials of the RTA [Royal Thai Army], BPP [Border Patrol Police] and Customs at the several checkpoints on the route to Bangkok are usually bribed. 'Protection' fees are either prepaid by the smuggling syndicate or paid by the driver at the checkpoints."

16. Alvin M. Shuster, "G.I. Heroin Addiction Epidemic in Vietnam," *New York Times*, May 16, 1971. Once smuggled to Vietnam, a heroin brick worth $1,000 in Bangkok sold for $5,000. Saigon street gangs could then dilute the heroin to make three bricks and sell it off in $2 vials.

17. Based on extrapolations from CIA data, the Exiles cartel's combined operations likely enjoyed revenues in the hundreds of millions during the heyday of the late 1960s to early 1970s. In today's money, this would be somewhere between $3 billion and $5 billion. Precise figures are almost impossible to determine.

18. CIA, "Overseas Chinese Involvement in the Narcotics Traffic," January 1972. Accessed from the CIA's Freedom of Information Act Online Reading Room.

19. "If we were not here, the communists would be. We are watchdogs at the northern gate." So said Gen. Tuan Shi-wen, who ran one half of the Exiles. Tuan was speaking to Peter Braestrup of the *New York Times* for an article titled "Exiles from China Wait in Thailand," September 8, 1966.

20. John D. Marks and Victor Marchetti, *The CIA and the Cult of Intelligence* (New York: Dell Publishing, 1980), 256. Marchetti was a former special assistant to the CIA's director. In the book, he describes the CIA-Taiwan relationship during the 1950s and 1960s.

21. Richard M. Gibson, a former State Department official on the Thai-Burma desk from 1975 to 1977, described this operation to the Association for Diplomatic Studies and Training (ADST) in January 1998: "The CIA used to run intelligence operations from [Chiang Mai province, northern Thailand] into China. . . . It's an open secret that the CIA is there. Everybody in Chiang Mai knows it. We were there for drugs. . . . What we could also do was monitor the radio communication. As I understand it, the Chinese were pretty slick, the KMT [ex-Kuomintang] guys, because they had guys being trained in Taiwan. They had codes and they were really tough ones to break" (ADST, Foreign Oral History Project, 1998).

22. *Penthouse* magazine interview with Victor Marchetti, special assistant to the CIA's deputy director circa 1968. "Interview with Morton Kondracke," January 1975 issue. From the interview: "The CIA used to support the Kuomintang gang down in Burma. They were a bunch of dope runners too. In fighting communism, the spooks make some very strange bedfellows."

23. CIA, "[REDACTED] Situation on the Burmese-Chinese Border and the Position of the Chinese Nationalist Troops," March 8, 1954. Accessed from the CIA's Freedom of Information Act Online Reading Room.

THE LEAGUE OF WARLORDS

1. Young, *Burma Headhunters*, 14: The Young missionaries praised the headhunting Wa for abstaining from opium. Harold Young, son of the Man-God, wrote of the drug's "taming" effects, noting that "taming a wild animal takes away from the magnificence of its wild nature."

2. Ka Kwe Ye was the formal Burmese name of these self-defense force units.

3. There were many Shan royal families, some co-opted or dominated by Burma's military. Others openly rebelled for independence.

4. The Wa warlord Shah's raids into China ran concurrent with a similar CIA operation, based in Laos, that sent ethnic Yao and Lahu assets deep into China to tap telegraph lines and sabotage communist infrastructure. Described in Michael Morrow, "CIA-Backed Laotians Said Entering China," *Washington Post*, January 26, 1971.

5. A former associate of Shah named Ai Nap Khun Nyi said, "Shah is like a brother to those who are close to him. Kindly even. But to the masses, to the little people, he portrayed himself as extremely cruel. He needed that reputation because his militia was small." Author interview, 2020.

6. The aforementioned Ai Nap Khun Nyi, who also knew Mahasang, corroborates Saw Lu's appraisal. "Mahasang was very business minded. If you were friendly with him, he was alright. Even kind of funny. But you better not disturb his business, or he'd pull his pistol out and shoot you." Author interview, 2020.

7. "League of Warlords" is an interpretation of the loose, shifting titles this co-alition used. Each warlord came up with his own pet name for the League, usually something like "the Wa Leaders' Group." Saw Lu colloquially called it "Saw Lu's Ka Kwe Ye group."

ENSLAVED NO MORE

1. Details of Zhao Nyi Lai's early life were provided by his daughter, Ei Phong Lai, and Ai Nap Khun Nyi, a relative close in age who lived with Lai on a farm in China. Author interviews, 2020.

2. China's Wa colonization peaked in violence in 1958. Before, there were some efforts by Chinese officials to dominate the Wa in a less aggressive manner, but the Maoist government was fed up by 1958. As anthropologist Magnus Fiskesjö has observed, Wa on the Chinese side view the year 1958 as cleaving the past from the present, not unlike BC and AD.

3. People's Liberation Army troop figures are from the CIA report "Construction of Military Installations and Transportation Facilities in the China-Burma Area," September 9, 1985. Accessed from the CIA's Freedom of Information Act Online Reading Room.

4. This book focuses on Wa guerrilla cells fighting for the Communist Party of Burma, but the party had cells in other borderland zones—Kachin, Kokang, Mong La—each led by a different indigenous commander. The Wa peaks were the most important battleground. That is where the Communist Party of Burma planted its headquarters, in Panghsang, a Wa settlement stuck to the Chinese border.

5. The land was a gift from Burma's military, according to Saw Lu.

UNSPEAKABLE

1. I usually called her Daw Mary. *Daw*, meaning "auntie" in Burmese, is the polite honorific for an older woman.

THE PRODIGY

1. CIA officers don't call themselves "agents." Confusingly, they use the word *agent* to refer to human assets, say, a foreign bureaucrat or merchant who provides them with secrets.

2. According to one former Bangkok-based CIA contractor, "Job number one for the CIA is to gather intelligence. They don't necessarily have to do anything with that intel. They'll only use it to make mischief if it's in the national interest. But bottom line, the last thing they want is anyone shutting down the flow of that intelligence." Author interview, 2020.

3. Barry Broman, CIA station chief in Burma during the mid-1990s. Author interview, 2021.

4. Wei's early years remain the most mysterious chapter of his already inscrutable life. This account is crafted from secondhand details recalled by past associates. Sources on Wei's early years include author interviews with a former senior Shanland officer, a Wa National Army officer, members of Lee Wen-huan's family living in Thailand, a Burmese intelligence chief, and others. On certain facts, their versions do not agree, so I have prioritized details most strongly corroborated by multiple sources and other evidence.

5. It is possible Wei's listening post collected a lot of encrypted signals that the Taiwanese and American spies couldn't decode. In Marks and Marchetti, *The CIA and the Cult of Intelligence*, former CIA official Victor Marchetti wrote that, in the 1960s, US intelligence amassed tapes of uncrackable Soviet and Chinese signals that filled warehouses, all in hopes of one day decoding the encryption.

6. Police colonel Hkam Awng, former narcotics agent under Burma's government: "He was adopted by Khun Sa when Wei was quite young, in his teenage years. Khun Sa liked his initiative. His smarts. That's how Wei became his right-hand man." Author interview, 2019.

7. In the late 1960s, after Saw Lu created the League of Warlords, he was propositioned by Zhang Qifu, later known as Khun Sa. Zhang visited Saw Lu in the Wa highlands and offered vast sums of money if Saw Lu could provide exclusive access to the Wa opium crop. "He said, 'How much money do you need? How many weapons? Whatever you want, I'll take care of you.' I told him, 'Look, we're opposites. You're a businessman. You want to buy up all the opium in Burma, that's your business. That's your right. But my job is to secure a future for my race.'" Saw Lu rejected the offer. It was their one and only encounter. Author interview with Saw Lu, 2020.

8. Author interview with Gen. Lee Wen-huan's children in 2020. The quotes are secondhand remembrances.

9. CIA, "Opium Production and Movement in Southeast Asia," January 1971, contains details of the Lao military's narcotics-trafficking operations: "The narcotics are then assembled in Vientiane [the Lao capital] for shipment, often in RLAF [Royal Lao Air Force] aircraft, to other cities in Laos such as Savannakhet of Pakse or to international markets." Accessed from the CIA's Freedom of Information Act Online Reading Room.

10. Alfred McCoy, *The Politics of Heroin in Southeast Asia* (Brooklyn, NY: Lawrence Hill Books, 1972). T-28s were the aircraft used by the Lao military to bomb communists, while C-47s were used to move heroin from Laos to South Vietnam. McCoy was the first to provide a detailed account of the lumberyard battle in Laos.

11. CIA, "Opium Production and Movement in Southeast Asia," describes Zhang Qifu's followers in this period as having "gone underground," formerly "traversing well-trafficked roads [in Burma]" but now "forced into clandestine operations."

12. Levine was drawing on the Italian phrase *Capo di tutti i capi*, meaning "boss of all bosses."

13. In 1972, $1 million was worth roughly $7 million in 2024 dollars.

14. CIA, "CIF Involvement in Narcotics Trafficking," date obscured, likely 1985–1986. Accessed from the CIA's Freedom of Information Act Online Reading Room: "Soon after the agreement [to stop trafficking opium] the CIF turned over 26 tons of opium to the Royal Thai Government for destruction, but CIF trafficking activity resumed almost immediately. . . . Strong ties with Chinese syndicates in Bangkok and Hong Kong allowed the CIF to keep its leadership as the best trafficker to the international market."

15. William F. Mooney and William Clements, "CIA Linked to Killing of Drug Charge," *Chicago Daily News*, June 19, 1975.

16. Khun Sa, *General Khun Sa—His Life and Speeches* (Shan State, Burma: Shan Herald Agency for News, 1993).

17. Khun Sa, *General Khun Sa*. Khun Sa said his jailers allowed him only one book in prison: the fourteenth-century Chinese novel *Romance of the Three Kingdoms*, a treatise on statecraft vaster in scope than *War and Peace*. He claimed the book as an inspiration, though many confidants say he could barely read.

18. Jao Kai Wa was dragooned from Yunnan back in the 1950s at the age of fifteen. At the time of this incident, he was a platoon leader in his late thirties. Author interview in Chiang Rai, 2020.

19. Khun Sa's nation went by several titles over the years (such as "Muang Tai," or Land of the Shan). Most of them roughly translate as "Shanland." His army was known as the Shanland United Army (SUA).

20. Bo Gritz, speaking to US Congress, "U.S. Narcotics Control Efforts in Southeast Asia: Hearing Before the Committee on Foreign Affairs, House of Representatives, One Hundredth Congress, First Session, June 30 and July 15, 1987." Gritz, a former US Special Forces officer who met Khun Sa in the mid-1980s, said his real ambition was to "be George Washington." Both Khun Sa and Washington were armed rebel leaders, the wealthiest men in their would-be countries, who got rich from addictive plants, tobacco in Washington's case. Neither was fond of paying taxes.

21. This red-lion crest may not have originated in Shanland but was adopted by Khun Sa's operation and others to indicate high-purity heroin.

22. CIA, "The Golden Triangle: New Developments in Narcotics Trafficking," September 1978. Accessed from the CIA's Freedom of Information Act Online Reading Room. The report describes Shanland overtaking the opium market from the Exiles, known as the Chinese Irregular Forces, or CIF, by US intelligence.

23. Author interviews with Khuensai Jaiyen, Khun Sa's former secretary, in 2019 and 2020.

24. Speaking of the US consulate in Chiang Mai, Victor Tomseth, the State Department's East Asia Bureau officer for Thailand, said, "The Agency had a big

operation there and there was—and still is—a listening operation there. They ran [agents] in and out and had various, nefarious people on their payroll." Tomseth interview with the ADST, May 13, 1999. (ADST, Foreign Oral History Project, 1999).

25. Former State Department official speaking on background. Author interview, 2022.

26. James Mills, *Underground Empire: Where Crime and Governments Embrace* (New York: Doubleday 1986).

27. US Congress, "World Drug Traffic and Its Impact on US Security: Hearings: Ninety-Second Congress, Second Session. 1, Southeast Asia. August 14, 1972" (Washington, DC: US Government Printing Office, 1972). At the hearings, Gen. Lewis Walt said there was "no precedent in history . . . under which government A gives government B the right to station law enforcement representatives on its territory, who operate their own intelligence system and their own network of informers. About the only power they lack is the power of arrest." He was referring to the DEA's predecessor agency, the Bureau of Narcotics and Dangerous Drugs, with which he cooperated extensively.

28. CIA, "Worldwide Report: Narcotics and Dangerous Drugs," March 17, 1982. Accessed from the CIA's Freedom of Information Act Online Reading Room.

29. This underground prison was known as a "gourd prison." Its chamber was shaped like a gourd. Occupancy was limited to three men. Standing on one another's shoulders, they still couldn't reach the top and escape.

30. Thomas Miller, former vice consul of the US consulate in Chiang Mai—who was friends with Mike Powers—described him to the ADST in 2010.

31. Powers has since divulged, cryptically, that the CIA paired him with a secret force of "Vietnamese irregulars . . . former convicts and stuff like that. . . . [T]hey were tough people." Powers speaking to Larry Forletta, a fellow ex-DEA officer, for "Mike Powers: A True Legend of DEA," *Forletta Investigates* (podcast), May 18, 2021. Accessed on Apple Podcasts.

32. Richard LaMagna, former deputy chief of Worldwide Heroin Investigations, speaking in the 2021 HBO documentary *Traffickers: Inside the Golden Triangle*.

33. Whether Wei actually embezzled money from Shanland is unclear. That he was not executed outright suggests Khun Sa wasn't fully convinced of his guilt. In an alternate version of this incident, told to me by a former Burmese military intelligence agent named San Pwint, Khun Sa decided to replace Wei with his nephew—again, because the drug lord grew paranoid about his financier's loyalties. "But Wei did nothing wrong," San Pwint said. "He did everything right. Khun Sa had to invent some reason to get rid of him." Author interview, 2020.

MR. SUCCESS

1. The proctor's name is Kheunduan Tungkham, a close Khun Sa confidant. Author interview, 2019.

2. CIA, "Political Stability: The Narcotics Connection," March 1968. Accessed from the CIA's Freedom of Information Act Online Reading Room. "In the past, high-ranking officers of the Thai military, including Prime Minister Kriengsak, were implicated in the narcotics trade."

3. US Congress, "Drug Enforcement Activities in Southeast Asia: Hearing Before the Subcommitte on Crime," December 1982.

4. Anonymous op-ed in *Ban Muang*, a Bangkok-based newspaper, January 28, 1982.

5. Gritz, "U.S. Narcotics Control Efforts in Southeast Asia."

6. Former DEA chief Thomas Constantine, speaking to Reuters in 1994. Quote cited in "Myanmar Drug Lord Khun Sa Dead" by Reuters staff, October 30, 2007.

7. Bertil Lintner, "The Politics of the Drug Trade in Burma," Indian Ocean Centre for Peace Studies, 1993. Khun Sa had "several soldiers executed" following Wei Xuegang's jailbreak, according to Lintner.

8. The name Wa National Army was loosely shared between two gangs, one led by Shah, another headed by Mahasang the Prince. They were brothers-in-law. The latter hunkered down on opium trails around the Thai province of Mae Hong Son. Shah inhabited Ang Khang mountain around provincial Chiang Mai. Wei Xuegang joined Shah's faction.

9. General Tuan, who led the Exiles' "Fifth Army" faction in Chiang Rai, had been dead since 1980, and his successor favored turning their domain into a tea farm/tourist retreat. Today, Tuan's headquarters, known as Mae Salong, is one of the most beautiful mountain resort towns in Thailand. Some call it "Little Switzerland."

10. "I need a man who has powerful friends. I need a million dollars in cash. I need, Don Corleone, those politicians you carry in your pockets like so many nickels and dimes." Virgil Sollozzo in Mario Puzo, *The Godfather* (New York: G. P. Putnam's Sons, 1969).

11. CIA, "Narcotics Review [REDACTED]," August 1968. Accessed from the CIA's Freedom of Information Act Online Reading Room: "Following a failed attempt on the life of [General Lee Wen-huan], the CIF [Chinese Irregular Forces] assassinated a number of SUA [Shanland United Army] brokers and operatives. Both sides have now deployed hit teams to eliminate key enemy personnel."

12. CIA, "CIF Involvement in Narcotics Trafficking."

13. Author interview in 2019 with a former high-ranking Thai antinarcotics official.

14. CIA, "Thailand's Changing Strategic Outlook: Implications for Thai-US Security Relations," November 1987. Accessed from the CIA's Freedom of Information Act Online Reading Room. As the file notes, Thailand's military had "nearly total dependence on the United States" during the 1980s.

15. Unsigned report in *Siam Rat Sappada Wichan* (newspaper), March 14, 1982. The Thai-language article reported that the Wa National Army "worked for the Americans and the [Thai] narcotics suppression units by providing information for the attack on Ban Hin Taek [Broken Rock]." More information about the Wa National Army's links to the Thai army appears in the CIA report, "Narcotics Review,"

October 1985. Accessed from the CIA's Freedom of Information Act Online Reading Room: "When fighting [between the Wa National Army and Khun Sa's Shanland United Army] spilled over into Thailand and threatened a village, Royal Thai Army troops joined the fight against the SUA."

16. The Wa National Army also received Fabrique Nationale rifles, another weapon used by the Thai military. As for AK-47s, the Wa mercenaries bought them from the black market or took them from enemy corpses.

17. The boat's name was *Jai Rak Samut*, Thai for "sea-loving heart."

NATIVITY

1. The Communist Party of Burma controlled an area roughly the size of the US state of New Jersey.

2. Phoenix Television, a Chinese-language channel, interviewed Bao Youxiang in 2005 for a segment called "Two Heroes": "We used to live like monkeys, two or three homes forming a community, and there was a great distance between each community. The long journey to find your neighbor will cost you sweat and patience and you would be in no mood to communicate. . . . [L]ook at city people, talking all the time, absorbing a lot of information. Monkey-like villagers don't see others for days and they fall behind in development." Video in author's possession.

3. Ibid. As a child in the 1950s, Bao tended poppies with his family, scraping opium into big pots, which they sold for food. No one was allowed to imbibe the drug. "My father hated opium smokers," Bao told Phoenix Television. "He said they're shameful. So we obeyed him. Because if we disobeyed him, he kicked us hard and told us to go eat shit."

4. Rogue Wa elements within the Communist Party of Burma attempted to synthesize heroin in the late 1980s but could not master the process. Their powder was crude, with low purity, and often came out light pink.

5. From a 2020 author interview with Than Soe Naing, a former high-ranking Communist Party of Burma official: "At around 6 p.m. . . . Zhao Nyi-lai, the northern commander, was very drunk, saying things like 'I'll kill them all' and 'They oppressed us for too long.' Bao Youxiang conferred with him and led him away from the frontlines." Than Soe Naing provided other firsthand details of the revolt, which he witnessed. He was given amnesty by the mutineers and remained in Panghsang after its liberation.

6. The destruction of Communist Party of Burma records was a great loss, one lamented by historians and even Burmese military intelligence officers. Decades' worth of documents, photos, and manifestos were incinerated.

7. Tom Kramer, "The United Wa State Party: Narco-Army or Ethnic Nationalist Party?," East-West Center, January 1, 2007.

8. This was an unorthodox arrangement, but versions exist even in Western countries. The United States contains the Navajo Nation. To a degree, the nation can observe some of its own laws. But the Wa, unlike the Navajo and other American tribes, maintain their own private army and total control of indigenous lands.

9. In lieu of Wa State, a term that makes Burma's officials uncomfortable, the military regime calls it Special Region Two.

10. Wa State government, *Thirty Years of Endeavoring to Paint a New Image of Wa State*, a historical film released in 2019. Copy in the author's possession.

11. Wa State's northern motherland on the Burma-China border encompasses roughly sixty-five hundred square miles, according to United Wa State Army records. Wa Southern Command, at the time, covered only about one hundred square miles, less than Brooklyn.

12. Wa Southern Command headquarters was located due north of Mae Ai, Chiang Mai province, in Thailand.

13. Wa State's government has a political wing called the United Wa State Party (UWSP), but it is not really distinct from the UWSA. Initially Zhao was the leader of the UWSA and the UWSP. Today, Bao leads both. The two groups' leadership is so intermingled that many observers, then and now, refer to the entire governing institution as the UWSA. UN workers will sometimes use the phrase "Wa Central Authority" to refer to the UWSP-UWSA.

14. Lai and Wei always conversed in Chinese, Wei's preferred language, in which Lai was fluent, even though he struggled to read and write.

15. McCoy, *The Politics of Heroin*. McCoy asserts that the UWSA opened at least seventeen new heroin refineries within a year of its founding in 1989. Burma's junta even allowed the Wa to truck opium southward on government roads, so long as Burmese cops received kickbacks.

16. "Myanmar," *Global Illicit Drug Trends 2001*, United Nations Office on Drugs and Crime.

17. "US Urges More Anti-drug Efforts in Pakistan," UPI, August 8, 1991.

18. The figure on armed groups in Burma producing nearly two thousand tons of opium in 1990 comes from the United Nations Office on Drugs and Crime (UNODC; *Global Illicit Drug Trends 2001*). As for how much of that heroin made it to the United States, the CIA reports that, in 1982, roughly 15 percent of heroin sold in the country came from Burma. By 1990, Burma supplied 56 percent of American-sold heroin, according to the aforementioned UNODC report. See also CIA, "Golden Triangle: Increased Military Actions Against Narcotics Traffickers," October 1983. Accessed from the CIA's Freedom of Information Act Online Reading Room.

19. A. W. McCoy, "Lord of the Drug Lords: One Life as Lesson for US Drug Policy," published in the journal *Crime, Law, and Social Change* (University of Wisconsin, Madison, 1998). New York City was especially deluged with Golden Triangle heroin. In 1984, Southeast Asian heroin accounted for just 5 percent of the heroin sold there. By 1990, the figure was 80 percent.

20. American suppliers almost always bought UWSA and Shanland heroin from ethnic Chinese smugglers. This lent the false impression that the heroin was Chinese in origin.

21. Ronald J. Ostrow, "Casual Drug Users Should Be Shot," *Los Angeles Times*, September 6, 1990. Los Angeles police chief Daryl Gates said this at a Senate hearing in September 1990.

KICK THE CAT

1. Asked to appraise Saladino's work, a former DEA official leading international operations, Matty Maher, said, "Good agent. He's got the skills. He's got the expertise. Knows how to handle informants. He can run an operation with lots of problems in it and find ways to work through them." Author interview, 2022.

2. This rumor was ubiquitous in Burma. General Ne Win, head of the Burmese junta at the time, was believed to bathe in dolphin blood. Presumably this referred to the Irrawaddy dolphin, a species native to Burma.

3. Interview with Burton Levin by the ADST, July 2010. Death-toll estimates for the August 1988 massacre in Burma range between three thousand and ten thousand people. According to Levin, "The bloody terror . . . was probably on a scale larger than Tiananmen."

4. ADST interview with US career diplomat Victor Tomseth, May 13, 1999.

5. Quotes from Huddle are from two sources: an author interview with Huddle in 2021 and a 2015 interview between Huddle and the ADST. He attributed the "cat to kick" quote to an unnamed "Australian ambassador."

6. The ousted DEA agent's name was Greg Korniloff. Angelo Saladino was Korniloff's successor.

7. Saw Lu was at one point running more than one hundred local informers for the DEA. Author interview, 2021.

8. Bian's recollection to me about where she'd meet Saw Lu differs from Saladino's. She recalls the rendezvous occurring inside one of their embassy-appointed homes and said, "I don't remember a safe house." Internal DEA reports from that period mention the existence of a safe house. Author interview, 2021.

9. These forms are officially called "DEA 103 forms . . . a voucher for payment for information and purchase of evidence."

10. According to Saw Lu, Chairman Lai let him keep the money. He spent most of it on creating an all-Wa political party in Burma—one ready to stand for election if Burma's regime ever allowed an election. It did in 1990. The Wa party won no seats, but this was hardly eventful because the junta quickly voided the election. Author interview, 2021.

11. The DEA's office in Burma estimated fifteen hundred to eighteen hundred tons of opium were produced Burma in 1990. Classified source obtained by author.

12. CIA, "1986 International Narcotics Control Strategy Report—Burma," December 1985: The CIA's own file laments an "almost complete dependence on aerial photography to arrive at crop estimates" in Burma.

13. Roughly speaking, a poppy pod yields a little under one gram of opium. A hectare of poppies will yield an average of eleven or twelve kilos of opium. But these figures vary from year to year.

14. "Listen. Take anything from [Bian's real name]—who should be in prison—with a grain of salt. She or anybody else in their [DEA] office would not have a fucking clue what we're doing, OK? Because it's fucking secret." Author interview with former CIA officer stationed in Burma, 2021.

15. Assistant Secretary of State Melvyn Levitsky speaking at a press conference in Washington, DC. His comments were broadcast on a *CBS News* report that aired May 1, 1990. Video acquired from Vanderbilt Television News Archives in 2022.

16. The CIA had a "big section" circa 1993 controlling "17 of the 53 people" working at the US embassy in Burma, according to Franklin "Pancho" Huddle, the former chargé d'affaires. Author interview, 2021.

17. The CIA spy who nearly became US ambassador to Burma was Frederick Vreeland. The son of a fashion icon, he later opened up about his work as a CIA asset inside the State Department. On his Twitter account, @FreckVreeland, he posted on October 26, 2021, that he lived a "double life" at the time.

THE BURN

1. There were six or seven labs burned altogether on this trip: some in UWSA-run areas, a few in neighboring Kokang and Mong La. The UWSA lab was located in an area called Na Sai. On the same trip, Saladino and Stubbs also participated in the burning of heroin refineries in areas adjacent to Wa State. They included the Kokang region to the north and the Mong La region to the south. Burma's regime oversaw these eradications under its "Border Area Development Plan," a largely ineffective project to bring infrastructure to the Chinese border. In general, any Burmese military development deal with the Wa government would involve these adjacent areas—Kokang and Mong La—which were governed by their own respective warlords, both of them UWSA allies. The UWSA policy is to treat both the Mong La and Kokang zones as a sphere of Wa influence.

2. The DEA officials were John Andrejko, Far East section chief, and Felix Jimenez, chief of global heroin investigations. They met SLORC counterintelligence chief Col. Than Tun in October 1990. From a classified DEA memo about the meeting: "Chiefs Jimenez and Andrejko expressed a strong desire to expand DEA/Burmese narcotics intelligence sharing and to identify specific needs that the Burmese government might perceive as areas in which the DEA could provide narcotics assistance and expertise."

3. US Congress, "Review of the 1992 International Narcotics Control Strategy Report: Hearings Before the Committee on Foreign Affairs and the Subcommittee on Western Hemisphere Affairs, House of Representatives, One Hundred Second Congress, Second Session, March 3, 4, 11, and 12, 1992" (Washington, DC: US Government Printing Office, 1992).

4. Bertil Lintner, *Burma in Revolt: Opium and Insurgency Since 1948* (Bangkok: Silkworm Books, 1999).

5. United Nations Office on Drugs and Crime, "Opium Poppy Cultivation in the Golden Triangle," October 2006.

6. Huddle specifically noted New York congressman Charles Rangel as a die-hard DEA supporter. Author interview, 2021.

7. A junta mouthpiece newspaper, the *Working People's Daily*, said of the VOA report in March 1990 that America had lobbed "unfounded lies" at the SLORC,

including allegations that incinerated labs were "mere showpieces" and that "a certain insurgent group, the Wa, are permitted to trade narcotics." The "real causes of the narcotic problem are, firstly, the imperialists [meaning the British Empire] who introduced opium to Myanmar. Second, the imperialists' godsons, the White Chinese Kuomintangs [meaning the CIA-backed Exiles]. Thirdly, multi-colored insurgents."

8. DEA headquarters did eventually read the letter but for not another six weeks, when Saladino faxed an encrypted copy. One DEA chief who reviewed the letter said the intent was justified but the language was too strong: "I would've written it differently." Author interview with Saladino, 2022.

9. At the time, Parker Borg, working in the State Department's own antinarcotics division, was angling hard to become the US ambassador to Burma. The position was still unfilled. Borg was a counterterrorism specialist in the State Department and already well acquainted with the intelligence community, including the CIA. He spoke about this in an August 12, 2002, interview with the ADST, as part of its Foreign Affairs Oral History project.

10. An internal DEA investigation into Bian's whistle-blowing claims concluded, "There is no dispute that on June 18 and 19, 1991, the appellant, in her meeting with Matthew Maher, made numerous allegations to the DEA's Office of Inspection and later to the General Accounting Office. During this period, the appellant raised questions regarding [country attaché] Saladino and the Burmese government, as referenced in a March 15, 1991, memorandum to [Secretary One] Khin Nyunt, and also raised questions concerning his handling of a DEA confidential informant." The investigation concluded that Bian's allegation against Saladino regarding a "sham" heroin lab was spun from a "conspiracy theory [that] is supported and premised on her sheer conjecture."

11. Maher, contacted by the author in 2022, claimed he did not recall demanding signatures from Saw Lu. Saladino vividly recalls Maher demanding the signatures in a Yangon safe house. Asked about Bian's allegations, Maher said, "We'd be remiss" to ignore them, adding, "People like that will say anything to support their case. Whether it's true, false or irrelevant."

TORPEDO

1. "I knew exactly how many millions [of kyat, Burma's currency] Major Than Aye received for letting trucks pass. They wanted to kill me for interfering with their earnings." Author interview with Saw Lu, 2020.

2. Benjamin Min, an assistant to Saw Lu, described the incident in his personal files. According to a July 1993 document titled "Saw Lu (Saul) Arrested by MI" (meaning "military intelligence"), one of the officers told Saw Lu that, for the equivalent of a few hundred bucks, he could convince the guards to leave Mary alone. Saw Lu scrawled a note to his children, asking them to hand over cash to any soldier bearing the IOU. They retrieved their bribe, and Mary was spared. File in author's possession.

3. Gen. Colin Powell, then chairman of the Joints Chiefs of Staff, speaking to the *Army Times*, April 1991. Quotes reprinted in Fred Kaplan, "Powell: The US Is Running Out of Demons," *Boston Globe*, April 9, 1991.

4. President George H. W. Bush had already designated Burma a "drug-producing country" under the Foreign Assistance Act of 1961. The act requires the United States to oppose loans from "international financial institutions" unless the president offers a waiver for improving narcotics enforcement. In August 1991, Bush also invoked the Customs and Trade Act of 1990, which mentioned Burma by name, giving the president the power to impose "such economic sanctions upon Burma as the President determines to be appropriate, including any sanctions appropriate under the Narcotics Control Trade Act of 1986."

5. David Sikorra, *Search for the Authentic: Navigating the Currents of Life for Meaning and Purpose* (Searcy, AR: Resource Publications, 2021).

6. This conversation was later related to Saw Lu by Zhao Nyi Lai. Author interview with Saw Lu, 2021.

7. Brian Leighton, Rick Horn's attorney, in a letter to the Senate Select Committee on Intelligence, October 25, 1996: "Dedicated to protecting what was left of DEA's reputation and initiatives, Agent Horn reassessed the security of DEA's operations at post. Agent Horn learned that the [chief of station's] predecessor had established a procedure whereby he was routed a copy of all DEA's teletypes each morning." Copy in author's possession.

8. Ibid.

9. US Court of Appeals, District of Columbia Circuit, "Declaration of Plaintiff Richard A. Horn in Support of Plaintiff's Supplemental Reply" (signed by Horn on July 7, 1995).

10. More directly translated, Saw Lu's "foreign minister" title was more like "special foreign affairs chief." His other title was "chief of the United Wa State Anti-Drug Legion," referring to his DEA-like armed division: UWADO.

11. Benjamin Min, "Saw Lu (Saul) Arrested by MI," July 1993: "SLORC officers soon began asking Tax Lai [Chairman Lai; *tax* is an honorific] and Tax Pang [Pang is Bao's nickname] for Saw Lu's return to Lashio. SLORC was told that it was now very touchy issue as Wa followers of Saw Lu would object to his departure. Moreover, both agreed that Saw Lu should remain in Wa State. After all, he was a Wa leader. One month later, SLORC message received by Tax Lai stating Saw Lu is actually a CIA agent and troublemaker in Wa state, and insisted he be turned over to SLORC. Both leaders again rejected the demand and countered that SLORC should come and speak to Saw Lu personally and ask him to voluntarily return to Lashio."

12. "Opium's Destitutes," *Bangkok Post*, April 2, 1995, quotes Chairman Lai as saying, "We know that we are considered as the bad guys but our people are the last ones to profit from drug money. So we are ready to convince them to give up opium production and shift to other activities but for that we need outside help. We need agronomists, geologists, doctors and any other kind of know-how."

13. The UWSA's opium profits likely ranged between $10 million and $20 million at the time. The "Opium's Destitutes" article states that the UWSA raked in at

least $9 million from opium in 1994. A State Department report titled "A Wa Self-Portrait," December 4, 2002, cites UWSA internal figures in estimating its opium revenue at $20 million, which is "a good deal less than many assume." Report released by WikiLeaks.

14. Brian Leighton, "The Facts: Letter to Senator Shelby," January 21, 1997: During Horn's time in Burma, the SLORC "increased the number of drug task forces in the country from five in 1988 to sixteen in 1993," increased heroin seizures by 50 percent in 1992, and completed a "first of its kind" opium-yield study.

THE SUMMIT

1. In 1993, from January to May, Saw Lu and Agent Stubbs held several marathon meetings in Bill's house. Saw Lu traveled back and forth from Pang Wai to Chiang Mai multiple times. Stubbs would fly to and from Yangon. Author interview with Saw Lu, 2020.

2. Read the entire text of "The Bondage of Opium" in the appendix.

3. According to Maher, State Department resistance to the plan was deemed a near certainty. "That was foremost in their mind. We knew they'd go, 'Wait a minute, if GOB [government of Burma] decides to cooperate, and we're OK with it too, then we've lost the nightstick we keep beating them on the head with, saying they're not doing anything.'" This "nightstick" refers to a State Department refrain that Burmese officials were hopelessly corrupted by the drug trade and had zero intention of actually allowing a mass eradication to occur. Author interview with Maher, 2022.

4. Then and now, the United States is the largest donor to the United Nations' antinarcotics office and can sway its policy. Then called the UNDCP (International Drug Control Program), its current title is the United Nations Office on Drugs and Crime. "The UN goals were in line with our long vision. You think about DEA, you think putting guys in jail. But the overarching idea of replacing poppies with something else, they knew it was brilliant." Author interview with David Sikorra, 2022.

5. Huddle said his personal views about US policy in Burma were more pragmatic. He didn't believe sanctions—or the threat of sanctions—would change regime behavior. "You have an austere population in Burma, a rich resource base, and neighbors who are happy to trade with them. It's the worst possible case for sanctions. You're just punishing people for having a poor government." Still, the State Department felt "it had to do something. To make a difference. It just wasn't in the cards." Author interview with Huddle, 2021.

6. Leighton, "The Facts": "Brown . . . assured Horn he was strongly supportive of the program, but behind Horn's back assisted Huddle in deriding the program and sent messages to his Washington headquarters that the project was unworthy of support or consideration."

7. Records and various sources' recollections differ on the summit's exact date, though there is general agreement it took place in late June 1993.

8. No DEA source interviewed by the author corroborates this $50 million figure, though Saw Lu is confident this was promised by the DEA in informal conversations. Author interviews, 2020 and 2021.

9. Leighton, "The Facts": "From DEA's perspective, the goal was for DEA to serve as a mere facilitator for meetings between the leaders of the opium producers, ranking figures of the Central Government of Burma and a representative of UNDCP. . . . The local UNDCP rep and his headquarters were cautiously optimistic. They viewed it as a unique opportunity to begin a program to phase the opium producers out of narcotics. The government of Burma was suspicious of the plan but, in the end, was willing to give it a fair hearing."

10. Leighton, "The Facts."

11. As for how the CIA allegedly acquired the compromising version of "The Bondage of Opium," this is an account based on statements from Matty Maher and Brian Leighton, Horn's attorney, who described the events to a US Senate committee. In 1993, the DEA's Yangon office employed a secretary—a longtimer adept at handling secret files. "She knew our rules," Maher said, "and would abide by them." When the secretary was ready to move on, the DEA tried to replace her with another DEA loyalist. "But the embassy fought us on that. They said, 'We don't want any new Americans in the country.'" On personnel matters, State Department diktats were supreme. "They told us, 'Just hire one of the embassy wives,'" meaning any woman married to a US staffer stationed in Burma. Paperwork piled up. "We were up against it," Maher said. The DEA gave in, hiring a woman whose husband worked for the State Department and answered to Huddle, the chargé. According to Leighton, Huddle pressured the new secretary to access and hand over the original copy of "The Bondage of Opium," and the file was passed through Huddle to the CIA and finally to SLORC officials. Leighton stated that this betrayal risked violent retaliation against Saw Lu, while simultaneously "depreciating DEA's credibility with the GOB [Government of Burma] and derailing the entire project—all at once." Maher quotes derived from author interview, 2022.

12. Before ordering Horn's removal from the embassy, the State Department leaned on the DEA to transfer him out, according to Maher. "They were the ones who said you gotta take Rick Horn out of Burma. And I said, I'm not doing it. And they said, well, if you don't do it, we'll PNG [persona non grata] him"—diplomat speak for blackballing someone, rendering them unable to function. "I said, 'Go ahead and PNG him. Because I'm not taking him out. I don't want him thinking he did something wrong. Because he didn't.'" Author interview, 2022.

13. Matthew Heller, "The Coffee Table with Ears," *Daily Journal*, June 2010.

14. US Court of Appeals, District of Columbia Circuit, "Re: Sealed Case: No. 04-5313," December 14, 2006: "Releasing those portions of the [Investigator General] reports would create the risk of revealing covert operatives, organizational structure and functions, and intelligence-gathering sources, methods, and capabilities."

15. "Art Brown did not do whatever Horn imagines happened in 1993 and the settlement agreement does not contain any admissions or otherwise validate Horn's bizarre

allegations." Statement from Morrison & Foerster, a law office representing former CIA officer Arthur Brown, published by American Lawyer Media, November 4, 2009.

16. US Court of Appeals, "Re: Sealed Case: No. 04-5313": Judges note the "seeming impossibility that Huddle would have learned of the conversation by lawful means."

17. Huddle denies Horn's allegations to this day. "If you were wiretapping somebody, would you include the fact that you were wiretapping them in a cable? Think about it. You're a smart guy, I assume. Nothing could be stupider." The suit, he said, was "probably the worst thing I've ever seen in government. A nutcase with a free lawyer . . . a one-man law firm who's not in Martindale-Hubbell." Author interview with Franklin "Pancho" Huddle, 2021.

18. Judge Royce Lamberth, Chief Judge of the US District Court, "Memorandum—Horn v. Huddle," March 30, 2010.

19. Ko-lin Chin, *The Golden Triangle: Inside Southeast Asia's Drug Trade* (Ithaca, NY: Cornell University Press, 2009): "The two sides [China and the UWSA] signed a memorandum stipulating that the Wa leaders would not use the Chinese route to smuggle heroin." Criminologist Chin quotes a UWSA official describing a 1996 meeting between Bao Youxiang, Li Ziru, and Liu Shuanyueh, then Yunnan province's security chief.

20. Wei's older brother, Wei Xuelong, moved to Panghsang in the early 1990s to smooth the Wei brothers' relations with UWSA headquarters. Throughout the 1990s, Wei Xuegang mostly stayed in Wa South.

21. Clinton's election victory over George H. W. Bush may have saved Khun Sa's life. "We needed that lethal finding and we weren't getting it from Clinton. Bush would have given it." Author interview with former CIA officer Barry Broman, 2022.

22. As if attacking a multiheaded Hydra, the DEA and Thai police captured a dozen Khun Sa lieutenants all at once, to "cut off all the heads and put the monster out of commission." Richard LaMagna, former deputy chief of Worldwide Heroin Investigations, speaking in the 2021 HBO documentary *Traffickers: Inside the Golden Triangle*.

23. Author interview with Broman, 2022. Burma's military had officially agreed to fight alongside the UWSA in wiping out Shanland, but Broman said, "The Burma army didn't really mount serious attacks. The Wa did the fighting."

24. United Wa State Party, "Monument of Peace Forged in Flames of War and Hardship," a UWSA/UWSP propaganda video celebrating Wa State's thirtieth anniversary, released in April 2019. Originally posted to Chinese-language social media application Weixin. Video in author's possession.

MANIFEST DESTINY

1. The Mong La Army is a colloquial term. The organization's official title is a word salad: National Democratic Alliance Army. It is led by a former Chinese Red Guard turned heroin trafficker named Lin Mingxian.

2. Pastor John Cao, based in North Carolina, was arrested in 2017. "John Cao," US Commission on International Religious Freedom, 2022.

THE GREAT MIGRATION

1. Chin, *The Golden Triangle*.

2. Wa leaders had maintained sporadic contact with the UN antidrug agency (then called the UNDCP) since 1995, but no serious cooperative project kicked off until 1998.

3. US State Department, "Evaluation of the Wa Alternative Development Project," January 17, 2003. The United Nations' Wa Alternative Development Project annual budget wavered over the years, later reaching an average of roughly $2.5 million in the early 2000s, before the project collapsed in 2007.

4. From the video "Monument of Peace Forged in Flames of War and Hardship": "This great migration . . . was indeed something magnificent in the world history of migrations. . . . [T]he former poppy farmers said farewell to opium and started a new life."

5. Poppy farmer quotes taken from the Lahu National Development Organization's April 2002 "Unsettling Moves," the most exhaustive report on this forced migration.

6. Ibid. The Lahu National Development Organization estimates that roughly four thousand Wa died from malaria in Wa South in 2000 alone.

VANILLA SPEED

1. US House of Representatives, "Drug Trade and the Terror Network: Hearing Before the Subcommittee on Criminal Justice, Drug Policy and Human Resources of the Committee on Government Reform House of Representatives, One Hundred Seventh Congress, First Session, October 3, 2001" (Washington, DC: US Government Printing Office, 2002).

2. Chin, *The Golden Triangle*.

3. Smuggling Southeast Asian heroin to Europe was not a favorable option. Heroin trade routes to Europe are traditionally dominated by syndicates sourcing from the Golden Crescent: Iran, Pakistan, and Afghanistan.

WHISKEY ALPHA

1. The more than fifty-billion-pills figure is based on seizure data compiled by the UNODC as well as Thailand's Office of the Narcotics Control Board. Since 2000 at least six billion ya-ba pills have been seized by authorities in East and Southeast Asia. Estimating actual narcotics-production figures is notoriously tricky, but the UNODC relies on the 10 percent rule: they assume authorities catch roughly 10 percent of all trafficked narcotics and extrapolate from there. Six billion ya-ba pills seized would suggest the manufacture of roughly sixty billion pills, though the exact figure is impossible to determine. The UNODC's Southeast Asia representative, Jeremy

Douglas, told the author in 2021 that his office estimates all Myanmar-based organizations (including the UWSA and smaller players) produce between two billion and six billion ya-ba pills per year. Fentanyl may be perceived as more consequential than meth simply because it's highly lethal, kills a lot of Americans, and dominates headlines. But when it comes to the number of actual users, fentanyl can't touch meth. As the United Nations puts it, meth "dominates the synthetic drug market" worldwide. And in the top methamphetamine market, Southeast Asia, ya-ba is king. Even in the United States, the prime fentanyl market, only one-tenth of 1 percent of the population uses the drug, according to US Department of Health and Human Services data from 2020. In countries such as Thailand—where ya-ba dominates— the rate of meth use has at times reached 3 to 5 percent of the population, according to the UNODC. See United Nations Office on Drugs and Crime, "Global Illicit Drug Trends 2003."

2. Starbucks seldom releases specific sales data, but in 2016 the corporation posted to Facebook that it had sold more than 671 million cups of coffee worldwide the previous year. Also in 2016, McDonald's revealed that it sells 550 million Big Macs every year. See "Creator of McDonald's Big Mac Dies at 98, Ate One Burger a Week: Family," *CNBC*, November 30, 2016.

3. UNODC, "Global Illicit Drug Trends 2003": "Thailand also reported the highest methamphetamine prevalence rate worldwide (2.5 million people or 5.6 percent of the population aged 15–64) though some estimates reported in the press go up to 3 million people." Golden Triangle meth production, measured by the volume of seizures in Southeast Asia, has exploded since this statistic was recorded.

4. Heavy ya-ba use can cause severe psychological problems, but compared to opioids, addiction is far less lethal. Thailand and other Southeast Asian countries lack solid statistics on drug-related fatalities, but US data show alcohol and opioids dominating overdose deaths. Most meth-related deaths involve the user mixing meth with other drugs.

5. "New Roles of the Thai Military: Readjusting for the 21st Century," National Defense College of Thailand, 2002.

6. Wassana Nanuam, "Army Alert for Wa Infiltrators," *Bangkok Post*, February 15, 2001.

7. Jok is a pseudonym for an active-duty Thai soldier who requested anonymity. He served in the Third Army Region, Thailand's northern division, which contains its best-equipped antinarcotics units.

8. Activists groups include nongovernmental organizations (NGOs), such as nonprofit charities.

9. Maxmillian Wechsler, "Maha Sang: Man of the People? Or Drug Runner," *The Big Chilli Magazine*, January 2000.

10. Whether Bao Youxiang could retain a lesser position on this theoretical ruling council was never fully determined. In general, Saw Lu was sympathetic toward Bao. Bill Young was not.

11. Estimates of the UWSA leaders' earnings vary wildly. Research commissioned by *Time* magazine in 2002 suggests they may, in that year, have amassed roughly

$550 million. See Andrew Marshall and Anthony Davis, "Soldiers of Fortune," *Time*, December 16, 2002. The US Treasury, in targeting assets owned by UWSA leaders in 2005, sought $103 million from their corporate ventures.

12. Bao Youxiang speaking to Phoenix Television for a 2005 segment titled "Two Heroes of Wa State."

13. Wei has been married and perhaps had multiple wives, one of whom is accused by the United States of helping him launder money in Thailand. Whether he has children is unclear, only that any sons or daughters—should they exist—have no public profile. A March 2007 intelligence report in *Jane's Defence Weekly*, titled "Wei Xuegang: The UWSA's Narcotics Kingpin," reported that Wei has one son born to a Thai mistress in 1988.

14. "I personally encouraged Wei to leave [Wa South]. I thought, hell, the CIA or DEA or the Thais might try to go across and kill him." San Pwint, former top intelligence officer under Secretary One Khin Nyunt, speaking to the author in 2020.

15. Leaked US State Department cables, "GOB Cancels UNODC Trip to WA Territory," January 18, 2005, and "UWSA Drug Indictments: One Week Later," February 1, 2005. Both reports released by WikiLeaks.

16. Author interview with UN aid worker formerly assigned to Wa State, 2019.

17. Associated Press video, "Suspected Asian Drug Lord Indicted," January 25, 2005.

18. DEA, "Eight High-Ranking Leaders of Southeast Asia's Largest Narcotics Trafficking Organization Indicted by a Federal Grand Jury in Brooklyn, New York," press release, January 24, 2005.

19. Bao Youxiang, "Two Heroes of Wa State," Phoenix Television, 2005. Copy in author's possession.

20. Ronald Renard, UNODC Wa project manager in 2006–2007, "The Wa Authority and Good Governance, 1989–2007," *Journal of Burma Studies* 17, no. 1 (2013): 141–180.

21. UWSP, "Monument of Peace Forged in Flames of War and Hardship."

22. James Risen, "Poppy Fields Are Now a Front Line in Afghan War," *New York Times*, May 16, 2007. "The C.I.A. and military turned a blind eye to drug-related activities by prominent warlords or political figures they had installed in power, Afghan and American officials say."

23. Scott Baldauf, "Afghanistan Riddled with Drug Ties," *Christian Science Monitor*, May 13, 2005.

24. Treasury Department, "Treasury Action Targets Southeast Asian Narcotics Traffickers," press release, November 3, 2005.

MOUNTAIN FORTRESS CHINA

1. This is a condensed synopsis of the Burma military's campaign to create new militia in the borderlands circa 2009. It was essentially a replay of the 1960s-era campaign to turn mountain-dwelling minority armed groups into *Ka Kwe Ye*, or "self-defense forces." The army urged groups to form *Pyi Thu Sit* (Burmese for "people's war"

units, typically no larger than a hundred fighters, some only fielding a dozen or so men) and the larger Border Guard Forces (BGFs), battalion-sized militia with more than three hundred soldiers occupying border zones with high strategic value. In 2009, Burmese officials pressured the UWSA to transition into a BGF. Insulted, the Wa refused outright, with Chairman Bao insisting on Wa State's position as "democratic self-ruled autonomous region."

2. "Data Set: Deaths Due to Homicides," National Institute of Statistics and Geography (INEGI), an autonomous Mexican government agency.

THE RECKONING

1. Operation Hotspot began on August 25, 2010, and continued for several months. "The concept for Operation Hot Spot is to target the largest drug trafficker in the region, WEI HSUEH KANG, the UNITED WA STATE ARMY, and other high level drug trafficking organizations within Asia. The DEA and NSB [Royal Thai Police Narcotics Suppression Bureau] have produced informational products for distribution in areas with a high propensity for drug trafficking" (US Embassy of Thailand, press release, November 26, 2010).

2. US State Department, "Implications of Operation Warlord Indictments," cable, January 14, 2005. The cable refers to long-standing Bao-Wei turf battles arising from "senior-level financial and policy disagreements," adding, "Many observers believe that Wa territory . . . is a powder keg."

3. Rajeev Bhattacharyya, "Decapitation Video Points to Increasing Military Atrocities in Myanmar," *The Diplomat*, July 6, 2022.

EPILOGUE

1. "Remarks at a White House Kickoff Ceremony for National Drug Abuse Education and Prevention Week," Ronald Reagan Presidential Library, October 6, 1986.

2. In Wa State, Wei is also known as a philanthropist, financing roads, dams, and bridges across the neglected peaks. A UN official named Jeremy Milsom, who once ran the Wa development project for the UNODC, once said, "Wei Xuegang has done more to support impoverished poppy farmers in breaking their dependence on the crop than any other single person or institution in Burma." See Jeremy Milsom, "Trouble in the Triangle: Opium and Conflict in Burma," Transnational Institute, July, 22, 2005.

3. World Food Programme, "Wa Self-Administered Division: WFP Myanmar," Operational Brief 2019.

4. Andrew Ong and Hans Steinmüller, "Communities of Care: Public Donations, Development Assistance, and Independent Philanthropy in the Wa State of Myanmar," *Critique of Anthropology* 41, no. 1 (March 2021): 65–87.

5. This public execution took place on May 14, 2020, in the Wa State town of Namtip.

6. As of 2023, the highest-ranking liaison to the UWSA is Deng Xijun, a prominent Chinese diplomat previously assigned to Afghanistan and as an envoy to the Association of Southeast Asian Nations.

APPENDIX: "BONDAGE OF OPIUM"

1. Saw Lu misrepresented the Communist Party of Burma's antiopium policy, perhaps to push all blame for the drug on non-Wa outsiders. At times, the party tolerated Wa villagers harvesting opium—and even taxed it—but it generally forbade large-scale trafficking. Some ethnic Wa commanders engaged in heavy trafficking against the party's wishes.

2. In pointing to a "Wa State" prior to the 1989 revolution, Saw Lu referred to what the colonial British called the "Wa States," described by UK surveyors as "numerous statelets" at a "lower stage of development" than other parts of Burma at the time. Essentially Saw Lu meant to say that the Wa were ungoverned by any country and ruled themselves in a constellation of warlord fiefdoms and fortress towns—minuscule "states" for lack of a better word. He did not mean there was a "Wa State" with a fully functional government, as the terms now implies. Saw Lu's point was that the Burmese military, after seizing total power in 1962, should have carved out a separate zone or state and given the Wa some degree of self-rule.

INDEX

ABC News, 134
Afghanistan, opium of, 275
America. *See* United States of America
amphetamine, 252. *See also*
 methamphetamine

Banna, 26, 28, 32, 64, 206, 209
Bao Youxiang, 201
 assumption of throne by, 219
 child cadets of, 240–241
 claim to Chinese media of Wei's
  disappearance, 269–270
 cold marriage of Wei Xuegang and,
  251
 comments about the Wa by, 125
 crumbling of politburo's defenses
  before, 128
 DEA's take on, 16
 deputy of, 256
 as face of the Wa nation, 16
 hiding of Saw Lu by, 238
 inner circle of, 295
 kinglike system of, 241
 Lai's confiding to, 126
 nepotism of, 272
 photograph of, 141
 remarks taunting US government, 274
 reputation for fearlessness solidified
  in war against League of Warlords,
  127
 revolt led by, 128
 right-hand man of, 219
 Tet Kham run by clan of, 267
 top political strategist of, 256
 upbringing of, 126
 Wa villagers complaining to, 127

as Wei's boss, 242
 Whalen sitting in helicopter next to,
  269
Ba Thein Tin, 318
BCP. *See* Burma Communist Party
Bian, 156, 159
 anger at not being sent to Wa State,
  168–169, 173
 arrival in Burma office, 172
 background on, 157
 backstory of, 171
 campaign to discredit boss, 173
 damning allegation about Saladino
  by, 185–186, 188
 as DEA intelligence analyst, 156
 DEA's dismissal of, 179
 "ongoing personal vendetta" against
  Saladino, 183
 Stubbs's upstaging of, 167–168
 threat to, 166
 as whistle-blower, 185
Border Patrol Police (Thailand), 45, 111
Borg, Parker, 184
Braox clan, 81
Brown, Art, 199, 216
Brown, John, 52
Bureau of Narcotics and Dangerous
  Drugs, 99
Burma
 arrivals of Bian and Saladino in, 172
 as country in flux, 299
 Covid-19 virus sweeping through, 305
 crossings from Thailand into rebel
  territories in, 231
 DEA's intensifying fixation on, 177
 DEA's state of play in, 195

Burma *(continued)*
  DEA's status in, 162
  dissolving of junta of, 299
  foreign media in, 162
  George H. W. Bush's sanctioning of, 194
  government of, need for buy-in of, 212
  as hidden gem (per Stubbs), 195
  Huddle's existence in, 213
  junta of, 164, 166
  junta atrocity of, 155
  junta's decades-long despising of CIA, 199
  Khun Sa's escape to, 112
  known as Myanmar, 2
  massacre in (1988), 157
  network of CIs in, 183
  revolt of the masses in (2021), 305
  ruler of a mini-country inside, 176
  Saladino's move to, 154
  State department's position on, 178
  totalitarian misery of, 243
  US brands pulled out of, 249
  US embassy in, 177
  –US lovefest, 300
  Wa State's position inside, 312
  Wei's movements restricted in, 123
  Xi in, 228
Burma Communist Party (BCP), 318
Burma Socialist Program Party, 318
Burroughs Wellcome, 252
Bush, George H. W., 154, 194
Bush, George W., 250

Castro, Fidel, 16, 194
CBS News, 162
Central Intelligence Agency (CIA)
  antijunta agenda of, 165
  backstory of involvement of, 39–40
  Bill Young's falling out with, 207, 262
  Border Patrol Police created by, 45
  care packages dropped by, 40
  close call for, 98
  conditions for UWSA's inception created by, 4
  conflict between DEA and, 88, 100
  -contracted planes running drugs for an armed group, 42
  creation of the Exiles by, 40
  -DEA friction, 250
  DEA threat to narco-espionage system of, 88
  drug-trafficking assets of, 46
  employment of Bill Young by, 206
  enterprise run by, 39
  establishment of radio outposts by, 47
  the Exiles' relationship with, 43
  first instance of planes running drugs for an armed group, 42
  formula to estimate heroin yield, 160
  guns provided by, 38, 39
  ideal smuggling territory described by, 259
  junta's decades-long despising of, 199
  listening post, 89
  memo by, 41
  motives of for seeking Wei's downfall, 250
  narco-armies favored by, 275
  obsession with peering inside Mao's kingdom, 46
  officers, job of, 87
  operations, 39–49
  operation of State Department and, 156, 196
  recruitment of Bian by, 171–172
  sabotage against Saw Lu by, 218–219
  sanitized role of in Golden Triangle, 86
  Saw Lu's being accused of contact with, 292–293
  Saw Lu's first time hearing about, 56
  source of friction between DEA and, 250
  -Taiwan intelligence apparatus, 56, 67, 126
  UWSA considered a menace by, 259
  Whalen's relationship with, 249–250
Chaichamrunphan, Warin, 277
Chiang Mai province (Thailand), 43, 92, 99, 207, 260

China
  cash crop shipped to, 235, 243
  consumer market of, Wa State's
    production of goods for, 243
  as co-opting the most fearsome drug
    cartel in Asia, 286
  focus on hard infrastructure in Wa
    nation, 279
  forbidding of drug trafficking in, 285
  -friendly narco-army, UWSA as, 250
  inability of to swallow Wa State, 312
  mysterious virus emanating from
    Wuhan, 228
  UWSA befriended by government
    of, 287
  UWSA's new ban on trafficking
    to, 220
  Wa dependence on, 278
  Wa State's main portal to, 297
  wildcats and hustlers in, view of Wa
    State by, 271
China White, 134, 175, 302
  discontinuing of, 255
  labs rendering opium into, 251
  peddling of in California, 248
  photograph of, 140
  production of, 272, 296–297
  refineries, 246
  value of, 196
Chinese Communist Party
  -approved textbooks, 281
  consultation of UWSA with, 312
  Li Ziru's understanding of, 219
  officials regularly attending UWSA
    ceremonies, 286
  takeover of family farm by, 66
  trouncing of Kuomintang by, 28
  UWSA and, 287, 312
Chinese Irregular Forces (CIF), 47, 117
CI. See confidential informant
CIF. See Chinese Irregular Forces
Clapp, Priscilla, 268
Clinton, Bill, 222
Clinton, Hillary, 299
"cloud sea," 229

Cobain, Kurt, 134
Commander Long Legs, 63, 70, 124.
    See also Lai, Zhao Nyi
Communist Party of Burma, 124
  Commander Long Legs of, 63
  composition of, 71
  goading of Wa masses by, 73
  guidance of from China, 61
  League of Warlords and, 62
  Marxist representing, 62
  politburo of, 124, 127
  as puppet group of China, 69–70
  security squadron, 128
  terrain claimed by, 114
Communist Party of China. See Chinese
    Communist Party
confidential informant (CI), 5,
    149–153, 156, 182, 196, 209,
    260, 283
Covid-19, 228, 305
crack cocaine era (America), 258
cryptocurrency, 310
crystal meth, 16, 227, 252, 284, 309

da Gama, Vasco, 1, 3
DEA. See Drug Enforcement
    Administration
Deng Xiaoping, 127
Douyin, 311
Drug Enforcement Administration
    (DEA)
  agents, backgrounds of, 87
  agents and UWSA troops helping to
    set refinery aflame, 174
  "aggressive community outreach" of,
    293
  Bian as intelligence analyst for, 156
  Bian's deep knowledge of, 171
  Bill Young as secret weapon of, 207
  chief of global operations, 211–212
  -CIA friction, 250
  CIA's sabotage against, 216
  closely guarded document of, 159
  conflict between CIA and, 88, 100
  continued pursuit of UWSA by, 308

Drug Enforcement Administration
(DEA) *(continued)*
as covert to operational status in
Burma, 162
creation of, 100
declaration drawing laughs from, 243
description of UWSA by, 77
failure to protect Saw Lu, 153
as first Americans stepping on Wa
soil, 169
frustration of, 284
hierarchy of, drug lord in, 16
inspector, Burmese spies trailing, 191
intensifying fixation on Burma, 177
irony of plan proposed by, 165
John Tin Aung as superfixer for, 157,
183
most irksome bit about working for,
105
most wanted man in Asia, 16
name for Saw Lu, 6
Operation Hotspot, 293
Operation Warlord, 273–276
plan to make junta feel in control, 164
plans to besiege Shanland by, 111
power of State Department vs. power
of, 154
predecessor of, 99
reverence of Superstar by, 5
Saladino transferred stateside by, 195
sanitized role of in Golden Triangle, 86
satellite images of Wei's whereabouts
possessed by, 249
Saw Lu's dangerous relationship with,
158–159
Saw Lu's intel produced for, 182
Saw Lu's proposal to, 317–321
Saw Lu's request for contact with,
151–152
Saw Lu wanting to upgrade
relationship with, 137
source of friction between CIA and,
250
Spot a Druglord, 293
statement on Wa by, 2

subsources of, 283
tape recording of Wei's speech shared
with, 246
transfer of Bian by, 179
"Tiger Trap" launched by, 222
top-ranking internal inspector for,
186
tracking of Wei by John Whalen, 248
trying to scale up in Burma, 178
UWSA considered a menace by, 259
War on Drugs dogma brought to
Thailand by, 252
warning of imminent American
operation against Wa State, 273
Wei as target of, 246

education, UWSA's apathy toward, 289
Escobar, Pablo, 86
the Exiles
acquisition of opium, 42
as America-backed narco-army, 60
anti–Khun Sa alliance of Wa
National Army and, 119
Broken Rock let go by, 103
burdening of with post–War on
Drugs strictures, 101
business of, internal feud within the
US government and, 98
business model of, 42
CIA protection of, 46
collapse of, 119
control of the Thai-Burma border
monopolized by, 92
creators of, 40
demand for tribute, 94
drugs as new raison d'être, 42
entire stockpile of, 99
focus on heroin, 44–45, 97
incursions into China, 41
League of Warlords' trade with, 60
monopoly of, shattering of, 104
most influential leader of, 43
motivations of, 48
mule caravans launched by, 100
names for, 47

photograph of, 142
radio bases manned by, 89, 93
relationship with CIA, 43
selling of heroin by, 45
as shrinking organization, 116–117,
    127
stretch of border ruled by, 259
trade with the League of Warlords, 60
extortion rackets, 310

freebasing, 253

Gandhi, Mahatma, 136
General Lee. *See* Lee Wen-huan
    (General Lee)
Gen Z, 312
Golden Crescent, 134, 275
Golden Triangle, American officials'
    depiction of, 86
    American strategies in, 87
    arrival of dope in United States, 134
    attack dogs of last resort, 117
    CIA's preference that the Exiles
        dominate, 112
    communist-free (need of United
        States to keep), 48
    conflict between tribes of (CIA and
        DEA), 88
    DEA assets covering, 207
    drug lord, Wei as protégé of, 82
    General Lee of, 91, 92
    most disreputable band of drug
        runners in, 114
    most powerful figure of, 91
    narcotics cartel (Lai's envisioned
        model of), 132
    narcotics cartel (progenitors of), 142
    narcotics trade (infrastructure of), 45
    narcotics trafficker, Wei as all-time
        greatest, 86
    prime smuggling trails of, 266
    responsibility of CIA in, 46
    shock waves from America hitting, 96
    UWSA as apex predator of, 311
gospel rock, 150

Grace (Saw Lu's daughter), 237–238,
    241, 290
"great migration," 236–247
Guangzhou, 285

headhunters, 19–38, 241
    baptism of, 57
    bureaucratic tribes and, 86
    Chinese exiles trying to evade, 40
    most prolific of, 54
    procedure of, 23
    raiding parties, 41
    Saw Lu's orders to assimilate
        among, 20
    skulls arrayed by, 19
    souls of, 206, 266
    stories, 119
    Stubbs and, 167
    teams sent into China, 48
    Wei among, 89
Hello, Shadowlands, 3
heroin
    attempts to smuggle across the
        Pacific, 104
    Bao's need to rebalance economy
        away from, 242
    CIA's formula to produce, 160
    as economic engine for Wa State, 136
    focus of the Exiles on, 44–45
    Horn's project to devastate global
        trade of, 204
    largest eradication of in Burmese
        history, 162
    Mexican black tar, 175
    -producing leviathan, UWSA as, 134
    refinery, torching of (photograph), 145
    selling of to one type of customer, 45
    shutting down of pipeline to United
        States, 255
    smuggling of from Burma into the
        United States, 154
    Wa, purity of, 165
    Wa National Army's involvement in
        exporting of, 120
"heroin chic," 134

Hong Pang, 267, 277, 284
Horn, Rick, 198–200, 203–205,
     210–214, 216
  accomplishments of, 203–204
  claims about CIA by, 216
  coffee table incident at home of, 200
  as conflict-prone boss, 217
  as DEA's new lead agent in Burma,
     198–200
  discussions with Art Brown, 199
  encrypted communications devices
     ordered from, 204
  ensuing lawsuit by, 217
  goal of, 204, 212
  honorific for, 213, 217
  mission of, 212
  project to devastate the global heroin
     trade mobilized by, 204
Huddle, Franklin "Pancho," 155, 198
  alibi of, 218
  background on, 177
  as de facto ambassador, 183, 213
  job of, 213
  successor to, 268
Huli, 229, 230, 309, 310
Hussein, Saddam, 86, 274
Hutchinson, Asa, 250

information technology, vicious side of,
     310
Inmarsat phone, 212
insanity pills, 254
Isaac (Saw Lu's son), 189–190, 197

Jacob, 74, 149, 257, 271, 296
  at age eighteen, 237
  backstory on, 15
  Baptist belief about Chinese visitors,
     279
  consolation prize offered to, 80
  depression of, 300
  difficulty in talking about Wei
     Xuegang, 82
  doubts about having moved to Wa
     State, 240

enhanced status of, 297
enlistment in UWSA, 240
envoys tracked down by, 77
epiphany of, 281–282
heroin habit of, 297, 302
impression of Wei on, 270
imprisonment of, 301
as interpreter, 10
middle-school curriculum of, 288
muted ethnicity of, 236
as official in Wa State's literacy
     department, 280
prayers of, 281
public execution witnessed by, 239
salary of, 296
Saw Lu living vicariously through, 256
Saw Lu's advice to, 272
Saw Lu's forgiveness of, 303
time spent at Baptist rehab by, 303
withdrawal symptoms of, 301
Jao Kai Wa, 102
Jinawat, Pittaya, 259
Jok, 259
  description of, 260
  grenade detonation under truck of, 261
  need for vengeance explained by, 261
  orders to, 262
junta, 164, 166
  atrocity of, 155, 164, 166
  decades-long despising of CIA, 199
  dissolving, 299
  highest tier of, 199
  officers, as toll collectors, 192
  Saw Lu as agent of, 49
"Just Say No" campaign (US
     government), 118

Kengtung, 25, 31, 33, 50, 55, 209
Khin Nyunt. See Secretary One
Khuensai Jaiyen, 110
Khun Sa, 101, 111–123
  admiration of Wei by, 104
  credit taken for defeat of, 223
  DEA operation to wipe out network
     of, 222

DEA proclamation about, 112, 222
empire of, plan to wreak havoc in, 118
escape to Burma, 112
incentive to capture, 176
interviews to American TV crews, 134
mention of in Saw Lu's manifesto, 211
naming of Shanland by, 103
as newly reinvented Robin Hood, 102
offer to make peace with General
    Lee, 116
Powers' threat to, 108
pressure on, 109–110
proposal of corporate buyout, 116
as ruler of a mini-country inside
    Burma, 176
secrets blurted out by, 113
as shapeshifter, 106
State Department statement about, 177
State Department's label for, 177
suggestion to meet General Lee, 116
Thailand's mountain passages
    dominated by, 132, 208
toppling of, 222
toppling of, requirements for, 222
Wei, as protégé of, 82, 86
Kim Il Sung, 194
Kingpin Act, 10
K-TVs, 271
Kuomintang government
    Chinese Communist Party's
        trouncing of, 28
    creation of the Exiles by, 40
    remnants of in Taiwan, 115
    rottenness of, 29
Kyaw Thein (KT), 161, 179, 249

Lahu, 11, 26, 31, 58, 201, 206, 209,
    257, 263, 283
Lai, Zhao Nyi, 64–74, 124, 131, 146,
    163, 176, 208, 214, 263, 288, 304
    accumulation of followers of, 69
    acute sense of politics and power
        possessed by, 135
    aid-for-eradication program, 182,
        197

alcoholism of, 219
ancestral region of, 200
arrival of Saw Lu to home of, 200
banditry of, 68
burial of, 288
ceremonial position of, 266
coming of age of, 66
description of, 52
enslavement of, 64
experience with Maoist China, 66
feuding with Saw Lu, 136
formal title of government settled on
    by, 133
as founding father (photograph), 146
hardening of heart against
    communism, 125–126
in charge of first Wa nation in
    history, 129
Khun Sa's braggadocio of benefit to,
    135
as lone desperado, 67
meeting with Secretary One, 197
model envisioned for perfect Golden
    Triangle narcotics cartel, 132
negotiating for the Wa by, 130
nom de guerre, 63, 70
offer made to Secretary One, 168
photograph of, 146
plan for harvesting opium, 131
rage burning inside, 53
request for opium production in Wa
    nation, 130
reunion with Saw Lu, 135–136
Saw Lu marked for death by, 72
Saw Lu's plan endorsed by, 203
Saw Lu's recognition of, 63
securing of highlands by, 73
spiel of, 69
strategy revealed to, 69
stroke suffered by, 263, 288
subversive tone of, 126
troubling concession made by, 136
Wa villagers complaining to, 127
Laos, contestants wrestling for control
    of, 94

Lashio, 73, 77, 82, 135, 200
  de facto UWSA embassy in, 9
  guest coming to see Saw Lu in,
    303–304
  Jacob's upbringing in, 236
  last evening in, 151
  Saw Lu and family's return to home
    in, 300
  subjugation drive in, 11
  troops summoning Saw Lu at home
    in, 189
League of Warlords, 50–63
  ban on head-hunting enacted by, 74
  Bao's reputation for fearlessness
    solidified in war against, 127
  Communist Party of Burma and, 62
  defeat of, 70
  Mahasang the Prince as veteran of, 165
  Mahasang's joining of, 265
  orders to wipe out, 70
  poppy harvesters paying taxes to, 69
  as proto-government, 60, 69
  reassembly of, 264
  Saw Lu's former partner in, 114
  trade with the Exiles, 60
Lee Wen-huan (General Lee)
  aging of, 116
  blast at estate of, 117
  estate of, 105
  headquarters of, 92
  intelligence operatives of, 93
  Khun Sa's offer to make peace with,
    116
  as leader of the Exiles, 43, 99, 119
  photograph of, 142
  Wei's burning of, 114
  Zhang's relationship with, 91
Leun clan, 81
Levin, Burt, 154, 162, 163, 177
Levine, Mike, 96–99, 100
Li Ziru, 219, 222
  stroke suffered by, 256
  understanding of China's Communist
    Party by, 219
  unnerving of Saw Lu by, 220

Mae Hong Son province (Thailand), 112
Mahasang the Prince
  death of, 288
  domination of Ving Ngun by, 54
  fleeing of Red Guard uprising by, 71
  followers' name for, 265
  interest in assisting CIA-Taiwan
    operations, 58
  joining of Whiskey Alpha coup plot
    by, 266
  legitimacy as member of new ruling
    council, 266
  Master of Creation as opposite of, 60
  orders to wipe out, 70
  Saw Lu's meeting with, 58
  territory of, 89
  as veteran of League of Warlords, 165
Maher, Matty, 185, 186, 187, 191, 212
Man-God, 26, 206. See also Young,
    William Marcus
  dogma of, 28
  dream prophesized by, 49
  mistake of, 32
  prediction of, 38
  spirit of, 202
  warnings to, 27
Mao Zedong, 65, 73, 127, 136
  army of, CIA backstory and, 39–40
  currency bearing face of, 221
  incomplete revolution of, 29
  leadership of, 20, 28
Marx, Karl, 73
Mary (wife of Saw Lu), 19–24, 31, 50,
    63, 83, 144, 151, 200, 193, 197,
    219, 290, 305
Master of Creation, 264
  beliefs of, 59
  communists sparing life of, 71
  followers of, 55
  impromptu marriage ceremony
    enforced by, 59
  magnetism of, 60
  as most peculiar warlord, 55
  orders to wipe out, 70
  response to Saw Lu's message, 55

seducing of, 57
willing hostage in lair of, 59
McCain, John, 299
McConnell, Mitch, 180, 249
methamphetamine, 252–257
  as modest vice, 253
  as perfect drug for Asia's modern
    workforce, 254
  volume of pouring out of Wa State,
    309
  Wei's drug-producing machine
    oriented toward, 247
  Wei's strategy to produce, 251
meth labs, 253, 259
  capital and manpower necessary to
    start, 273
  photograph of, 143
  run by Chinese syndicates, 313
  superlabs, 309
  water needed for, 285
Mong La Army, 227
Mong Yawn, 248
Moynihan, Daniel Patrick, 180–181
Myanmar, 2, 180

Naung Khit (UWSA Western Sector),
  296, 301
new-age alchemy, 309
Ne Win, 318, 320
Nixon, Richard, 96, 98, 100, 307
Noriega, Manuel, 86
Northeast Command HQ, 12, 189,
  191–192, 197
Northern Alliance, 275

Obama, Barack, 299
Operation Hotspot, 293, 295
Operation Warlord, 273–276, 278, 284
opium
  of Afghanistan, 275
  -eradication scheme, 242–244
  the Exiles' acquisition of, 42
  the Exiles' stockpile of, burning of,
    99–100
  Lai's plan for harvesting, 131

Lai's request for production of in Wa
  nation, 130
  as lifeblood of Wa, 51
  Maoists despising of, 56
  Mao's gospel on, 66
  as perfect means of exchange, 64
  pipeline, 650-mile-long, 45
  -producing region, Golden Crescent
    as, 275
  Saw Lu raised to fear, 51
  Taliban's taxing of, 250
  tax on, 52
  transporters, cash installments doled
    out by, 192
  Wa battalion leaders selling, 127
  Wa-grown, swept into labs in Laos, 95
  Wa slavery and, 64
  as Wa State's only viable export, 131
Ouan Rattikone, 94–95

Panghsang
  description of, 278
  Jacob instructed to walk streets of,
    238–239
  K-TVs in, 271
  Lai's confiding to Bao in, 126
  outskirts of, mutineers amassed in,
    127–128
  as rogue capital, 124
  Saw Lu fraternizing at private
    gatherings in, 283
  Saw Lu's family slipping out of, 300
  Wei Xuegang's arrival in, 131–132
Pang Wai, 13
  burial of Lai at, 288
  church built in, 61
  CIA crates dropped near, 40
  class of person in, 21
  cloistered interior of, 22
  Lai's familiarity with, 67
  Lai's family home in, 200
  Lai's Morse code message from, 125
  outer defensive walls of, 20
  prior scene of intense humiliation at,
    201

Pang Wai *(continued)*
  protection of, 32
  Saw Lu in, 19–38
  Saw Lu driven out of, 71
  Saw Lu's first months in, 294
  Saw Lu's plan to infiltrate, 31
  Saw Lu's trek to, 20
Papaver somniferum, 1. *See also* opium
People's Liberation Army (PLA), 279
  radio transmissions by, 48
  Saw Lu's fear of, 63
  soldiers, communist officer traveling
    with, 56
pig abattoirs, 310
PLA. *See* People's Liberation Army
Powell, Colin, 194
Powers, Joyce, 109, 153
prayer, 150–151
Prem Tinsulanonda, 111
propionyl chloride, 309
pseudoephedrine, 251, 309

Qing dynasty (China), 1, 99
quid pro quo arrangements, 180

Rang, 51, 61, 68
Rather, Dan, 162
Reagan, Nancy, 118
Reagan, Ronald, 109, 111, 308

Saladino, Angelo, 152, 195
  arrival in Burma office, 172
  being transferred stateside by DEA,
    195
  Bian's damning allegation about,
    185–186, 188
  Bian working with, 157
  bugged house of, 185
  camaraderie with Saw Lu, 163
  as DEA agent sent to Wa State, 168
  determination of to expand
    cooperation with Burma's military,
    177
  failed efforts by to free Saw Lu, 194
  first glimpse of Shanland by, 105

first sit-down with Saw Lu, 157–158
  irony of plan of, 165
  Kyaw Thein told to cultivate
    relationship with, 161
  Maher's questions about activity of, 187
  mission of, 162
  move to Burma, 154
  need for Congress and White House
    to endorse experiment, 165
  obsequious letter sent to Secretary
    One, 179
  old drug war stories shared by, 153
  as participant in mission to destroy
    refinery, 174
  photograph of, 146
  premonition felt by, 182
  pressure on DEA to fire, 186
  reason for meeting Saw Lu in secret,
    164
  receipt for "purchase of evidence"
    produced by, 159
  relationship with Saw Lu hidden
    from ambassador, 160
  reputation of, Saw Lu's clearing of, 188
  Saw Lu's enterprise impressing, 158
  Secretary One's "extreme displeasure"
    conveyed to, 179
  Secretary One's relationship with,
    161–162
  as sole US narcotics agent in Burma,
    156
  warning of Bian's "ongoing personal
    vendetta" against him, 183
  warning to Saw Lu by, 191
Saladino, Barbara, 153, 154, 156, 157,
    184, 195
San Pwint, 130
Saw Lu
  abduction of, 196
  adoration of America by, 219
  as agent of Burma's junta, 49
  ailments of, 151
  ambition of, 202
  Angelo Saladino's first sit-down with,
    157–158

argument about head-hunting, 61
argument about Wa State, 203
arrival at home of Lai, 200
assembly of recruits by, 201
Baptist fervency of, 243
beatings of, 294
belief in War in Drugs, 307
big obstacle to dream of, 164–165
Bill Young's discussion of plot with, 257
Bill Young's last conversation with, 298
charges against, 292
children of, 189
CIA sabotage against, 218–219, 222
code name for, 158
as confidential informant, 153, 182, 283
confiscation of report by, 191
conveying of minutia about UWSA, 192
as crown jewel for Bill Young, 283
death of, 305–306
degradation of, 219
downfall of, 222
dream of erecting welfare state, 243
entombed in Wa soil, 222
evacuation of under cover of darkness, 300, 301
exodus of, 72
face-to-face debriefings with John Whalen, 283
failure of, 73
failure of DEA to protect, 153
feuding with, 136
first encounter with, 9–18
first killing of a human, 63
first months in Pang Wai, 294
first time hearing about Central Intelligence Agency, 56
as foreign minister of Wa State, 202
as founding father, 17
getting started as warlord, 50–51
grave of, 306
as "history-making man," 307
hospitalization of, 297

imprisonment of, 292
inability to contact, 158
intel produced for DEA by, 182
interrogation of, 292–293
Jacob forgiven by, 303
job of, 158
journey through Shanland, 207
junta's abduction of, 196
as junta's golden boy, 53
Lai's opinion of, 68
Lai's warning about US aid, 203
legitimacy as member of new ruling council, 266
Li Ziru's unnerving of, 220
long game of, 163
manifesto of, 210–211, 317–321
marked for death by Lai, 72
meeting with Mahasang the Prince, 58
message to opium workers from, 208–209
messages sent to warlords by, 55
movement to reject the opium poppy set in motion by, 307
network of drug-trade informants mobilized by, 158
new plan of, 39
as Old Testament prophet, 236
orders to assimilate among headhunters, 20
orders to wipe out, 70
personal agenda of, 20, 54
photograph of, 144
plague disregarded by, 305
rapport of Bill Young and, 209
reason for meeting Saladino in secret, 164
recovery at home, 298
reentry to society by, 255–256
refusal to talk about Wei, 95
release of, 197
request to reconnect with DEA, 151–152
reunion with Lai, 135–136
Saladino's camaraderie with, 163

Saw Lu *(continued)*
  Saladino's reputation cleared by, 188
  self-defense force concept explained
    by, 56, 57
  shame of, 73
  signatures of, Saladino's reputation
    cleared by, 188
  speeches of, 52
  survival of, 299
  torture of, 190–198
  "unauthorized contact" offense of,
    295
  unfurling of plan of, 168
  UWSA officials machinating to
    secure freedom of, 299
  UWSA's stripping of authority of,
    220
  vision of, 214
  vision of America by, 56
  waiting for arrival of DEA, 215–216
  Wa State's future predicted by, 309
  Whalen's not sensing malaise of, 287
Secretary One
  exposure of Saladino's unsent memo
    to, 184
  "extreme displeasure" conveyed by
    Kyaw Thein to Saladino, 179
  fear of America by, 161
  focus on DEA, 161
  hopes of "reform" dangled by, 243
  Lai convinced to contact, 168
  Lai's meeting with, 197
  Lai's offer to, 168
  need for DEA, 194
  obsequious letter sent to, 179
  office of, as junta's highest tier, 199
  paranoia of, 164
  Than Aye as disciple of, 191
self-defense force concept, 53, 54, 56,
    80, 95, 130
September 11 attacks, mood of US
    government following, 250
Shah
  being overlooked by Wa society, 264
  clan of, 54

as contractor working for the CIA-
    Taiwan intelligence apparatus, 56
espionage collected on communist
    China by, 115
fleeing of communist uprising by, 71
illness from natural causes, 288
jubilation at creation of new Wa
    nation, 123
legitimacy as member of new ruling
    council, 266
as most ferocious warlord, 54
orders to wipe out, 70
response to Saw Lu's message, 55
retribution of, 264
as Saw Lu's former partner in League
    of Warlords, 114
stories told to Saw Lu by, 56
title given in Wa government, 133
Shanland
  Bao convinced to eliminate, 222
  buildup of nation of, 132
  as Burma's largest cartel, 163
  conquering of, 112, 274
  invasion of, 111
  naming of, 103
  recruitment blitz of, 117
  rivalry with UWSA, 176
  Saladino's first glimpse of, 105
  Saw Lu's journey through, 207
  Shanland 2.0, 112
  special prison in, 107
  UWSA's swallowing of, 223
Shan State
  northern, Than Aye as spymaster of,
    191
  Saw Lu sent into, 84
  the Youngs' focus on converting, 25
Shanzhai China, 279, 312
Shinawatra, Thaksin, 258
Sikorra, Dave, 195, 204
  apprehension of, 196
  loyalty oath requested of, 204
  message of inner voice screaming at,
    205
  Stubbs's mysterious talk around, 205

SLORC. *See* State Law and Order
    Restoration Council
speed pills, 252, 254
Spot a Druglord (DEA), 293
Stalin, Joseph, 73
State Department
    antijunta agenda of, 165
    cat-kicking policy of, 156, 177
    label for Khun Sa, 177
    as obstacle to proposal, 212
    Pancho Huddle as de facto
        ambassador, 183, 213
    position on Burma, 178
    pressure on DEA to fire Saladino,
        186
    as saber-toothed tiger, 164–165
State Law and Order Restoration
    Council (SLORC), 156
    American visitors to, 176
    bad news from, 179
    choices Lai offered to, 197
    Lai's offer to, 197
    naming of Myanmar by, 180
    Saladino's expectation of help from,
        162
    sham "democracy" of, 320
    show put on by, 321
    Wa's peace agreement with, 318
STU-III (Secure Telephone Unit), 204
Stubbs, Bruce, 152, 204
    background on, 166
    Bian's derision of, 172
    as DEA agent sent to Wa State, 168
    involvement of in Horn's project,
        205
    as participant in mission to destroy
        refinery, 174
    premonition felt by, 182
    upstaging of Bian by, 167–168
    warning to Saw Lu by, 191
Stubbs, Su Yon, 166–167, 175
Sule Pagoda, 157
Superstar, 5–6, 158, 159. *See also* Saw Lu
Suu Kyi, Aung San, 155, 181, 299, 304,
    320

Taliban, 250, 275
Tang, baptism of, 57
Team America, privileges of belonging
    to, 48
Tet Kham, 267
Thailand
    Border Patrol Police, 45, 111
    Chiang Mai, Stubbs's meeting with
        Superstar in, 205, 210
    criminalization of amphetamine in,
        252
    crossings into rebel territories in
        Burma, 231
    DEA operation executed in, 293
    divide between Wa South and, 259
    moral panic over ya-ba in, 258
    number of ya-ba pills seized by, 260
    Saw Lu seeking treatment in, 257
    Stubbs as agent transferred from, 166
    underground entrepreneurs
        producing horse pills in, 252
    UWSA heroin flown into, 220
    War on Drugs dogma brought to, 252
    Wei facing death penalty in, 246
Than Aye, 191, 192, 197
Thingyan, 128
TikTok, 311
Time magazine, 162
Tin Aung, John, 157, 183
torture of Saw Lu, 190–198

UN Drug Control Program, 212
United Nations Office on Drugs and
    Crime (UNODC), 273
United States of America
    as abstract, distant threat to Wa
        officer corps, 295
    arrival of Golden Triangle dope in, 134
    as country most contaminated with
        Wa heroin, 137
    dark power managed by, 88
    defining of, 276
    duty to "disrupt and dismantle" the
        UWSA, 274
    goading of the Exiles by, 41

United States of America *(continued)*
  as hidden force in the Wa peaks, 29
  as latest empire to pick on the Wa, 2
  Mexican border tactics employed by,
    286–287
  notoriety of, 164
  Reagan's statement on, 308
  Saw Lu's adoration of, 219
  Saw Lu's divine abstraction of, 307
  Saw Lu's dream of a drug-free Wa
    nation embraced by, 257
  Saw Lu's vision of, 56
  Secretary One's fear of, 161
  shock waves rippling out from, 96
  shutting down of heroin pipeline to,
    255
  struggle to traffic heroin to, 97
  supercartel led by men with a
    personal grievance toward, 223
  treatment of Thailand by, 44
  view of Mao's kingdom by, 46
  as voracious narcotics consumer, 254
United Wa State Anti-Drug
    Organization (UWADO), 20, 202,
    208, 209, 215, 220
United Wa State Army (UWSA), 1–2,
    77–85
  America's duty to "disrupt and
    dismantle," 274
  apathy of toward education, 289
  as apex predator of Golden Triangle,
    311
  battle emblem of, 174
  camps, 231
  capture of meth traffickers
    (photograph), 145
  child soldier of (photograph), 140
  China's government befriending of,
    287
  CIA's sabotage against, 216
  DEA branding Wei as "financial
    genius" behind, 293
  DEA's continued pursuit of, 308
  "embassy" of, 77, 78
  establishment of, 74

  exchange of gifts with envoy of, 79
  as formal title of government, 133
  going corporate, 267
  as government, 2
  government, as "kingpin," 276
  headquarters of, 13
  heroin lab, offered to Secretary One,
    168
  as heroin-producing leviathan, 134
  illegal drugs as a top revenue source
    in, 2
  inquiries about mastermind of, 77
  kingpin of, 16
  leadership, claims to outsiders of
    Wei's disappearance, 269–270
  making contact with, 9
  minutia conveyed about, 192
  new ban on trafficking to China, 220
  nurturing of by past US operations, 4
  officers, public execution by, 239
  officials machinating to secure
    freedom of Saw Lu, 299
  as patrons of Huli, 229
  PLA weaponry sold to, 279
  plans to meet top envoy of, 77
  priorities of (listed in Saw Lu's
    manifesto), 321
  reason for Jacob's enlistment in, 240
  reliance on Wei's fortunes, 149
  rivalry with Shanland, 176
  running of Wa State by, 2
  Saw Lu declared a great leader by,
    237
  Saw Lu's affiliation with, 159
  Saw Lu's joining of, 74
  Saw Lu's return to Burma proper
    requested by, 300
  signature drug in the twenty-first
    century, 143
  social engineering feat of, 244
  swallowing of Shanland by, 223
  text message from, 227
  troops setting refinery aflame, 174
  Wei Xuegang as longtime financier
    of (photograph), 146

Western Sector (Naung Khit), 296
    ya-ba as North Star for, 254
United Wa State Party (UWSP), 317,
    321
UNODC. *See* United Nations Office on
    Drugs and Crime
U Nu, 320
US client states, 312
US Customs, Hard Narcotics
    Smuggling Division, 97
US News & World Report, 113
US Treasury Department, 277
U Tin Oo, 320
UWADO. *See* United Wa State
    Anti-Drug Organization
UWSA. *See* United Wa State Army
UWSP. *See* United Wa State Party

vanilla speed
    demand for, 254
    production of, 252–253
Vietnam War, 45–46, 98, 171
Ving Ngun, 54, 89
Voice of America (VOA), 179–180, 194

Wa
    America as latest empire to pick on, 2
    ancestral lands, 67, 84
    autonomy, dream achieved for, 313
    battalion leaders, selling of opium
        by, 127
    China's dream for, 70
    Christianized, 241
    comeuppance for, 123
    estrangement of people of, 125
    first nation of, Lai in charge of, 129
    government, 263, 313
    heroin, purity of, 165
    heroin production as temporary
        embarrassment for, 163
    heroin refinery, torching of
        (photograph), 145
    Lai as founding father (photograph),
        146
    leaders, DEA announcement to, 274
    Mahasang's view of, 58
    middle schools, 281, 288
    as narco-tribe, 1
    nation, 277, 278
    nationhood, epoch of, 74
    officer corps, America as abstract,
        distant threat, 295
    officialdom, schools of thought
        reigning among, 279
    opium (photograph), 143
    opium as lifeblood of, 51
    peace agreement with SLORC, 318
    peasants, as involuntary pioneers, 245
    people, loyalty of, 262
    People's Republic of China and, 129
    person, typical, 311
    "planning operations" against Khun
        Sa's forces, 118
    poverty and degradation in, 124
    proposal, actions nuking, 216
    race, Saw Lu's contributions to, 82
    refinery, Saladino's first look at, 173
    slavery, 64
    unity, Saw Lu's vision of, 63
    uprising of, 129, 131
    as vilified people, 1–2
    William Marcus Young as oracle
        of, 25
Wa Alternative Development Project,
    242–243
Wa National Army, 114, 264
    anti–Khun Sa alliance of the Exiles
        and, 119
    devolving of, 119
    heroin exported to United States
        through, 120
    involvement in plan to wreak havoc
        in Khun Sa's empire, 118
    Khun Sa's troops sent to wipe out,
        123
    as most disreputable band of drug
        runners in Golden Triangle, 114
    numbers in, 119
    opportunity for, 117
    stronghold, 132

War on Drugs
  as America's longest running war, 307
  dogma brought into Thailand, 252
  expectation of junta receiving
    adulation for assisting, 176
  glimmers of bloodless alternative
    to, 6
  Hollywood portrayal of, 3
  Jok's take on, 260
  Lai's fear of, 135
  lesson emerging about, 275
  madness of, 88
  Nancy Reagan's campaign in, 118
  Nixon's declaration of, 96
  Saw Lu's belief in, 307
  three years into, 101
Washington, George, 136
Wa South, 133, 134, 208
  divide between Thailand and, 259
  governor of, 253
  highlanders told about, 244
  as owner of prime smuggling trails,
    266
  Wei as governor of, 246
  Wei's establishment of, 250
  Wei's ruling of by remote control, 270
Wa State
  army of, 2
  biggest threat to, 312
  birth of, 129, 131
  capital of, 81
  cartography of, 133
  central committee of, 201, 203
  DEA handlers sent to, 168
  demarcation of, 80
  difficulty of traveling to, 3
  doomed pilgrimage to, 228
  economy of, 131
  factories opened by, 243
  first steps toward industrialization of,
    268
  fresh-air ghetto of, 232
  geographical problem of, 132
  heroin as economic engine for, 136
  as imitation mini-country, 279

  imminent American operation
    against, 273
  Jacob's doubts about moving to, 240
  Lai's request for opium production
    in, 130
  main portal to China from, 297
  muscle and brains of, 287
  opium as only viable export, 131
  political future of, 312
  position of inside Burma, 312
  recurring DEA trips to, 175
  risk of associating with, 276
  Saw Lu as foreign minister of, 202
  Saw Lu's argument about, 203
  syndicates welcome to set up shop in,
    285, 286
  third anniversary celebration, 200
  tragedy of, 311
  triumvirate of, 201
  United Nations' relationship with,
    312
  as utopia under construction, 237
  voice of the masses of, 311
  volume of methamphetamine
    pouring out of, 309
  Wei's assessment of, 132
watchdogs, 47
WeChat, 311
Wei Xuegang, 77, 86–110, 209
  apprenticeship of, 90
  as architect of Yanda's dispossession,
    235
  arrival in Panghsang, 131–132
  asking Jacob about, 16
  background of, 89
  as benefactor of anti–Khun Sa
    alliance, 119
  biography of, 86
  bribery of jailers by, 122
  burning of Gen. Lee Wen-huan, 114
  business mind of, 83
  as Chinese intelligence asset, 286
  CIA's motives to see downfall of,
    250
  copycats of, 285

DEA head price on, 78, 273
DEA's satellite images of whereabouts of, 249
description of, 247
dream of, 222
drug-producing machine, 247
economic recovery plan of, 224
escape by, 113
as everything CIA's Cold War–era planners once feared, 223
evolving strategy of, 284–285
experience working at CIA listening post, 89
as finance czar of UWSA, 16, 77
financial brilliance of, 242
as germaphobe in the company of killers, 107
grander vision to make speed pills, 252
as greatest Golden Triangle narcotics trafficker of all time, 86
Hong Pang as multinational founded by, 267
imprisonment of, 110
Khun Sa's admiration of, 104
as kingpin of UWSA, 16
"landlord" model of, 285
lesson learned from Operation Warlord, 284
as longtime financier of UWSA (photograph), 146
mansion of, 270
media reports of disappearance of, 269–270
meeting General Lee, 92
as Mr. Success, 111–123
as nation's treasurer, 103
new labs of, 251
officers trying to imitate, 242
origin story of, 88–90
overhauling of gang into proper trafficking syndicate, 115
pathological condition of, 251
personal ambitions of, 133
photograph of, 146

pill factories of, along Thai-Burma border, 255, 258
preferred language of, 133
as protégé of the infamous Golden Triangle drug lord, 82, 86
rejoicing over creation of new Wa nation, 123
release of, 122
resentment building toward, 110
reuniting with Zhang, 101
as Robin Hood–like figure, 270
as runner-up prize for DEA, 113
Saw Lu's inability to talk about, 85
Saw Lu's warning to Lai about, 136
servile subjects needed by, 244
shattering of the Exiles' monopoly by, 104
shift to synthetics by, 253
smuggling system of, 260
statesmanship approach of, 246
supposed embezzling by, 110
transplants divvied out by, 245
trying to speak to Saw Lu about, 82
uncommon intelligence of, 88
vast business empire of, 263
Wa South regiments of, 280
Zhang Qifu and, 90–91, 93
Wei Xueyin, 270
welfare state
funding of through meth, 311
Saw Lu's dream of erecting, 243
Whalen, John
Bao sitting in helicopter next to, 269
marathon hang with Bill Young and, 282–283
photograph of, 141
relationship between regime counterparts and, 249
relationship with Central Intelligence Agency, 249–250
responsibility of, 250
Saw Lu's face-to-face debriefings with, 283
tracking of Wei by, 248, 268

Whiskey Alpha rebellion, 257, 258–277
     coup plot, 295
     dismissal of, 288
     early days for, 267
     gist of, 263
     lead architect of, 262
     operations of, 264
     playbook of, 263
     raison d'être of, 264
     as Shah's shot at retribution, 264
The World, 3

Xiao Minliang, 256, 268, 287, 300
Xi Jinping, surprise visit to Yangon, 228

ya-ba, 80, 254, 255, 258, 284, 309. *See
     also* Whiskey Alpha rebellion
Yanda, 232–234, 244
Yangon, 61
     bugging of Saladino's house in, 185
     DEA office in, 137
     diplomatic quarter of, 154
     downtown, 157
     embassy at, 165
     praise for Wa State from, 129
     rebooting of DEA office in, 195
     stimulating atmosphere of, 195
     Stubbs's move to, 166
     UN Drug Control Program offices
          in, 212
     US embassy, John Whalen at, 248
     Xi Jinping's surprise visit to, 228
Young, Bill
     appetite for risk inherited by, 206
     bitter parting with CIA, 262
     CIA's employment of, 206
     drafting of Saw Lu's manifesto, 317
     falling out with CIA, 207
     as Golden Triangle native, 263
     as lead architect of Whiskey Alpha
          rebellion, 262

     morose comment made to Saw Lu
          by, 288
     as Moses, 282–283
     rapport of Saw Lu and, 209
     sacred heirloom bequeathed by
          grandfather to, 206
     Saw Lu as crown jewel for, 283
     Saw Lu's last conversation with, 298
     Saw Lu's meeting with, 257
     Saw Lu's request to connect with,
          152
     as secret weapon of DEA, 207
     speech ghostwritten by, 215
     subsources of, 283
     suicide of, 299
     upbringing of, 206
Young, Harold, 27
Young, William Marcus, 206. *See also*
     Man-God
     belief in saving souls of headhunters,
          206, 266
     converts of, 201
     family lore of, 25
     growing flock of, 26–27
     mission held sacred since the days of,
          282
     as oracle among his
          Wa followers, 25
     original converts of, 236
     sacred heirloom worn by, 206

Zhang Qifu, 89. *See also* Khun Sa
     ambition of, 90
     charge of treason against, 96
     defiled reputation of, 95
     hostage swap for release of, 101
     imprisonment of, 96
     megasale plans of, 93–94
     reuniting with Wei, 101
     Wei Xuegang and, 90–91, 93
Zhao Nyi Lai. *See* Lai, Zhao Nyi

Credit: Pailin Wedel

Patrick Winn is an award-winning investigative journalist who covers rebellion and black markets in Southeast Asia. He enters the worlds of guerrillas and vigilantes to mine stories that might otherwise go ignored. Winn is a three-time winner of the Human Rights Press Awards, presented by Amnesty International, and has received the Robert F. Kennedy Journalism Award (also known as the "poor man's Pulitzer") and a National Press Club award, among other prizes. He lives in Bangkok.

PublicAffairs is a publishing house founded in 1997. It is a tribute to the standards, values, and flair of three persons who have served as mentors to countless reporters, writers, editors, and book people of all kinds, including me.

I. F. STONE, proprietor of *I. F. Stone's Weekly*, combined a commitment to the First Amendment with entrepreneurial zeal and reporting skill and became one of the great independent journalists in American history. At the age of eighty, Izzy published *The Trial of Socrates*, which was a national bestseller. He wrote the book after he taught himself ancient Greek.

BENJAMIN C. BRADLEE was for nearly thirty years the charismatic editorial leader of *The Washington Post*. It was Ben who gave the *Post* the range and courage to pursue such historic issues as Watergate. He supported his reporters with a tenacity that made them fearless and it is no accident that so many became authors of influential, best-selling books.

ROBERT L. BERNSTEIN, the chief executive of Random House for more than a quarter century, guided one of the nation's premier publishing houses. Bob was personally responsible for many books of political dissent and argument that challenged tyranny around the globe. He is also the founder and longtime chair of Human Rights Watch, one of the most respected human rights organizations in the world.

• • •

For fifty years, the banner of Public Affairs Press was carried by its owner Morris B. Schnapper, who published Gandhi, Nasser, Toynbee, Truman, and about 1,500 other authors. In 1983, Schnapper was described by *The Washington Post* as "a redoubtable gadfly." His legacy will endure in the books to come.

Peter Osnos, *Founder*